BUILDING THE UNION

A volume in the

CLASS AND CULTURE Series

Milton Cantor and Bruce Laurie,

series editors

Chevrolet Die Maker: Circa 1930 (courtesy of the National Automotive History Collection of the Detroit Public Library).

BUILDING THE UNION

Skilled Workers and Anglo-Gaelic Immigrants in the Rise of the UAW

STEVE BABSON

RUTGERS UNIVERSITY PRESS
New Brunswick and London

Library of Congress Cataloging-in-Publication Data

Babson, Steve.
  Building the union : skilled workers and Anglo-Gaelic immigrants
in the rise of UAW / by Steve Babson.
    p.   cm. — (Class and culture series)
  Includes bibliographical references and index.
  ISBN 0-8135-1657-9
  1. International Union, United Automobile, Aerospace, and
Agricultural Implement Workers of America—History.   2. Automobile
industry workers—Michigan—Detroit—History.   3. Tool and die
makers—Michigan—Detroit—History.   4. Skilled labor—Michigan—
Detroit—History.   5. Alien labor—Michigan—Detroit—History.
I. Title. II. Series.
HD6515.A82I573   1991
331.88'1292'097734—dc20   90-45947
                                                                           CIP

British Cataloging-in-Publication information available

To the memory of Bernie Firestone

CONTENTS

LIST OF TABLES

ACKNOWLEDGMENTS

Among the individuals and institutions that assisted this work, the role of my dissertation committee at Wayne State University deserves special mention. Chris Johnson first directed my attention to the role of Anglo-Gaelic immigrants in the UAW and urged me to make this study the focus of my dissertation. Robert Ziegar drew upon his own extensive research in the labor history of the twentieth century to provide critical and detailed evaluations of early drafts. Charlie Hyde shared his considerable knowledge of manufacturing technology, and Doug Fraser contributed his unique insights as a participant in the events described in this book.

Additionally, I owe a special debt to Wayne State University's Labor Studies Center, where I currently work. Hal Stack, the center's director, recognized the continuing demands on my time represented by this research, and provided two successive summer leaves to complete the work. My co-workers have also been supportive throughout, with Bob Cunningham in particular providing timely assistance troubleshooting my uncooperative computer.

Several research libraries were indispensable to the completion of this book. Chief among these was the Archives of Labor and Urban affairs at Wayne State's Walter Reuther Library. A casual review of the notes in this book will indicate how heavily I relied on the staff and resources of this first-rate institution. Likewise, staff members at the National Archives' Chicago branch and the Burton Collection of the Detroit Public Library facilitated my research of, respectively, the immigration records and Detroit subculture of foreign-born metalworkers.

Portions of the Introduction are excerpted from an article of mine, "Class, Craft and Culture: Tool and Die Makers and the Organization of the UAW", *Michigan Historical Review* 14 (Spring 1988). Portions of Chapters 3 and 4 previously appeared in Chapter 12 of *Labor Divided:*

Race and Ethnicity in United States Labor Struggles, 1840–1970 (Albany, 1990). I thank the *Michigan Historical Review* and The State University of New York Press for permission to excerpt from these materials.

Milton Cantor, Bruce Laurie, and Nelson Lichtenstein gave particularly close scrutinies of the manuscript and helped improve the final version in innumerable ways. Milton was especially supportive, reading my overlong dissertation not once but twice, and providing extensive guidance for editing it down to manageable size.

As with any research into the past, this book relies on the preceding work of many historians. In a profession and a society where knowledge becomes property, the contributions of those who haven't yet published their research deserve special thanks. Tom Klug, a fellow graduate student at Wayne State, has been most comradely, sharing his findings on Detroit management's rationalization of metalworking between 1900 and 1920, as well as his extensive research on the Employers Association of Detroit.

I gained a unique insight on this city's interwar decades from the oral histories of people who built cars and joined unions in the 1930s. Among the Detroit toolmakers and organizers I interviewed, Russell Leach, the late Blaine Marrin, Irv Iverson, Walter Dorosh, Leonard Woodcock, Dorothy Kraus, Henry Kraus, and the late Geoffrey Snudden gave me detailed accounts of events they knew first hand. Oscar Paskal's gift of his toolmaking manuals and apprentice textbooks provided additional perspective on the mid-twentieth-century practices of Detroit's toolmakers.

Finally, I would like to thank two people I have relied on in my work over the last ten years, one personally, the other professionally. Nancy Brigham is not a historian and she is not my typist, but in addition to being a supportive spouse, urging me forward while accepting the latest excuse for delay, her skills as a writer and her commitment to trade unionism have made her a valued sounding board for many of the ideas expressed in this book. Bernie Firestone never read the completed manuscript and didn't live to see it published, but he was the sort of union leader who still inspires hope and "points the way" for the rest of us. I am one of many people in a beleaguered city and a struggling labor movement who miss him.

BUILDING THE UNION

INTRODUCTION

"As though they were one man the workers of Detroit got in motion . . . all in one mass, men and women, Negro and white, all together."

The *United Auto Worker*, national newspaper of the UAW, projected this stirring image of worker unity in 1937. The tone of the passage is inspirational, the perspective is class-bound, and the myth is enduring: the union organizing drives of the 1930s, we are told, mobilized workers "all in one mass." Popular histories abound with such imagery of unified and spontaneous militancy, much of it originating with participants and reported subsequently by journalists, partisans, and finally, some historians.[1]

There is an opposing vision of the 1930s labor movement that rejects this popular myth. Articulated by some participants and by a growing number of labor historians, this contrary perspective focuses on the role of an activist minority in sparking the mass actions of the 1930s. Instead of a spontaneously unified rank and file "acting as one," it stresses the uneven development of militancy, the calculation and hesitancy of the majority of workers, and the initiating role played by strategic groups.[2]

This book falls within the second perspective. Examining the growth of auto-worker unionism in Detroit during the 1930s, it focuses on the dynamics of craft, class, and culture that propelled two overlapping groups, skilled workers and Anglo-Gaelic immigrants, into prominent leadership roles within the UAW.

There is, of course, something paradoxical in these two numerically insignificant groups taking leadership in an industry known in Detroit for its "de-skilled" jobs and its Eastern European workers. While craft labor and British immigrants are known to have played a critical role in the nineteenth-century history of American industry and labor, they are usually presumed absent from twentieth-century events. Yet, however incongruous, skilled tradesmen and Anglo-Gaelic immigrants stand out like colored yarn in the warp and weave of Detroit's auto-union history.[3]

The initiating role of tool and die makers is especially visible. It was 500 tool and die makers in the Vernor Avenue plant of Briggs Manufacturing who, by successfully striking against a wage cut in January of 1933, inspired 15,000 production workers to walk out on Briggs and other employers—the first mass strike in Detroit's depression-era auto industry. It was tool and die makers who, in the fall of 1933, established the Mechanics Educational Society of America (MESA) as the first auto union to successfully strike and negotiate on an industry-wide basis. It was the UAW's East Side Tool and Die Local 155, formed by former MESA activists, that organized and led Detroit's first sit-down strike at Midland Steel in November 1936. It was pro-CIO tool and die makers at General Motors who, by striking during model changeover in the summer of 1939, forced the industry's leading employer to recognize the UAW-CIO over the discredited UAW-AFL. And it was a tool and die maker, Walter Reuther, who rose from the presidency of Detroit's West Side Local 174 to leadership of the striking tool and die makers in 1939—and from there, to leadership of the UAW International in 1946.

Reuther was American-born, but most of the strikers he led in 1939 were Northern European immigrants, and prominent among these were Anglo-Gaelic craftsmen. Bill Stevenson, and Scots-born chairman of the GM Bargaining Committee and president of Detroit's West Side Tool and Die Local 157, was Reuther's equal in devising the strategy that made the UAW-CIO victorious in 1939. Another Scotsman, John Anderson, president of the East Side Tool and Die Local, was chief organizer of the pivotal Midland Steel sit-down in 1936. And yet another Britisher, Matthew Smith, was the founding leader of the Mechanics Educational Society of America, a union in which European-born workers were a majority and British workers a plurality.

Many of Detroit's biggest factory locals also drew upon Anglo-Gaelic immigrants for leadership. From the Scotsman Bill McKie, leader of the first union at Ford Rouge, to the Irishman and IRA veteran Pat Quinn, leader of the Dodge sit-down strike in 1937, there was hardly a UAW plant committee or local executive board that didn't have at least one member who spoke with a brogue or a Yorkshire accent, or answered to the name "Scotty." The five biggest UAW locals in Detroit—Ford Local 600, West Side Local 174, Dodge Local 3, Packard Local 190, and Tool and Die Local 157—each had at least one Anglo-Gaelic president in the union's first dozen years. Plant committees, steward bodies, and executive boards in each of these locals also had a disproportionately large number of Anglo-Gaelic leaders. Some of these immigrants rose to the union's International Executive Board, and some of their offspring rose still higher. Leonard Woodcock, the union's fourth president, was born in Rhode Island but raised in Europe by his English parents; his father, a diemaker, brought the family to Detroit in 1928 and later became an early strike leader at the Motor Products Corporation. Doug Fraser, the union's fifth president, was born in Glasgow; his father, an electrician, was a strike leader in the DeSoto plant during the 1937 sit-down.[4]

What brought these Anglo-Gaelic immigrants to Detroit? And why did they, particularly the tool and die makers among them, play such a prominent leadership role in the city's auto unions?

Answering these questions requires two kinds of investigation. On the one hand, the dynamics of union formation and shop-floor leadership can be isolated by what anthropologist Clifford Geertz calls "thick description." As cultural interpretation, it moves from a "thin" recital of behaviors and formal institutions to a detailed reconstruction of the conceptual structures that make social life meaningful. Since these structures of meaning can be unstated and contradictory, thick description has to be sufficiently "microscopic" to capture minute variations of language and behavior. "The aim," says Geertz, "is to draw large conclusions from small but very densely textured facts." Applied to the shop-floor milieu of Detroit's auto factories, the methodology calls for a detailed investigation of the workplace culture lying beneath the formal, institutional norms of factory administration. Thick description, by exposing the contradictory and inexplicit meanings in working-class practice, takes the researcher beyond the impressionistic or naively empirical objectives of institutional and populist history and focuses on the ethnocultural, occupational, and fraternal relations structuring mass mobilization.[5]

But which shop floor should the historian choose for this inquiry? If it is assumed that any one factory, picked at random or selected because of available data, will reveal the same essential "inner dynamic," the choice hardly matters. But the evidence indicates that factories, like neighborhoods and nation-states, each represent the unique crystallization of their particular history, even as they also represent the prevailing dynamics of the surrounding world. Machine shops are different from foundries, and both are unlike assembly plants. In the

1920s and 1930s, a factory toolroom with a German supervisor would hire more Germans, whereas a neighboring plant with a Polish toolroom supervisor might exclude Germans altogether. A factory with its own inside toolroom (a "captive-shop") had a different work force from one that relied on outside job shops—and so on.

To account for these and other variations, thick description has to be partially diluted with a wider selection of shop floors. But how much wider? The question raises both practical and methodological issues, for unless the investigator has unlimited access to graduate research assistants, a wide-ranging survey necessarily turns thick description into thin generalization.

This book will try to split the difference between thick and thin description by focusing on a limited number of factory environments and events. It is hoped that a compromise of thick description's microscopic focus on a single workplace with a more telescopic survey of contrasting environments and pivotal events will exploit the strengths, rather than the weaknesses, of these two approaches.

The boundaries of analysis are defined by geographic, chronological, methodological, and practical limits. Geographically, this book concentrates on the Detroit area, including Hamtramck and Dearborn; it makes occasional and brief excursions to other Michigan auto centers, and frequent trans-Atlantic leaps to Britain and Ireland. Chronologically, it begins with a review of early twentieth-century craft production in the auto industry and narrows to an intensive focus on toolroom practice and union formation in the 1920s and 1930s. Methodologically, it selects for study individual leaders and strategic groups drawn from a limited number of pivotal organizations and events, with "pivotal" crudely defined as "biggest," "first," and "definitive." The biggest Detroit auto factories in the 1930s were Ford Dearborn, Dodge Main, and Packard; the biggest auto-union organizations included the uaw locals at these three factories and the Amalgamated Locals 174, 155, and 157; the biggest sit-down strike in the 1930s (and in u.s. history) occurred at Dodge Main in 1937. The first union organizations to gain a mass following in the 1930s included the Auto Workers Union (awu) and the Mechanics Educational Society of America (mesa). The first strikes included the walkouts at Briggs, Motor Products, Murray Body, and Hudson Motors in the winter of 1933, as well as mesa's industry-wide strike in the fall of that year and the Midland Steel sit-down in 1936. The definitive events of these years included the aforesaid events, as well as the strikes by tool and die makers at General Motors and by Dodge Local 3, both in 1939, which reestablished the uaw-cio's base and shaped the initial boundaries of collective bargaining. Equally definitive were the "Labor party" initiatives that established a union presence in Detroit politics from 1934 to 1937, but which also failed to win majority support. Practically, constraints of time and energy mean some of these pivotal events and organizations receive less attention than others. Packard Local 190, for example, is hardly touched on; the AWU and West Side Local 174 get only spotty coverage; and examination of Ford Dearborn ends in 1939, two years before Local 600 won recognition.

As indicated, this book examines the role of strategic groups in building Detroit's auto unions. Four such groups deserve attention: members of left-wing organizations, particularly the Socialist and Communist parties; skilled workers, particularly tool and die makers; aspiring professionals; and Anglo-Gaelic immigrants. The first of these four has long attracted the attention of historians and draws further comment here only when it overlaps with other groups. Accordingly, little attention is paid to the programmatic differences between left parties. For the purposes of this book, party organizations are less determining than the wider left-wing subculture from which they sprang. Skilled metalworkers and Anglo-Gaelic immigrants straddled this left-wing subculture, and it is these groups that predominate in this book; aspiring professionals are sketched only as a contrasting case.

This approach reverses the order of things in many histories of Detroit's auto unionism. Compared with the celebrated role of left-wing union organizers, skilled workers have received less attention and Anglo-Gaelic immigrants virtually none. There are several reasons for this lopsided coverage. First, many studies of mass production and industrial unionism assume from the start that skilled workers must be marginal actors in a "modern" industry. Scientific management and Fordism are assumed to be inevitable outgrowths of capitalist development, the necessary expressions of its inner logic. Since the elimination of skilled labor from production is a paramount aim of Fordist management, skilled workers are expected to disappear; their continued presence, when acknowledged, is treated as anomalous or peripheral. It follows that industrial unionism is "modern," while the craft-conscious unionism of skilled workers is "archaic," one-dimensional, and less deserving of attention. Even studies that explicitly reject this logic are swayed by its explanatory appeal. In *Work and Politics*, Charles Sabel rejects technological determinism and situates the division of labor in a historically determined medley of sociopolitical-economic factors. But despite his recognition that skilled workers play an equivocal role in modern industry, with potentially wide variations in their behavior and goals, when Sabel turns to 1930s Detroit he uncritically accepts the populist version of union formation: Slavic and Appalachian autoworkers, in his account, confronted Northern European craftsmen "who were willing neither to open their unions to the unskilled nor to let the latter organize themselves independently"; these production workers therefore had to organize the UAW by "sweeping aside the craftsmen's objections to an independent union."[6]

This is not how it happened. It must be acknowledged, however, that identifying the role of skilled workers and Anglo-Gaelic immigrants in the process of union formation is no easy task when these leaders purposefully downplayed their identity. As a movement built on the shared grievances of factor life and the general goal of worker empowerment, industrial unionism generated symbols and concepts that emphasized the solidarity of all workers and minimized the appeal of competing craft, ethnic, gender, and racial identities. The achievement of the union's goal—maximum unity—depended on language and symbols that obscured the uneven development of its social base. Skilled workers in leadership emphasized their common cause with production workers, not their vanguard position in the factory hierarchy. Immigrant union leaders were equally reticent about their "un-American" origins. British-born Stan Coulthard, who emigrated to Detroit in 1921 and later organized auto- and dairyworkers, recalled how the antiunion media stigmatized foreign-born organizers. "You see, the press editorials at this time were full of innuendos about alien agitators and how true Americans would never follow an alien like me. If this sort of thing came up once in the *Detroit [Free] Press* or the *Detroit Times* it came up a dozen times." Anglo-Gaelic leaders at least had a common language with native-born co-workers, though dialect and accent set them apart. A brogue could even be an asset in Detroit's union halls, but few Scotsmen dwelled on their foreign birth and heritage. Their reticence in this regard contrasted with the Polish-Americans, Italian-Americans, and other hyphenated "ethnics" who predominated in Detroit's biggest production-worker locals. When Hamtramck's autoworkers organized their first UAW affiliate, their ethnic and class identities both found expression in the "Polish Workers Local 187"; likewise, Italian-Americans at Ford initially organized under the banner of the UAW's Italian Organizing Committee. Anglo-Gaelic union activists, on the other hand, rarely identified themselves as immigrant/ethnic workers, with the notable exception of some Irish nationalists. In a unique parallax of consciousness, Anglo-Gaelic immigrants developed a sensibility that synthesized their old-country experience as workers but denied the immigrant/ethnic dimension of their lives. The very stress they placed on class and craft meant they denied or downplayed their identity as immigrants. Other factors contributed to this self-denial: the greater ease of assimilation for English-speaking immigrants, particularly for the Anglo-Saxon Protestants among them; the stigma placed on "alien" status by antiunion employers and federal authorities, particularly the FBI; and the imperial status of Great Britain, which made nationalism a jingoistic rather than adversarial movement for British workers.[7]

Among those few Anglo-Gaelic leaders who publicly identified their immigrant roots, some had reason to misrepresent this dimension of their past. Bill McKie, the only Anglo-Gaelic union leader in Detroit to be featured in a book-length biography, had much to say in prepublication interviews with author Philip Bonosky about his first fifty years in Scotland, but Bonosky (and/or International Publishers) excised most of this material from the book. In its place, Bonosky gave a superficial and misleading picture of McKie's Scottish experience, portraying him in terms suited to the polemical intentions of a pro-Communist tract. According to Bonosky, McKie was simply a rank-and-file union "member" in Scotland, when he was actually a national leader of the Sheet Metal Workers; McKie, we are told, had the honor to "meet" William Morris at a street-corner meeting, when actually McKie had organized the meeting and introduced Morris to the crowd; McKie's wife, Bess, had always known and shared McKie's life "as a young militant Scottish worker," when in fact they had initially shared a religious life bounded by their participation in the Salvation Army Band and choir. To acknowledge the complex reality of McKie's life, Bonosky would have had to abandon the fictional claim that all workers "naturally" gravitate toward militancy. According to Bonosky, McKie did not join the Communist party until 1935, after his experience at Ford "naturally" persuaded this class-conscious worker "that it was time to join more closely with those who were equipped to give leadership and direction through the stormy days to come." The fact that McKie had been a founding member of the British Communist party in 1921 did not square with this inspirational tale; consequently, the lengthy description of his experiences in the Scottish left, which McKie provided Bonosky in prepublication interviews, found no place in the "official" biography of his life.[8]

Fortunately, verbatim transcripts of McKie's recollections have survived. Unfortunately, there is no comparable record for other Anglo-Gaelic leaders. The absence of such documentary material is especially frustrating when evaluating the role of a man like John Anderson, the MESA leader and UAW organizer who played such a pivotal role in Detroit's labor movement. Because Anderson remained silent about his preimmigration life, we are again left with the image of the militant worker who "naturally" turned to radical politics. And because he was a loser in the factional wars of the late 1940s, Anderson did not attract the attention of historians who could plum this biographical void. The only available sources of information on his life are the spotty and contradictory impressions of contemporaries, including the speculations of one labor spy who misidentified Anderson as "an American-born Red of Finnish parents."[9]

All these factors make it difficult to identify the real nature of union formation and leadership. This task is all the harder if the historian assumes that most union leaders inhibit or distort the "true" aspirations of union members. Labor historians have sometimes been guilty of this predisposition, particularly those who want to vindicate factional viewpoints or serve the cause. If they were left-wing activists who suffered defeat in the 1940s and 1950s, or if they were New Left activists confronting the establishment in the 1960s and early 1970s, they had reason to resent the Red baiters and Cold Warriors they opposed. But by uncritically positing a unitary "rank and file" as the natural enemy of bureaucracy, populist historians have obscured the actual dynamics of union formation.

The Chrysler sit-down strikes of 1937 are a case in point. In March of 1937, UAW leaders told the *New York Times* that the sit-downs "were not ordered by it [the union], but represented the logical result of a spontaneous movement of the rank and file." The *Times* repeated this statement as part of its coverage, producing a "fact" which, for the unwary historian, confirms a supposition of leadership timidity and spontaneous worker militancy. This "fact," however, does not survive cross examination. UAW leaders did order the sit-down. They then lied to the press, and for the best of reasons: they faced conspiracy charges for their actual role in organizing and calling the sit-downs, and their bargaining leverage could only be enhanced by the image of a unified, independently militant rank and file.[10]

In this and in many other cases, the articulated intentions of key individuals and groups, all readily available to "thin" description, often contradicted the actual dynamics of auto production and union formation. In many cases, the commonly held "facts" do not speak for themselves. Everybody "knows," for example, that scientific management and mass production reduced the auto industry's reliance on skilled workers—and yet, in contradiction of this commonsense fact, employers were also becoming increasingly dependent on skilled tool and die makers. Likewise, the 1930s was a decade of mass unemployment and labor surplus—yet workers struck in 1937 when auto employment was at an all-time high, and skilled labor was in short supply during retooling. The UAW, like other CIO unions, found its base among production workers, many of them Eastern Europeans—yet skilled workers and Anglo-Gaelic immigrants were predominant in its leadership.

Some facts do speak for themselves, though they say less than is commonly held. There is little doubt that the 1930s was a decade of misery for many Americans, especially workers. It is equally clear that this experience, as many participants said then and now, fueled the growth of the CIO and other protest movements. However, it is also clear to some participants (and labor historians) that these protest movements were not an unmediated reaction to suffering. The truth is that suffering can be endured with little or no protest if people believe conditions should not be changed or cannot be changed or can only be changed at the risk of life and security. The firm conviction that change is both necessary and winnable is comparatively rare, a fact obscured when the 1930s are recalled by the sheer magnitude of suffering and the massive scale of popular protest. Yet even in some of the most militant of these demonstrations, the protesters lacked the resources or the opportunity to sustain a successful challenge of the status quo. This was certainly the case in Detroit in 1933, when both production workers and skilled tradesmen struck the auto industry. For both, the strikes put management on notice that further wage cutting carried the risk of further turmoil—but only the skilled workers emerged with an organization that could sustain and direct their protest.[11]

The tool and die makers who founded MESA in the fall of 1933 not only wielded a unique bargaining leverage in the tool-dependent auto industry but also possessed cultural resources uniquely suited to union organization and leadership. For the Anglo-Gaelic leaders who predominated in this fledgling organization, that culture bore the mark of their old-country roots. The pattern of symbols and concepts that gave meaning to their social lives had taken form in an environment of working-class and secular associations: the Odd Fellows hall, the craft society, the co-op store, the workingmen's club, the sympathy strike, the Labour party. The coherence of this culture should not be overstated; its variations and contradictions cannot be ignored. But even with the necessary qualifications, there remain some irreducible contrasts in the aptitudes and abilities of Anglo-Gaelic union leaders compared with their Eastern European and American-born counterparts. Whereas the former possessed the languages of craft and class and the repertoires of collective action especially suited to union leadership, the latter more often spoke the languages of ethno-religious identity or individual opportunity. Since culture is constitutive as well as reflective of social practice, Anglo-Gaelic immigrants continued to project their unique sensibility onto the world even as they adjusted to the altered social terrain of Detroit. The result, in MESA and much of the UAW's early structure, was a hybrid of British practice and American adaptation.

Isolating the Anglo-Gaelic contribution to this outcome is no easy matter. First, the diversity of Anglo-Gaelic culture seems to mock generalization. Among workers, a deep gulf divided the social and workplace existence of unskilled laborers and "respectable" craftsmen; compared with the United States, the wage differential between the two was greater and the number of semiskilled jobs bridging the gap was smaller. Among unions, the very size of the British labor movement produced a dizzying array of organizational forms; in engineering alone, forty-two different unions claimed membership in 1913–1915. Within the Amalgamated Engineers, the largest of these unions, syndicalists, industrial unionists, and craft-amalgamationists fought a many-sided battle over strategy and structure: national agreements versus local autonomy, militant action versus prudent organization, the general strike versus parliamentary reform. Political diversity could even penetrate the family. Billy Allan, the Glasgow baker who emigrated to Detroit in 1928 and rose to leadership in the city's Communist party, recalled a politically divided household. "My father voted Independent Labour, my uncle Alec, a skilled metal worker, voted Tory, as did my grandfather, a retired army man." Other social cleavages divided the United Kingdom's diverse populations—Presbyterian from Anglican, Protestant from Catholic, Highlander from lowlander, Londoner from provincial. And overshadowing all these in the ferocity of its conflict was the struggle between Ireland and England.[12]

No effort to generalize can ignore this diversity, but a mere cataloging of variance would be equally misleading. Commerce and migration interwove the diverse cultures of the United Kingdom, and common organization and experience linked the social movements of its constituent populations. A Belfast engineer belonged to the same union and joined the same strike movements as his Glasgow counterpart; the Dublin stevedore and member of the Transport Workers could cross to Liverpool and find countrymen, union comrades, and family in abundance. Irish rebellion and British repression produced an enduring bitterness among combatants, but the working-class wing of the nationalist movement found British allies among the same workers and socialists who organized relief ships for Dublin during the 1913 lockout. Tom Mann, engineer and socialist, was one of many craftsmen who retained his membership in the Engineers while organizing and leading new unions for laborers and semiskilled machine hands. James Larkin, founder of the Irish Transport Workers, was born in Liverpool; James Connolly, coleader of the Transport Workers and martyred commander of the Easter Rising, was born in Scotland and grew to political maturity in Edinburgh's Social Democratic Federation. Bill McKie, grandson of an Irish Fenian, was born and raised in a town straddling the border—and the cultures—of Scotland and England.)

For the Anglo-Gaelic immigrant who rose to auto-union leadership, the boundaries that distinguished these separate cultures partially merged in Detroit's melting pot. The result was not assimilation to Hooverite Americanism but formulation of another hyphenated sensibility—the Anglo-Gaelic-American labor unionist. This hybrid species was numerically dwarfed by the dominant "Birds of Passage" migrating to North America, and its unique camouflage further obscured its presence. But Detroit's auto factories were not the only place where English-speaking immigrants played a crucial role in twentieth-century unions and protest movements. Historian Ron Schatz also identified their presence in the cadre of organizers who founded the United Electrical Workers. In the population of organizers he identified for their pioneering role, six of the twenty-five for whom he could find information on place of birth were Anglo-Gaelic; half of twenty-eight were skilled tradesmen (seven of these were tool and die makers) in an industry where only 12 percent of the work force was skilled; and five were known members of the Communist or Socialist parties. Joshua Freeman identified a parallel case in the New York City Transit Workers Union, whose founders in the 1930s included nearly two-dozen veterans of the Irish Republican Army, joined by Communists and skilled tradesmen in the repair shops.[13]

Identifying the subgroups that contributed a disproportionate share of their members to union leadership is one thing; specifying the relative weights of these leadership groups is far more difficult. Schatz estimated that roughly half of the United Electrical Workers' pioneering leaders were skilled tradesmen and a quarter were Anglo-Gaelic immigrants. These are acceptable estimates for the UAW case, but there is no effort to back this claim with quantitative data. The boundaries of "leadership" are simply too diffuse at the local level to allow for such precision. At Dodge Main alone, there were nearly 1,000 stewards and dozens of local officers in 1937. One might assume that the formal hierarchy of leadership gave greater prominence to the Executive Board member than the chief steward—but this assumption would ignore the actual role of David McIntyre, the Clydeside tradesman and previously unheralded chief steward whose role in the 1937 sit-down surpassed many of his "superiors" on the Executive Board. Likewise, the Scotsman John Anderson was the *acknowledged* leader of UAW Local 155 in 1936, even if he had not yet departed his *formal* position on the International UAW staff. To accommodate these and other cases where the formal ranking of leaders obscured the actual practice of leadership, the definition of the latter has to be situational: who made the critical decisions and who actually wielded authority at pivotal moments of crisis and opportunity? This means that the leadership population expands and contracts over time and in ways that preclude stable quantification. There is, therefore, no fixed proportion that describes the comparative weight of leadership subgroups in all Detroit locals at all times in the 1930s; it is possible, however, to know with reasonable certainty that in pivotal locals at key moments, skilled workers and Anglo-Gaelic immigrants were two of the four groups that wielded predominant authority.[14]

The American unions that Anglo-Gaelic immigrants helped found were no more "foreign" because of their role than the Model T was "Hungarian" simply because three immigrants, Joseph Galamb, Charles Balogh, and Julius Haltenberger, helped Henry Ford design the car. American conditions defined the unique environment in which these two constellations of social practice, auto unionism and the Model T, were possible. But the elaboration of these possibilities gained momentum as strategic groups proved capable of identifying and realizing certain of these potentials. It may be that "foreign" sensibilities, under particular circumstances, help catalyze a redefinition of what is known and possible, accelerating the decay of routine expectations. The wider implications of this dynamic are suggested by another parallel case, the role of English-speaking Caribbean immigrants in founding the Universal Negro Improvement Association and the Harlem branch of the Communist party.[15]

Because collective action occurs in shop-floor and neighborhood environments imperfectly known to contemporary observers and the historians who follow, it can appear as a spontaneous eruption of impersonal forces, suddenly galvanizing protest with no significant leadership or forethought. "Spontaneity" becomes a rubbery concept, stretched over the many gaps in available evidence to explain what is actually unknown. By exalting the heroism of the rank and file, the myth of spontaneity reduces them—by their very spontaneity—to unwitting ciphers of "underlying forces." Spontaneity is the wrong term for collective actions, which can be fast-paced, exhilarating, and turn on unexpected contingencies, but which begin with people who think before they "spontaneously" act. Under these circumstances, certain groups articulate their response with greater certainty and decisiveness than others. These initiating groups may seek contradictory goals and their actions may produce unintended outcomes, but they set events in motion.

This book focuses on two such groups, skilled workers and Anglo-Gaelic immigrants. Chapter 1 describes the management innovations that transformed craft production of automobiles after 1907 and elevated tool and die makers to prominence within the industry. Chapter 2 details the nature of tool and die work in the 1920s and 1930s, the characteristic attitudes and aptitudes of toolroom workers, and industry's growing dependence on immigrants to meet the demand for skilled workers and white-collar engineers. In this and subsequent chapters the words "toolroom" and "toolmaker" will, for narrative convenience, substitute for the longer "tool and die," except where specific distinctions are drawn between the general category of toolmaking and its specific form in diemaking. Chapter 3 recounts the events of the early 1920s that pushed Anglo-Gaelic workers from their homeland, and describes the ethnic and craft dimensions of the subculture they established in Detroit. Chapter 4 specifies the craft sensibilities, class consciousness, and organizational know-how that made these Anglo-Gaelic immigrants uniquely suited as union organizers. Chapter 5 describes their particular abilities in Direct Action strategies that challenged the liberal State, and contrasts this dimension of their leadership with the predominant practice of American-born union leaders and production workers in the years 1933–1937. Finally, Chapter 6 focuses on the leading role of skilled workers and Anglo-Gaelic immigrants in the UAW's 1939 recovery and contrasts the cultural baggage that German and British workers brought to Detroit. To avoid repetitive citation of documentary sources, biographical information for selected Anglo-Gaelic immigrants is summarized in Appendix A.[16]

1

SKILLED WORKERS AND THE RISE OF AUTO

Racy Cadillacs, sleek Buicks, Chevrolets that look like a million dollars! Turret tops, streamlined fenders, one-piece-all-steel bodies! These marvels of modern production are made possible only by highly skilled engineering, tool, die, and maintenance workers.

Fisher Strike News, UAW, 21 July 1939[1]

So economical and rapid is manufacturing by the use of dies that wherever possible this method is used. . . . In fact, "Always say 'Die'" might be accepted as a cardinal principle of the industry.

Chrysler Motors Magazine, September 1935[2]

At a time when workers and managers confronted each other across a wide terrain of disagreement, they could still see eye to eye on at least this one issue: tool and die makers, "the magicians of the shop," as the UAW strike bulletin dubbed them, played a pivotal role in auto production.

Here and in other industries producing durable metal goods, tool-making was the foundation of mass production. As such, it marked a recent innovation in manufacturing practice. Until well after the Civil War, metalworking had proceeded in a craftsman's realm that encompassed the shop owner, the foreman, and the journeyman. After 1890, however, "scientific management" aimed at a total transformation of metalworking by removing skills from production and reconstituting authority in a new strata of white-collar engineers. This managerial revolution steadily gained momentum after the turn of the century, but it was in the rise of the auto industry after 1910 that the assault on craft production proceeded with particular urgency and spectacular results. Inspired by the example of Henry Ford, carmakers introduced jigs, fixtures, stamping dies, and other specialized tools and machines that helped eliminate craft skills from production. Yet ironically, even as scientific management carried the day on the shop floor, it could not escape its dependence on the new strata of skilled workers its methods and machines relied on: the toolmakers and maintenance workers who engineered the instruments of control.

Auto and Skilled Labor
in Detroit, 1899–1907

In 1899, Ransom Olds opened the first Detroit factory to make "self-driven wagons." Producing one or two cars a day, the new plant launched Detroit into the Automotive Age, but its production methods harkened back to the craft techniques of a not-so-distant past. Compared with the mechanized and management-controlled practices advocated by Frederick Taylor and other proselytizers of scientific management, the Olds plant, like most in the early auto industry, employed artisan methods and craft labor. The very cars produced by these pioneer automakers also borrowed from the past. Mechanically, they were a crude amalgam of components adapted from the bicycle and marine-launch industries: sprocket and chain drives, ball bearings, tubular frames, wire wheels, and pneumatic tires came from the former, and engine components came from the latter. Outwardly, the lineage of the "horseless carriage" was easily traced to the wagon industry: the open bodies were made of wood, with a single or two-cylinder engine mounted horizontally beneath the buggy-style seat.[3]

Together with the technology of these older modes of transportation came a trained work force of skilled craftsmen. "The mechanics who could do the work in the bicycle shops," *Iron Age* reported in 1903, "could easily turn their hands to the work required of them in the automobile plant. In a half dozen of the latter it was found that half of the workmen and skilled mechanics had formerly worked in the bicycle shops." Likewise, body making relied on the skills and capital of the carriage industry. But in contrast to the more standardized and large-scale production runs in bicycle and wagon making, production in the early years of automaking reflected the primitive and unsettled nature of the product. While manufacturers tested alternative means of powering the vehicle (steam, electric, or gas-fueled engines), cooling its power plant (air or water), and steering it (tiller or wheel), production methods necessarily remained chaotic and experimental.[4]

Under these conditions, auto manufacturing reproduced the basic elements of craft production, a form of workplace organization characteristic of metalworking before 1890. Until the movement for scientific management gained a substantial following in the new century, most managers delegated shop-floor authority and initiative to skilled workers acting as foremen, master mechanics, or inside contractors. In some industries, notably gun making, machine tools, bicycle manufacturing, and sewing machines, "armory practice" had modified this system to include machinery with special tools and fixtures for interchangeable manufacturing. But many sectors of metalworking still relied on hand tools and general-purpose machines.[5]

Such was the case in auto. Since production runs were minuscule and product modifications were continual, heavy investment in specialized machine tools and automatic methods was out of the question. Production barely moved beyond the prototype stage, and in most cases the chief innovators were not the white-collar engineers rising to prominence in some large-scale metalworking firms, but craftsmen trained in the shop. Some had been formally apprenticed: Henry Ford at the Detroit Shipbuilding Company; Henry Leland, founder of Cadillac and Lincoln, in the gun factories and machine-tool shops of New England; David Buick (reportedly) at the James Flowers and Brothers Machine Shop in Detroit; and Jonathan Maxwell, cofounder of the Maxwell-Briscoe Motor Company (forerunner of Chrysler) in the machine shops of northern Indiana. Others, including Ransom Olds, Henry and Clement Studebaker, and the Dodge brothers, apprenticed in their fathers' blacksmith shops.[6]

The production process these pioneer automakers supervised was relatively unmechanized and highly skill-dependent. The patternmakers who carved wooden replicas of a part; the foundry molders and coremakers who used these patterns to make sand molds for casting; the forge workers who pounded hot metal into shape with their steam hammers; the machinists and metal polishers who removed excess metal with general-purpose machines and hand tools; the carpenters who built the bodies; the painters who hand-brushed the slow-drying lacquers on the cars' exteriors; and the upholsterers who hand-stitched the interiors—all worked according to craft norms that defied scientific management. Since these craft workers varied in their skills, attitudes, and performance on the job, the parts and components they produced also varied in their approximation of the blueprinted design. Consequently, they were not interchangeable, and the assembly process involved far more than simply bolting components together. In addition to the wrench and the riveter, assemblers had to wield the hammer and the file to force ill-fitting parts into proper alignment. "Proper alignment" wasn't precisely defined in any case. "The mechanic fastened it the way he thought best," recalled Bredo Berghoff of assembly methods prevailing at the Hewitt Automobile Company in 1906. "There was no particular rule about how things had to be done."[7]

Of necessity, these assemblers had to be skilled mechanics, capable of conceptualizing how the finished component would work, and therefore able to realign the imperfect parts. "I made complete carburetors for each engine," Joseph Galamb remembered of his stint at the Stearns Automobile Company in Cleveland, where he worked briefly in 1904. "They had to be all built up from the machine parts. Nobody had an assembly line in those days. . . . They all just built up each car separately." Some workers, like Galamb, assembled entire components—carburetors, engines, rear axles. Others worked in teams, as in the body-making shops. William Chalmers, who took a job at Packard in the 1920s to research the industry's personnel policies, described how one older co-worker recalled the early production methods: "He could remember when the wooden frame for a body was brought to two men working at a 'stand,' a location on the floor, and then all of the various materials necessary were deposited around the body. The two men worked for three and a half days on the same job, and turned out a complete automobile body at the end of that time." In final assembly, Henry Ford recalled a similar process. "We simply started to put a car together at a spot on the floor and workmen brought to it the parts as they were needed in exactly the same way that one builds a house."[8]

Such work was difficult to subdivide, since at any point in the process only the craft worker and his teammates knew the unique sequence of adjustments already made to "fit" the components together. At each stage in the production process, whether pattern shop, foundry, forge, machine shop, body plant, or final assembly, this "unitary" feature of craft production was evident to varying degrees. But few of these production steps took place under the same roof or, for that matter, within the same firm. Automakers, as noted above, borrowed heavily from preexisting technologies, and in practice this meant they relied on preexisting firms to supply them with castings, forgings, machined parts, and finished bodies. Among the hundreds of car companies that appeared after the turn of the century, most were small assembly plants with only a smattering of machine tools. With so little production done in-house, the average firm employed only eighty-five workers in 1904.[9]

Detroit soon established itself as the favored location for the industry's leading companies. There were several reasons for this. As auto historian George May notes, the machine shops of southeastern Michigan had already developed a unique ability to cast, machine, and assemble gasoline engines.

While highly talented mechanics and automobile experimenters elsewhere continued . . . trying to work out the problems of developing road vehicles powered by steam or electricity, the same type of individuals in Michigan, almost without exception, were working with gasoline engines—first, perhaps, to develop small engines for marine uses. . . . Sintz, Worth, King, Ford, Brush, Murray, Buick, Joy, Dodge, Leland, Marr, Richard, Maxwell—the list goes on.[10]

Drawing on a rich hinterland of hardwood forests, the nearby cities of Pontiac and Flint hosted a flourishing wagon industry, and Detroit was second only to Connecticut in fabricating Michigan copper into a wide range of metal goods. Like Chicago and Cleveland, Detroit had easy access to lake-born transport of iron ore from Lake Superior and coal from Ohio, and its central location in the Midwest gave it uniform access to a national market—something New England's early automakers sorely lacked. Other midwestern cities had greater concentrations of wealth, but Detroit's industrial base was diversified across a wider spectrum of metalworking trades, providing ample latitude and resources for new initiatives.[11]

The city's budding auto industry expanded accordingly, relying on a work force that grew with the arrival of immigrants from Britain, Germany, Poland, Italy, and Russia. In 1901, Oldsmobile's Detroit plant assembled 400 cars, second only to the Connecticut-based Locomobile, builder of the famous steam-powered car, in U.S. production. Two years later, Olds produced 4,000 cars in its Detroit and Lansing plants and became the industry's undisputed leader, followed by Cadillac's annual production of 1,700 automobiles. Together, these two Michigan firms produced over half the national total of 11,200 cars sold in 1903, and as national sales tripled in the next three years, Detroit's auto industry grew apace.[12]

There were, however, problems that plagued Detroit's automakers from the start. Their market was growing, but it was still restricted to wealthy sports enthusiasts, thrill seekers, and professionals. A far larger market awaited if the industry could produce a simplified, low-cost, and reliable car, but none of these conditions were easily achieved before 1907–1910. Reliability was a particularly vexing problem, since improving any one element of a car's design often produced or aggravated some other difficulty. When automakers replaced wire spokes with wooden artillery wheels in 1903, they gained strength but added considerable weight to the car and stress to the already overtaxed engine; when they enlarged the engine to four cylinders, the power plant no longer fit under the carriage seat, and the entire body had to be redesigned. Most troublesome of all, the metals that had proved adequate for the bicycle frequently fatigued and fractured when used to produce camshafts, axles, gears, and other high-stress components. The only known alternative to carbon steel for producing these parts was a nickel alloy used to make locomotive axles, but this nickel steel was so tough that machining of parts became extremely difficult.[13]

Matters were not always helped by the automakers' dependence on outside suppliers. As manufacturers strove to secure the volume of castings they needed, foundry owners discovered they could raise prices and lower quality without losing customers. Automakers, anxious to meet rising demand and acutely aware that other car manufacturers were searching for castings, accepted the shoddy work because, as one observer wrote in 1906, "they were afraid that if they sent them back, the foundry would refuse to cast any more for them." Since many foundries also specialized in particular metals and particular kinds of work, car manufacturers had to rely on as many as a dozen suppliers to secure the iron, steel, brass, and aluminum castings they needed. Multiple sourcing, in turn, produced multiple variations in the castings' approximation of the blueprinted design, requiring additional fitting and trimming of dissimilar parts during assembly.[14]

With these production bottlenecks added to the already time-consuming work of building, trimming, and painting car bodies—some wooden carriages required as many as eleven coats of varnish and more than six weeks for the seventy-five pounds of pigment to dry—the result was an exceedingly low level of productivity. In 1899, industry-wide production amounted to 1.66 cars per worker per year; five years later, total output had jumped 482 percent, but productivity barely climbed 8 percent in the same period, rising to just 1.8 cars per worker per year. To raise output, management had to add labor in lockstep with rising production: from 2,240 workers industry-wide in 1899 to 12,000 workers by 1904—or from 4,050 to 36,000 over the same period counting workers in body and parts plants. Finding this many skilled workers was no easy task, and managing them presented the profit-conscious employer with even greater headaches.[15]

This was especially so after 1901, when Detroit's metalworkers redoubled their efforts to enforce craft control of production. Buoyed by the heavy demand for their skills and a nationwide upsurge in union organizing, they challenged management in a wide range of areas, including work rules, methods, hours, wages, and closed-shop hiring. Their efforts met with considerable success. In May 1901, Detroit's International Association of Machinists (IAM) struck for shorter hours, and although it failed at several big plants, the union eventually forced twenty-eight metalworking shops to reduce the mandatory work day from ten hours to nine. That summer, striking members of the Amalgamated Iron, Steel, and Tin Workers Union forced two of the city's major employers, Detroit Spring & Steel and American Car & Foundry, to honor the union wage scale and grant 5 percent pay increases. In December, the Iron Molders began a six-month strike against the Buhl Malleable Iron Works and, after several violent confrontations with strikebreakers, finally forced the company to grant their Shop Committee authority over wage rates on new work. Rejuvenated by these victories, Detroit's unions grew from a citywide membership of 8,000 in 1901 to 14,000 in 1903, representing 9.5 percent of the city's total work force and considerably higher percentages in construction, transportation, and metalworking.[16]

Faced with these union gains, management spokesman John Whirl complained that Detroit's employers "had no more real control than if they were in no way connected with the shop." Especially critical of union work rules that regulated the introduction of machinery, he concluded that in a closed shop "the proprietors were merely the financial agents" for a production process controlled by union tradesmen. "It was for them [managers] to find out the cost of production as arranged by organized labor, and then make the selling price sufficient to leave them a profit."[17]

In metalworking, this upswing in union power was concentrated in the established foundries and machine shops that automakers relied on. A few auto assembly plants were affected by the 1901 strikes, including a temporary disruption at the Olds factory during the Machinists' walkout, but craft unions established no significant degree of organization in the still chaotic environment of this new industry. Yet even without formal organization, skilled autoworkers wielded considerable power, especially when automakers were as desperate to find competent machinists as they were to secure good castings. Ill-defined and constantly changing work procedures, combined with the craft methods prevailing in the industry, gave the skilled worker substantial latitude in the pacing and the organization of his work. A single episode, reported in 1906 by a plant spy in the Ford Motor Company, gives ample testimony to this distinctive feature of automobile production during the industry's early years. When a foreman and an engine tester argued, and then wagered, over how a particular engine part worked, they hit upon a logical means for settling the dispute: they stopped production for a half hour to dismantle the motor and explore its inner workings.[18]

Management Takes Control

There was no single point where these problems of craft production, union power, restricted markets, inadequate machine tools, and overdependence on outside suppliers suddenly coalesced into a distinct crisis. Rather, these problems were recognized very nearly at the start of the auto industry's life, and the crisis they produced was, in a sense, perpetual.

Efforts to correct the situation also began early. In December 1902, the city's brass manufacturers and foundry owners formed the Employers Association of Detroit (EAD), and the following year this organization launched a concerted campaign to counterattack the unions and establish the open shop. Between 1903 and 1907, companies fired union supporters and refused to renew closed-shop agreements, provoking dozens of major strikes. To ensure that unions, once driven from the workplace, would not stage a comeback, the EAD also established a citywide Labor Bureau to recruit strikebreakers and screen out "troublemakers." By 1906, the Labor Bureau had files on 40,000 people—nearly half of Detroit's work force.[19]

The decisive turning point came in 1907, when virtually all of Detroit's organized trades—including boilermakers, machinists, molders, patternmakers, metal polishers, painters, upholsterers—struck to defend their craft organizations. These sustained and often violent confrontations underlined both the strengths and the fatal weaknesses of craft unionism. In Detroit's machine shops, shipyards, and foundries, craft workers frequently came to the aid of fellow unionists with sympathy strikes that widened a single craft's dispute into a general work stoppage. But solidarity usually stopped short of including the unskilled and sometimes explicitly excluded the foreign-born. In 1904, Detroit's Boilermakers had adopted a resolution opposing "the employment of foreigners in the building of iron ships." The foreign-born were hired just same, and fighting between Italian strikebreakers and native-born craft unionists punctuated the Boilermakers' strike defeat at the Great Lakes Engineering Company in June 1907. The Metal Polishers also lost an eight-week strike that spring as police escorted Hungarian strikebreakers into the plants. Plagued by inter-ethnic conflict and their own exclusive practices, and overwhelmed by court injunctions, heavy police patrolling, and the Labor Bureau's tightening control of the labor marker, Detroit's craft unions met with crushing defeat in 1907.[20]

Simultaneously, Detroit's metalworking companies launched a technical revolution that swept through every sector of the auto industry— a revolution that began with the very nature of metal itself, and which found its most complete expression in the near total revamping of the machine-tool industry.[21]

New alloys of vanadium, chromium, and tungsten made automobile components stronger and more reliable as American steelmakers developed alloying technologies originating in Europe. After 1907, alloy steels found wide application in all the mechanical stress points of the automobile. Body and frame construction also changed: structural steel had already replaced tubular frames for holding the engine, drive train, and wheel components, and while car bodies retained their wood frames, steel panels now began to replace wood in the body's outer skin. But as so often proved to be the case in building a complex machine like the automobile, solving one problem only aggravated another. Precisely the same qualities that made the new alloys strong enough to stand the stress and loadings of the automobile also made them difficult to machine. "We found it a hopeless task to attempt to turn a piece of alloy steel in one of our old, small lathes," said one manufacturer in 1907. "The machine chattered and jumped, threatening to go to pieces every minute." Yet, as the *American Machinist* later observed, the cause of these difficulties also provided their solution. "The alloy steels, developed in the first place for automobile use, were the answer." Employers downgraded or replaced an entire generation of machine tools with new machines made from alloy steels. In addition to being stronger and heavier, they were designed with faster speeds and feeds to utilize the benefits of high-speed cutting steels. Multiple tooling that allowed simultaneous drilling of several parts or rapid change from one tool to another also became more common.[22]

Contemporary observers had little doubt where the stimulus for these changes came from. "As in steel making," *Automobile* magazine reported in 1907, "machine tool design has advanced more under the influence of the automobile than it would have in several times as many years otherwise." Not only did the needs of automobile production generate technological innovation in these related industries, it also provided the specific model for solving many technical problems. As machine tools, for example, grew larger, faster, and more powerful, the old means of lubricating the machine's bearings with a hand-held oil can no longer proved adequate. "In casting about for an answer to this problem," the *American Machinist* reported, "the machine-tool designer found a suggestion in the multiple jet, drip, and force-feed oiling systems which were being developed to such a great degree in automobile design."[23]

The auto industry, once dependent on production technologies derived from previous modes of transportation, was now generating its own distinctive production methods. Multiple-head and specialized machine tools predated the auto industry, but it was auto manufacturing that developed these innovations with an unprecedented scope. The pace of technical change quickened after mid-decade, and by the recession of 1907 auto manufacturers were installing a whole new generation of turret lathes, radial drills, borers, grinders, and drill presses. As they retooled, many also reorganized their machine shops to replace the previous grouping of machines by function with a sequential arrangement that mirrored the production process and eliminated the need for trucking parts from one department to another.[24]

As in older metalworking industries where extensive mechanization began before 1900, the introduction of new and more numerous machine tools in auto manufacturing produced several new occupational stratums within the factory. Increasingly, the individual pioneers who designed and built their first cars by cut-and-try methods had to turn to hired engineers and tool designers to blueprint an ever more complex production process. Between 1905 and 1907, Henry Ford established a design department and hired the draftsmen who would go on to produce the Model T and the Model A; by the latter year, Ford's General Drafting room had a staff of fourteen, half of them working on car design, and half on tool design. At this point, Ford was actually less inclined to delegate authority than most manufacturers, for in the same year, Maxwell-Briscoe already had twenty-four draftsmen and Cadillac had nearly fifty.[25]

In redesigning the work process for cutting metal, these engineers had at least six interconnected goals: first, to replace handwork with machines; second, to design holding fixtures to quickly locate and clamp the metal stock into the machine tool and reduce set-up time to a bare minimum; third, to increase the machine tool's cutting precision; fourth, to simplify its operations; fifth, to increase its cutting or grinding speed; and sixth, to make it fully automatic. In addition to speed and reduced labor costs, a critical focus of these innovations was interchangeable parts. Where skilled craftsmen using hand tools and general-purpose machines had previously produced parts that varied as much as their individual skills, now special machines using holding fixtures and automatic controls would consistently drive the cutting tool through the same precise motions, time after time.

The Ford Motor Company moved fastest and farthest in this direction between 1907 and 1917, surpassing all others in its commitment to designing and installing its own specialized tools and fixtures. As the Model T, introduced in 1908, tapped a fast-growing market for low-cost automobiles, this spiraling demand drove Ford engineers to adopt unprecedented levels of mechanization. By 1914, the same company that eight years before had owned virtually no production machines had installed 15,000 machine tools and other devices in its Highland Park factory. The company's expanded tool design room was "constantly designing new machines," as one stockholder report later observed. "The trend always was to cut down the number of operations to the smallest possible unit and then design a machine to do that operation with unskilled labor."[26]

As the stockholders well understood, rapid mechanization proceeded with the detailed division of labor, a process that found its most celebrated expression in the moving assembly line. But although the assembly line took center stage in the public imagination, it was a subsidiary development of the more fundamental innovations in machine tools and special fixtures. Assembly-line methods were only possible with interchangeable parts—parts that did not require last-minute fitting and filing by hand. "In mass production," as Henry Ford put it, "there are no fitters," and it was the new generation of machine tools and fixtures that made this possible. Here again, the auto industry was leading the way. "Probably one of the most extensive and far reaching effects of the development of automobile manufacturing," as the *American Machinist* saw it, "is the growth of the jig and fixture and other methods of securing interchangeability of parts."[27]

To produce interchangeable parts in large volume, automakers reduced their reliance on outside machine shops. Only when machine tools were tailored to the specific needs and pace of the production process could the assembly line be assured of a continuous supply of parts, and while outside contracting continued (and increased in absolute volume), low-cost, high-volume manufacturers increasingly shifted to in-house production. For much the same reason, automakers were also integrating the preceding steps of the manufacturing process into their firms. If improving the precision and increasing the output of machined parts was important, the quality and the volume of the inputs to the machining process also demanded closer attention. Bad castings with hard spots, blowholes, and imperfect dimensions required extra machining, and if the output from foundry and forge could not keep pace with the accelerated methods in the machine shop and final assembly, production ground to a halt. Recognizing the need to coordinate the quality and quantity of each phase of production, the larger automakers who could afford the necessary capital investment expanded their plants and incorporated much of the production process under their corporate roof. Before 1906, Cadillac was one of the few automakers with its own foundry; by 1921, all the major manufacturers had built pattern works, foundries, and forges.[28]

With these operations in-house, automakers could concentrate on innovations that, by making the machining of parts less necessary, contributed to the accelerated pace of automobile production. Chief among these were die casting, cold stamping, and electric welding.

Die Casting.   This process, first used in the production of cash registers in 1904, used a metal mold, or "die," instead of a sand mold to cast metal parts. The process had many advantages over sand casting, including the reuse of the mold and the capacity to cast a part that was closer to its finished size, thereby reducing the amount of machining that was required before assembly. After initial difficulties controlling for warpage, caused as the die and casting cooled at different rates, the process found wide applications in the auto industry. By the early 1920s, an unskilled laborer could turn out 900 piston castings per eight-hour shift on a die-casting machine, compared with 200 pistons per eight-hour shift by sand casting—and the latter process still required some expensive molding skills.[29]

Drawing the obvious conclusion from such comparisons, one contemporary observer summed up the essence of what die casting represented: "The skill of the tool maker, embodied in the construction of intricate dies, is used by the unskilled worker in producing and reproducing castings ranking high in quality and quantity."[30]

Pressed Steel.   For centuries, casting and forging hot metal were the only known methods for producing parts. Early clock makers first developed cold stamping to punch out gear blanks and clock plates, but the stamping of larger parts began with the wagon and bicycle industries in the late nineteenth century. Midwestern manufacturers were the first to use it as an alternative to forging, and automakers initially adopted the process to produce clips, braces, and brackets. As they searched for alternatives to the heavy castings then in use, they began to employ pressed steel to produce rear-axle housings (beginning in 1907), body panels (beginning 1907–1909), body frames (Ford in 1925), and flywheel covers, brake drums, oil pans, piston rods, and other major components. Again, the use of a metal die—in this case a stamping die—made it possible to expand the volume and quality of metal parts while reducing the required number of molders, forgers, and machinists. Not only did pressed steel save weight, but, as the *American Machinist* noted, "many machining operations were eliminated and parts were delivered to the plant ready for assembly."[31]

Welding. Before 1885, forging hammers were the only means available for welding metal. With the invention of electric-resistance welding by 1888 and acetylene welding around 1900, manufacturers of metal machinery acquired a much faster and more flexible means of joining parts. Automakers first used acetylene and then electric welding to replace riveting and bolting. Gas torches required some skill to produce a good weld, but the development of electric welding machines and special jigs and fixtures to hold the work made possible the mass production of welded parts by less skilled labor. Welding, in turn, made the use of pressed steel all the more attractive, since it enabled automakers to produce a complete axle housing, for example, by welding separate stampings.[32]

Together, these innovations produced a spectacular increase in productivity. As indicated in Table 1.1., the most rapid improvement occurred in the five-year-period between 1909 and 1914, during which the Ford Motor Company developed the moving assembly line and captured 48 percent of the industry's market. Henry Ford certainly was enriched by this success, but as unit costs tumbled he also cut the price of his Model T, thereby widening the market and boosting employment even as labor productivity soared. As competing companies emulated this strategy (to varying degrees), the auto industry grew by leaps and bounds, catalyzing a stunning transformation of America's social and economic life.

Detroit Transformed

With the auto industry's new methods came new jobs, new immigrants, and new threats to craft unionism.

TABLE 1.1
OUTPUT PER AUTOWORKER, 1899–1921

Year	No. wage earners	Annual production	Cars per worker	Percentage increase
1899	2,241	3,723	1.66	—
1904	12,049	21,692	1.80	8.4
1909	51,294	126,570	2.47	37.2
1914	79,307	568,781	7.17	190.3
1919	210,559	1,888,059	8.97	25.1
1921	143,658	1,602,336	11.15	24.3

SOURCE: Mortimer La Fever, "Workers, Machinery, and Production in the Auto Industry," *Monthly Labor Review* 19 (October 1924): 736.

NOTE: Figures do not include body and parts plants.

As late as 1910, three-quarters of the auto industry's labor force could still be classified as skilled tradesmen; by 1913, however, the Ford Motor Company's chief stockholders claimed that 70 percent of the firm's 15,000 workers "could be taught their operation in less than two days time and did not need to be able to read, write, or speak the English language. . . . Very few skilled workmen were necessary," the stockholder analysis concluded, "except in the tool room."[33]

In the toolroom, Ford employed some 250 highly skilled workers by 1915, all of them "first class mechanics" in the estimation of Horace Arnold and Fay Leone Faurote, authors of *Ford Methods and Ford Shops*. But elsewhere, the company applied a different criteria in selecting its work force: "The Ford Motor Company has no use for experience, in the working ranks, anyway. It desires and prefers machine-tool operators who have nothing to unlearn, who have no theories of correct surface speeds for metal finishing, and will simply do what they are told to do, over and over again, from bell-time to bell-time."[34]

In a normal industrial environment, finding such workers would not be difficult. But Detroit was not a normal industrial environment. In 1908, the city's booming auto factories produced 20,000 cars; ten years later, production topped one million—a staggering 4,900 percent increase. Even with the rapid advances in worker productivity, Detroit's seventy car companies had to expand their total work force to 135,000, nearly quadruple the *entire* manufacturing labor force in all Detroit industries in 1900. The industry's high wages drew thousands of metalworkers, midwestern farmhands, and southern farm laborers to Detroit, but employers constantly strove to expand this migratory stream. As early as 1907, Detroit's Board of Commerce asked immigration officials on New York's Ellis Island to steer foreign workers to the city, while the EAD placed ads in nearly 200 newspapers across the country encouraging both skilled workers and immigrant laborers to come to the Motor City.[35]

They came in droves, swelling the city's population from less than 300,000 at the turn of the century to over 1.5 million by 1927. Open fields and dirt roads on the edge of town gave way to subdivisions of brick cottages, bungalows, and two-family homes. In some years, the Detroit Department of Buildings issued twenty-one permits for new construction every day. "Families unable to rent," the *Detroit Free Press* reported in the summer of 1913, "have purchased sites and lived on them in tents or shacks while their homes were being rushed to completion." Like prospecting towns of the old West, Detroit was full of single men. Some never intended to stay: they planned to work several years, save money, and return to Europe or the South. Others hoped to bring wives and families to Detroit once they established themselves, and others, part of a growing "suitcase brigade," regularly commuted back to their rural (usually southern) homes between jobs. By 1920, Detroit had 119 males for every 100 females—an imbalance surpassed only by Akron, Ohio, among the nation's seventy largest cities.[36]

Detroit's industrialists soon came to regard this mass of immigrant and migratory workers as an unpredictable genie—at once a highly profitable source of labor power, but also a volatile, alien force that could not always be controlled. High absenteeism, rapid turnover, poor discipline, and the myriad problems caused by a multilingual work force absorbed the energies of every company. For factory owners seeking to mass-produce a standardized automobile, their solution to this "labor problem" was the social equivalent of their production strategy: they would mass-produce standardized "Americans." Ford, the acknowledged leader in mass production, also led the way in this social engineering of an entire work force, doubling wages to five dollars a day to encourage conformity, and installing both a "Sociological Department" and a mandatory English School to enforce it.[37]

Craft unions fared even worse than ethnic subcultures. The latter, though hard-pressed by the social engineering of corporate Americanizers, were at least outside the immediate bounds of management authority. Craft workers, in contrast, experienced the unmediated impact of management's production engineering, and the transformation of metalworking between 1900 and 1920 all but obliterated the jurisdictional coherence of craft unionism. Between 1904 and 1919, the average auto assembly plant's work force grew eightfold, to 668 workers, and as jobs were subdivided and skills fragmented, the old distinctions between crafts and between skilled and unskilled were correspondingly muddied. It was soon apparent to many trade unionists that no one of the seventeen different craft unions claiming some portion of the auto work force could win recognition from the powerful corporations that now dominated the industry. As early as 1905, the Detroit Federation of Labor endorsed the growing sentiment for a unified movement, declaring it "the duty of every honorable laboring man to devote his energy and attention to the concentration of all unions into one solid union."[38]

Unity was easier to invoke as an abstract ideal than achieve in practice. The IAM seemed prepared to make the transition to a class-bound industrial union in 1911 with the election of a socialist president, William Johnston, and the decision to open its ranks to women and unskilled helpers (while still excluding blacks). Membership soared from 63,000 in 1912 to 127,000 in 1917 and, after especially rapid growth during World War I, to 331,000 members in 1919. But with the dismantling of wartime regulations, the IAM lost the legal protections that favored its growth in federal arsenals and on government-controlled railroads, and postwar layoffs and strikebreaking reversed the gains of the preceding years. The defeat of the nationwide railroad shopmen's strike in 1922 was the most definitive setback in a long slide, which by 1925 had reduced national membership to barely 72,000. When the ailing Johnston stepped down in 1926 and died soon after, Arthur Wharton, his conservative replacement, steered the IAM toward the calmer backwaters of pure and simple craft unionism.[39]

It remained for the union of Carriage, Wagon, and Automobile Workers (CWAW), a left-wing organization outside the AFL, to demonstrate the potential of industrial unionism in Detroit. Not coincidentally, the one sector of the industry where this maverick union nearly achieved a significant and stable presence also happened to be the one sector least affected by the mechanized and machine-tooled methods introduced before World War I: body making.

Body making resisted mechanization and skill dilution for several reasons. Chief among them was the fact that the automobile's body and passenger compartment served as the car's visible standard in the marketplace, and its finish and trim therefore required more attention than the exteriors of most mechanical components. Many of the irregular surfaces under the hood and beneath the floorboards could be left rough and unadorned. "What is the use of finishing up the hidden parts of a chassis as if you are going to put it in a parlor?" Walter Chrysler told Buick paint-shop workers when he became factory manager in 1912. "This stuff is caked with road mud on the first day it is used." Exterior body panels, however, had to be carefully smoothed, polished, and painted by hand. Likewise with body seams: it hardly mattered whether the welds on a rear axle housing were visible, but it mattered a great deal if the seams between body panels were not properly joined. Such work demanded a certain degree of skill from the metal finisher, who used hammer, soldering iron, and file to produce a smooth seam. Installing interior trim also required skill in securing fabric, moldings, and upholstery to the irregular surfaces of the passenger compartment. Many aspects of these varied trades were subdivided before World War I, but most of it was still performed with hand tools at fixed work stations. The demand for painters, metal finishers, frame builders, trimmers, and other skilled and semiskilled workers to perform these tasks was all the greater in firms that frequently changed the body styling.[40]

It was among these body workers that the CWAW established its base. Founded in 1886 as a union of carriage builders, this organization had a unique history which would carry it through every phase of the modern labor movement's organizational development. Starting as a Knights of Labor assembly, it reorganized its faltering membership into the AFL in 1891. In 1899, in a remarkably prophetic assessment, the union's journal predicted "beyond a shadow of a doubt, that [automobiles] will be the means of throwing the present constructed [sic] carriage or wagon on the scrap pile in the very near future." The union immediately began to recruit members in this growing industry, and in 1909 added "Automobile" to its name. Until 1913, its publications were printed in both German and English and included frequent reprints of articles by Karl Marx, Ferdinand Lassalle, and Karl Kautsky.[41]

From the beginning, the union was embroiled in jurisdictional disputes with the many AFL crafts claiming membership in auto-body manufacturing. The CWAW's socialist leaders, including William Logan, the English-born president elected in 1913, refused to recognize these claims and contemptuously dismissed the AFL's 1914 order to abandon industrial unionism and surrender its members. Craft unions, the CWAW countered, had no commitment to organizing in auto: the Blacksmiths were "practically out of business"; the Metal Polishers "stand on poverty row"; the Patternmakers "as auto factory organizers are a joke"; the Machinists charged a $200 initiation fee and had "only one of three machinists organized"; and the Painters "did not have 500 carriage painters in the U.S." and should stick to the "lowly" house painters they represented. This was not what the AFL wanted to hear, and it expelled the CWAW in 1918.[42]

"No organization that pulls out of the A.F. of L. ever has cause to regret it," William Logan declared on behalf of his "outlaw" union, now rechristened the United Automobile, Aircraft, and Vehicle Workers of America (UAAVWA). Apparently fulfilling Logan's brave words, the UAAVWA prospered outside the AFL and blossomed in 1919, when union organizing drives and mass strikes also swept the nation's steel, railroad, coal, and other industries. Spurred by this national movement, the UAAVWA organized some 40,000 workers into thirty-five locals, with sizable memberships in New York City, Cincinnati, Flint, and above all, in Detroit Local 127. The union's Detroit membership was concentrated in the body-making plants, and between 1918 and 1921, all of Local 127's major strikes took place in this sector of the industry, from the Wadsworth manufacturing and Wilson Body strikes of 1919 (both companies made bodies for Ford), to the 1921 strikes at Fisher Body, Packard, and Hupp. While strikes did occur among other sectors of the auto work force in these years, the body workers in the UAAVWA were the only group with sufficient leverage to force their employers into bargaining over hours, wages, and working conditions.[43]

For a brief moment, it appeared the UAAVWA might establish a continuing presence in Detroit's factories and working-class neighborhoods. Inside the plants, Local 127 had a membership of between 30,000 and 35,000 and was growing at the rate of 1,000 members a month in late 1919, early 1920. Outside the shop, the union organized a Tenants League to counter rent gouging in Detroit's crowded housing market and a Private Soldiers and Sailors Legion to counter the right-wing veterans organizations formed after the war. When postwar layoffs began late in 1920, Local 127 organized a "Stew Club" to feed the unemployed; when the local issued its bylaws the same year, they were printed in Polish as well as English. But the UAAVWA's gains were short-lived. As an avowedly left-wing union, with frequent reprints of Lenin, Trotsky, and Liebnicht in its paper, the Detroit local took its share of abuse during the nationwide Red Scare following World War I. By late 1919, police were arresting union members for selling the *Auto Workers News* and charging them under Michigan's Criminal Syndicalism Act. When the economy slumped in 1921 and employers began laying off workers and cutting wages, the union became embroiled in a series of bitter and largely unsuccessful strikes.[44]

The New Model: Body Making

The severe depression of 1921 destroyed the UAAVWA's momentum, and membership quickly plummeted to roughly 1,500. Fundamental changes in the production process thereafter reduced the UAAVWA's old constituency in the body plants. As with previous innovations in forming and machining metal parts, a key step in that transformation was the successful effort by major auto manufacturers to consolidate the production process under one roof and replace production skills with new tools, fixtures, and machines.[45]

Until 1919, body making was the single largest sector of the auto industry still dominated by independent suppliers. Several factors accounted for the decision by most large automakers to absorb a portion of this production after World War I. The very strikes that demonstrated the power of the UAAVWA helped motivate Ford to reduce its dependence on outside suppliers and accelerate plans to install body-making capacity at its new Dearborn complex. In August 1919, three months after Local 127 struck Wadsworth and Wilson, the body plant in B-Building began producing 800 touring car and sedan bodies a day. General Motors gained control of Fisher Body by the end of 1921 and immediately reorganized, subdivided, and mechanized as much of the work as it could. Ensuring stability of supply was a chief motive behind this move, and the direct integration of body making into GM's production process also facilitated the planning and coordination of annual model changes. Similar considerations impelled Chrysler to buy the American Body Company's plant in 1925 and retool it to build Chrysler bodies. Ford and Chrysler still bought a considerable portion of their bodies or body parts from independent suppliers, but the independents were also consolidating their operations as Briggs Manufacturing and Murray Body led the way in absorbing smaller firms. Using their own internal capacity as a lever, the big automakers could foster competition among these independents and saddle them with the stigma of being low-wage employers.[46]

An additional impetus for this consolidating movement among automakers and independent suppliers was the demand for closed bodies. More powerful engines, stronger pressed-steel frames, and better roads all made the closed body more feasible, and the postwar success of the Hudson Motor Car Company in selling such a design made production of closed bodies a market imperative. Production of closed bodies soared correspondingly, from 30 percent of total output in 1922 to 85 percent in 1928.[47]

The high cost of this changeover drove many firms out of the business; the technical revolution that accompanied the changeover did the same for many skilled and semiskilled workers. The new bodies, for example, were increasingly made of steel. The use of wood to build body frames, still common at the beginning of the 1920s, was declining by the end of the decade and was virtually extinct after the mid-1930s. Ford converted to an all-steel body and frame in 1925; ten years later, Fisher Body replaced wooden body frames with its all-steel "Turret Top" body for Chevrolets, Oldsmobiles, and Pontiacs. Metal stampings made body frames both stronger and lighter, and demand for skilled woodworkers declined accordingly.[48]

Closed bodies made of pressed steel panels required considerably more welding than open bodies, and the need to join these panels as quickly as possible led to more extensive use of jigs and fixtures. As in the machining of engine parts and other mechanical components, jigs and fixtures ensured uniform and exact placement of the work without human judgment. By also replacing the skilled welder using an acetylene torch with an unskilled worker using an electric seam welder, the combined result was a significant increase in productivity. By 1924, a man using an electric welder and fixtures could weld sixty rear-quarter panels an hour, compared with only twelve and a half such welds by a skilled man using a torch.[49]

Ten years later, the development of electric welding and special jigs and fixtures had reached the point where automated welding machines in the Dodge Body shop could join nine body parts together with 160 spot welds in just forty-five seconds. "Welding guns start in sequence and when the welds are completed, the fixture opens automatically, ready for the removal of the finished part," *Automotive Industries* reported. Such automated methods ensured standardization by "eliminating the human element that is now usually present in welding work. The function of the operator is now limited to loading, starting, and unloading, with no variable time allowance for the handling of welding tools, maneuvering into difficult places, etc."[50] After reviewing similar innovations in body making between 1921 and 1936, auto analyst Blanche Bernstein aptly observed that "skill has been shifted and restricted to the preparation of tools and dies."[51]

Among the skills "shifted and restricted" were those of metal finishers. Their numbers grew as closed steel bodies replaced open carriages, but their skills declined in the late 1920s as pneumatic belt sanders began to replace the hand files they had previously wielded. The same process of mechanization and deskilling awaited trimmers.

Where before, they had worked in teams and trimmed complete bodies at stationary work stations, after 1921, the bodies were mounted on conveyors and the work subdivided into detailed tasks.[52]

By 1930, *Automotive Industries* could report that in the Dodge trim department, "following the straight-line production methods so eminently successful in chassis departments, all trim operations have been finely sub-divided, mechanized as far as possible, and arranged in logical sequence along the body trim line."[53]

Of all the skilled body-making trades, painters suffered the most spectacular decline after 1921. The cause of their demise was simple: the spray gun. One paint sprayer could equal the output of seven men with brushes, and with the new pyroxylin lacquers developed in 1923, the paint dried fast and evenly.[54]

The simultaneous development of all these innovations in body making required a substantial investment—one that only the larger manufacturers could hope to recoup by spreading the cost over an extended production run. Smaller companies that could not afford the up-front cost in tooling either failed, or concentrated on custom work for the higher-priced end of the market. Many of these custom builders were concentrated in New York City, which remained, not coincidentally, the last bastion of the old UAAVWA/Auto Workers Union in the late 1920s. Otherwise, according to *Automotive Industries*, "all through the East where bodies have been made in small quantities on a semi-special design basis, factories have closed up and the proprietors have abandoned the business because they were unable to find a market for bodies made at the old price."[55] "Detroit," the *American Machinist* observed in the same years, "is now . . . the center of the body industry." With this geographic shift came a transformation in methods. In one body plant where a "progressive" system of conveyors, elevators, sequential flow, and coordinated delivery of parts replaced the prewar method of hand-trucking the bodies to stationary work sites, the time required to turn raw material into a finished body fell from 299 to eighty-three hours. After the reorganization, the plant produced fifty bodies an hour compared with seventeen an hour under the old methods, with no increase in the work force.[56]

Combined with the continuing investment in specialized and fully automated machine tools, these innovations in body making produced a spectacular payoff in productivity. In the industry's first two decades, output per worker had risen from less than two cars a year to more than eleven; it now took just four more years, to 1925, to nearly double that figure and push output per worker per year to twenty automobiles.

TABLE 1.2
Number of Workers in Selected Metalworking Crafts, Michigan
and Detroit, 1920 and 1930

	1920		1930		Percentage change	
Occupation	Michigan	Detroit	Michigan	Detroit	Michigan	Detroit
Machinists	60,878	31,855	58,936	28,577	−3.2%	−10.3%
Blacksmiths, forge, hammer	9,284[a]	2,812[a]	8,948	3,666	−3.6	30.4
Molders, casters, founders	10,091	4,087	8,624	2,539	−14.5	−37.9
Pattern/model makers	2,688	1,585	3,394	1,622	26.3	2.3
Millwrights	4,703	1,991	6,179	2,362	31.4	18.6
Toolmakers, die setters, die sinkers	11,794	7,709	25,285	16,060	114.4	108.3
Total	99,438	50,039	111,366	54,826	12.0	9.6

Source: Compiled from Bureau of the Census, *Fourteenth Census of the United States, Population*, Volume 4, *Occupations* (Washington, D.C., 1923), 947–948, 1101–1102; *Fifteenth Census of the United States, Population* , Volume 4, *Occupations by States* (Washington, D.C., 1933), 782–784.

Note: Figures for 1920 are males only: for 1930, males and females. Comparability is not significantly afffected, since only six women worked in these occupations in all of Michigan in 1930.

[a]Includes welders.

With this upward trend, the proportion of skilled metalworkers and machine-tool operators in the production work force fell throughout the decade.[57]

This rapid shift in occupations and skills riveted popular attention on Detroit. The mass-produced automobile and the assembly-line methods that made it possible had wide-ranging social and economic consequences, and observers from every point on the political spectrum felt compelled to judge the "auto revolution" for good or ill. Most would have agreed with Professor Charles Reitell's 1924 assessment of occupational trends in the auto industry. "We find," said Reitell, "skill or long experience at the top and brawn at the bottom both greatly lessened." In the first case, Reitell observed, skill shifted "from the trained workers into intricate and complex machines"; in the second case, "the brute force of physical labor" gave way to mechanical conveyors and transfer devices. "The natural concomitant of this," Reitell concluded, "is an increase in number and percentage of those who must operate or tend the machines and mechanical appliances."[58]

Reitell's assessment accurately portrayed the declining proportion of skilled metalworkers and unskilled laborers in auto *production*. But like many contemporary observers, Reitell drew the additional—and flawed—conclusion that skilled metalworkers, as individuals, could no longer find a place in the industry. "The 'all around machinist,'" said Reitell, "the machinist who has gone through years of apprenticeship and has finally learned his trade, finds a falling demand in the automobile industry."[59]

Such had been the hope of Frederick Taylor, Henry Ford, and others. "All possible brain work should be removed from the shop and centered in the planning or laying-out department," Taylor counseled in 1903, and over the next quarter century management replaced quite a bit of "brain work" with jigs, fixtures, dies, and other special tools. But before these instruments of management control could be installed on the shop floor (in lieu of "brains"), the planning department had to turn to a troublesome intermediary: the tool and die maker. Management thereby enhanced its control of the production process, but skill did not disappear from the industry. Indeed, even as the number of machinists, blacksmiths, and molders in Michigan and Detroit stagnated or declined during the 1920s, the spectacular jump in the number of tool and die makers (see Table 1.2) produced an overall *increase* in the number of skilled metalworkers during this decade.

Reitell and others simply missed the significance and the growing numbers of the "all around" machinist-as-toolmaker: understandably, for most of these craftsmen were segregated in specialized facilities and few of them found a place in popular accounts of mass-production wizardry. But management was well aware of their strategic importance—and of an increasingly acute shortage of these critical workers.

2

THE CITADEL OF CRAFT

Tool and die work included a wide range of skills and products, but the common denominator in any shop, large or small, was the value placed on the autonomous craftsman—the skilled worker who honored trade norms and worked without supervision. Self-directed (and sometimes aloof), strong willed (and often stubborn), outspoken (sometimes pedantically so), these craftsmen were prime recruits for industry leadership through the 1930s, in management as well as the union. The heavy demand for their skills allowed them to bid their wages up to "aristocratic" levels in the 1920s, and management, confronted by this spiraling cost, sought to subdivide jobs and "cheapen" the work along the same lines previously applied to production tasks. When this strategy further aggravated the long-term shortage of fully trained craftsmen, management had to look outside their industry—indeed, outside the United States—for their skilled labor.

Toolmaking

Detroit's toolrooms built a wide range of specialized equipment, but the predominant categories were jigs, fixtures, and dies. The first two were so closely related that in practice they referred simply to "smaller" and "larger" work-holding devices. On drills and boring machines, the "jigs" consisted of steel bushings that aligned the cutting shafts above the holes to be drilled, bored (enlarged), reamed (finished to require size), or tapped (provided with screw threads). In addition to these bushings, the jig's key elements consisted of "locating points" to ensure uniform placement of the piece, and clamps to hold it firmly in

39

place. In contrast to jigs, which guided the cutting tool while holding the work, fixtures simply held the work to the machine in the specified alignment for cutting or welding; the cutting edge or welding device operated according to internal controls set within the machine rather than external guides set in the fixture. Fixtures were commonly used on lathes (which cut revolving pieces with a rigid cutting tool), mills (which cut parts with a revolving cutting tool), planers (which scraped large flat surfaces with a fixed blade), shapers (which did the same to smaller pieces), and welding machines.[1]

By 1930, the dictum "Always say 'Die'" had produced an enormous variety of dies in all shapes and sizes, from simple hand-size dies mounted in bench presses, to thirty-ton body dies mounted in stamping presses weighing over 1,000 tons. Some dies did little more than punch a hole or trim the edges of a sheet metal part; "draw" dies, on the other hand, stretched the metal into complex curves. A simple die finished its work in a single downward stroke, while more complex dies used multiple rams and drivers to shape the metal from the top, bottom, and sides. Fixture building demanded considerable skill, but diemaking generally required the greatest precision, particularly for the draw dies that shaped fenders and other contoured parts. It was here, in fact, that the "magicians of the shop" practiced their most demanding art.[2]

For all their variation, draw dies had several common components. The "punch" was a hardened steel impact surface contoured in the shape of the part to be stamped; bolted to the end of a vertical "ram," the downward stroke of the punch pressed the sheet metal against the "die," a metal cavity that contoured the negative image of the part. The punch and the die were each mounted on cast-iron "shoes" ("punch shoe" and "die shoe"); vertical guide pins fastened to the die shoe controlled the punch's motion as it traveled up and down these shafts.[3]

In building these complex mechanisms, the diemaker (or "die sinker" if it was a forging die) planned the actual construction sequence and, if necessary, amended the tool designer's blueprints. These design adjustments were frequently required, since even the most skilled engineer could not always anticipate the complex interactions of metal under intense pressure. In some cases, particularly for smaller dies, an engineer or a foreman would simply sketch the finished piece and the diemaker would design and build the finished die.[4]

The first step was the production of templates and checking fixtures to ensure precision work. Templates profiled various outlines of the die's blueprinted elements and enabled the diemaker to measure the die against the original design; checking fixtures allowed the diemaker to measure the initial stampings produced by the die and compare them with the part's blueprinted dimensions. Once the templates were finished, the diemaker was ready to initiate the actual construction of the die. In the early years of the auto industry, skilled diemakers performed virtually all these operations, from the machining, heat treating, and filing of the die "details" (as the various inserts and other components were called), to the fitting, assembly, and final tryout of the finished die. "In the old days," recalled Logan Miller, a Ford diemaker who later became general manager of the Rouge, "we did most of the work by hand with hammer and chisel. You had to work from templates on contour work, using a chisel and chipping by hand." On these complex draw dies, the sculpted shape of the punch and the die "had to be chipped and filed to blend the contour from one template to another. It took weeks and months to develop a die."[5]

As the industry expanded its use of dies, and as these became bigger and more complex, management introduced new machines and a more elaborate division of labor to boost the productivity of diemaking. A key innovation was the Pratt and Whitney "Keller" machine used to produce the huge, contoured draw dies for body stamping. Introduced in the mid-1920s, the Keller was essentially a large milling machine with a precision profiling attachment. The profiler's "tracer head" followed the outline of a wood or plaster model (the product of a highly skilled die model maker) and activated in tandem a revolving cutter that copied the tracer's movements and cut the required shape onto the punch or die. "This machine," the UAW's *Tool and Die Engineering News* reported in 1940, "can do in 100 hours what tool and die makers did in 2,000 hours."[6]

By the late 1920s, toolroom management had also broken diemaking down into several specialized tasks, particularly in the construction of large body-stamping dies. The growing complexity and increasing demand for precision in the construction of such dies meant that many of these specialized tasks still required considerable craft knowledge and skill. But among skilled workers, a rudimentary job hierarchy was visible nevertheless. At the top of this job ladder was the "die leader" (or, in shops making other tools, the "tool leader"). Highly trained, experienced, and usually recruited from the older members of the work force, the leader took his job assignments from die-room supervisors but planned the actual work of producing the die himself. In addition to redesigning die components as needed, the leader might produce templates and gauges, though in some plants skilled specialists took responsibility for this work. The leader's main task was to allocate and direct the work of three to ten "diemakers," also called "bench hands."

On small dies, either the foreman or the leader decided which bench hand produced which die; on large dies, the leader divided the "detail" work among his bench hands and directed the final assembly of the die. "The die leaders," Irv Iverson recalled of the men he knew in Detroit's toolrooms, "in a way were like straw bosses. They gave instructions." The leader directed the work of others—but he was not a foreman. He was an hourly worker and wore a blue collar—yet he worked without direct supervision. The ambiguity of his position might appear strange to the outsider, but the nineteenth-century observer would immediately recognize the autonomous craftsman, wielding much the same authority—but none of the managerial or entrepreneurial functions—that inside contractors once possessed. Management had to rely on his skill, initiative, and authority for the same reason that nineteenth-century metalworking firms built their initial enterprise within the craftsman's realm: the varied and small-batch work of diemaking demanded a constant application of judgment and skill that could not be fully blueprinted in the engineering department. Ironically, the very work process that underpinned interchangeable manufacturing and destroyed the craftsman's realm in production reconstituted that realm in the die room.[7]

The die leader allocated the work of producing die details to his bench hands. For large draw dies, these details would later be assembled into Kellered and finished castings; for small and simple dies that required no Kellering, the bench hand might take responsibility for building the entire die. In either case, the bench hand studied the relevant blueprints, determined the sequence of work to be performed, and assembled the necessary materials and tools. Following the blueprinted design of the part, he would "lay out" or mark on the metal the precise outline of drill holes and other specified cuts to be made. In the large die rooms of Ford, General Motors, Chrysler, and other major auto and supplier plants, specialized "machine hands" made these cuts, not the bench worker. The machine tools they operated were distinguished from production machines by their greater capacity for precision and for variation of cutting angles and speeds. There were none of the mechanical devices found on production machines that restricted operations and guided the tool through narrowly prescribed motions. Accordingly, the skill of these workers, who usually specialized in the operation of a particular machine, consisted of their ability to read blueprints and *quickly* set up and perform precise, varied, and often complicated cuts.[8]

After the machine hand performed the necessary "rough" cuts along the specified dimensions, most die details required some form of "heat

treating." This work consisted of three separate operations: "annealing" removed the internal stresses in the machined metal by heating
the piece to moderate temperatures and allowing it to cool slowly;
"hardening" strengthened steel by first heating it to a temperature that
merged its iron and carbon in a single grain structure, and then
quenching the metal to trap it in this hardened condition; "tempering"
removed the internal stresses caused by hardening in a process of heating and slow cooling similar to annealing. In the early years of the auto
industry, the diemaker performed some or all of this work, but as the
range of alloy steels grew in number and complexity—by the 1930s,
Ford used forty different kinds of alloy steel in the production of its cars
and tools—the work more often required the specialized knowledge of
skilled "hardeners." After heat treating, the parts were ready for final
finishing, assembly, and die tryout.

From initial layout and template making to finished die, this entire
process required the coordinated labor of many different kinds of
workers. In addition to the jobs already described, the work force included the maintenance tradesmen who installed, moved, and
repaired the machinery: blacksmiths, electricians, millwrights, machine repairmen, pipe fitters, and repair-maintenance welders. These
skilled tradesmen worked in production departments as well as toolrooms and were a necessary complement to the growth of mechanized
mass production. Semiskilled machine operators, cranemen, truck
drivers, crib men, and unskilled sweepers and laborers rounded out
the toolroom work force. The actual mix of these classifications varied
from plant to plant, with every trade represented in large die shops
and only a handful in smaller shops. In general, however, the two predominant categories of labor were diemaker and skilled machine hand,
each representing roughly 40 percent of the work force in a large die
shop. The overall division of labor in fixture building and other categories of toolmaking roughly paralleled the job classifications in
diemaking (tool leader, toolmaker, etc.), with a somewhat larger minority of semiskilled workers operating cutter grinders and other
specialized machines for repetitive work.

Aptitudes and Attitudes

Compared with the minutely subdivided and repetitive jobs in production, tool and die making required certain aptitudes and, in turn,
generated certain attitudes that set the craftsman apart from the production worker.

Chief among these was the craftsman's conception of work. For the skilled tool and die maker, work was defined by craft norms and shop skills learned in a long apprenticeship, and the worker's substantial investment of time and energy in acquiring this knowledge meant the craft he performed was a central feature of his identity and economic well-being. Craft work confirmed the craftsman's individuality and gave meaning to the "craft pride" he frequently invoked against skill dilution. Deskilling undermined the marketability of his trade and jeopardized his economic security; it also challenged the craftsman's sense of self. The result was the tool and die maker's characteristic defensiveness toward any innovation that subverted his craft autonomy, whether it be new machinery or increased supervision.

Production workers were no more inclined to welcome new machines or increased supervision, but their opposition to both focused more often on the economic or stress-producing consequences (physical and psychic) of these events. The job represented the necessary means to secure a wage, and the particular content of the work had less to do with the production worker's sense of self. Metal finishers, upholsterers, and other craftsmen in deskilled jobs might retain certain features of the craftsman's identity, and new hires to these semiskilled jobs might acquire a hybrid status as "intermediate" (task-specific) tradesmen. But most production workers confirmed their identity outside the factory. Particularly for those who had migrated from rural towns and farm communities, factory wages provided the means for paying off debts and buying land when they returned home; for many immigrants, wages also provided the means for bringing additional family members to Detroit. So long as the industry was buoyant and jobs were available, their "instrumentalist" attitude toward work produced a relative indifference to the job requirements—though not the intensity—of their labor. A temporary downturn in auto production or the appearance of alternative prospects could persuade many to leave the industry. For tool and die makers, on the other hand, their investment of time and effort in acquiring the skills of the trade represented a commitment to the craft and the industry; for management (and later the union), the toolroom was therefore a natural seedbed for new leaders.[9]

Tool and die work also reinforced certain peculiarities of temperament, including a near compulsive attachment to orderliness, deliberation, and, above all, precision. Whereas the initial "rough cuts" taken by the machine hand may only have required him to leave 1/32 of an inch on the scribed line, the "finishing" cuts of the tool and die maker often required precision measured in thousandths of an inch. For template makers, the standards were even more exacting, sometimes requiring use of specially machined "Jo Block" gauges that could measure 1/100,000 of an inch. This kind of precision demanded extreme care in housekeeping: a poorly maintained tool, a faulty micrometer, or a metal filing lodged beneath a height gauge could ruin a job. "Cultivate habits of carefulness, keep the tools in good shape, and make your work right," Henry Burghardt advised in his much-used manual on toolroom practice. "Be orderly and careful; it pays." Toolroom manuals were full of injunctions promoting this fastidious attention to detail. At the same time, they also emphasized the self-directed planning and "laying out" of work required in precision tool-making. If the tool and die maker sometimes fancied himself as the "magician of the shop," in practice there was considerable science in his wizardry. He had to be a problem solver, able to read engineering instructions, correct for unexpected design flaws, and select the proper tools for translating blueprint into hardened steel. Rationality and logic were prized accordingly and served as the necessary prerequisites for effectively deploying subsidiary skills in blueprint reading, trigonometry, and machine-tool operation.[10]

These attributes of their work cultivated a distinctive self-assertiveness among tool and die makers. While the average production worker learned only the repetitive movements of his or her narrowly prescribed task, and generally knew less about the technical and organizational demands of production than the supervisor, the tool and die maker, in contrast, knew how to complete complex and lengthy engineering tasks, and often understood at least as much about the technical intricacies of mass production as his supervisor. As a fully trained craftsman, not only did he not need to be told how to do a job, he positively resented it when white-collar supervision meddled in his work.

Knowing "the right tool for the job" was a hallmark of the craftsman's knowledge, but it was also the basis for a certain conservatism in methods. "Skill means the knowledge of the proper tool to use and how to use it in the right way," Burghardt observed, but "it means more than this—it means a positive unwillingness to use a tool that is not right." In an industrial environment where technological change was a constant, this craft dictum could produce considerable conflict. After all, which tool was "right?": the tool the craftsman had learned to use in a particular way, or the tool that management wanted to introduce or redefine? As a problem solver, the tool and die maker could readily embrace those innovations that he had initiated to improve his work; but as a craftsman, schooled in the norms and traditions of a particular shop practice, he often viewed innovations originating outside the craft with considerable alarm.[11]

Two features of the auto industry's toolmaking sector influenced this ambivalence toward innovation. First, as wage earners dependent on factory owners for their jobs, tool and die makers confronted their employer's demonstrated preference for deskilled workers. Second, in an industry dependent on tools and dies, skilled workers enjoyed substantial opportunities for advancement: from one job to a better job, from the toolroom into engineering, from wage labor into supervision, and from wage labor into entrepreneurship. Under certain circumstances, the first of these two dynamics could reinforce support for collective action against management-controlled innovations. But under different circumstances, the second dynamic could encourage individualistic responses to the same management initiatives.

The structure of the auto industry's toolmaking sector reinforced both of these dynamics. Certain firms, notably General Motors and Ford, produced a sizable amount of their own tools and dies. Most firms, however, did not, and even GM and Ford contracted some of their work to independent "job shops." The tool and die industry, then, was characterized by extreme variations in plant size and in the corresponding opportunities for collective action or individual initiative. At the one extreme was General Motors, with tool and die making concentrated in two Fisher Body factories located in Detroit: Plant 21 (known as Plant 1 in the 1920s), making jigs, fixtures, welding bucks, and templates; and Plant 23, making body dies for most of the GM line. The latter was reputedly the biggest diemaking plant in the world, employing roughly 3,000 workers in a multistory plant several blocks east of the Detroit headquarters of General Motors. Ford also employed a huge work force of tool and die makers—peaking at 17,000 when the company retooled the Rouge for Model A production in 1927. In normal years, the smaller (though still sizable) toolroom work force at the Rouge was scattered among the complex's major plants, with more than 1,100 tool and die makers employed on three shifts at the Pressed Steel Building in the 1920s. Several major supplier firms also maintained their own "captive" plants for tool and die making, including Murray Body, Briggs, and Motor Products.[12]

Typically, the captive shops at General Motors, Ford, and other major firms concentrated on the larger and more complicated welding bucks and body dies, especially those requiring work on the enormous boring mills, radial drills, and Keller machines that few job shops could afford. Smaller fixtures, "rush" jobs at the peak of the retooling season, and many of the die "details" that went into the larger body dies were often contracted out. Chrysler, Hudson, Hupp, and other carmakers depended even more on outside suppliers and turned to independent job shops for much of their tooling.

The 133 Michigan shops surveyed by the Census of Manufacturers made the wolverine state the nation's leading builder of tools and dies in 1929, producing 40 percent of total value added (Ohio was second with 20 percent, Illinois third with 8.4 percent). The average Michigan job shop employed sixty-eight workers that year, nearly double the national average of thirty-seven, but these averages concealed a wide range of firm sizes. Star Tool and Die, one of Detroit's largest job shops, employed more than 300 workers in its West Side plant, producing not only dies and tools but also short production runs of stamped parts for General Motors and other customers. At the other end of the scale were dozens of shops employing fewer than twenty workers. The division of labor in these job shops varied according to product specialization, but in general, their work force differed in two respects from captive shops: first, the owners often worked in the shop, and second, there was little white-collar engineering, since much of the design work was provided by the customer.[13]

"Division of labor" hardly existed in a third category of toolmaking firm, the "alley shop." These were small shops with a handful of old machines and three or four workers, often housed in a converted storefront, an old warehouse, or some other ad hoc quarters. The alley shop where Irv Iverson worked in the 1930s was housed in an abandoned milk depot—surroundings which belied the company's exalted title of "Associated Tool and Gear Engineering." Contrary to its stated specialization, the firm did not have the machinery to cut its own gears and had to subcontract this work to another shop. "The man that ran the place was quite an able salesman," recalled Iverson, the youngest of four employees. "He did his own contact work as well as running the shop. He'd just assign work and then he'd leave." He was apparently as good a salesman as Iverson recalled, securing contracts with Pontiac, Murray Body, Ford, and several other firms to produce alloy steel replacement parts for aging machine tools. His success may have been temporary (alley shops had a notoriously short life span), but firms like "Associated Tool and Gear Engineering" still represented a first step into entrepreneurship.[14]

Even if most tool and die makers did not venture into business, they invariably knew someone who had. If they worked in a job shop, it was usually their boss, who more often than not was a former toolroom worker and one-time alley shop proprietor. These men were, as the *American Machinist* put it, "individualists. In countless cases shop owners and executives have risen from the ranks and a great majority of these contract shops are built around the owners, a 'master mechanic.'" The tool and die industry also offered other avenues for individual advancement. Job switching was the most common of these individualistic options: in a buoyant economy, a competent job-shop tradesmen seeking better work or higher pay could easily find alternative employment during the diemaking season. Some could step up to supervision, and those with experience or training in drafting could move into the growing ranks of white-collar engineers.[15]

Job switching and promotion into salaried positions were options for production workers as well, but in neither case were these avenues for individual advancement as wide or as long as they were for the skilled tool and die maker. The pivotal role and growing demand for dies, fixtures, and other instruments of interchangeable manufacture gave the experienced toolmaker considerably greater leverage in advancing his career, and management ranks were correspondingly populated with many of these upwardly mobile tradesmen. The case of Logan Miller has already been referred to. Trained as a railroad machinist on the Illinois Central, he hired into the Ford toolroom in 1914 as a lathe hand, rose to assistant general foreman of tool and die operations by 1916, and after transferring to Dearborn in 1924, rose to assistant superintendent of the Rouge in 1935, general manager of the Rouge Division in 1949, and Ford vice president in 1952. Though he rose farthest, he was by no means the only tool and die maker to ascend through Ford's management hierarchy. William Pioch, beginning as a fully apprenticed toolmaker at a Detroit parts supplier, entered the Ford toolroom in 1912 as a diemaker and tool designer and quickly rose to superintendent of tool designing, assistant chief tool engineer, and, in 1926, director of production engineering at the Rouge. E. A. Walters, the son of a toolmaker, first apprenticed in the toolroom of Buffalo's Keim Mills and, after Ford bought Keim and moved operations to Highland Park, soon became foreman and then superintendent in the pressroom of the "X Building" before transferring to the Rouge and becoming superintendent of pressed steel in 1924. John Findlater, another skilled diemaker from Keim, became superintendent of both the forge and the toolroom at Highland Park before transferring to the Rouge and taking over the Steel Division. He was joined by his friend Alex Lumsden, an apprenticed blacksmith and toolroom worker at Highland Park, who became head of the Rouge open hearth department in 1925.[16]

For several of these men, the choice between collective action and individual advancement came early in life. Logan Miller, like Walter Chrysler, joined the IAM during his early years as a railroad mechanic and, as a union picketer in 1912, witnessed several violent confrontations with company detectives during the ill-fated strike of the Harriman lines. Alex Lumsden also honored the picket lines during a strike in New York at the U.S. Light and Heat Company; Charles Sorensen, first production manager at the Rouge and a former journeyman patternmaker, briefly served as an officer of the Detroit patternmakers' union before hiring into Ford. Logan Miller later admitted to his youthful support for the Socialist party, and John Findlater had actively campaigned for socialist candidates while living in Buffalo.[17]

Findlater apparently retained some vestige of his youthful politics. After quitting Ford in 1929, he took a leave of absence from the forging company he founded with Alex Lumsden and spent 1932–1933 in the Soviet Union, consulting on forging and steels. But he was the exception. For his former colleagues in Ford management, the opportunities for individual advancement entirely overshadowed their youthful experimenting with radical politics or union activism. Logan Miller claims to have turned away from the union after his 1912 experience in the sometimes violent and ultimately unsuccessful Harriman strike. Sorensen, the former union officer, turned full circle and became one of the leading adversaries of union organization at the Ford Motor Company. For these men, the principles of worker solidarity ran counter to the celebrated and tangible opportunities for individual advancement. They had, after all, experienced the very success promised by the dominant ideology of private enterprise and individual striving.[18]

A Seller's Market

For the majority of tool and die makers who never left the ranks of blue-collar labor, "success" was just as tangible, if also more modest. "These constitute the aristocracy of every shop," Horace Arnold said of the auto industry's toolroom workers in 1915. It was an apt phrase, for in the two decades before 1929, they prospered as no other group of workers did.[19]

In these years, the demand for their vital skills appeared to be insatiable. "About 1910," according to the *American Machinist*, "the need for skilled workers in Detroit, including tool and die makers, was so great due to the growing auto industry that men imported from all parts of the country had temporarily to be housed in tents." Three years later,

Harry Jewett, president of the Lozier Motor Company, told the *Detroit Free Press* that his personnel director was "actually forced to undertaking scouting expeditions of his own in order to obtain skilled machinists and tool makers." Two years later, in 1915, the *Detroit Labor News* reported that the Employers Association of Detroit was advertising for skilled mechanics in New York, Chicago, Philadelphia, Cincinnati, and other cities. According to the *Labor News*, an EAD form letter sent to respondents discouraged them from coming to Detroit if they were workmen of only average skill. "If, however, you are a high-grade mechanic, tool maker, die maker or machinist . . . provided you have no objection to working under open shop conditions, then within a reasonable time you would secure employment to your liking."[20]

The *Detroit Labor News* insisted there was no shortage of tool and die makers and accused the EAD of trying to flood Detroit with surplus tradesmen. This may well have been the EAD's intention, but its persistent search for tool and die makers suggests the seller's market continued. Indeed, by the 1920s, the EAD had devoted its primary attention to securing skilled labor for Detroit's factories. Unskilled labor was no longer its concern. "When men are too plentiful," the EAD's general manager observed in 1927, "the employment office of each plant is surrounded and our bureau is not required to supply ordinary help." According to the secretary of the EAD's Employment Department, most employers in 1928 called upon the bureau only when they needed machinists, diemakers, and semiskilled metal finishers.[21]

The Ford Motor Company was especially eager to secure tool and die makers as it retooled for the Model A. Hyacinth Dubreuil, a French machinist and union official seeking work in Detroit, recalled the advice of an American worker in 1927. "'You can't find work? . . . The situation in general is bad for unskilled workers, [but] it isn't so much so for those who are skilled. At Ford's . . . you ought to try to get in by saying you are a die maker.'" Despite his lack of experience in diemaking, Dubreuil was immediately hired, no questions asked. Frank Muellner, also a machinist, recalled much the same experience looking for work in 1926. "I went over to the Ford Motor Company and they had a big [employment] line out there on Miller Road. Then finally they called out, 'Anybody here a die maker or a skilled man?' So I raised my hand and the guy comes and says, 'Ok, follow me.'" Henry Geile, another skilled machinist, recalled that he "had never seen so many people" in his life when he went to the Rouge in 1928 to find a job. "Only in the army." But unlike most of these industrial recruits, Geile did not have to wait in line. "A gentleman passed by and calls 'Mechanics here? Mechanics here?'" Geile reported to work the next morning.[22]

With their skills in heavy demand, toolmakers commanded above-average wages. At a time when Michigan's auto industry paid the highest manufacturing wages in the world, and when Ford paid production workers the industry's highest starting wage at 62.5 cents an hour, Ford in 1928 was recruiting tool and die makers at $1.00 an hour. While minimum wages for production workers rose to 75 cents an hour in 1928 and to 87 cents in 1929, Edwin Norwood reported in the latter year that some tool and die makers at Ford earned as much as $350 a month, or $2.19 an hour on a straight-time basis. In other auto companies, the wage differential between production workers and tool and die makers was roughly comparable. Unlike Ford, which paid all employees an hourly wage, the rest of the industry had shifted after World War I to piecework and group-bonus pay for production workers, while retaining hourly wages for skilled workers. Since the various incentive pay schemes for production workers produced a lower hourly average than at Ford (in supplier plants, *much* lower), the contrast was all the greater with toolroom wages, which more nearly tracked the $1.00-an-hour minimum paid at the Rouge. Captive toolrooms rarely paid the $2.00-plus hourly wage that Norwood reported at Ford, but weekly earnings in many shops were boosted by the considerable overtime that prevailed everywhere but at Ford, which limited the workweek to forty hours in 1925.[23]

The wage differential with production workers was higher still when measured against toolroom wages in Detroit's job shops. A die sinker could scan the *Detroit News* classifieds and find work for $1.20 an hour in 1926, well above the national average for toolmakers of 75.6 cents an hour. In addition to paying 5–10 cents an hour more than captive toolrooms, job shops offered the additional incentive of less supervision and, in many die shops, more varied work. On the other hand, job-shop work was less secure. Like the rest of the auto industry, tool and die making had seasonal peaks and valleys that significantly affected employment. These swings became more pronounced in the 1920s as automakers followed the lead of General Motors and began to introduce annual model changes. The timing of such changes varied from company to company, but most shut down their plants after Labor Day and introduced their new models after Christmas. This production cycle created yet another distinction between tool and die makers and production hands: the former worked most intensively in the summer and fall as new tooling was prepared and installed, the latter during the winter and spring when new models appeared and sales peaked. Employment in Michigan's tool and die shops fluctuated dramatically with these seasonal variations. In 1929, auto sales broke four million for the first time and toolroom employment peaked early, in April and May, perhaps because die repair and emergency tooling for the record-setting production run added to new-model tooling for 1930. But by December, with completion of new-model tooling, employment in Michigan's tool and die shops fell to little more than half (56 percent) of its peak.[24]

Some job-shop tradesmen might not work for several months during the slack season, but the enormous overtime they worked in the summer and fall compensated for part of the loss. After the intensive pace of the rush season, many workers didn't mind this time off, particularly when the end of the die "program" coincided with Michigan's late-fall hunting season. The trade-off between the relative security of the captive shop, where employers more often retained their hard-to-find skilled workers, and the higher pay and looser supervision of the job shop, where employers could not afford the fixed cost of year-round employment, produced a keen sensitivity in the tool and die maker to the comparative advantages of each sector. Buoyant years that promised ample employment options in the job shops produced significant crossover from the captive plants; at the first hint of a bad year, the job hoppers moved in the opposite direction.[25]

Averaging for all this variation in hours and wage rates, Detroit's tool and die makers earned a median annual income of roughly $2,400 in 1929, and a significant minority earned $3,000 or more. Compared with the $1,400 to $1,700 that *full-time* production workers earned, and considering that most production workers were chronically underemployed, the tool and die maker's high earnings made him far and away the best-paid worker in the world's richest industry.[26]

As such, he was a prime target for profit-conscious employers seeking to cut their costs. "The way to relieve the shortage of skilled labor," said *Automotive Industries* in 1925, was "in the opinion of a good many automotive engineers, . . . to devote even more time and attention to the development of labor-saving equipment." In the production trades, this strategy had produced spectacular results; in the toolroom, it promised future inroads against skilled labor. But weighed against these immediate gains, mechanization and specialization had long-term effects that aggravated the very problem these strategies were supposed to solve. The *American Machinist* hinted at this paradoxical dynamic in 1935: "New industries, new processes, new machinery, new materials require great numbers of skilled workers and at the same time create much obsolescence among craftsmen, particularly since the pre-Depression era was characterized by over-specialization."

In sum, specialization had produced spectacular short-term productivity gains, but by killing apprenticeship and producing "more half-baked mechanics than any other country in the world," as one writer in the *American Machinist* put it, such specialization had undermined the industry's long-term capacity to implement new technologies. "Half-baked" tradesmen with task-specific skills could not respond to the continually evolving parameters of tool and die making. "The country has paid dearly for its preponderance of half-trained workmen," the *American Machinist* concluded. "From the apprentices of today are drawn the inspectors, the foremen and the executives of tomorrow"—and without a continued replenishment of fully trained metalworkers, this seedbed of management would fall barren.[27]

"The Trained Man Wins"

A few employers tried to counter this trend by training their own skilled work force. One of the first was Henry Leland, the former New England mechanic and founder of Cadillac, who established the School of Applied Mechanics in 1907. Offering a two-year course that combined shop training with classroom instruction in mechanical drawing and other engineering subjects, the school placed a heavy emphasis on "character building" by stressing the virtues of individual striving and prohibiting the use of tobacco and liquor. Students worked a fifty-six-hour week and received wage increases and bonuses according to their grades.[28]

Leland's Calvinist pedagogy was reproduced on a far larger scale by Henry Ford's Trade School. Founded in 1916 as a component of the company's welfare work, it also combined shop training and classroom instruction with heavy drilling in the virtues of thrift, cleanliness, and individualism. By 1929, Trade School enrollment had grown to 2,800 students, most of them entering the program at ages twelve to fourteen. During the four-year curriculum, they alternated between one week in the classroom, where they took instruction in high-school English, civics (of the Henry Ford "school"), geography, shop-algebra, trigonometry, metallurgy, and other topics, and two weeks in the shop, where they worked on shaper, lathe, bench, and heat treating. Paid twenty cents an hour their first year and raised in stages to a fifty-one-cent maximum if they got satisfactory grades, the students made the Trade School a profitable venture for Ford by producing tools and making repairs on a wide range of equipment. To supplement the supply of tool and die makers graduated from the Trade School, Ford also founded the Apprentice School in the Rouge "B Building" in 1923. In addition to taking Trade School graduates for advanced instruction, the Apprentice School recruited adult students from the Rouge work force and provided remedial training in mathematics before moving on to trigonometry, drafting, and shop theory. By 1926, Apprentice School enrollment had grown from thirty to 1,500 students.[29]

Among Detroit automakers, only Studebaker, Hudson, and a handful of others organized apprenticeship programs before 1929. In Flint, General Motors established the "Institute of Technology," which rivaled Ford's program in size and scope, though it focused exclusively on adults rather than boys. Unlike the Ford program, the one at GM stressed training for white-collar management as well as the skilled trades. A featured offering in the latter category was "The Complete Machinists' and Toolmakers' Course," costing roughly $300 for six hours a week of training stretched over four years. The "skilled specialist," as the *Bulletin* described him, "in the past . . . came up through an apprenticeship . . . under the guidance of expert mechanics." But "the changing conditions in industry have so broken down the apprenticeship system that it is now employed in only a few cases." Yet the *Bulletin* added, "even in this modern age of specialized production the all-around mechanic is in constant demand." The program at GM probably included less of the school-boy emphasis on "character building" found at Ford or Cadillac, but the *Bulletin* did urge potential students to consider the time spent in training as "your days of opportunity. Every man is the director of his own destiny. . . . Remember, 'The Trained Man Wins.' "[30]

Trained women did not. Indeed, at no point was training offered or seriously considered for women, though nearly 14,000 worked in the auto factories of Wayne County by 1930. This 5.6 percent of the factory labor force, modest as it was, dwarfed the nonexistent representation of women in the auto industry's toolrooms: Census figures for 1930 list just two women among Michigan's 25,000 tool and die makers. The years of training required for toolmaking or any other skilled trade implied a commitment to factory work that no one expected from a woman. Single girls and young women might make a temporary excursion into the most thoroughly deskilled jobs as upholstery stitchers and machine operators, and employers were happy to hire them in growing numbers—and then pay them a third or a half less than they paid men for comparable work. But for employers, male workers, and all but a handful of women, apprenticing a female toolmaker was an unthinkable violation of her "natural" role as homemaker, wife, and mother.[31]

Blacks were also unwelcome in the toolroom. Here again, prevailing norms outside the plant regulated the supply of labor within the factory. According to the deeply imbedded racial stereotyping of the time, African-Americans were mentally incapable of precision work but physically suited to the foundry, where they supposedly could withstand the intense heat better than whites. Some employers claimed they had no such prejudice against apprenticing blacks into skilled jobs, but when Lloyd Cofer, representing the Detroit Urban League and Board of Education, presented them with qualified applicants, "these men," Cofer observed in 1937, "maintained that after these boys were trained, the skilled white craftsmen would refuse to work with them." There was ample evidence to support this claim, including, as Cofer found, "that certain of the craft unions affiliated with the A.F. of L. were closed to Negroes." In a racist society that relegated African-Americans to inferior status, many skilled tradesman would have interpreted their presence in the toolroom as a personal affront and a demeaning of their craft. White production workers, who were far more likely to find black workers competing for the same jobs, also preferred the segregated hiring practices that minimized this competition and soothed the intense "Negrophobia" plaguing whites at all levels of society. One factory engineer, in a statement that probably said as much about his own feelings as those of his plant's employees, insisted that any mixing of blacks into white departments, where they "hung their coats touching those of whites," would produce an immediate reaction, particularly among southern whites: "You know, 'that nigger is poison. . . . God damn, I don't want that black SOB to sit on my toilet seat. . . . I've got to hang my coat along side of his over there. I've got to handle tools that a nigger handled.' "[32]

The sole exception to the auto industry's segregated hiring practices was the Ford Rouge plant. Henry Ford believed that for the white race "dominance is an obligation" requiring "the stronger [to] serve the weaker." Accordingly, Ford hired black workers into the production departments and skilled trades at the Rouge. Still, nearly half of the 10,000 black workers in the Dearborn plant worked in the foundry, and only token numbers made it into the skilled trades. Willis Ward, a University of Michigan graduate who hired into the Ford Motor Company Employment Department in 1935, later recalled that Ford had 100 black tool and die makers in 1941. On the other hand, Bill McKie, an early union leader at the Rouge, recalled only a handful of black skilled tradesmen in the early 1930s, and one, a leader, was forced to relinquish his position when whites objected to working under his direction. Walter Dorosh likewise recalled only two blacks in his 1939

Trade School graduating class. Robert Robinson, a black tool and die maker from Jamaica who came to Detroit in the 1920s, was initially refused work when he applied for a toolroom job at the Rouge. "I stood in line at the employment office and each time I reached the front, I was told they were not hiring, even though they had advertised for the job." Eventually hired as a sweeper, he entered the toolroom only after enrolling in the Trade School and relearning the skills he already knew. In 1930, as he recalled, there were no other black tool and die makers in the entire plant. The same year, the Census counted only seventy-two black tool and die makers in all of Michigan, sixty-seven of them concentrated in Detroit.[33]

Although Ford's Trade School restricted black entry to the toolroom, the company was still one of the few that trained workers of *any* race for tool and die work. Among most employers, as *Automotive Industries* reported in 1925, there prevailed "an attitude of extreme apathy toward the question of training of skilled workers. . . . Production men in general seem to be content to hire those men who have been trained by other industries." Compared with this cost-free "poaching" of skilled workers, internal training programs were expensive and risky ventures, for there was no guarantee a skilled worker would remain with the firm that trained him. Employers more often used "apprentices" as low-wage alternatives to adult labor and simply ignored their training—so much so, the 1920 Census felt compelled to note that "many of those returned as . . . *machinists' apprentices* were, in fact, only *machine tenders.*"[34]

For those workers who could not enroll in or afford the training programs offered by Ford, General Motors, and a few other companies, there were only limited alternatives. Some workers supplemented whatever on-the-job training they could find with shop-related classes at Cass Technical, Wilbur Wright, and other public high schools. Others, including future Ford executives William Pioch, E. A. Walters, and Charles Sorensen, rounded out their shop training with mail-order engineering courses from the International Correspondence School. Workers scanning the newspaper classifieds could also take up the invitation to "EARN MORE MONEY" from the Michigan State Auto School, which promised to teach the aspiring tradesman "Machine Shop and Bench Work" and the intricacies of the "Special Lathe Machine." Given the compressed curriculum of these commercial trade schools—the Detroit "Trades Bureau" specified a mere "3 to 4 months of evenings"—the training could only have produced the sort of "half-baked" mechanics the *American Machinist* complained of.[35]

Some workers had to settle for less than this. Joe Oberg served an "unorganized apprenticeship," as he called it, at Detroit's Swedish Crucible Steel during the 1920s. Working in the shop during summers while he attended high school, he spent much of his time as a mere "go-for." "If a journeyman wanted a pack of tobacco, he'd send me to the store to get him tobacco. And I can still remember cleaning their shoes. . . . But then they'd give me a job to drill some holes on a drill press, then a little work on the lathe, then a little milling machine and shaper. . . . It was just basic tool shop machinery." Under these circumstances, the quality of the training depended not only on the skills of the adult journeymen but also on their willingness to pass these along to a potential competitor. Irv Iverson recalled the reticence of his adult co-workers in the alley shop where he apprenticed. "Some of these guys were afraid, 'if I teach this guy too much he'll have my job, the boss will keep him because he's young and impressionable and he'll do what he's told without arguments.' "[36]

For all these reasons, the unskilled worker often made his way into toolmaking not by formal training in the trade but by "stealing it." Frank Marquart described the process as he knew it in 1916:

A young man hired out in a factory as a toolmaker. He was placed on a machine and, with the help of the man working on the next machine, picked up a little skill—until the foreman discovered that he was a "shyster" and fired him. Then he hired out in another plant, picked up a little more skill, and so on, until he acquired enough competence to hold down a toolroom job.[37]

The man who "stole a trade" could sometimes work his way into the toolroom as a machine hand, but only rarely could he learn the combination of skills—blueprint reading, trigonometry, layout, bench work, and precision fitting—necessary to produce a template, a die, or a complicated fixture. For these skilled workers, employers had to look elsewhere.

Workers of the World

Most looked to Europe, where engineering practices surpassed American norms in many areas of advanced industrial engineering, but where the organization of these innovations into a system of mass production progressed at a far slower pace. Consequently, many of Europe's engineers and toolmakers saw a greater demand for their skills in North America than in their native lands. "Like most young engineers, I wanted to get some experience in the United States," recalled

TABLE 2.1
FOREIGN-BORN ENGINEERS AND PRODUCTION MANAGERS AT FORD

Name	Position	Country of origin
Bredo Berghoff	director, Apprenticeship School	Norway
Carl Johansson	lead engineer, Ford Laboratories	Sweden
Joseph Galamb	director, Ford engineering	Hungary
Eugene Farkas	director, experimental engineering	Hungary
Carl Emde	chief tool designer	Germany
John Findlater	supt., toolroom, forge, steel	Scotland
Alex Lumsden	supt., forge, open hearth	Scotland
P. E. Martin	production manager, Highland Park	Canada
Charles Sorensen	production manager, Dearborn	Denmark
William Knudsen	supt., branch assembly plants	Denmark

NOTE: The positions listed suggest greater precision in job titles than was actually the case, since Henry Ford opposed formal titles. See Eugene Farkas, "Reminiscences," Accession 65, Henry Ford Museum, 43–45; Logan Miller, "Reminiscences," Accession 65–146, Henry Ford Museum, 11.

Bredo Berghoff, a graduate of the technical school in Porsgrunn, Norway. "It was a common experience for a young Norwegian engineer to go to the United States to complete his technical education." Berghoff, like many other Europeans who set out for North America, intended to stay only "a couple of years." The years stretched into a lifetime, the bulk of it spent at the Ford Motor Company.[38]

He was not alone, for as indicated in Table 2.1, the core of Ford's engineering and production staff was also foreign-born. Two of these men, Findlater and Sorensen, came to the United States as young boys, but their upbringing still bore the stamp of an immigrant heritage. Sorensen was apprenticed by two foreign-born tradesmen, his Danish father and a German patternmaker. Findlater, only five years old when his family arrived in the United States, had a different sort of old-world tutelage. According to fellow Scotsman and business partner Alex Lumsden, Findlater, raised by his father and grandmother, "was more replete with some of the Scots sayings than I was due to his grandmother, who was of a more ancient vintage." William Knudsen, age twenty when he arrived in Buffalo, was prominently involved in that city's Danish immigrant societies according to E. A. Walters, his coworker at the Keim Mills.[39]

The Ford Motor Company would have been a very different organization without its foreign-born engineers, many of them trained in Europe's outstanding technical institutes. It was, after all, Joseph

TABLE 2.2
NUMBER AND PERCENTAGE OF FOREIGN-BORN CRAFTSMEN, MICHIGAN
AND DETROIT, 1930

Occupation	Michigan		Detroit	
	No.	Percentage[a]	No.	Percentage[b]
Machinists	19,445	33%	12,367	43%
Pattern/model makers	1,202	35	702	43
Tookmakers, die setters, die sinkers	11,110	44	8,061	50

SOURCE: Bureau of the Census, *Fifteenth Census of the United States*, Volume 4, *Population: Occupations by States* (Washington, D.C., 1933), 800, 803.

NOTE: Figures are for males only.

[a]Of total work force in Michigan.

[b]Of total work force in Detroit.

Galamb and two other Hungarians, Charles Balogh and Julius Haltenberger, who designed the Model T with Harold Willis and Henry Ford, and it was Galamb and Eugene Farkas who made up half of the four-man team that designed the Model A. These Europeans had no trouble finding work in Detroit's rapidly expanding auto industry. On Galamb's first day in Detroit in 1905, he was offered a job as tool designer at three different plants—Cadillac, Silent Northern, and Ford. Carl Johansson, the former toolroom foreman at Sweden's Eskilstuna Arsenal and inventor of the famous "Jo Block" gauges, came to Detroit in 1919 when Ford purchased his gauge-making company and moved it from New York to Dearborn.[40]

The toolrooms at Ford and throughout Detroit were no less dependent on foreign-born craftsmen, as indicated in Table 2.2. "In our die room, we had essentially Scotchmen, Germans, and Englishmen," recalled Walter Dorosh of the Ford Rouge die operation in the 1930s. "Most of them came from Europe." When Henry Geile, a German toolmaker, arrived from Europe in 1928 and got hired at Ford's Machine Building, the first words he heard on the job took him by surprise. "On the bench, I put my tool box here," he recalled, "and then the other fellow, he looked at me, says 'Sprechen sie Deutsch?'" Geile's surprise was compounded when he discovered his bench mate came from the same town in Westphalia where Geile learned his trade. Frank Muellner, another German-born machinist working at the Rouge in the mid-1920s, felt equally at home in the die room: his die leader was German, and one of his three benchmates was Austrian. Of the remaining two, one was Yugoslav and the other was the sole American-born worker in the five-man group. Fifteen years later, when the UAW first surveyed Ford's toolrooms for foreign-born aliens, it found twenty countries represented among the 184 immigrant tradesmen who had not yet become citizens. British and Canadian craftsmen (some of the latter British-born) accounted for nearly two-thirds of the total.[41]

Every die room and tool shop in Detroit had its distinctive mixture of nationalities, with Germans, English, and Scots predominant in most. The exact proportion of foreign- and native-born workers is difficult to measure in all cases, except one: at the Briggs Corporation's tool and die plant on Vernor Avenue, of the 499 workers surveyed by the union in 1934, 61 percent were foreign-born. Impressionistic accounts of the plant population in other shops roughly match this figure. Blaine Marrin, a toolmaker at Fisher Body, recalled a work force in Plant 21 that was 70 percent foreign-born, led by Germans and followed in close order by Scots, English, and Danes; in contrast, the nearby Plant 23, making body dies, was 60 percent Scots and English, with far fewer Germans. Leonard Woodcock remembered that over half of the approximately 350 workers in the Motor Products toolroom were English, including his Oldham-born and -apprenticed father. Russell Leach recalled that among tool and die makers at Murray Body, roughly 30 percent were Germans and 15 percent Scots.[42]

Leach also remembered that the distinctive mix of nationalities in a shop often reflected the particular preference of the owner or supervisor. "The old hiring system was that the personnel man who did the hiring would always take the recommendation of the supervision in a given plant. He [the supervisor] would pick up the phone and say, 'Hey, I want you to hire my brother, hire my nephew,' etcetera, etcetera." Owners of job shops had no personnel department and hired whomever they pleased; since many owners were German-born, they tended to hire fellow countrymen. At Active Tool and Die, Snyder Tool, and several other German-owned job shops, the work force was so overwhelmingly German-born that even the blueprints were in the mother tongue.[43]

"These Danes," Irv Iverson recalled of the two Danish-born craftsmen who owned Redford Tool and Die, "they were somewhat prejudiced against other nationalities. . . . If a guy could do the job, they would take him in there, but the Danes particularly disliked the English. . . . They were more partial towards the Germans." As a result, the Redford work force was dominated by Danish and German workers, with a sprinkling of native-born toolmakers and only one Englishman. In the toolroom at Hudson Motors, on the other hand, Joe Oberg remembered that "we did not have too many Germans. . . . The

TABLE 2.3
NUMBER AND PERCENTAGE OF FOREIGN-BORN WORKERS, DETROIT,
1920 AND 1930

Occupation	1920		1930	
	No.	Percentage	No.	Percentage
All manufacturing	109,636	45%	129,089	41%
Semiskilled operatives, auto[a]	13,146	41	17,991	41
Laborers, auto[a]	18,702	65	22,349	46
Toolmakers, die setters, die sinkers	2,694	35	8,061	50

SOURCE: Bureau of the Census, *Fourteenth Census of the United States*, Volume 4, *Population, 1920: Occupations* (Washington, D.C., 1923), 1101–1102; Bureau of the Census, *Fifteenth Census of the United States*, Volume 4, *Population: Occupations by States* (Washington, D.C., 1933), 803.

NOTE: Figures are for males only. Percentages apply to total work force of Detroit.

[a]Not otherwise specified.

Master Mechanic was Polish, a fellow by the name of Zelinski, and he was from the old school of classical Polaks. Maybe that's why there weren't too many Germans there." Blaine Marrin also recalled that the mixture of nationalities at Fisher Body was not the result of random selection: "The guy who was the head of Fisher Body . . . went over to Germany and brought these fellows [back]. . . . They were concentrated . . . in Plant 1 [later called Plant 21], the checking fixture department."[44]

However much the precise blend of nationalities varied from shop to shop, the striking feature of this toolroom work force was the rapid increase in the proportion of immigrant tradesmen during the 1920s, as indicated in Table 2.3. This increase is especially notable given the declining proportion in the same years of foreign-born manufacturing workers and unskilled auto factory laborers, and the unvaried proportion of foreign-born semiskilled machine operators in the auto industry. In 1920, the proportion of immigrant craftsmen in Detroit's toolrooms was little more than half the proportion of foreign-born workers among auto-industry laborers; ten years later, immigrant tool and die makers represented half their trade in Detroit, surpassing the proportion of foreign-born workers in every other category of manufacturing labor.

A second anomaly is revealed in the overall trend for immigration to Detroit in the same years. Traditionally, historians have dichotomized

TABLE 2.4
RATIO OF FOREIGN-BORN TO
SECOND-GENERATION RESIDENTS, DETROIT AREA, 1930

Nationality	No. foreign-born	No. second generation	Ratio[a]
Canadian	88,904	71,364	1.25
English	32,215	31,705	1.02
Scottish	25,555	13,842	1.85
German	34,594	100,262	.35
Irish Free State	6,832	19,533	.35
Italian	30,591	35,512	.86
Polish	83,985	132,132	.64
Russian	23,761	26,018	.91
Total	447,063	561,378	.80

NOTE: Detroit area includes Highland Park, Hamtramck, and Dearborn.

[a]Number of foreign-born residents divided by number of second-generation residents.

immigration to the United States into "old" immigration from Northern Europe and "new" immigration from Southern and Eastern Europe, with the latter overtaking the former around 1890 and becoming dominant and characteristic until the end of mass immigration in 1921. Considered against this background, Detroit's experience appears quite peculiar. Table 2.4 measures the ratio of foreign-born residents in 1930 against the number of native-born descendants of immigrant parents for each of Detroit's major nationality groups. As a rough indicator of "old" and "new" immigration, it indicates a striking reversal of the usual dichotomy, for it is the Scots and the English, joined by the Canadians, who have the highest ratio of new immigrants by 1930. These Britishers were among the one million emigrants (net) who left the United kingdom in the decade before 1930, and roughly a quarter of those departing for the United States were skilled workers. Combined with the figures in Table 2.3 and the impressionistic—but consistent—recollections of men who worked in Detroit's toolrooms, the evidence indicates that a large minority of British immigrants coming to Detroit were skilled metalworkers.[45]

Their arrival was perfectly consistent with the needs of Detroit's auto industry, but this fortuitous conjunction raises at least three questions. First, why did they leave Britain in such large numbers? Second, how did they then make their way to Detroit? And third, what mental and ideological "baggage" did they bring along that equipped them so readily for leadership in Detroit's soon-to-be-reborn union movement?

3

LABOR ROUTES

Harold Snudden left Great Britain in 1919. He was twenty-seven years old, a fully apprenticed toolmaker, and, according to his surviving family, a strong union man. With his wife, Gertrude Miles, a skilled dressmaker, and their two-year-old son Geoff, Harold boarded a converted troop ship and crossed the Atlantic to Halifax, Nova Scotia.[1]

Four years later, after brief residencies in Montreal and Toronto, Snudden crossed the Detroit River from Windsor in the winter of 1923 and began a thirty-year work life in Detroit's toolrooms, never rising to prominence in the union or the industry, but representing, with his fellow immigrant tradesmen, the larger population from which Detroit auto unions drew their Anglo-Gaelic leadership. This immigrant stream widened dramatically in the early 1920s as economic collapse pushed thousands of skilled metalworkers, coal miners, and other unemployed workers across the Atlantic. Union defeat and Irish civil war both added their exile contingents. Crossing to North America on routes defined by British imperial policy and U.S. immigration law, most Anglo-Gaelic emigrants arrived in Canada and came to Detroit through Windsor, Ontario. An increasingly dense thicket of immigration restrictions delayed their crossing at the Detroit River, forcing many to consider illegal entry or daily "commuting" to Detroit-side jobs. But most of Detroit's future Anglo-Gaelic union organizers managed to cross in this postwar decade, contradicting the "antisubversive" intentions of the Quota Act. As they found jobs in Detroit's booming economy, Anglo-Gaelic workers settled into a transitional world of immigrant rooming houses, Odd Fellow lodges, and favored saloons. Most found homes and apartments in neighborhoods on the northwest side of Detroit where previous British immigrants had congregated, and many married immigrant spouses. Newly prosperous after prolonged unemployment, and still adjusting to an alien world, Anglo-Gaelic craftsmen were as conspicuously absent in the sporadic auto strikes of the 1920s as their American-born co-workers in Detroit's toolrooms. Temporarily quiescent to open-shop norms, they still maintained a skilled-trades subculture demarcated from elite circles by occupational lines and class sensibilities.

The Immigrant Stream

Harold Snudden's postwar trek to North America was not his first. In 1910, after apprenticing at a local lathe manufacturer in his native Surrey, outside London, Snudden had crossed to Canada and traveled the eastern provinces looking for toolroom work. Failing to find steady or acceptable employment, he returned to England before 1914 and, in the early war years, worked at the Royal Aircraft Factory in Woolwich near London. But the Canadian experience had already changed his loyalties and options, and when young Snudden became eligible for conscription, he joined the Canadian Army in England—an option which prewar residency in Canada made possible, and which the higher pay and (reputedly) milder discipline of that country's army made preferable.

Snudden's combat experience marked another watershed in his life. During a particularly fierce battle in Belgium, British officers ordered his regiment to cross a canal and charge into German machine guns at the top of a railroad grading. Virtually the entire unit was wiped out. "There were 15 men left out of 1200," son Geoffrey recalled of his father's combat experience, "and he was one of them." Private Snudden blamed his British officers for failing to call up supportive artillery— "they must have hated their men to do this"—and he bore a lasting grudge against the establishment they represented. "My father lost his religion in the trenches," according to his son. "He figured that God shouldn't have allowed that kind of slaughter. . . . He became a socialist."

After the war, Harold thought he might also become a Canadian. In his eyes, a Britain marked by class snobbery and industrial unrest offered little future; Canada, by contrast, seemed to offer wider opportunities and more peaceable prospects. But the four years following the Snuddens' 1919 departure for the Dominion were not a happy time. In the postwar economy, jobs were not easy to get and hold in Canada, and Harold, between bouts of unemployment, bounced from one job to the next—from locomotive repair shops, to farm-machine toolrooms, to low-wage job shops. In Toronto, to help bridge the months of unemployment, the Snuddens rented the upstairs room of their home to a boarder. Gertrude put an "Alterations and Dressmaking" sign in the front window and took in tailoring, but the birth and death of a baby girl interrupted this income.

Toronto, where the Snuddens lived longest, was still a British world in many ways. Son Geoffrey recalls a neighborhood filled with English and Irish immigrants, most of them living in single and semi-detached homes and many, like his parents, spending a weekend evening at the Odd Fellows Lodge. But not every reminder of Britain was welcome. When Harold applied for work in the repair shops of Toronto's streetcar system, he learned that only members of the Sons of England were favored for the job; Harold would have nothing to do with the "Sons of Bitches," as he called this patriot organization, and searched elsewhere for work.

Being British, he found, made this search more difficult in the wider world where Canadian employers sometimes shunned immigrant Englishmen. Years later, Geoffrey's father still bitterly recalled that some job listings specifically told English workers they "need not apply." Veterans seemed to be especially unwelcome. "These guys had been through the mill and they weren't going to take any crap," Geoffrey Snudden recalled of his father's generation. "They had risked their lives and they expected a little consideration, which they didn't get."

The elder Snudden apparently gave little in return. In one low-wage shop where the owner conducted lunchtime prayer meetings, Harold, the day he was asked to rise and pray aloud, responded with a unique plea: "he got up," as Geoffrey recalled the episode, "and prayed for more money."

Fired from this job and laid off from many others, Harold finally decided to try his luck in Detroit. The Motor City was reportedly hiring toolmakers, and the pay was much higher than in Canada. Snudden left his family behind and crossed the border as a "visitor" in December 1923. He immediately found a job in Fisher Body's Detroit toolrooms and returned to Toronto to move his family west. Arriving in Windsor early in 1924—along with thousands of British immigrants moving in the same direction—the Snudden family applied at the American consul for an immigrant visa but had to wait nearly twenty months for their turn on the quota list. While they waited, Harold worked in the United States and then hired into the Windsor toolrooms of the Ford Motor Company. In June of 1924, he took out papers in Detroit declaring his intention to become a U.S. citizen.

When his family cleared quota the following year and crossed to the United States, Snudden's life merged with the Detroit experience of his fellow tradesmen. Seven years after coming to Detroit, he petitioned for U.S. citizenship. Like many other immigrant toolmakers, he often changed jobs each season and each new die program, moving back and forth between the "captive" toolrooms of Briggs, Murray Body, and other large corporations. Before 1935, he joined thousands of immigrant toolmakers in the newly organized Mechanics Educational Society of America; after 1935, he and thousands like him switched their membership to the United Auto Workers.

Snudden followed a path traveled by many of the Anglo-Gaelic workers who rose to leadership in Detroit's unions. Table 3.1 indicates the map-points of that migration for thirty of these British- and Irish-born union leaders. However sketchy, this collective profile suggests that British-born union leaders in Detroit's labor movement had much

TABLE 3.1
SUMMARY OF BIOGRAPHICAL DATA
ON SELECTED DETROIT MESA/UAW LEADERS

	Scottish (N = 13)	English (N = 13)	Irish (N = 4)	Total (N = 30)
U.K. Trade				
Tool/machinst	6	9	1	16
Coal miner	3	1	0	4
Electrician	1	1	0	2
Other/skill	2	2	1	5
Laborer	0	0	2	2
Transport	1	0	0	1
Year Emigrated[a]	1923	1924	1923–1924	1923
Age[b]	26	28	23	26
Marital status[c]				
Single	7	6	3	16
Married	3	5	1	9
No data	3	2	0	5
Port of entry				
Canada	7	6	2	15
New York	0	4	2	6
Other U.S.	2	0	0	2
No data	4	3	0	7

SOURCE: Appendix A.

[a]Median.

[b]Median age at time of emigration.

[c]At time of emigration.

the same immigrant experience as Harold Snudden. Like Snudden, the majority were toolmakers/machinists (sixteen of thirty) and skilled (twenty-three of thirty); most emigrated in the early 1920s before reaching age thirty; and most, like Snudden, came via Canada (fifteen of the twenty-three for whom there is data). Unlike Snudden, a majority of those for whom there is available data were single, and most came from Scotland and north England (see Appendix A for hometown or region).

They were all part of the last surge in mass emigration from the United Kingdom to North America. Beginning in 1920, peaking in 1924, and continuing until 1930, postwar emigration in these eleven years brought some 370,000 men, women, and children from Great Britain to the United States. Immigration figures varied widely according to alternative measures used by the U.S. Bureau of Immigration, but by any standard, the level of emigration from Britain—as well as Germany—was substantial. British immigration to the United States would never again reach the numbers indicated in Table 3.2, and though previous periods of mass immigration saw many more Britons

TABLE 3.2
NUMBER OF IMMIGRANTS TO THE UNITED STATES,
BY COUNTRY OF ORIGIN, 1919–1933

Year	Great Britain	Ireland[a]	Germany
1919	6,797	474	52
1920	38,471	9,591	1,001
1921	51,142	28,435	6,803
1922	25,153	10,579	17,931
1923	45,759	15,740	48,277
1924	59,490	17,111	75,091
1925	27,172	26,650	46,068
1926	25,528	24,897	50,421
1927	23,669	28,545	48,513
1928	19,958	25,268	45,778
1929	21,327	19,921	46,751
1930	31,015	23,445	26,569
1931	9,110	7,305	10,401
1932	2,057	539	2,670
1933	979	338	1,919

SOURCE: U.S. Department of Commerce, Bureau of Census, *Historical Statistics of the United States, Colonial Times to 1970*, Part I, 105–106, Series C 89–119.

NOTE: Country of origin is defined as "country of last permanent residence."

[a]Includes Northern Ireland and the Irish Free State.

cross to America—880,000, for example, in the eleven years 1880–1890—the 1920s migration roughly matched the levels of 1890–1913.[2]

Like their prewar and nineteenth-century counterparts, postwar British and German immigrants to the United States were disproportionately drawn from the ranks of skilled and professional labor. In the years of peak immigration, 1923 and 1924, "skilled" workers (meaning, as measured by the Bureau of Immigration, blue- and white-collar, skilled and semiskilled) averaged 35 percent of the ethnic Scottish, 25 percent of the ethnic English, 20 percent of the ethnic Irish, and 30 percent of the ethnic German immigration—compared with 16 percent for all other ethnic groups entering the United States. Reflecting the highly developed industrial and relatively bureaucratized economies from which they came, Anglo-Gaelic immigrants were also disproportionately white-collar and proletarian. In 1924, skilled Anglo-Gaelic immigrants, by "race," were substantially underrepresented in the artisan trades of shoemaking and tailoring, which together represented less than 2 percent of their number, compared with 6 percent of skilled Germans and 13 percent of all other skilled immigrants. In contrast, skilled Anglo-Gaelic immigrants were significantly overrepresented by clerks, miners, and especially metalworkers. Whereas more than 7 percent of skilled Anglo-Gaelic immigrants were machinists and 10 percent were iron and steel workers, the comparable figures for all other skilled immigrants were, respectively, 3 and 2 percent.[3]

Not surprisingly, these metalworkers did not distribute themselves equally among the forty-eight states but concentrated instead on key industrial centers. In 1924, when a postwar record of 6,616 immigrant machinists came to the United States, 25 percent of these foreign-born metalworkers—the largest single group—declared themselves bound for Michigan.[4]

"Psychologically, these people are less averse to changing their abode," the American vice consul in Manchester said in 1923 of the skilled workers applying for U.S. visas, "than they are to changing their occupations." These were precisely the alternatives that confronted Harold Snudden and many other skilled workers in postwar Britain: to remain in the land of their birth, in which case they might have to leave their trade or adjust to radically different terms of work, or stick with their craft and venture across oceans and continents looking for acceptable employment. For those who chose the second course and crossed to North America, there was the compensating promise of a better life in their new home—plentiful jobs, higher wages, wider opportunities. But these were only promises and, more often, rumors; what the emigrant tradesman left behind was the known world, the world he had grown up in. It is a measure of the severity of Britain's postwar crisis that to Harold Snudden and many of his fellow craftsmen, this world appeared to be a dead end. Opportunity beckoned in North America, but this "pull" must have been less persuasive for each emigrant than the "push" of economic collapse and union defeat.[5]

Push

For the generation of British workers who played such a key role in the rise of the UAW in Detroit, the decision to emigrate was shaped by the devastating collapse of Britain's economy in 1921. Where unemployment during the prewar economic boom had never exceeded 3.3 percent, by June of 1921, 23 percent of all trade unionists suddenly found themselves on indefinite layoff. Overall unemployment among insured workers reached two million by December, representing nearly 18 percent of the work force. It was, some claimed, the worst unemployment in 100 years, and the statistics from Britain's major industries gave ample testimony for this grim assessment: 38 percent out of work in iron and steel; 20 percent laid off on the docks and 25 percent from merchant shipping; 310,000 unemployed in engineering (as the British termed metalworking), representing 25 percent of the work force. The economy bottomed out that winter, and the unemployment rate for insured workers fell to 13 percent in 1922. But there was no lasting recovery for metalworking engineers; between 1922 and 1935, unemployment among these skilled workers was never below 8 percent and in bad years hit 30 percent. For those still on the job, money wages spiraled downward. Since prices fell as well, real wages actually increased in many sectors of the economy, particularly for the lowest-paid unskilled workers. For skilled engineers, however, the 35 percent cut in money wages between 1920 and 1922 outpaced the fall in the cost of living, and real wages fell below 1914 levels. Thereafter, the number of engineers working for piece-rate wages grew by 25–30 percent between 1923 and 1927, until half of all fitters (skilled assemblers) and two-thirds of all turners (skilled lathe hands) worked for wages tied to productivity.[6]

Recovery began in 1922–1923 for several sectors of the British economy, particularly the new scientific-technical and consumer-oriented industries of the Midlands and the Southeast. But sustained economic recovery never reached the North, whose industries had long focused on foreign markets and, particularly in Scotland, capital goods. In the postwar years, as these sectors faced mounting competition from foreign rivals, British capitalism seemed unprepared for the challenge. While U.S. and German corporations in the prewar years had bought up rival firms and expanded vertically into every stage of manufacturing and marketing, Britain's industrial enterprises retained many of their mid-Victorian characteristics: small-scale, family-owned, and craft-based, with much of their market still concentrated in the "pioneer" sectors of industrialization: textiles, steam engines, and coal.[7]

In the prewar years, only British shipbuilding had retained its lead over American and German competitors, and for reasons peculiar to this capital-goods sector. Unlike the new consumer-oriented industries, which used specialized machinery to produce standardized goods, shipbuilding required specialized craft labor to produce a single, nonstandardized product. Skilled workers dominated the industry, and by the early 1890s the merchant steamships these craftsmen built accounted for 82 percent of world production. Scotland's Clydeside grew accordingly, since this region offered key advantages that attracted shipbuilders from the 1830s onward: nearby deposits of coal and iron ore; a river opening onto North Atlantic trade routes and offering more abundant and cheaper sites than London for building large ships; a reservoir of low-wage laborers driven from the Highlands and immigrating from Ireland; a ready supply of skilled engineers with experience constructing steam engines and other machines for the textile industry; and the success of Robert Napier's Clyde-based Cunard Lines, which generated ample orders for Clydeside shipyards owned by Napier and others. Clydeside engineering also dominated British production of locomotives, railroad rolling stock, hydraulic equipment, steam engines, cranes, pumps, and other varieties of capital equipment, much of it for export to developing economies. Manufactured in relatively small batches, these capital goods required skilled metalworkers producing to close tolerances. Before World War I, as many as 80 percent of Glasgow's insured wage earners were skilled tradesmen, and the metalworkers among them still produced innovations that gave British engineering a worldwide preeminence.[8]

Yet the Clydeside in particular and Britain in general lagged behind the United States and Germany in virtually every sector of the "Second Industrial Revolution," as economists have labeled the comprehensive shift in Europe's economic growth after 1890. The once dominant centers of the First Industrial Revolution—iron, textiles, steam engines, railroads, and coal—gave way to steel, chemicals, gasoline engines, electric motors, automobiles, and oil, and though British companies gradually reoriented themselves toward these new sectors, they did so on a smaller scale and at a slower pace than their German and American rivals. Even Britain's shipbuilding industry faced a troubled future in the prewar years, for the Clydeside yards had clung too long to the old technology of steam reciprocating engines and correspondingly lagged in their transition to turbine and diesel power. By 1911–1913, British shipbuilders still accounted for 62 percent of world production, but their competitive lead had narrowed substantially from the 1890s.[9]

"Businessmen will be dynamic," Eric Hobsbawm has observed, "only in so far as this is rational by the criterion of the individual firm." By this criterion, the conservatism of British industry was sensible and practical, even if it weakened the economy in the long run. Britain's smaller internal market constricted the demand for mass-produced goods and increased the unit cost of innovation. Meanwhile, the old technologies and markets of the First Industrial Revolution still produced profits, whereas the new technologies and markets of the Second Industrial Revolution sometimes threatened the value of existing plant and usually required considerable capital investment. Since craft labor was relatively abundant in Britain and wages were lower than in the United States, there was also less incentive to replace labor with fixed capital. When pressed by new rivals—many of them using British capital and machinery—some British firms shunned the expense and trouble of retooling and turned instead to the protected markets of the Empire. "The traditional methods of making profits," as Hobsbawm puts it, "had as yet not been exhausted, and provided a cheaper and more convenient alternative to modernization—for a while."[10]

Such an economy was ill-prepared for the postwar world. Demobilization not only killed production of warships but also swamped the world market with a glut of underutilized merchant shipping. The heavy reparations demanded of Germany stunted the postwar recovery of the European economy and produced mountains of Ruhr coal to undersell Britain's output. Government policy favoring a strong pound and return to the gold standard also saddled British exports with unfavorable exchange rates, and stagnant colonial economies further curtailed the demand for machinery exports.[11]

For skilled workers along the Clyde, future prospects in the postwar economy looked bleak indeed. Glasgow's jobless rate peaked at 25 percent in 1923, and Scottish unemployment between then and 1930 averaged 14 percent against the United Kingdom's 11.4 percent. Scotland, long known for its consistently high rate of emigration, sent thousands more of its citizens "on the tramp" in search of work. Among them was Bill Stevenson, the future president of UAW Local 157. As luck would have it, Stevenson finished his five-year apprenticeship as a fitter-turner in 1921, the very year the bottom fell out of the market. "The depression was in its full depth," he later recalled. "As a matter of fact, I never worked in the trade in Scotland." After two years of unbroken joblessness, Stevenson, at age twenty-two, decided "to escape boredom": he booked passage on a steamer from Glasgow to Montreal in September 1923 and crossed the river from Windsor to Detroit the following month.[12]

Henry McCusker emigrated the same year, one of 50,000 Scottish coal miners who left the industry during the 1920s. A member of the Lanarkshire County Miners Union and a nine-year veteran of the pits by age twenty-three, he surveyed the bleak conditions in his undercapitalized, pick-and-shovel industry and decided he'd had enough. "I thought there were some better horizons," as he put it, "than to be continually working like a mole in the coal mines of Great Britain." In 1923, he left the twenty-seven-inch-high tunnels where he had worked with his father and three brothers and emigrated to Pennsylvania. After a temporary return to coal mining, during which he joined the United Mine Workers, McCusker moved to Detroit in 1925 and bluffed his way into the Ford Motor Company as a grinder hand. By then, coal miners and family members "by the hundreds" had emigrated to the United States from his Clyde Valley town of Tannochside, including his brothers, his fiancée, and her entire family. Henry's younger brother Joe—the future president of Ford Local 600—arrived in Detroit in 1927, enrolled in the Ford Apprentice School, and got a job at the Rouge Tool and Die Building.[13]

English workers, particularly in the North, had nearly as much reason to emigrate as the Scots. Harry Southwell, an apprenticed cabinetmaker, tram driver, and member of the Transport Workers Union, did so in 1923. Like Harold Snudden, Southwell had been disillusioned by his combat experience, but nevertheless stayed in the army after the war. "Thousands of people were being released for employment in civilian life," he recalled years later, "and there was not a sufficient number of jobs to accommodate them." Things looked no better when he finally returned to civilian life, and Southwell resolved to leave for Australia or America. America had the stronger appeal, and Southwell and his wife landed in Detroit the same year as Bill Stevenson, Harold Snudden, and thousands of other British immigrants. After hiring into Maxwell Motors, the future president of UAW Local 174 learned machine grinding and eventually became an "expert" grinder hand.[14]

For Ernie Woodcock, a skilled toolmaker apprenticed in an Oldham engineering firm, emigration was a familiar option. Like Harold Snudden, he had already crossed to Canada before World War I and searched for work. From Canada, he had followed his craft to Rhode Island (where his son, Leonard, the future international president of the UAW, was born) and to Germany, where the outbreak of World War I found him employed in a German metalworking firm. After wartime internment, Woodcock returned to England in 1918, opened his own shop manufacturing silver-mesh handbags, and promptly joined the unemployed when the postwar slump and a change in fashion drove him out of business. In 1924, Woodcock took his family to Canada and from there made his way to Detroit.[15]

Unemployment was not the only factor that pushed British and Irish emigrants across the Atlantic. In the United Kingdom (and for that matter, across Europe) union activists and socialists had pinned their hopes for the future on the continued growth of labor and left-wing organization, but in the years after 1919 they saw the gains of 1900–1918 partially disintegrate during a sustained confrontation with employers and the State.

At its peak in 1918–1919, British labor seemed poised for an ever-widening challenge to the status quo. Less than two decades after its founding in 1900, the Labour party had won 22 percent of the vote in 1918 on a platform proclaiming its socialist goals. Simultaneously, union membership had ballooned toward eight million, double its size in 1914 and three times greater than in 1910. British workers were riding the crest of a sustained and growing strike wave, building from 235,000 strikers in 1916 to 2.4 million in 1919. The wartime government viewed these militant actions with mounting apprehension, particularly after the Dublin uprising in April 1916 cast an insurrectionary glow on any strike action. Conservatives saw special cause for alarm in the movement of dissident shop stewards that began with the formation of the Clyde Workers Committee (CWC) in 1915 and subsequently spread to other metalworking centers. In the winter of 1919, militant shop stewards on the Clydeside took center stage when they defied their national union leaders and launched a general strike for the forty-hour week. More than 100,000 workers responded to the call in Scotland and Belfast, most of them skilled metalworkers who hoped a shorter workweek would reduce unemployment. This modest agenda took a violent turn, however, when police attacked a mass demonstration of 50,000 strikers in Glasgow's St. George's Square, provoking chaotic street battles, the arrest of left-wing shop stewards, and the deployment of tanks and soldiers around City Hall.[16]

These events confirmed the image of "Red Clydeside" and set the stage for a year of industrial unrest, punctuated by mass strikes of railroad workers, Yorkshire miners, Lancashire cotton workers—even

London policemen. Although many observers feared or hoped that these confrontations presaged a revolutionary upheaval, events soon proved otherwise. Economic collapse and mass layoffs emptied the shops of left-wing stewards after 1920 and cooled the militancy of many workers. Thereafter, hopes for a radical transformation of British society suffered repeated disappointment. In 1921, the celebrated "Triple Alliance" of the railway, transport, and miners unions collapsed when the Miners struck and their allies refused to halt the shipment of coal. The following year, the powerful Engineers lost a thirteen-week lockout and conceded management control over hiring, manning of machines, and overtime. The Labour party won 31 percent of the vote in 1923 but demoralized an entire generation of labor militants when it formed a minority government the following year. With no program for socializing the economy and no parliamentary majority to advance its agenda, the Labour government floundered. In October 1924, after ten months of indecisive rule, new elections gave the Conservative party an overwhelming majority in Parliament. The culminating defeat of the postwar labor movement came eighteen months later. In May of 1926, after the Conservative government rejected nationalization of the coal mines and withdrew its wage subsidy, the Trade Union Congress called a general strike in support of the striking Miners. The walkout surprised all observers for its size and enthusiasm; nevertheless, nine days later the TUC's cautious leaders, confronted by the government's success in maintaining food supplies and transport, rejected calls for more militant tactics and terminated the strike.

Demoralization and victimization followed, driving thousands of militants out of their jobs and some of them overseas. Mat Smith was one of the latter. The Manchester-born engineer had led wartime strikes against skill "dilution" and had refused conscription, spending much of World War I in and out of jail. In the fall of 1926, "after a period of insecurity," according to MESA office manager Elizabeth McCracken, "in which he had seven jobs in three weeks," Smith emigrated to Canada, the apparent victim of poststrike blacklisting. Bill McKie, chairman of the Edinburgh City Central Strike Committee in 1926, emigrated the following year, as did George Handyside, the Glasgow machinist and future officer of Local 157. Joe McCusker, the future president of Ford Local 600, left the Lanarkshire mines the same year to join his brother Henry in Detroit.[17]

They followed a small group of Irish emigrants who also left behind disappointment and defeat. Among them were Cornelius Quinn and Patrick Rice, both veterans of the Irish Republican Army who had joined the independence movement as teenagers and lived through the rise and fall of radical republicanism. By September of 1919, the British government had outlawed Sinn Fein, the Irish Volunteers (later the IRA), and the Dail (the Irish Republic's first governing body), prompting a bloody insurrection as IRA ambushes, assaults on police stations, and assassinations of British officers were answered by retaliatory raids on Irish civilians. The Treaty of December 1921, which kept Ulster under British rule and gave the twenty-six counties restricted independence, ignited inter-Irish feuding and civil war, ending in 1923 with the defeat of the antitreaty forces.

Many IRA refugees made their way to New York City, where they hired into municipal transport companies and later played a pivotal role in organizing the Transport Workers under Mike Quill. Others moved on to the Midwest. Among them was Pat Rice, the Belfast-born industrial laborer (his immigration papers identify him as an "iron ore assembler") who emigrated from Liverpool in 1922 on the steamship *Celtic*. Arriving in New York City that August, he eventually made his way to Detroit, acquired training as an electrician, and hired into the Ford Rouge power plant as a substation operator. When the UAW organized Ford, this IRA veteran became president of Local 600's Maintenance and Construction Unit, and he eventually rose to vice president of the local. Hugh Thompson, another IRA veteran, emigrated to the United States in 1925, came to Detroit and hired on at Murray Body, where he helped organize the federal AFL local at that plant in 1934. Cornelius "Pat" Quinn, son of a Donegal farm laborer and the future president of Dodge Local 3, was another of the IRA refugees arriving in Detroit after 1921. Quinn had joined the IRA at age seventeen and eventually rose to captain, leading raids on police barracks during the Black and Tan wars. After the 1921 treaty, he allied himself with the diehard IRA faction opposing the partition. Captured and imprisoned by the new Irish government, he contracted pneumonia and was released after six months. With the defeat of IRA resistance to the treaty, and with rumors of rearrest hanging over his head, Quinn sailed in 1924 from Cork, bound for Montreal. Two years later, he crossed to Detroit on the Windsor ferry.[18]

Most of his fellow Irishmen arriving in Detroit came from far less radical backgrounds. Jack Thompson, for one, joined the British Army during World War I and fought in France before coming to Detroit in the early 1920s and hiring on at Ford. Fired in 1922, he moved to Toledo, took an active part in the 1934 Auto Lite strike, and eventually rose from UAW Local 12 to Region 2B director and member of the union's International Executive Board. Michael Magee also served in the British Army during World War I, spending much of the war in France in the

Irish Brigade. A Belfast-born automobile mechanic and member of the Transport Workers Union, Magee was active in the Labour party after the war and, he claimed, "took a leading part in the General Strike of 1926" before emigrating to Canada. In 1930, he crossed to Detroit from Windsor and got a job at Ford's Dearborn Assembly plant as a production worker. Robert Crothers, another Belfast Irishman, apparently left for economic rather than political reasons; a skilled toolmaker, he emigrated during the postwar slump in Great Britain's metalworking centers, boarding the *S.S. Leviathan* in Southampton and sailing to New York City in 1923. By January of the following year he was in Detroit, where he hired into GM's Fisher Plant 23.[19]

Crossing State Lines

These Anglo-Gaelic immigrant workers joined the larger immigrant stream making its way to America after the war. In 1919, only 25,000 Europeans could manage the transatlantic crossing, but their numbers grew dramatically thereafter. In the twelve months ending in June 1921, 652,000 Europeans entered the United States, representing 81 percent of total immigration. The 51,000 British among them nearly matched the prewar immigration from England and Scotland, but their number fell far short of the 222,000 immigrants from Italy and the 95,000 from Poland.[20]

This revival of mass immigration from Eastern and Southern Europe rekindled a bitter debate over U.S. policy. Employers who wanted to draw on foreign labor supplies, and foreign-born U.S. residents who wanted their kindred to follow, together opposed immigrant restriction. But they could not turn back a growing anti-immigrant sentiment, fueled in the immediate postwar period by fears that foreign-born radicals and immigrant workers threatened America's political and economic stability. "We do not want to be a dumping ground," said General Leonard Wood, the federal commander who imposed martial law on Gary, Indiana, during the 1919 steel strike, "for radicals, agitators, [and] Reds, who do not understand our ideals." Most congressmen agreed, and in May 1921 they voted by lopsided majorities for the first across-the-board limits on European immigration. The 1921 Quota Act did so by restricting immigration from any particular country to 3 percent of the foreign-born population from that nation already resident in the United States in 1910; in 1924, Congress further tightened these restrictions by reducing the quotas to only 2 percent of the foreign-born population living in the United States in 1890. The intention was clear: not only to restrict the total number of immigrants but also to reduce the proportion coming from Eastern and Southern Europe. Based on this explicitly biased formula, the United Kingdom's 1921 quota of 77,342 surpassed all others, more than doubling the Italian quota of 34,007 and dwarfing the Polish quota of 30,977.[21]

Judged by the criteria of those who framed it, the 1921 Quota Act was only a qualified success. As intended, the proportion of immigrants from Southern and Eastern Europe fell dramatically, from 64 percent of total immigration in 1921 to 23 percent in 1924. But total immigration fell only in 1922 and rose thereafter to 706,896 by 1924—a level approaching the postwar peak of 1921, before implementation of the Quota Act. In his 1924 *Annual Report* to the secretary of labor, the commissioner general of immigration acknowledged that this "great, perhaps almost startling increase in immigration during the past two years might very naturally suggest a substantial breakdown of the per centium limit law." But "such is not the fact," the commissioner reassured the secretary. Total immigration increased only because of new factors that Congress could not have anticipated: an unexpected jump in emigration from Northern Europe, exceeding even the overly generous quotas of 1921, and an equally sudden increase in Canadian immigration, which Congress exempted (together with Latin American immigration) from quota restrictions. Ironically, while General Wood and others had focused on the subversive potential of immigration from southern and eastern Europe, it was this postwar surge in preferred immigration from Britain and Canada that brought Anglo-Gaelic labor "agitators" to Detroit.[22]

The simultaneous rise of immigration from Canada and Britain was not coincidental, for many emigrants leaving the United Kingdom after World War I went to Canada first and then made their way to the United States. As a Dominion of Great Britain, Canada offered several advantages as a first stop in North America. Its institutions, laws, and customs were more familiar to the British emigrant, and steamship fares to Canada were generally lower than passage to New York. Government policy also favored emigration to the sparsely populated farmlands of the Dominions. Consequently, Canada in 1905 surpassed the United States as the favored destination for English emigrants and in 1907 captured first place among the Scottish as well.[23]

The 1921 Quota Act swelled Canadian immigration all the more, for at the very moment when economic depression and union defeat swelled the ranks of British emigrants, the Quota Act now put a ceiling on how many could enter the United States. Even the anglophile bias of the British quota was unequal to the sudden jump in visa requests from Great Britain, and in 1923 and 1924 the United Kingdom quota was quickly oversubscribed. The result, as the *Liverpool Journal of Commerce* summarized in 1924, was that "eminently desirable immigrants . . . have been diverted to the Dominion [of Canada] by the many harassing conditions which the people of the United States have thought fit to impose on the passenger traffic to their country." The same year, the American consul-general in Liverpool reported that the Cunard Line and other steamship companies had diverted some of their largest liners from the U.S. trade to the Liverpool-St. Lawrence route. Immigrant arrivals at the St. Lawrence ports jumped 100 percent in 1923 according to the consul-general, "and indications are that the figures will again be doubled this year."[24]

As a Dominion of the British Empire, Canada was freely accessible to British subjects. Many of the thousands who crossed to Montreal and other St. Lawrence ports intended to settle in Canada, but it quickly became apparent that a sizable number of these British immigrants had no intention of staying north of the border. Many thought that because Canadian immigration to the United States was exempt from the Quota Act, they had only to get to Canada and they could enter the United States without scrutiny. In fact, the British quota applied to all native-born emigrants from the United Kingdom, whether they crossed to the United States from Great Britain or Canada. The 1921 act originally required residency of only one year in Canada to exempt European immigrants from their quota, but Congress lengthened this to five years when it renewed the Quota Act in 1922. Many emigrants were simply unaware of this change—or were misled by those who profited by their ignorance. "If the stories we hear from British emigrants are true," the American consul in Windsor, Ontario, reported to his Manchester counterpart in 1923, "the steamship and booking agencies are giving out misleading information, as we are told that they tell the emigrant that it is not necessary for a British subject to have a [visaed] passport going into the United States from Canada. This of course is not so."[25]

Drawn, as the *Hamilton Herald* put it, by "white lights, abundance of money, and ample opportunities," immigration from Canada to the United States climbed from 32,452 people in 1918 to a record high of 200,690 in 1924. If not for the 1921 Quota Act, the number would have been higher. Native-born Canadians as well as Europeans who had lived five years in British North America had only to pay an $8.00 head tax to cross the border, but 16,236 immigrants who had only recently arrived in Canada were denied entry at northern land-border crossings in 1924—more than double the next highest total of 6,370 immigrant rejections at New York City, and four times higher than rejections at the Mexican border. "The unfortunate experience of the past year in this respect," the commissioner-general reported, "reflects increasingly desperate efforts on the part of various European peoples to get into the United States." Significantly, the two largest groups of debarred immigrants were the English and the Scottish, together representing two-thirds of all quota-excess immigrants denied entry.[26]

The commissioner-general of immigration was especially attuned to the presence of these debarred emigrants. "There are," he reported in 1924, "a large number of inadmissable aliens, chiefly natives of the United Kingdom, now in Canada . . . who cannot obtain quota certificates and who are awaiting an opportunity to enter the United States unlawfully." He knew also that most would try to cross at Detroit. "It is doubtful whether any portion of the United States border affords better opportunities for evasion of the law by smugglers." Some 500,000 nonimmigrant commuters crossed the Detroit River every month on the Windsor ferry, and illegal immigrants could easily lose themselves in "this turbulent mass of humanity surging forward for quick passage through the gates." During winter months, the more daring could walk across the frozen river; in the summer, "it was not unusual to receive reports of boat loads containing as many as thirty aliens being landed." With no effective Border Patrol to police this brazen smuggling, an estimated 50,000 illegal aliens crossed the Canadian border into the United States in 1924 alone. In the early 1920s, the Detroit River was to these illegal immigrants what the Rio Grande would become to the "wetbacks" of later years.[27]

For British emigrants waiting to cross legally from Canada to Detroit, the small number of quota slots allocated to Windsor and other border cities proved to be a formidable obstacle. Whereas the total British quota was only 90 percent filled in 1925, Windsor's allotment of just thirty nonpreference slots was exhausted in the first week of the fiscal year (starting July 1). By November, there were already 1,187 applicants for the *next* year's allotment. "We have sufficient now on our waiting list," the Windsor consul wrote U.S. Representative John Rogers in that month, "to exhaust a similar allotment from the British quota for slightly over 39 years to come. Our waiting list is believed to be longer than any other consulate in proportion to the number of visas we may issue." Windsor's urgent pleading for more quota slots produced results the following year, when the number was raised to 400. A June 1925 letter to the Windsor Consulate from the American

Consular Service in London expressed the hope that this would help relieve the visa situation, but regretted that the consulate could do no more because of heavy visa demands in Scotland—"the Consulate at Glasgow alone having a waiting list of twenty thousand." Windsor was swamped by the continuing high demand for visas: by 1926 its waiting list for the British quota had grown to 5,538. Heavy demands on the Irish quota also required a reapportionment of slots to Windsor, raising its annual quota allotment to 300.[28]

Ernie Woodcock was among those thousands on the Windsor waiting list. Arriving in Canada in 1924, he worked briefly for Massey Ferguson before moving to Windsor and hiring into the toolroom of Ford's Windsor plant. It took three years, 1925–1928, before he and his family could obtain quota certificates and cross to Detroit. Robert Allison, the Clydeside toolmaker who emigrated to Canada in 1924, waited three years before crossing to Detroit, and his family remained in Windsor until at least 1931. Mat Smith, the left-wing engineer, also had to wait two years in Canada before he crossed from the Border Cities to the United States in 1928.

Once they had legally arrived in Detroit, these immigrant workers had to continually reevaluate the permanency of their stay. At least initially, many British immigrants hedged their bets. Bill McKie and his wife first came to Detroit only to "visit" their daughter, and McKie's 1928 dues book for the Edinburgh Branch of the Sheet Metal Workers bears entries from his Detroit address on Cabot Avenue—suggesting he may well have contemplated a return to Edinburgh. Shortly afterward, however, he applied for citizenship. Others postponed this formal and, it must have seemed, irrevocable transition to a new life. Bill Stevenson waited nine years (1923–1932), David McIntyre eighteen years, (1919–1937), and Robert Crothers eighteen years (1923–1941) before submitting their Declarations of Intention. Matthew Smith, the future leader of the Mechanics Educational Society of America, never filed.[29]

Others knew with relative certainty when they arrived in Detroit that this was their new home. Tom Hanlon, the Tyneside toolmaker and future sit-down leader at Dodge Main, submitted his Declaration of Intention within three months of arriving in January 1926. Norman Mathews, the Cornwall electrician and future president of Packard Local 190, took even less time: just three days after landing on Ellis Island, Mathews arrived in Detroit, went directly to Circuit Court, and declared his "intention to renounce forever all allegiance and fidelity to George V, King of Great Britain and Ireland."

Settling In

In Detroit, the leadership potential of these Anglo-Gaelic immigrants would be realized in the union organizing drives of the 1930s. In the 1920s, however, it was a different matter. In these years, as they settled into their new surroundings, immigrant tradesmen had neither the resources nor the opportunity to challenge Detroit's open shop. In all likelihood, most were still too demoralized by the twin disasters of long-term unemployment and trade-union defeat. The immigration process, with its heavy emphasis on exclusion of alien radicals, also gave the recent immigrant reason to pause before initiating protest action. "I had the feeling, rightly or wrongly, that it was better for Americans to do the job," recalled Stan Coulthard, the young Merseysider who arrived in Detroit in 1923. "I thought that a foreigner, a Britisher, would have a handicap in that being an alien Americans wouldn't follow him." At the same time, Coulthard and his fellow countrymen in Detroit's auto plants had less reason and fewer opportunities to challenge the status quo during the boom conditions of the 1920s. Compared with Britain and Ireland, the status quo looked pretty good to Anglo-Gaelic immigrants, especially to the skilled tool and die makers among them.[30]

In this first postwar decade there is only sporadic evidence of their presence in Detroit's hard-pressed labor movement. William Logan, an English-born worker, rose to the presidency of the United Automobile, Aircraft, and Vehicle Workers of America and helped build a shop-based organization "much like the steward system in England," according to Detroit labor journalist Joe Brown. Logan's own description of the UAAVWA's internal structure does bear a striking resemblance to the cross-craft and shop-based structure of Britain's wartime stewards councils. "Under this system," Logan said of Detroit Local 127 in 1920, "there is one committeeman or woman for every ten workers or a fraction thereof. . . . These committeemen comprise what is known as the Board of Administration, which is the governing body of the local."[31]

But tool and die makers, and the British among them, were generally absent in the organizing campaigns of the UAAVWA and its successor organization, the Auto Workers Union (AWU). Formed by the small nucleus of organizers who survived the UAAVWA's post-1921 collapse, the AWU under Communist leadership sustained an underground network of shop newspapers and organizing committees in the late 1920s. Sporadic strikes and departmental walkouts disrupted auto production in these years, but most such job actions were limited to the body-making plants, where metal finishers, trimmers, and upholsters confronted technological change and cuts in piecework wages. Many autoworkers recognized the pivotal role that tool and die makers could have played in these strikes. As one AWU organizer put it, "the assembly men and others who dare not risk their jobs always asked, if they struck, 'would the tool and die makers strike too?' " The answer was no in all but a handful of cases. Of sixteen departmental strikes in Michigan's auto industry between 1926 and 1928, the AWU identified the leading occupational groups as metalworkers (five walkouts) and wet sanders (three), followed by trimmers, molders, and assembly-line workers. Only one recorded walkout involved tool and die makers: a strike by the second shift at Fisher Body Plant 23 in March 1928, protesting a cut in the overtime premium for Saturday night work. Industry observer William Chalmers compiled a similar list of eleven auto-industry walkouts between 1918 and 1929—none included tool and die makers.[32]

Initially, the immigrant toolmaker had trouble comprehending, much less challenging, the working conditions he found in Detroit's toolrooms. Even the language was bewildering, as Alan Strachan recalled: "In my own case, I had served a legitimate apprenticeship and had papers to prove that I was a qualified 'fitter and turner.' But who in Detroit had ever heard of that job description? I was to learn later that most 'fitters and turners' had become tool and die makers.[33]

Strachan could at least recognize, "albeit sometimes with great difficulty," the English language he shared with native Detroiters. But many of his fellow countrymen must have found the cityscapes of North America strangely huge and a little intimidating. "The city worker from Manchester or Birmingham, from Glasgow or Dundee, comes, it is true, from a relatively large and crowded center," observed British journalist S. K. Ratcliffe in 1927. "But the scale to which he is accustomed is still very small, and for him, the mass and clangor of New York or Chicago, even of Cleveland and Detroit, cannot fail to be a crushing experience."[34]

Homesickness and loneliness were alleviated for immigrants whose relatives had already established themselves in these strange surroundings. Strachan could look to his uncle; McKie and his wife to their daughter; Joe McCusker to his brother. For single workers with no such family contacts, the likely first stop was one of the many rooming houses near the plants or downtown. If they were Irish or Scots-Irish, they would probably find one in Corktown. This once predominantly Irish neighborhood immediately west of downtown had lost much of its residential cohesion but still contained such distinctively Irish institutions as Holy Trinity church and St. Vincent's parish. In the twentieth century it represented a gateway to Detroit for many English-speaking immigrants, much as the East Side "Black Bottom" had served, in turn, immigrants from Germany, Italy, and Eastern Europe, and African-American migrants from the southern United States. Henry McCusker, the Scottish coal miner, spent his first months in Detroit living in an all-Scottish boardinghouse on Corktown's Pine Street; Pat Quinn, the Irish laborer from Donegal, first lodged in a Wabash Street rooming house owned by a County Sligo immigrant. Many other immigrant workers in Corktown found a bed, a meal, and, in the nearby pubs, familiar accents and fellow countrymen.[35]

In these contacts, many also found their first lead to a job. The "English" rooming house where Stan Coulthard first lived after arriving in 1923 "was like a second home for me," and Coulthard counted among its blessings the help his fellow countrymen gave him "to get jobs and find my way around." Finding a job was a relatively easy matter in Detroit during the 1920s, particularly for Anglo-Gaelic immigrants who were fitters and turners/tool and die makers. These "aristocrats" of labor must have been troubled by some aspects of their new work environment: the extraordinary degree of mechanization and subdivision of labor they saw in Detroit's auto plants, some of it even entering the toolrooms; the pervasive individualism that prompted Mat Smith, the Manchester toolmaker, to dub Detroit's tool and die makers "overtime hogs" and "dog-eat-dog . . . reactionaries"; above all, as we'll see in Chapter 4, the absence of unions. But these were caveats on a situation that must otherwise have looked good to work-starved tradesmen.[36]

It was this relative prosperity, added to the characteristic insecurity and caution of the adjusting immigrant, that stilled worker protest in Detroit's toolrooms. Their labor-market leverage put tool and die makers in a strategic position, allowing them to win good wages and generally favorable conditions with minimal organization, mobilization, or strikes. They could turn instead to the "good life" promised by the new mass-consumer advertising of the 1920s. Many did so with a vengeance. "In 1929," Bill McKie later recalled, "many skilled workers' yearly income ran $2,340. Everybody knows that this particular year . . . was what we look back upon as a period of prosperity. Houses were built, the installment man was busy on the job, we were all buying radios, we were all buying cars." Some were even buying stocks. "Playing the market became an obsession with them," Alan

Strachan recalled of the many "speculators" he knew in Detroit's tool-rooms. "They had a way of disappearing at least once during the morning, usually into the toilet, where they studied the previous day's market activities before calling their stockbroker." Their speculative spirit reminded Strachan of the gamblers he had known among British engineers. "There was, however, a significant difference—where the American toolmaker was speculating in the major financial markets, his British counterpart was spending his hard-earned shillings with an illicit bookmaker betting on the horses." Labor journalist Joe Brown, looking back on the 1920s, sardonically recalled how toolroom entre-preneurs "kept 'cool with Coolidge,' asked 'Who but Hoover,' joined the Masonic and other fraternal orders, and learned to play golf and bridge. The mass of tool and die makers," he concluded, "had no more conception of a common interest as craftsmen than a tom cat has of chastity."[37]

Predictably, employers celebrated this entrepreneurial spirit. "De-troit's Open Shop workers," enthused one business magazine, "are Capitalists. It is they who have closed the gap between classes that were once known as Capital and Labor." Henry Ford went to some lengths to advance this image and purchase the goodwill of his em-ployees, including the Anglo-Gaelic immigrants in Ford's toolrooms. "The Ford Motor Company bought and paid for the Scottish Pipes," explained Bill McKie, recalling the company's lavish subsidy of the St. Andrews Society band. "They paid for the uniforms and bagpipes and everything, and they used to send this large band to all the cities [where] they were having a showing of cars." George Campbell, the Clydeside engineer and St. Andrews member who worked in Ford's toolrooms, had further reason to identify with Ford management. As a member of the Masonic Order, Thirty-second Degree, he and other toolroom Masons shared the rituals of Freemasonry with their fraternal brothers in Ford management—Henry Sr. included. Many non-Masons also saw an identity of interests between themselves and the elder Ford. "When I leave this lousy place, wash-up, change my clothes and go out for the evening," one Ford toolmaker told Alan Strachan in 1928, "you can't tell me from Henry Ford." You probably also couldn't distinguish his home from that of a Ford supervisor. Detroit's low-density neighborhoods, with tree-lined streets and grass berms, of-fered substantial dwellings that were far superior to working-class houses in Britain and Ireland. More so than most workers, the high-wage British tradesman could afford the better of these homes. Some moved to solid and comparatively spacious walk-up apartments. Oth-ers moved to cottages, one-and-a-half-story bungalows, or moderately sized houses: single-family or duplex, frame or brick, many of the latter in a Tudor-revival style, and some with driveways and garages.[38]

Most Anglo-Gaelic immigrants found these homes in Northwest Detroit, though few moved there without intermediate stops. Harold Snudden, like many other tool and die makers, relocated his family from one place to the next as he changed jobs, moving from the far East Side through a succession of addresses to the house he bought on the upper West Side in 1929. Many of his fellow countrymen were heading in the same direction. Among those Anglo-Gaelic immigrants who later rose to leadership in Detroit's autoworker unions, nineteen of twenty-seven for whom addresses could be found in the 1928–1932 city directories lived west of Brush and north of Michigan Avenue (See Appendix B). Pre-1920 immigrants from English Canada, Britain, and Ireland had already settled in this northwestern quadrant of the city, and postwar arrivals gravitated toward relatives and compatriots. The streets above Grand Boulevard, west of Woodward, and along Grand River Avenue were especially favored in the 1920s, as developers put up block after block of new housing in the area. Here and in neighboring Highland Park, British and Irish immigrant workers lived among the native-white Americans who predominated in this quadrant of the city. The better-paid occupational groups also predominated in the area, with white-collar clerks and independent professionals sharing neighborhoods with blue-collar tradesmen. In this regard, the experience of Anglo-Gaelic immigrant workers contrasted sharply with that of autoworkers in Poletown, Hamtramck, Delray, and other immigrant enclaves. In these latter settlements, the outward movement of white-collar residents had gradually produced neighborhoods where the working-class ethnic majority predominated; on the Northwest side, in contrast, British tradesmen lived among white-collar professionals and businessmen.[39]

If spatial relations determined social consciousness, Anglo-Gaelic immigrants would have assimilated with the native-born, white-collar residents who were numerically predominant in their neighborhoods and socially predominant in "mainstream" culture. The evidence, however, indicates that assimilation depended on a wide range of perceived opportunities, both social and economic. Among Anglo-Gaelic immigrants, these opportunities varied by occupation and class. White-collar clerks and professionals looked to downtown employers and business partners for opportunities to advance their careers. Opportunities for most skilled metalworkers veered off in a different direction: some could move into lower-level factory supervision and a few could open job shops, but the majority sought opportunities as journeymen tradesmen. Toolmakers, patternmakers, and other metal-working tradesmen worked in a craftsman's realm that included job-shop owners and skilled foremen, but not doctors, bank managers, and realtors. Living in "respectable" homes with white-collar neigh-bors was an opportunity these tradesmen could afford; some, like George Campbell, went a step farther and crossed into a social world that linked them with the white-collar businessmen and professionals who predominated in the St. Andrews Society and Scottish Rite Ma-sonry. Yet most tradesmen remained in a social world defined by the values and associations of skilled workers, a world that was proximate to the bourgeois universe of St. Andrews and shared some of its at-tributes (Protestant, white, male-dominated), but which was otherwise demarcated by class.

Some individuals moved back and forth between these worlds. Like George Campbell, Harold Snudden joined the Masons, but for very different reasons. "He didn't like 'em," his son Geoffrey recalls of the "businessmen" in the Masons. "But he thought . . . he could get a job easier through their influence." When this calculated strategy pro-duced unsatisfactory results, Snudden quit.[40]

His membership in the Odd Fellows, on the other hand, represented something different. At the East Side Amity Lodge, the membership included, by Geoffrey Snudden's recollection, a large number of his father's shopmates and fellow craftsmen. Many were also fellow immigrants—"all I had to do was listen to them," recalled Geoffrey of the distinctively British accents at the Odd Fellow dances where his father played trumpet. By this rough measure, Geoffrey estimates at least 20 percent of his father's 2,200 lodge mates were British immigrants.[41]

His recollections are consistent with the known facts concerning the Odd Fellows. This mutual-aid organization traced its origins to Brit-ain's industrial revolution, when artisan workers established "Box Clubs" to provide sickness and funeral benefits for tramping journey-men. When the Combination Acts made unions illegal between 1799 and 1824, these "friendly" societies provided cover and strike benefits for protesting workers; they also gave the early labor movement much of its organizational structure, including "stewards" (officers), benefit plans, "clearance certificates" and "traveling cards" for tramping mem-bers moving to another lodge's jurisdiction. The Odd Fellows, founded in Manchester and growing to more than 400,000 members by 1870, was the largest of Britain's "affiliated orders." For a time, it was also the focus of considerable government concern. Secret rituals borrowed from the Masons (a vestigial link still visible in Detroit, where Amity provided space for the "Paul Revere" Masonic Lodge) gave the Odd Fellows a conspiratorial hue, while the district-wide organization and noisy gatherings of Odd Fellowship (usually in a tavern) violated laws against corresponding societies and seditious meetings. The Odd Fellows grew nonetheless, in part because some government leaders saw them as a means to keep down the tax levy (the "Poor Rates") to support the unemployed, and in part because workers saw them as the only alternative to the stigma of poor relief. After 1850, the Odd Fellows and other friendly societies submitted to protective legislation; after 1911, many became official agents for the state insurance program established by the National Insurance Act. By then, the Odd Fellows' nearly one million members and hundreds of lodges made it a significant institution in Britain's working-class neighborhoods, particularly among the better-paid workers who could afford the initiation fees and dues.[42]

In the United States, the British immigrants who dominated Odd Fellowship before 1840 gave way to American-born members who favored the Masonic form of cross-class fraternalism. But Odd Fellow membership remained predominantly blue collar compared to the Masons, and immigrant workers like Harold Snudden could join one of thirty lodges in Detroit offering comradeship and insurance benefits for sickness and death. The Amity Lodge's 1918 bylaws devoted the better part of fifty-six pages to the rules, procedures, and conditions for providing this mutual insurance. New applicants were eligible for membership only if they were "free white males, not under 21 years of age, of good moral character, not engaged in the business of saloon keeper, bartender, professional gambler, or a hotel keeper having a liquor license." Furthermore, "All persons admitted to membership must believe in a Supreme Being . . . and have some known, reputable means of support." Those who passed this muster—and a medical exam—were accepted "if less than two black balls appear" in the required balloting of incumbent members. Upon payment of an age-defined initiation fee, five dollars for those aged thirty-six years or less, up to fifty dollars for fifty or more years, the dues-paying member (seven dollars annually) was eligible for benefits: five dollars a week for the first fourteen weeks of sickness and two dollars a week for thirty-nine weeks; seventy dollars for burial expenses; thirty dollars for surviving family; and emergency loans for members in distress, subject to the vote of the lodge.[43]

As indicated by the composition of the By-Law Committee that formulated these rules, the Amity Lodge was a predominantly blue-collar and skilled-trades organization: the six-man committee included two molders (one of them was also an officer in the Stove Mounters International Union), one machinist, one pressman, one shipbuilder, and one white-collar member, a secretary for an electroplating firm. The same was true for one of Detroit's biggest lodges, American Eagle 441: in 1918, of fifteen officers whose occupations can be identified with reasonable certainty, eleven worked in blue-collar occupations (seven as skilled tradesmen and two of these as foremen), three in white-collar jobs (two clerks and a lawyer), and one as a self-employed photographer. Available evidence strongly suggests that the American Eagle Lodge, located in the proximate neighborhood where Anglo-Gaelic immigrants clustered (see Appendix B), also drew many British tradesmen into its ranks. The April 1918 issue of the lodge's *American Eagle Bulletin* was full of patriotic news concerning membership service in World War I: significantly, of nineteen excerpted letters from members in military service, two were from men serving the British Army in France (one remarking that he met others from Detroit lodges). A third member, Andrew Smith, was featured with a photo and accompanying story explaining that "he joined the British Army soon after the war broke out and has fought in every battlefront on the British line in France." Of thirty-four change-of-addresses given for members in the military, four were Canadian units (two of them Engineers), and three were units stationed in England and Scotland. The presence of these British members suggests that some of those who volunteered for American service may also have been British immigrants who had already gained U.S. citizenship or wished to acquire it through special provisions favoring enlistees.[44]

A second Odd Fellow lodge is worthy of note in this and other regards: Scotia 488, whose very name, as well as its location on the near Northwest Side (Appendix B), suggests immigrant ties. In 1933, it was here and at the not-too-distant American Eagle Lodge that the Mechanics Educational Society of America, the forerunner union of the UAW, established two of its six Detroit locals. Over the previous dozen years, both these lodges must have gained many new Odd Fellow members and future MESA recruits, particularly in the peak years of Anglo-Gaelic immigration, 1921–1924. Their leadership certainly reflected a continuing blue-collar infusion. The ten officers of the Scotia and American Eagle Lodge in 1924–1926 for whom there is occupational evidence included six with blue-collar backgrounds: an autoworker (the 1924 lodge leader—"noble grand"—at Eagle), a patternmaker (eagle vice grand), a toolmaker, a welder, an auto mechanic, and a railroad policeman. One officer, the treasurer at American Eagle, was a white-collar clerk. Three others occupied more ambiguous positions: a "decorator" (perhaps of store windows or interior furnishings); a former glazier apparently elevated to petty proprietorship as owner of a small glass company; and a plastering contractor who worked at his home address.[45]

His home address, like that of fellow officers from the Scotia and American Eagle lodges, was proximate to the same neighborhood on the Northwest Side where Anglo-Gaelic immigrants congregated. This was also where the officers of Scottish Rite Masonry and the St. Andrews Society lived (see Appendix B). But Masonic and St. Andrews Society officers had very different occupations from their Odd Fellow counterparts. The Masons' Scottish Rite Consistory counted diemaker George Campbell among its members, but its fifteen officers in 1924–1926 were exclusively white-collar: four government employees (justice of the peace, deputy sheriff, police engineer, and secretary of the water commissioners), three downtown lawyers, three insurance executives, two contractor suppliers, a minister, a physician, and the proprietor of a tailoring business. The officers of St. Andrews were drawn from roughly the same occupations: in the three years, 1925–1926 and 1930, covered by available evidence, only four of eighteen known occupations among St. Andrews officers (one carpenter, two clerks, and one inspector) overlapped with the occupations of Odd Fellow leaders. The rest of St. Andrews' officers were either government officials and employees (a justice of the peace, the chairman of the City Election Commission, his clerk, a library carpenter, and a DPW foreman), professionals (a bank-branch manager and a physician), or real estate entrepreneurs (two contractors, three contractor-suppliers, and two realtors). The location of St. Andrews Hall was consistent with the social composition of this leadership: situated on East Congress (see Appendix B) in Detroit's commercial center, it was easily accessible from downtown offices and government buildings.

The activities and goals of St. Andrews also differed from Odd Fellowship. St. Andrews held charity balls to help, as the program put it, Scotsmen "who are not so well intrenched [*sic*] financially" as the Society's upper-income members; their social calendar focused on the annual Robert Burns Birthday Concert at the General Motors auditorium, featuring traditional Highland reels, Scottish ballads, and bagpipe music. The Odd Fellows do not appear to have explicitly opposed this emphasis on benevolence and "old world" culture—the Scotia Lodge, for one, chose a name that also marked its members' ties with the old world. But the values the Odd Fellows stressed were different: self-help and mutual aid, not charity and commerce. Bowling, weekend dances, and Bob-Lo cruises were the standard fare of Odd

Fellow sociability, not formal concerts and gala balls at the General Motors building. Assimilation was proudly proclaimed in lodge titles linking "American eagle" members with their affiliated "Old Glory Encampment," but Odd Fellow assimilation was more democratic and collective than the process at St. Andrews. Whereas the St. Andrews Hall hosted the Sons of St. George, the Order of the Scottish Clans, and other British-only groups heralding Imperial-Clan values, the Amity Lodge, in contrast, housed an Employment Bureau and Fraternity Council 1556 of the Security Benefit Association. The latter was a citywide organization with branches open to native- and foreign-born members.[46]

In all these regards, the Odd Fellows sustained a skilled-trades subculture that partially absorbed the ideological blandishments of open-shop Detroit, but which also partially countered and redefined these values by stressing mutualistic norms. The ideological links with Detroit's business leaders were clear enough. When the Diamond Lodge, located on the Northwest Side, celebrated the 1919 Centenary of Odd Fellowship, members marched in a body to Calvary Presbyterian Church, underscoring the Protestant faith that set them apart from Polish and other immigrant Catholic production workers. The marchers were all white, and if women participated it was only as members of their separate auxiliary, the Daughters of Rebekah. Available evidence suggests the Odd Fellows were also prowar in 1917 and pro-Republican in the 1920s. The American Eagle Lodge, for one, filled its wartime *Bulletin* with patriotic news and a "Roll of Honor" listing 128 members in the Allied Armies; ten years later, the lodge sponsored McKinley Council 8 of the Junior Order of United American Mechanics. Since this and other councils of the Junior Mechanics were named after Republican presidents (Lincoln, Roosevelt, Grant, etc.), the Eagle Lodge was apparently in sympathy with the Grand Old Party.[47]

But this does not mean the Eagle Lodge endorsed the same value systems as Henry Ford. The Republican party was not a monolith, exclusively dominated by conservative businessmen; in Detroit, the party had a history since 1890 of Progressive reform linked with Hazen Pingree, Teddy Roosevelt, and a thirty-year crusade (ending in 1922) to municipalize the streetcar system. While statewide Republicans advocated temperance and probusiness tax measures, Mayor Pingree, in contrast, built a mass base among Detroit's immigrant workers with populist attacks on "rich corporations [and] corrupt wire-pullers," and periodic visits to popular taverns. Until the mid-1930s, the Detroit Federation of Labor allied itself with this Progressive wing of the party, and the same brand of cautious reformism probably appealed to the Odd Fellows' blue-collar members. The Eagle Lodge's prowar stance also bears closer scrutiny, for in the midst of a wartime hysteria aimed at all things German, the *American Eagle Bulletin* warned against proposals that the Odd Fellows should expel their German lodges. These nuances of moderation would not have satisfied left-wing Anglo-Gaelic militants, but their moderate compatriots found in Odd Fellowship a blue-collar comraderie that set them apart from the business-professional outlook of St. Andrews and the Masons. Significantly, when Detroit's fledgling unions sought shelter in the 1930s, at least seven Odd Fellow lodges opened their doors and provided space for meetings, strike kitchens, or local offices; in contrast, St. Andrews Hall and the Masons remained barred to union gatherings. As available sites close to factories and open to union business, and as social organizations that sustained worker sociability, the Odd Fellows would play the same role as the Polish National Alliance, the Polish Falcons, and other immigrant societies that opened their doors to union meetings.[48]

Other organizations also sustained a skilled-trades subculture in the 1920s, though the scope, nature, and even the timing of their impact are only dimly recalled by former members and their surviving families or friends. Albert Kanarz, a German-American toolmaker, recalls the Eagles "Nest" (no relation to the Odd Fellow Lodge) on the near East Side where some 100–150 members gathered to watch weekly wrestling matches and drink bootleg beer. "They were from Fisher Body, Packard, Murray Body, different plants," says Kanarz, who was fuzzy on dates but emphatic on at least one point: "they were tool and die makers," not production workers. Like the Odd Fellows, the Eagles organized a womens' auxiliary for the wives and provided comraderie and a free meal for tramping members from out of town. Kanarz cannot recall any one ethnic group that predominated, though, not surprisingly in Jim Crow Detroit, "there were no coloreds."[49]

Joe Oberg, an American-born precision grinder, does remember a particular ethnic group predominating at the Patternmakers lodge he frequented as a boy in the 1920s. "They were all Scottish," he recalls of these die-model and foundry patternmakers, whose vital skills were in such demand that antiunion employers sometimes looked to the Patternmakers for skilled labor in the 1920s. Bill Stannis, a Scottish patternmaker who boarded in Oberg's home, took young Joe to the union's picnics and Bob-Lo cruises, where members engaged in "drinking, games, and 'tossing the Gabor.'" Particular saloons also catered to immigrant tradesmen. The Detroit branch of the Amalgamated Society of Engineers (ASE), one of Britain's most powerful skilled-trades unions, held meetings for its Anglo-Gaelic membership at the "Anglim Hall," better known as the Anglim Saloon after its owner, Edwin Anglim. The American branches of the ASE merged with the Machinists in 1920, but Anglim's saloon probably retained its immigrant clientele. In the 1930s, Bob Bolton's bar in Highland Park, located in an empty bank-branch building on Puritan and Hamilton, was also known as a congregating point for Scottish and English workers.[50]

This was a blue-collar world, far removed from the social networks of white-collar professionals and entrepreneurs, even if they lived next door to British toolmakers. Irish and Scots-Irish Catholics may also have moved in different circles from the British toolmaker, but their social world was even farther removed from the values and institutions of WASP culture. Although the Catholic Church was not a worker-controlled institution like the Odd Fellows, neither was it a mainstream organization akin to the Masons. In the 1930s, the church produced such conservative leaders as Father Coughlin and Archbishop Gallagher, but it also produced New Deal liberals like Archbishop Mooney, the utopian socialists of the Catholic Worker movement, and the liberal anti-Communists of the Association of Catholic Trade Unionists (ACTU). Henry McCusker, his brother Joe, and Pat Hamilton would gravitate toward ACTU; Pat Quinn, as he aligned himself with the left, ultimately became their political opponent in the UAW. But Quinn could still find a place in the ethnic subculture of Irish Detroit, rising through the membership ranks of the Gaelic League to eventually become its president.[51]

Through the same subculture he found his wife—Lil Howley, a co-resident of the Corktown rooming house where Quinn lived and a frequent dance partner at the Gaelic League hall on Grand River Avenue. As indicated in Table 3.3, other Anglo-Gaelic immigrants also found their wives in Detroit's ethnic subculture. Among those who later rose to leadership in Detroit's labor movement, the thirteen known cases of men who married in North America include nine who married women from Great Britain and Ireland.

Information about the immigrant wives in these marriages is difficult to find. In general, women were expected to fulfill family-bound roles as homemakers and mothers, and the high incomes that skilled tradesman earned in good years made this wife-at-home ideal attainable for many Anglo-Gaelic families. Consequently, there is less information about their lives available in the public record, and virtually none concerning their upbringing and experience before they emigrated.

Lil Howley, according to her children, was a nurse's aide in England before she emigrated in 1925 at the suggestion of her older sister, who

TABLE 3.3
IMMIGRANT MARRIAGES

Husband's name and nationality	Wife's name	Birthplace	Year and city of marriage
With American wives			
George Handyside Scottish	L. Pasquantonio	Roxborough, Massachusetts	1933 Detroit
Norman Mathews English	Eva Emma	Calumet, Michigan	No data
David McIntyre Scottish	Georgiana	Warsaw, Indiana	1926 Detroit
Alan Strachen English	Evelyn Bergland	—	1933 Detroit
With immigrant wives			
Robert Crothers Irish (Belfast)	Elizabeth	Dumbarton, Scotland	1935 Toledo
John Fairbairn Scottish	Letitia	Glasgow, Scotland	1926 Windsor
W.G. Grant English	Jessie	Wishaw, Scotland	1929 Detroit
Pat Hamilton English (Irish)	Marcella	Musselborough, Scotland	1932 Detroit
Michael Magee Irish (Belfast)	Elizabeth	Strathaven, Scotland	1935 Detroit
James Murdoch Scottish	Nell	Northampton, England	1927 Toledo
Pat Quinn Irish (Donegal)	Lil Howley	Sligo, Ireland	1930 No data
Pat Rice Irish	Bella Jack	Dundee, Scotland	1930 Toledo
William Stevenson Scottish	Jean	Ballymacnamee, Ireland	1927 Detroit

SOURCE: Steve Babson, "Pointing the Way: Skilled Workers and Anglo-Gaelic Immigrants in the Rise of the UAW" (Ph.D. diss., Wayne State University, 1989), Appendix A.

already lived in Detroit. Taking up initial residence in the Corktown rooming house her sister ran, Howley worked as a nanny for wealthy Grosse Pointe families until she married Pat Quinn in 1930. She probably had many immigrant companions working in neighboring Grosse Pointe homes as maids and nurses—as early as 1904, the leading occupation among women emigrating from the United Kingdom to North America was domestic servant. Job turnover was very high among these women, since many married soon after their arrival; finding a husband was reportedly a prime motive for emigrating in the first place. This may also have been a particularly compelling goal after World War I, since battlefield deaths left a surplus of nearly one million women aged twenty to forty in Great Britain (7,102,000 to 6,023,000 men), while Detroit's rapid industrialization produced a comparably disproportionate surplus of eligible bachelors. The prolonged economic slump of the 1920s gave added impetus for young women to emigrate and find work, since unemployment severely reduced the income of their parental family and increased the economic obstacles to starting a family of their own. For whatever reasons, the number of British and Irish servants emigrating to the United States jumped dramatically in 1921 to over 18,000, second only to the 20,000 coming from southern Italy. The quota law that subsequently restricted total immigration also reduced the absolute number of immigrants in this predominantly female occupation, but the total number of British and especially Irish servants entering the United States surpassed all other immigrant groups but Germans through the early 1920s.[52]

Significantly, seven of the nine cases where immigrant men married immigrant women represented cross-ethnic marriages: Irish men marrying Scottish women (three cases), English men marrying Scottish women (two), and Scottish men marrying English or Irish women (one each). The preliminary evidence from this small population suggests two hypotheses. First, that these marriages were not arranged before the couple emigrated. Since the husband and wife came from different parts of Great Britain or Ireland, and since most of these marriages occurred years after their arrival in North America, it seems likely these were couples that met and courted in Detroit. Second, given the above, they must have met in a social network that reinforced immigrant associations and sustained an Anglo-Gaelic presence in Detroit.

In the 1920s, the blue-collar dimensions of that presence were barely visible to the casual observer. Immigrant craftsmen merged with a skilled-trades subculture of native-born Protestants; Irish- and Scots-Catholic workers merged with an ethnic subculture dominated by their church. The characterological "fault lines" that distinguished Anglo-Gaelic workers from their shopmates were papered over by the 1920s prosperity and might have gradually disappeared if that decade's dynamic growth had continued indefinitely. Instead, the Great Depression came like an earthquake, rending the glib optimism of the Roaring Twenties and closing off the opportunities for individual advancement. In these changed circumstances, Anglo-Gaelic workers were among the first to act.

4

POINTING THE WAY

Bill McKie was fifty-one years old when he emigrated from Scotland to Detroit. In addition to a chest of books, tools of his trade, and other personal belongings, he brought "baggage" of another sort: the experience and knowledge of collective action.

No individual biography can fully represent the "average" for a group, and McKie's personal history is no exception. The particular contingencies of his life are irreducibly his own. But if his life was unique in many respects, the culture that defined his life choices was one he shared with many other immigrants. In this respect, McKie's personal history underlines those unique aspects of Anglo-Gaelic culture that prepared him and his compatriots for union leadership in Detroit. In the 1920s, as he and other Anglo-Gaelic immigrants settled into their new surroundings, there was little opportunity or call for them to unpack this cultural baggage. In the 1930s, however, crisis and opportunity merged in the Great Depression. In the general collapse of wages and the rapid deterioration of working conditions that followed the stock market crash, tool and die makers, formerly the favored elite of autoworkers, suffered the sharpest erosion of pre-1929 standards. Between 1933 and 1936, they took the lead in the strikes and organizing drives that galvanized autoworker militancy in Detroit. In doing so, they exploited both the political opportunities generated by the New Deal, and the labor-market leverage produced by a skilled-trades shortage. Anglo-Gaelic union leaders were especially suited for this mobilization by their unique consciousness of craft, class, and workplace organization. Compared with their American-born and rural-immigrant co-workers, they knew the rudiments of union organization through

95

sustained experience. With a "British model" to guide them, they helped point the way to a mass-based labor movement.

Brother Bill McKie

Like many of Britain's artisan radicals, Bill McKie began his life in a nineteenth-century world dominated by Protestant dissent. In Carlisle, the Scottish border town where he was born in 1876, "there were no socialists in my young days," McKie later recalled. Discussion in workingmen's clubs focused on "the question of religion in relation to workers, disputing what so and so said in the Bible, if it was correct." His father, a signalman for the Northeast Railroad, was an ardent Quaker; his mother was in the Salvation Army; and McKie played piccolo at Saturday night services of the Willow Home Mission. Evangelical views predominated but did not go uncontested in a town that equated self-improvement with earnest study and inquiry, and where self-proclaimed "Rationalists" sold popularizations of Darwin's theories. "I wasn't really sure what I was reading," McKie recalled of these sixpence books, "[but] I knew it was something different." Certainly different from the diet of religious reading his father still required of him. "Dean Farrer's *Life of Christ* and *Pilgrim's Progress* were my daily duty."[1]

At age twelve, McKie left school and entered the shop of a local iron monger, beginning a seven-year apprenticeship as a sheet metal worker.

Everything was made by hand, kettles, pails, buckets, milk cans, lamps, farmers' utensils. Anything used by the house. . . . The boss would say, "we judge an apprentice by the number of milk pails he turns out a day." The record was twenty-four pails. We had to get a [tin] sheet, roll the handle, put these studs on the bottom to keep away from the floor, and solder it all by hand. And I made the record, twenty-four a day. Sold for a shilling apiece, and I got three shillings a week.

On these nominal wages, McKie necessarily favored "amusements" that cost little or nothing—amateur rugby, the library, and election "tumults" pitting stick-wielding "blues," representing Liberals, against "yellows," representing Conservatives. "We were always Liberals on our street," McKie recalled. At age fifteen he found an outlet for his musical talent in the brass band of the Salvation Army, playing tenor horn. "I thought my mother would be pleased if I turned to the Salvation Army and proclaimed my sins."

McKie's life changed dramatically when he finished his apprenticeship at age nineteen. Unable to find work in his trade, he wrote the former manager of Carlisle's Gas Company, a Mr. Epworth, and asked for a job. Epworth, who had transferred to Edinburgh, knew McKie through Carlisle's "Pleasant Sunday Afternoon Brotherhood," and his affirmative answer brought the young sheet metal worker to Scotland's capital city. Mr. Epworth's sense of Brotherhood apparently had its limits, however: McKie was hired to fabricate gas meters at twenty-one shillings a week, three shillings less than the weekly wage for adult union members. When the union steward brought this discrepancy to his attention, McKie joined the Sheet Metal workers and his wages promptly rose. It was the start of a thirty-year career in the Scottish labor movement.[2]

His union was not opposed to new methods that subdivided work, but when one general manager tried to put unskilled workers on routine tasks and pay them below scale, McKie and his shopmates went on strike. "We weren't opposed to division," McKie recalled, "provided that their earnings were the same as skilled." As described by McKie, the conduct of the strike would have amazed observers from open-shop Detroit. "No need of a picket line because the general thought of the people was, they were in favor of the workers. There were no scabs. You would have been killed if you had scabbed." After union members petitioned the shareholders of the company explaining the situation, the offending manager was fired. From his participation on the strike committee during this walkout, McKie rose steadily through the union's leadership ranks.

It was through the union that McKie also transferred his evangelical concerns from the Salvation Army to socialism. For two years after moving to Edinburgh, McKie and his new wife, Bess, sang in the city's missions and preached the gospel of temperance and frugality. But McKie was troubled by the daily evidence that poverty still shadowed the lives of Edinburgh's temperate workers, no less so than the intemperate. Reading Adam Smith and Ricardo "until I was blind, deaf, and dumb" proved no more enlightening than the scriptures. It was the "father" of his union's chapel, William Angus, who turned his head.

He told me to read Bellamy's *Looking Backward*. So I read that and began groping, and then Angus came along and we would discuss all kinds of things. Then I made up my mind. I told my wife, "I don't think I can be a member of the Salvation Army any longer because I don't see what we are accomplishing to help the people I'm interested in. . . ." So I joined the Social Democratic Federation.

The year was 1897, and McKie found himself suddenly immersed in the vibrant growth of labor and socialist politics in Great Britain. From the formation of the Social Democratic Federation (SDF) as Britain's first Marxist party in 1883, socialism had steadily widened its influence to become, in the late 1890s, a significant minority movement among dissident workers and young intellectuals. As it grew, the movement also became more diverse. In 1893, mine leader Keir Hardie, fresh from his successful parliamentary campaign, broke with the Liberal hegemony in Scotland and formed the Independent Labour party, a diverse collection of former Liberal-Laborites and Christian Socialists. The ILP strove to become a national party but always found its biggest following in Scotland, where ILP and SDF candidates both contested municipal and parliamentary elections.

The two parties had overlapping memberships but distinctly different programs. The ILP favored a broad electoral coalition of trade unionists and middle-class professionals; independent labor action and progressive reform were the party's immediate goals—socialism was a distant and ill-defined future. The SDF, in contrast, rejected "practical" politics and lectured trade unionists on the futility of any strategy, including strikes, that tried to reform capitalist exploitation; the SDF entered elections not to win power but to propagandize for a socialist revolution.[3]

Accordingly, SDF vote totals varied from small to negligible, "but we didn't care," McKie recalled. Winning parliamentary power was the task of the Labour Representation Committee (later, Labour party), to which the SDF and ILP both sent founding delegates in 1900. But when the LRC failed to adopt a Marxist platform, the SDF withdrew and reaffirmed its primary task of "educating the masses." McKie, ever the evangelist, immersed himself in a constant round of socialist agitation.[4]

It was in this environment that he rose to leadership in both the SDF and the Sheet Metal workers. Tutored by the "old Fenian" John Leslie, whose singular blend of Marxism and Irish nationalism also influenced James Connolly and other Edinburgh SDF members, McKie gained his first grounding in socialist theory. It was rough going at first. "I read *Wage Labor and Capital* and couldn't understand it from Latin. The *Communist Manifesto*, yes. That made an impression on me." When Leslie and other SDF leaders urged him to become propaganda secretary for the Edinburgh branch, McKie had to overcome his natural reticence and learn the skills of public speaking. Bess, still devoted to the Church of Scotland, taught him the writing skills required of a propaganda secretary and sewed the gold-on-red SDF flag that McKie hoisted above outdoor meetings. After opening with a chorus of "The Red Flag," McKie and other SDF speakers took turns explaining socialism to the committed and the curious.[5]

After 1903, McKie and other SDF soapboxers had to compete with a new left-wing rival, the Socialist Labour party. Formed by dissident SDF members in Scotland, the SLP denounced the scholastic aloofness of the SDF's middle-class leaders in London and called for revolutionary politics focused on the shop floor, not parliament. Inspired by Daniel DeLeon, the sectarian leader of the American SLP, the Scottish branch drew a few hundred militants, led by James Connolly, to the banner of industrial unionism and the Industrial Workers of the World (IWW).[6]

Put off by the SLP's extreme sectarianism ("they out-Marxed us"), McKie remained with the SDF and its successor organization, the British Socialist party. The latter, formed in 1912 with an initial membership of 40,000, tried to overcome the SDF's isolation from organized workers by reaffiliating with the Labour party and pledging support for industrial as well as political action. But factional disputes pitting "old guard" parliamentarians against militant syndicalists left the BSP without a unified strategy and consigned the national party to its traditional role of agitational gadfly.[7]

In Scotland, however, the BSP's educational work developed a genuine base among left-wing workers, primarily through the efforts of John Maclean, the Glasgow schoolteacher, BSP leader, and founder of the Scottish Labour College. Maclean, fired for insubordination and barred from employment by any Scottish school board, set to work teaching Marxist economics to an entire generation of shop stewards, including Willie Gallacher and other future leaders of the Clyde Workers Committee. Able to link abstract theory with daily events, Maclean won a sizable following in Scottish revolutionary politics as a plant-gate agitator, strike-support organizer, and antiwar parliamentary candidate.

When the Scottish Labour College established its Edinburgh section, Maclean made McKie its chairman. As usual, McKie plunged headlong into the work, building the Edinburgh branch to a peak enrollment of 350 students and establishing extension courses in the surrounding mine villages. In the converted middle-class home that served the Edinburgh branch, dockworkers, skilled tradesmen, white-collar workers, and coal miners cycling in from nearby villages met three nights a week and all day Sunday to hear lectures and discuss political economy.

World War I brought an abrupt end to this educational work. Following Maclean's lead, McKie joined other Scottish BSP members in a left-wing faction that advocated "revolutionary defeatism" and active support for the Clydeside strikers. At age thirty-nine, McKie and several other skilled tradesmen in the BSP joined the army—as he put it, "not for the purpose of favoring the imperialistic war, but to be able to get among the soldiers and the navy and to carry on the education against the war."

In this, he was apparently successful. While training in Wales as an infantryman in the Royal Fusiliers, McKie organized successful protests against food shortages and irregular pay, and participated in a mass refusal to serve in Ireland after the Easter Rising. Sent to France, McKie was mustered out just as his regiment marched to the front. His union, the Sheet Metal workers, had challenged government claims of a skilled-trades shortage by citing information from McKie and others that many tradesmen were in France; the government responded by sending McKie back to Britain with orders to report for work in a Vickers aircraft factory. McKie organized the Sheet Metal workers in the previously nonunion plant and, as their shop representative, forced an end to the individual job-bidding that management had used to drive down wages.

Transferred near the end of the war to a Glasgow factory, McKie entered the final phase of his transition to Communist politics. During his absence, the government had hammered the Scottish BSP for its antiwar stance. Willie Gallacher, the Glasgow engineer and wartime strike leader, was jailed along with leading ILP and SLP stewards in the Clyde Workers Committee. Maclean, while serving as Lenin's first Soviet Consul to Scotland, was imprisoned for sedition. "John came out of prison when the war finished," McKie recalled. "I was alone. I was the one member of the British Socialist Party, all the rest had withered away." Maclean eventually recuperated from the prolonged hunger strike that had won his release, but he never recovered his prominent place on the left and in Scottish politics. Debilitated, according to some former colleagues, by depression and persecution mania brought on by prison, he slipped into obscurity. When McKie and other BSP stalwarts joined their SLP counterparts in founding the British Communist Party, Maclean held out for a separate Scottish party and refused to join. So too did McKie's other mentor, the Marxist "Fenian" John Leslie.[8]

McKie's subsequent leadership role in the Scottish branch of the Communist party not only marked a breach with these prewar comrades but also set him apart from other Anglo-Gaelic union leaders in Detroit. For most of these immigrants, the common denominator was a previous affiliation with the Labour party, ILP, or Sinn Fein, not the

Communist party. McKie's age also set him apart: few of the Scots workers emigrating to North America after World War I could recall Queen Victoria's reign. Few had risen as high in the labor movement as McKie, who served on the Executive Board of both the National Sheet Metal and Braziers Union and the Edinburgh Trades and Labour Council; and some Scots immigrants, coal miners and laborers among them, had no craft experience.

Yet in many respects, McKie's personal history paralleled the path traveled by other Anglo-Gaelic immigrants. While some had been raised in Catholic or nonreligious households, others had acquired the same amalgam of evangelical Protestantism and socialism that overlapped in McKie's upbringing. "In my early days, the church was the center of your life," recalled Merseysider Stan Coulthard, who once gave a paper in his bible class entitled "Jesus Christ, the Socialist." And for many of those who later rose to leadership in Detroit's labor movement, their previous experience in Britain had followed roughly the same lines as McKie's: most learned their trade in a shop environment where skilled workers still contended for control of production; most became local union activists and advocates of socialist and working-class politics; as such, most also became participants in collective action against employers and the State. If few traveled this path as long or as far as McKie, they had all traversed comparable terrain.[9]

Crisis

In the 1920s, Anglo-Gaelic immigrants had little call and less motivation to mobilize their co-workers around the goal of union organization. Particularly for the skilled tradesmen among them, relative prosperity made individual strategies for advancement more feasible and collective action less urgent. The still recent memory of the British labor movement's defeat in 1926 probably also gave pause to the Anglo-Gaelic union activist; certainly the indifference, hostility, or fluctuating commitment to unionism of many other immigrant groups and native-born workers discouraged action.

All this changed after the stock market crash of 1929 and the deepening economic crisis that followed. The Great Depression came "like an avalanche," as one survivor termed it, quickly smothering the buoyant individualism of the Roaring Twenties. After an extended period of confusion and demoralization, many Detroit autoworkers concluded by 1933 that militant action alone could improve their conditions. Since most autoworkers were relatively lacking in union experience and skills, they turned for leadership to the left-wing "deviants" in their midst—including the Anglo-Gaelic unionist.

These immigrant workers had their own good reasons to pursue organization after 1929. The depression hit Detroit harder than any other city of comparable size; having sped to prosperity on car sales, the Motor City's economy slowed to a crawl as consumers earmarked their dwindling resources for food and shelter, not cars. Compared with a nationwide unemployment rate that peaked at roughly 25 percent, Michigan's unemployment reached an estimated 46 percent in 1933. The auto cities in the southeastern corner of the state were hit especially hard as national sales fell from nearly 4.5 million cars in 1929 to barely one million in 1932. Metro Detroit's Industrial Employment Index fell accordingly, from 127 in August of 1929 to just 29 in the same month of 1932—a staggering 77 percent decline in three years.[10]

The depression's disastrous impact on autoworkers is well known. Detroit's tool and die makers shared in this general catastrophe and suffered particular hardships peculiar to their trade. Only a few were protected by the sort of arrangement Albert Kanarz recalled at Ford, where the company kept some tool and die workers on the payroll throughout the depression. Most toolroom workers experienced several bouts of unemployment between 1929 and 1933, including Ford worker Frank Muellner, laid off with other toolmakers when the company decided to postpone tooling for new models. Job-shop workers were especially vulnerable, since their work depended on contracts with General Motors, Chrysler, and other large firms where management was postponing new models. To keep their own "captive" shops going, some of these big companies brought back to their toolrooms work they had previously contracted out; to chop tooling expenses, others were developing look-alike models that could share stampings and reduce die work.[11]

Joseph Picconke, an American-born tool and die maker, had the misfortune of completing his apprenticeship at Hudson Motors in July 1931, as the economy continued its free-fall. He was immediately laid off. Finding a job at Fisher, he worked until August and was laid off again. It took him nine months before he found another job in May 1932, as a diemaker at Hudson Motors; five months later, he was laid off a third time. Six months later, Hudson recalled him to work; in December 1933, the company laid him off yet again. Picconke found a toolroom job four months later at Briggs and returned to Hudson two months after that when the company recalled him. In the three years following July 1931, Picconke was laid off from four different captive-shop jobs, spending a total of nineteen months unemployed—a year and a half out of three.[12]

Picconke and thousands of other tool and die makers now shared a fundamental condition with production workers: prolonged unemployment. The depression was in this regard a great leveler, establishing a common reference point for autoworkers of every skill and occupation. "They have lost their homes, they have had their automobiles repossessed, their furniture mortgaged," Mat Smith said of Detroit's tool and die makers during 1934 hearings on the auto industry. "To eke out an existence, these men, the 'aristocrats of automobile labor,' arrange to go on welfare, try door-to-door selling, or plead for odd jobs." Among 105 tool and die makers surveyed for the hearings, 24 reported they had gone on welfare at some point between 1930 and 1934, 21 reported losing their homes, 16 had lost autos, and the entire group had experienced a precipitous decline in earnings: from a $2,433 annual median in 1929 to just $636 in 1933.[13]

At the 1934 Presidential Commission Inquiry into the auto industry, held in Detroit, Smith and others representing tool and die makers testified to a long list of grievances their constituents had to confront once they got on a job. These included speedup, weekend work, ten- or twelve-hour shifts, mandatory fees for badges and tools, harassment of union supporters, company favoritism, and replacement of men with low-wage women workers. Production workers had similar complaints, but tool and die makers had to face two circumstances unique to their work. The first was the marked seasonality of toolroom employment. Although every autoworker experienced considerable job insecurity—in 1932, eighty-four of every 100 workers was laid off for some period—few experienced the extremes of extended unemployment and intense overtime that toolroom workers came to know in the early 1930s. As described in Chapter 2, the seasonality of tool and die work was already well established; during the depression, it simply became more pronounced. The season varied from one company to the next, but in the early 1930s most retooling occurred between September and January, alternating with a production season that started with the annual auto show in January and peaked between March and September. Some toolroom workers, particularly die leaders in the captive sector and the larger job shops, might get steady work throughout the year. But most faced six to seven months of idleness in the off-season, alternating with frenzied labor during the next cycle of toolmaking. According to the Patternmakers Association (one of the few craft unions to survive the early depression), "the large corporations are working patternmakers as high as seventy hours a week, paying some of them $60 or $65, while others, equally as skilled, are unemployed." Employers did not deny this charge, nor did they dispute the shortened toolmaking season. Economic necessity, they claimed, required both practices, since proprietary designs were easier to protect during a compressed diemaking season, and production of complex patterns and dies required the uninterrupted attention of a single craftsman, not the divided attention of shift workers. Mat Smith and others rejected these arguments as poor rationalizations for surplus labor and low wages.[14]

A second grievance that was unique to tool and die makers concerned the practice of inside contracting. This management strategy for lowering toolroom wages recalled the craft practices of the nineteenth century, when metalworking companies delegated shop-floor authority to skilled worker-contractors. The 1930s version of inside contracting, however, had little to do with craft control of production. Instead of the nineteenth-century practice of contracting out an entire department or processes, which skilled workers then managed for a year or more, job-shop owners solicited bids from individual workers on what they would charge to build a new die or fixture off a blueprint. By all accounts, the practice encouraged a continual bidding war between job-hungry tradesmen. Labor journalist Joe Brown described one outcome in the Excello Company's toolroom: "One worker bid $20 for doing a certain part of the work. Although a highly skilled worker, he had lots of trouble and the job took him eighty-nine hours. Two dollars were deducted from the price to pay for the tools that were damaged and he received $18 for eighty-nine hours work, approximately twenty cents an hour."[15] Orrin Peppler, a Canadian-born diemaker trained at Ford, fared even worse under the contract system at Buell Tool and Die: "If, after all expenses were paid and the overhead was taken care of, there was any money left, it would be divided up among those that worked on [the die]. But we found out later that there was just not any more than twelve and a half cents an hour."[16] Low-ball bidding by desperate toolroom workers was apparently endemic. Mat Smith and others representing tool and die makers at the commission hearings testified that the contract system drove effective wages in many job shops as low as twenty and thirty cents an hour by 1933.[17]

For these toolroom "aristocrats," the fall from prosperity had been harder than for most autoworkers. Toolmakers, after all, had farther to fall. In 1929, their annual earnings were more than 50 percent higher than the industry average; by 1933, the "differential" between toolroom and production wages had disappeared in job shops where contract-bidding had become the norm. For these toolmakers, the differential had actually turned from positive to negative. Captive toolroom workers were still paid by the hour, and their sixty-five to ninety-cent wage was still higher than the industry's fifty-eight-cent hourly average in 1933. But frequent layoffs cut into these wages as well, and overall, the ratio between average annual wages in the auto industry and in tool and die had slipped from better than 3:2 in 1929 to less than 50:50 by 1933.[18]

For the average tool and die maker, this was a stunning reversal of fortunes. All but nine of the sixty-five toolmakers who indicated their training in Mat Smith's survey had served apprenticeships of four years or longer, and this investment in skill was supposed to produce a significantly higher wage—the differential. That this had now disappeared in many job shops and had substantially declined elsewhere must have confirmed the toolmaker's sense of a monumentally disordered world. Every toolmaker experienced at least some aspect of this chaos—a sudden layoff or a seventy-hour week or a night-shift job or competitive underbidding on "inside" contracts. In the off-season, as month followed month with no job, thousands of unemployed toolmakers joined fellow Detroiters sifting through the debris of the Great Depression—bankrupt benefit societies that had exhausted their reserves, failed banks that could not recover their depositors' savings, and cash-starved city governments that closed schools and paid their workers in script. The house, the car, and the appliances he could no longer afford must have mocked the bewildered toolmaker; certainly the deflation of his breadwinner role must have been demoralizing. Back on the job during the frenzied toolroom season, he found a round-the-clock cycle of work that quickly sapped his strength. Fear of losing even the worst job kept him going. The result, as Mat Smith aptly phrased it, was "industrial psychosis, making mental cases of those workers who are harried by their troubles at home resulting from too-small wages."[19]

Thousands of workers fled Detroit to find jobs in other cities or other industries. Among them were Anglo-Gaelic immigrants who now faced the same job insecurity they had left in Britain a decade before. W. G. Grant, the British toolmaker and future president of Ford Local 600, married a Scottish-born bride in Detroit in 1929, marked the birth of a child two years later, and declared his intention of becoming a United States citizen in 1931. But the collapse of Detroit's economy apparently changed his plans: at some point in the next several years, he and his family returned to England and took up permanent residence in Creswell Green. The continuing depression in Britain's engineering trades apparently convinced Grant that he had no future in Scotland, for in 1934 he emigrated once again from Glasgow to Detroit; upon arrival, he filed a second Declaration of Intention. Two future officers in UAW Local 157, John Fairbairn, an Edinburgh toolmaker, and George

Handyside, a Glasgow machinist, also had second thoughts about remaining in Detroit during the early years of the depression. Fairbairn had married a Glasgow woman while living in Windsor in 1926, and after crossing to Detroit, he submitted his first Declaration of Intention to become a U.S. citizen in 1931. Like Grant, however, Fairbairn returned to Great Britain and established permanent residence in Glasgow before remigrating to Detroit and submitting a second declaration in 1934. Handyside submitted his first declaration six days after crossing from Windsor to Detroit in 1927, but in the next five years he apparently decided to retain his British citizenship and let this first application lapse. He waited eleven years before submitting a second Declaration of Intention for U.S. citizenship.

Opportunity

Workplace resistance to wage cuts, speedup, and layoffs must have seemed futile in the first three years of the depression. The only union attempting industry-wide organization, the Auto Workers Union, was virtually wiped out in 1930–1931 as layoffs removed its small cadre of left-wing workers from the plants. The Communist party shifted its emphasis to organizing Unemployed Councils, and these won a popular following in Detroit for blocking evictions and for demonstrations by the unemployed. But workplace organizing had virtually ceased: in early 1932, the AWU was publishing only one shop paper in Detroit, the *Ford Worker*, edited by Bill McKie. The AWU's situation improved only toward the end of the year as the Communist party, having adopted a new policy of "concentration," refocused its modest resources on mass-production industries in the Midwest. With a fresh cohort of organizers recently arrived from New York, the AWU targeted two companies: Ford and Briggs.[20]

"Toolmakers, Wake Up!," blared one AWU leaflet. "The bosses are sharply and bitterly conscious of the strategic position the toolmakers occupy in the industry. They know that even a 25 percent organization among the patternmakers, diemakers, and tool makers would put a definite check to . . . bullying tactics and [the] wage smashing campaign." The impact of this particular leaflet, with its clumsy outbursts against "the blood-sending Molachs [*sic*] of the auto industry!" isn't known. But when Briggs workers organized their first collective protest against "wage smashing," it was not the 10,000 production workers in the company's main plants that took this initial step, but 500 tool and die makers in Briggs' Vernor Highway shops.[21]

This was not a spontaneous rebellion. Briggs, a major supplier of auto bodies to Ford and Chrysler, had already forced two wage cuts in 1932 on its tool and die makers, the second averaging 10–25 percent. But these unilateral actions had produced only a diffuse and unfocused discontent, not a collective response. AWU leader Phil Raymond reported a significant turnout from the Vernor plant for the Unemployed Councils' Hunger March on Washington, but when the AWU called a shop meeting in November, only two workers attended. The AWU persisted nevertheless. The next meeting drew four workers, and a successful campaign against working two lathes at a time drew additional support. In early January, when Briggs announced a 15 percent wage cut at its main production plant on Mack Avenue, the AWU drew twenty-eight toolmakers from the Vernor plant to a meeting that planned strike action if the same cut was proposed for tool and die makers. A plant-gate rally boosted morale and brought sixty workers to the next AWU meeting; the subsequent election of departmental committees on each of the plant's four floors brought additional recruits.[22]

On 11 January 1933, when Briggs announced a 20 percent wage cut for the Vernor plant, virtually all these well-organized tool and die makers marched out of the factory. Most of them, as revealed in a subsequent union survey, were foreign-born tradesmen: naturalized citizens represented 40 percent of the plant population; another 19 percent had first papers; and 2 percent had no papers. It's unclear which immigrant group predominated among the 61 percent who were foreign-born, but British and German names stood out on the strike committee that was immediately established. AWU members predominated on the committee, but Socialist party and IWW activists also participated. All were well aware of their bargaining leverage. "A strategic moment had been selected for this first strike," Walter Reuther, a former Briggs diemaker, reported to his fellow socialists, "as the tools and dies for the new Ford car were about seventy-five percent complete and production could not begin on schedule without their completion." Bolstered by this knowledge, the strikers issued their demands to the company: rescind the wage cut and raise wages 10 percent; implement an eight-hour day and a forty-four-hour week; eliminate overtime except for emergency cases approved by the union's shop committee; pay time-and-a-half for overtime and double-time wages for weekend work; refrain from victimization of strikers; and recognize the union's grievance committees in every department. The company, after a futile attempt to split jig and fixture men away from diemakers by claiming the wage cut did not apply to the former, finally agreed to restore wages to their previous level and take back all strikers. Both the strike committee and the AWU organizers, recognizing the enormous significance of this company concession, recommended the membership accept the compromise. On 13 January, a mass meeting unanimously voted its approval of the settlement, and the workers returned to their jobs.[23]

"This strike proved to all automobile workers the possibility of winning strikes during this period of crisis," Phil Raymond observed in *Labor Unity*. It was no exaggeration. Less than a week after the settlement, a small group of diemakers from Motor Products met with the AWU and planned a protest action in response to wage cuts of 10–30 percent. Two days later, nearly half of the factory's 3,000 workers walked off the job. Among them was Ernie Woodcock, the Oldham-born engineer and die leader, whose hourly wage had been cut from seventy-one to sixty-four cents. At a subsequent mass meeting, Woodcock won election to the strike committee. "There were quite a few skilled trades people on that committee," recalls Leonard Woodcock, who accompanied his father to union meetings. "I suppose being skilled, people would be in the habit of having some deference to them. Anyway, there were quite a few . . . die makers, electricians, machine repair people." Since Woodcock also recalls that the majority of his father's skilled workmates were English-born tradesmen, it is highly probable that the strike committee also contained several other Anglo-Gaelic immigrants besides the senior Woodcock. Whatever their national background, these skilled tradesmen refused to be separated from their new allies in the production departments. "Tool and die makers, whose demands had been granted by the company," the AWU reported, "vote[d] solidly to stick it out with the unskilled workers until their demands were met." Their solidarity helped produce a second victory for the AWU when Motor Products agreed after three days of picketing to rescind the wage cuts, recognize the Shop Committee, and establish minimum wages of thirty cents an hour for women and forty cents for men on production.[24]

"Two successful and well-organized strikes within one week filled the workers of Detroit with a spirit of revolt against capitalist feudalism," twenty-five-year-old Walter Reuther reported that winter in *The Student Outlook*, published by the League for Industrial Democracy. Over the next month, that spirit of revolt motivated some 15,000 Detroit autoworkers to emulate the Briggs Vernor and Motor Products strikers: 10,000 in a massive walkout of production workers and toolmakers at the Briggs body plants; 3,000 in a complete shutdown of the Hudson Motors stamping plant; and 2,000 more in a partial walkout at the Murray Corporations body plant, led—again—by the tool and die makers. This first of several strike waves by Detroit autoworkers in the 1930s produced varied results: a compromise at Murray Body, a clear-cut victory at Hudson, and defeat at Briggs. In the latter case, the company's refusal to meet with Phil Raymond and other Communist leaders split the strike committee into warring camps, and the AWU's credibility soon plummeted when Communist party leader Earl Browder characterized the walkout as a "Communist strike." However mixed the results, the events of January and February 1933 marked a watershed. Like the AWU strikes in the 1920s, this rebellion was concentrated in the body plants, where metal finishers, trimmers, and other semiskilled production workers faced continuing automation and deskilling. But unlike the 1920s, the 1933 strikes were plant-wide walkouts, uniting skilled, semiskilled, and assembly labor. Equally telling, it was tool and die makers who now led the way, initiating the first walkouts and providing key leadership for the production worker strikes that followed. Encouraged by this first wave of militancy and the federal labor legislation that followed, union organization began to sprout in other Detroit plants, often from seed sown by skilled workers. At Kelsey Hayes Wheel, the union that first appeared in 1933 "had some of the people in the tool room organized," recalled Michael Manning, an early leader. "And of course, it spread to the shop."[25]

The AWU, discredited by Communist party sectarianism and the defeat at Briggs, accrued no permanent organizational gains from the 1933 strikes. But this ground swell of militancy prepared the soil for a particularly fertile seed—the Mechanics Educational Society of America, formed in February 1933, as the strike wave ran its course. The subsequent history of this organization, and the role its Detroit locals played in founding the UAW, has already been chronicled. The highlights of that history need only be summarized here and then reexamined for evidence of the role played by skilled workers and Anglo-Gaelic immigrants.[26]

The circumstances surrounding the actual founding of MESA remain obscured by the organization's apparent emphasis on "education." Some have claimed that this was a deliberate ruse, intended to conceal MESA's union aims and thereby protect members from employer retaliation; others have recalled more innocent intentions, with technical education and comraderie for toolmakers the sole aim of MESA's initial membership. The date of the first meeting is also unclear. Most say early 1933, but Elizabeth McCracken, MESA's office secretary (and daughter of Scots-born MESA leader Frank McCracken), recalled a 1932 meeting in someone's apartment which "broke up in disorder" and provoked several fistfights in the stairway. Even the identity of the founders is disputed. Mat Smith is often identified as a cofounder, but Smith later wrote that initially he was "cynical about the whole thing." It was not until a spirited meeting at Schiller Hall that Smith began, in his words, "dreaming the same dizzy picture as the [MESA] pioneers— of this hitherto unorganized mob of Detroit tool and diemakers suddenly transformed into a class conscious unit, taking their rightful place in the van of progressive unionism."[27]

It seems likely that a skilled-trades organization formed in the midst of the first mass auto strikes of the 1930s could not be innocent of union goals; technical education, moreover, rarely provokes fistfights among participating students. In any case, by the summer of 1933, the Mechanics Educational Society was identifiably a union, with organizers in Detroit, Pontiac, and Flint. Its membership was initially limited to tool and die makers, and its leadership was already dominated by Mat Smith, the Lancashire engineer. In the fall of 1933, he led MESA in its first and largest strike, a six-week walkout that began in Flint but quickly spread to Detroit, where tool and die work for all of southeastern Michigan was concentrated. The strike, punctuated by police violence and toolmaker assaults on a half-dozen Detroit factories (described in Chapter 5), closed more than 100 job shops and severely hampered operations at Fisher Body and other captive shops. Employers estimated the number of strikers at little more than 6,000; the union counted over 14,000. MESA failed to win an industry-wide settlement, but it did manage to negotiate individual agreements with fifty-one job shops and several captive shops, including Fisher, Pontiac, Murray Body, and Hudson. Gains were modest but significant, including some wage increases in smaller job shops (but none in captive shops), an end to contract work, and de facto recognition of the union—the latter a milestone, marking a tenuous first step toward collective bargaining in the auto industry.[28]

Responding to left-wing critics led by John Anderson—the Glasgow-born electrician, GM Ternstedt worker, and Communist party leader— MESA gradually opened its ranks to production workers. The union's Detroit locals claimed a combined membership of more than 21,000 by February of 1934, but as an organization still devoted primarily to skilled workers, MESA found itself dangerously isolated in the spring of that year. Over the previous ten months, the AFL had established catch-all "Federal Labor Unions" to organize both production and skilled workers in a particular plant, with an understanding that the skilled workers would later be parceled out to AFL craft organizations. In anticipation of a strike, these Federal Unions formulated wage demands, and MESA, expecting it would be drawn into this showdown battle, did so as well. When, instead of striking, the AFL accepted the federal government's promise in March 1934 to regulate working conditions through an Auto Labor Board, MESA was left on its own. Despite the fact that this was the off-season for toolmaking, MESA launched an ill-timed strike of job-shop toolmakers in April. After two weeks of uneven picketing and stalemated negotiations, MESA had to abandon its demand for an industry-wide wage increase and seek face-saving settlements with individual employers.[29]

This defeat sapped the organization's resources and aggravated the factional struggle between Mat Smith and John Anderson. Failed strikes at Burroughs Adding Machine and Motor Products further highlighted the union's narrow base. "The whole futility of craft unionism made itself felt," recalled Bill Stevenson, the Glasgow-born engineer and president of MESA's Detroit District Council. "For instance, in a plant like the Dodge plant with about ten or twelve entrances, nobody knew who was scabbing because the tool and die division . . . might be many small divisions in a plant of that character. Consequently, the few pickets we could get around could only identify people that they knew by sight." Elizabeth McCracken recalled the same dilemma. "They put a picket line on and the production workers walked through. It was very easy for a scab to go through with the production workers." MESA seemed able to organize production workers only in jobs shops and supplier firms where the toolroom work force was still relatively predominant or where particular organizers stressed the importance of industrial organization. Captive-shop toolmakers, in contrast, were often isolated in a plant population dominated by production workers. Many apparently felt neglected by their union. Diemaker Joseph Picconke reported that he and other toolroom workers at Hudson Motors joined MESA in 1933, but the union, "because of . . . lack of support from [the] parent body, failed to accomplish its purpose and disappeared from the plant." The following year, Picconke joined the plant-wide AFL Federal Labor Union for Hudson Motors.[30]

When the AFL finally gave its federal auto unions a national charter in 1935 and full autonomy in 1936, many local MESA leaders in Detroit urged their national organization to merge with the newly formed United Auto Workers. But MESA's National Administrative Council declined the UAW's merger offer in May of 1936, citing the AFL's failure to include skilled workers in the UAW's jurisdiction. Within days, three of MESA's six Detroit locals seceded from the organization and joined the UAW. MESA Local 7, led by John Anderson, became the UAW's East Side Tool and Die Local 155; MESA Local 9, led by Bill Stevenson, merged with Local 8 and became the West Side Tool and Die Local 157. As Chapters 5 and 6 will indicate in more detail, both locals played pivotal roles in the growth and survival of the UAW over the next three years: Local 155 organized Detroit's first sit-down strike at Midland Steel in November 1936 and, with Walter Reuther's West Side Local 174, catalyzed the UAW's phenomenal growth in Detroit during the spring of 1937; Local 157, as the leading local in the victorious 1939 tool and die strike at General Motors, reaffirmed the UAW's permanent presence in the auto industry. As described in Chapter 6, both locals also played leading roles in opposing Homer Martin and establishing the UAW-CIO as a militant, democratic union.[31]

Through all of this, tool and die makers were the cutting edge of auto unionism in Detroit. Production workers provided the critical mass that pushed the UAW forward, but as they stormed the walls of open-shop Detroit, they moved through breaches opened by the tool and die makers: from the first strike at Briggs Vernor in 1933, through the rise and fall of MESA and the sit-down wave of 1936–1937, to the General Motors strike of 1939. Elizabeth McCracken, trying to explain this record of militancy, stressed the previous suffering of the tool and die makers. "They were hungry, actually hungry, and they were looking for any way to hit back. There is a lot behind that phrase 'belly Communism.' I saw it." Her commonsense appraisal certainly captures the motivation that fueled the toolmaker's militancy, but it leaves two critical questions unanswered. First, why did that militancy explode in 1933 and again in 1936–1937, and not, say, 1931 and 1935? And second, why would that militancy be sustained by craft workers in (as Walter Reuther put it) a "craftless industry"?[32]

These questions can only be addressed by considering the varying opportunities for militancy that presented themselves in the 1930s. First among these was the changing political context. For good reason, historians have stressed the facilitating role of the New Deal in spurring worker militancy and protecting the fledgling union movement. Many have also recognized that the actual legislative action of the Roosevelt Administration was less determining than the political tone which New Deal rhetoric reinforced. Section 7a of the National Industrial Recovery Act certainly boosted the labor movement's morale, but administration of the law gave unions little help. The Automobile Code was virtually written by the industry's Chamber of Commerce, and President Roosevelt's Auto Labor Board sanctioned company-dominated employee associations as alternatives to legitimate unions. Moreover, passage of the NIRA *followed* the initial outburst of auto-worker militancy in the winter of 1933. It was the election of 1932 and

Roosevelt's fuzzy but evocative promise of a "New Deal" that fired the militancy of Detroit's autoworkers in the winter of 1933. In 1936, a similar political dynamic catalyzed worker militancy. As Roosevelt campaigned for reelection against Wall Street's "Economic Royalists," Frank Murphy campaigned for governor of Michigan with the prolabor slogan: "If I worked for a wage, I'd join my union." Less than three weeks after the landslide vote on 4 November 1936 that gave Roosevelt and Murphy their decisive victories, UAW Local 155 launched Detroit's first sit-down strike at Midland Steel.[33]

In addition to this political dimension, there was a second dynamic determining the timing and the breadth of the 1936–1937 strike wave. Contrary to the popular notion that the UAW was organized in the "depths of the Great Depression," the facts indicate the opposite. Auto production began to recover from depression lows in 1934 and 1935; 1936 was a near record year for sales, and 1937 was second only to 1929. Motor-vehicle industry employment of 459,000 was actually higher in 1936 than the 1929 labor force of 448,000, and although hourly wages in 1936 were still below 1929 levels, they had risen faster than prices since 1933—and represented an 11 percent increase over the purchasing power of 1929 wages. "Empty bellies" may have made Detroit's autoworkers militant in 1933, but workers joined the UAW in 1936–1937 with full stomachs (relatively speaking) and with less fear of losing their jobs. It was the *memory* of empty bellies that motivated them, and a resurgent economy that gave them the opportunity to act.[34]

This also applied to Detroit's tool and die makers, but with greater extremes and variation in the demand for their labor. As early as 1934, employers complained of an actual shortage of skilled labor. W. J. Cronin, secretary of the National Automobile Chamber of Commerce, predicted at the start of that year's tooling season that a shortage of tool and die makers "will shortly become apparent and continue in acute form until after the first of the year," caused by "the curtailment of immigration, death, promotion, transfer to other fields of activity, and other reasons." Under "other reasons" he might have added the companies' continuing failure to provide apprenticeship training. Even Detroit's business leaders acknowledged in a 1935 meeting, reported by the *Detroit News*, that "American industry has never developed any honest apprenticeship system or craftsmanship, preferring to draw on England, Scotland, the Scandinavian countries and Germany for its skilled . . . men."[35]

Union representatives bitterly disputed employer claims of a skilled-trades shortage. When the U.S. Employment Service drew attention to this scarcity in the spring of 1936, Frank Martel, president of the Detroit

Federation of Labor, denounced the agency as a tool of business. Its actions, he predicted, would "create an influx of labor flooding the already overcrowded labor field," making it possible "for the employers to take advantage." MESA leaders saw an additional motive behind employer complaints of a labor shortage: coupled with the frequent and, in MESA's opinion, unfounded claim by job-shop owners that customers demanded their die work on an "emergency" basis, employers used the alleged labor shortage as justification for exceeding National Recovery Administration (NRA) limitations on overtime. In a 1934 meeting at the NRA's Detroit Compliance Division, Mat Smith and other MESA officials countered claims of a skilled-trades shortage with evidence that some workers were unemployed because they had been blacklisted through the Tool and Die Manufacturers Association's job-referral system. "A man is not able to get a job under his own name," testified William Hulle, the London-born machinist. "But as soon as he changes his name, he gets a job."[36]

"Shortage" could mean one thing to employers and something else to union representatives. For the latter, there could be no shortage so long as some members remained unemployed; if there was a genuine and acute scarcity of skilled labor, the blacklist would have to go. For employers, on the other hand, a labor "shortage" could exist long before every available worker had been hired; once unemployment fell below a certain level, workers became more selective in their choice of jobs and more demanding about the pay they received. The perception of a labor shortage also varied between job-shop and captive-shop workers, and varied still more over time. In 1934, NRA investigator W. E. Chalmers, reporting on the tool and die job shops, found evidence of a skilled-trades shortage limited to only the highest classifications: die leader, template maker, and boring mill hand. Chalmers otherwise found strong evidence to buttress MESA's accusation that employers used their claim of a labor shortage to justify excessive overtime. However, as the auto industry expanded output over the next two years, the peak demand for skilled labor grew accordingly, even as the off-season demand remained quite low. Homer Coy of Studebaker, writing in the *American Machinist* in 1936, described these wide fluctuations in the demand for labor in an unusually frank acknowledgment of the industry's problem.[37]

Because . . . engineering departments will not release drawings for the new models until a short time before the change, too much work is created for skilled labor to handle during a short period. This causes a shortage of skilled labor during model changes and shortens the period of employment of the average skilled worker to not much over five months per year. . . . This condition is especially true of jobbing shops, because they depend on model changes for their work.[38]

The timing of these seasonal swings changed abruptly in 1935, when the industry moved the date for introducing new models from January to November. The new model year pushed back the tool and die season to a spring-summer peak and spread production-worker employment over the fall-winter months. Employers claimed this would benefit most workers by reducing their exposure to cold-weather layoffs (when heating and clothing bills rose) and by spreading the work more evenly over the year (since the usual sales peak in the spring would now be balanced by a fall season). The *American Machinist* reported mixed results. Overall employment did rise in the fall, but "pulling some of the spring peak over into the winter months, while a boon to production workers, will scarcely benefit the tool and die makers."[39]

Toolroom labor had more to gain from the upward trend in auto sales, both because more models could enter the market and because longer production runs meant more die repair work. At Fisher Body Plant 23, the major diemaking facility of General Motors and the stronghold of UAW Local 157, technological change also improved job prospects. Blaine Marrin, a toolmaker at the neighboring Plant 21, recalled a measurable jump in the work force of Plant 23 by 1935, after GM replaced wooden deck lids and roofs with pressed steel panels. It marked a radical change from the bodymaking procedures Marrin knew in the 1920s, when "80 percent of it was all wood," covered by leather or reinforced with metal panels. The 1935–1936 "Turret Top" marked another quantum leap in metal body construction. The *Fisher Body Service Manual* described this new departure. "Instead of building a Wooden Skeleton Framework complete, then applying the Panel Metal Stampings over it and attaching them with nails and screws as in former Models," now the body frame itself was made of metal stampings, fitted together with steel body panels "in a Body Jig and welded into one Solid Shell." Marrin recalled that the demand for diemakers was so great at Plant 23 that men were hired without the usual "screening" to keep out union sympathizers. By Marrin's recollection, 60 percent of the 2,000–3,000 workers in the plant were English and Scottish.[40]

The *American Machinist* summarized the impact of these diverse trends on the availability of skilled labor.

Restriction of immigration . . . , rapid recovery of the automobile industry in 1934 and 1935 from the depths of the depression with a consequent greatly increased demand for skilled workers of all kinds, and an almost complete secession of apprentice training programs within the past five years have resulted in a shortage of really skilled mechanics. This shortage is marked, especially in these past few months during the peak of preparation for the 1936 models.[41]

Unions were well aware of this cyclical upswing and urged their members to take advantage of it. MESA noted "the acute shortage of Tool and Die Makers in this area" in a leaflet issued near the end of the 1935 season, and called upon job-shop members to enforce a forty-hour week. A year later, the UAW also reminded skilled workers of their bargaining leverage. "You know that the employers are short of skilled men," the UAW's new Tool and Die Locals 155 and 157 announced in a joint leaflet at the start of the 1936 toolmaking season. "This gives you the advantage right now to sell your skilled labor at a higher wage."[42]

Leading the Way

Exploiting the favorable opportunities in both the labor market and the political arena, Detroit's tool and die makers helped catalyze a labor movement of extraordinary breadth and militancy between 1933 and 1939. Anglo-Gaelic immigrants, most of them also skilled tradesmen, were especially prominent in the leadership of that movement. The particular nature of their contribution to Detroit's auto unions must now be examined.

Charles Tilly provides a useful starting point with a model stressing "mobilization of resources" as the key element in collective action. Groups of people with shared interests and common organization mobilize their resources (labor, capital, know-how, or weapons) for common action when the collective goods to be won (a new contract, better wages, or a new government) are perceived to outweigh the potential costs (job loss, blacklisting, or arrest). Both the likelihood and the direction of a particular group's mobilization are defined by a wide range of factors, including the threats and opportunities that present themselves, the cohesiveness of the group, and the costs of building an organization. With respect to the latter, "newly mobilizing conflict groups usually reduce their organizing costs by building, intentionally or unintentionally, on existing group structure."[43]

MESA is a case in point. Like any union, it required offices and meeting space, and these were most economically secured through existing organizations. Two of MESA's six Detroit locals, as mentioned in Chapter 3, located their operations in Odd Fellow halls with a significant British membership and a predominantly skilled-trades leadership: the American Eagle Lodge, which housed Local 6, and the Scotia Lodge, which housed Local 8. Three other MESA locals located in East Side halls associated with German workers: Local 1 in Schiller Hall (see Appendix B), formerly the "House of the Masses" when it was owned by the Michigan Socialist party in 1919; Local 7 in the "ABC" Hall, or "Arbeiter Bildung [Workers Education] Club"; and MESA Local 9 in Carpathia Hall (also called Germania Hall). Local 13 found space at 3672 East Milwaukee, an address listed in Polk's City Directory as a restaurant owned by one Negos Baronian.[44]

For a union with a predominantly British and German membership, the selection of these halls (setting aside the question of Negos Baronian's links with MESA) was certainly no coincidence. The same could be said of the predominantly Polish production workers at Kelsey Hayes when they organized their 1936 strike at the West Side Polish Falcons Hall. But in addition to physical structures, Anglo-Gaelic immigrants contributed a sensibility and a "repertoire" of collective action that made them especially effective union organizers. Their subsequent leadership in MESA and in many of the UAW's first locals suggests that the principles of militant unionism were often articulated in Detroit with Anglo-Gaelic accents.

No such generalization can be made, however, without several qualifications. First, by the 1930s capitalism had long since become a global system, with Europe and North America its dynamic centers. Particularly within this North Atlantic "rim," mass emigration and transatlantic trade generalized social conditions, ideas, and political movements to the point where no *purely* national sensibility can be identified. In this respect, the postwar economic crisis that shaped the consciousness of British workers and sent many searching for work in Detroit was not just a "British" phenomenon but also a bellwether of the global crisis that engulfed in United States after 1929. The Great Depression generated among the native-born and immigrant workers of Detroit a new sensibility, one which rapidly narrowed the gap between Anglo-Gaelic activists and their increasingly militant co-workers.

This same world system that made economic crisis a global phenomenon, and which made feasible the mass emigration of Europeans to North America, also facilitated a reverse movement of people and ideas. From the time of the American Revolution, British radicals and trade unionists had found many of their most compelling models for social change in America. Radical reformers in particular automatically invoked American institutions—public education, universal manhood suffrage, Workingman's Democracy—in their efforts to widen the franchise. During the campaign for the Second Reform Act during the 1860s, the columns of radical weeklies like *Reynold's Newspaper* were filled, according to Henry Pelling, with a partisan enthusiasm for America "that can only be paralleled in modern times with the enthusiasm of the Communist *Daily Worker* for the Soviet way of life"; the only difference being that *Reynold's* had a weekly circulation of 350,000 at a time when the daily circulation of even *The Times* was only 70,000. At the mammoth reform demonstrations in London in 1867, the crowds, appropriately enough, sang "John Brown's Body" and "Yankee Doodle."[45]

Liberal enthusiasm for America dimmed in the late nineteenth century with the appearance of huge trusts and their steadily mounting war on American unions. But for British and Irish trade unionists, the American experience continued to provide a critical preview of ideological and organizational forms to counter industrial capitalism. A key influence was Henry George, "the prophet of San Francisco," whose book *Poverty and Progress* found a wide readership in England and Scotland. More than a few British socialists traced their rejection of laissez-faire liberalism to George's work. Bill McKie and James Connolly, among others, found the first model for their socialist utopia in the work of another American writer, Edward Bellamy's *Looking Backward*. American precedent was equally compelling as a guide for industrial unionism, so much so that among the industrial organizations in late nineteenth-century Britain, many consciously modeled themselves after the Knights of Labor. In the following century, when industrial unionism won wide appeal during the pre-World War I years, its advocates made repeated reference to their chief model and inspiration, the iww. The germ of Wobbly theory was spread by men like James Connolly, who lived in the United States between 1903 and 1910 and became a leading organizer for both the iww and the Socialist Labor party. After his return from North America, Connolly organized Belfast workers with tactics made popular by the iww: sympathy strikes uniting seamen and dockworkers across religious and craft lines, and community mobilization through neighborhood parades of the "Non-Sectarian Labor Band." James Larkin also borrowed iww ideas and tactics, and in 1913 welcomed the presence and the advice of Big Bill Haywood during the Dublin lockout.[46]

When Scottish militants and advocates of industrial unionism broke with the Social Democratic Federation in 1903, they readily took the name of their American mentor, Daniel DeLeon's Socialist Labor party. Copies of the *Weekly People*, the American party's newspaper, were regularly distributed in London and Glasgow; *The Socialist*, published by the Glasgow SLP, frequently reprinted DeLeon's articles while advertising "American pamphlets" for sale. In 1911, the SLP's Industrial Workers of Great Britain, modeled directly on the IWW, led a mass strike at the Singer Corporation's Clydebank plant. The strike failed, but the cross-craft unity of the strikers confirmed SLP militants in their advocacy of industrial unionism. The significance of their commitment to American models is underlined by their subsequent involvement in the wartime strikes along the Clyde, when the Clyde Workers Committee drew much of its leadership from SLP ranks.[47]

Any effort to identify the Anglo-Gaelic contribution to Detroit's auto unions has to acknowledge that industrial unionism, as advocated in the United Kingdom, was an amalgam of American, British, Irish, and French ideas. Bill McKie, John Anderson, Joe McCusker, and Pat Quinn all spoke with distinctly Scots or Irish accents when they advocated industrial organization in Detroit, but the discriminating ear could also pick out some of Haywood's western drawl.

The Anglo-Gaelic leaders named above were all prominent advocates of industrial unionism, but this did not distinguish them from the many American-born and immigrant workers who also favored industrial organization. Many Anglo-Gaelic workers, particularly among tool and die makers, actually opposed such an organizational strategy. As we'll see below, their opposition reflected the same preference for craft organization that characterized much of the TUC's leadership. A labor movement as large as Britain's naturally produced a wide spectrum of contending theories about union organization and strategy, from the cautious reformism of railway leader J. H. Thomas to the revolutionary syndicalism of Willie Gallacher. Anglo-Gaelic leaders in Detroit reflected the same diversity. What distinguished them from their American-born and rural-immigrant co-workers was not a particular political or union agenda but a unique sensibility of craft and class combined with an unmatched experience in workplace organization. They possessed, in short, both a language and a repertoire of collective action, and this cognitive orientation made them especially suited for leadership in Detroit's early auto unions.

Three elements of that Anglo-Gaelic "sensibility" stand out in this regard: craft consciousness, class consciousness, and organizational know-how. The first, craft consciousness, enhanced the cohesion of Anglo-Gaelic craftsmen; the second, class consciousness, expanded their vision to include allied tradesmen and, in some cases, the less skilled; the third, organizational know-how, gave Detroit's fledgling unions much of their initial structure and leadership. It should be emphasized that in no case did these attributes of Anglo-Gaelic leadership single-handedly "define" the outcome of union growth in Detroit. But the reverse is also true: in no case can Detroit's auto unions be understood without examining how Anglo-Gaelic influence reinforced certain trends and retarded others.

Craft Consciousness

In 1914, the Engineering Employers' Federation reported that 60 percent of Britain's engineering work force was still classified as skilled. The proportion was undoubtedly lower in the new consumer-durable industries of the Midlands, and significantly higher in the heavy and general engineering industries of the North and Scotland.[48]

Most of Detroit's Anglo-Gaelic immigrants came from these skill-intensive northern regions. When they arrived in Detroit during the early 1920s, they confronted a radically different environment. Skilled labor in Detroit's auto industry was only 5–10 percent of the total work force; by Henry Ford's estimate, 79 percent of all auto jobs took one week or less to learn. Surrounded by this sea of semi- and unskilled labor, the typical tradesman's sensitivity to "encroachment" by half-trained machine operators grew to an all-consuming obsession. "They wanted to build a fence around themselves," Nick DiGaetano recalled of the skilled metal polishers at Chrysler-Jefferson in the 1920s. His remarks describe the conservative potential of craft consciousness in any group of tradesmen, native- or foreign-born. " 'The foundry men?— hell with them. The assembly line men?—hell with them. . . . They have no trade. They are labor,' they said. The polisher was a big shot, like the molder, like the machinist, like the tool maker."[49]

This craft agenda was a losing strategy in Detroit, particularly in production departments where continual mechanization and redivision of labor overwhelmed the "fences" of craft unionism. But in Britain, where engineering craftsmen were better organized, unions were a substantial bulwark against unilateral subdivision of labor and introduction of low-wage "handymen." Craft consciousness was not just an individual sensibility or claim to status; in Britain more so than any other industrial economy, it was augmented by a collective consciousness of shop rules and practices that made craft a far more salient presence in British work life.

This salience of craft was not simply a *consequence* of union organization, however. Although engineering unions defended craft technologies, they did not initiate them and could not always "impose" them on those employers who chose to resist. The fact is, relatively few engineering employers chose to do so. Management did seek greater control of the division of labor, and craft unions did resist this trend, but British managers did not pursue the Fordist model of centralized command and wholesale mechanization with nearly the same conviction as American managers. British engineering firms had comparatively less capital, smaller markets, greater demands for precision production, and a far more established commitment to the socioeconomic structures of craft production. Wayne Lewchuk, in his comparative study of auto production in Britain and America, loses sight of this when he argues that British auto companies conceded partial control of the shop floor to workers only because union growth and the "syndicalist impulse" of 1910–1926 ruled out further subdivision of labor. As an example, Lewchuk cites the Daimler Company's use of incentive pay to spur productivity in a factory system that still delegated to workers considerable control over effort norms. Yet by Lewchuk's own account, Daimler installed this form of decentralized management between 1901 and 1906. The dates are important, since the "syndicalist impulse" in labor's upsurge during 1910–1926 cannot retroactively account for a process already in place by 1906. Daimler's location in the Midlands is also significant, since this region's light engineering industry had notoriously low levels of unionization before 1910 and after 1922. It was only in 1913 that the Workers Union could strike Daimler and other Conventry carmakers, and the main issue, according to historian Richard Hyman, was higher wages for semiskilled machine operators, not syndicalist control. The evidence suggests that even in auto, where "American methods" had relatively greater influence than most engineering industries, a residual reliance on partial shop-floor control of effort norms preceded union organization. It was a system management had long favored in metalworking, where craft production had a notable history. In the complex and volatile business of building cars, this system still afforded advantages of flexibility and low overhead, even as the relatively greater reliance on mechanized production reduced many production skills. Daimler's dependence on partial shop-floor control was neither new nor union-imposed; what was new about the management strategies at Daimler and elsewhere was the use of incentive pay to boost productivity.[50]

The remnants of craft production were far more evident in North England and Scotland, where the First Industrial Revolution had its deepest roots. As outlined in Chapter 3, the metalworking economy of the North was devoted primarily to the production of producer durables and military ordinance—steam engines, ships, armaments, locomotives, and textile machinery. This product mix, in turn, reinforced a continuing reliance on skill-intensive technologies. Special-purpose machines operated by less-skilled workers made sense only when lengthy production runs of standardized goods allowed employers to fully recover the expense of such a capital-intensive strategy. Since heavy and general engineering were low-volume industries, employers chose the craft-intensive option of general-purpose machines flexibly applied to many products. Skilled workers could produce the "varied and variable" output of these capital goods far more economically than alternative methods, and the demand for skilled labor was correspondingly high throughout the nineteenth and early twentieth centuries.[51]

This craft-intensive system became self-reinforcing, a point historian Charles More underlines by contrasting British and American engineering. In the former case, the early demand for skilled workers called forth a growing supply, which in turn made craft labor relatively cheap; in the American economy, on the other hand, employers confronted both an acute shortage of skilled workers and a relatively large supply of immigrant laborers. As a result, the wage differential between skilled and unskilled labor was higher in the United States during the nineteenth century. "Put very simply," More concludes, "just as the expense of skilled labor in America encouraged the development of mass production, so the cheapness of skilled labor in England meant that small-scale production did not impose any significant cost penalties, while producing a more tailor-made, and thus more desirable, product." Britain's pioneer role in producing capital goods for the First Industrial Revolution favored the use of skill-intensive technologies; the consequent growth of the skilled labor supply reinforced that choice by lowering the relative cost of its labor inputs.[52]

This growing supply of skilled engineers was a product of Britain's unique apprenticeship system. As late as 1925, there were 140,000 apprentices in British engineering and shipbuilding, representing 10.4 percent of the overall work force. In Michigan, by way of contrast, the 1,905 "machinists' apprentices" indicated in the 1920 Census represented a mere 2.6 percent of the state's 72,672 machinists and toolmakers, and less than 1 percent of the total metalworking labor force. Charles More's careful study of British apprenticeship indicates that contemporary perceptions of its near extinction focused too narrowly on London or on old-style indentures. The latter certainly were declining in the nineteenth century, and apprenticeship did virtually disappear in such industries as papermaking and boot and shoes. But "new-style" apprenticeship, based on verbal or written contracts rather than indenture, was actually growing in engineering, shipbuilding, and other industries. In these settings, management took boys aged fourteen to sixteen for an apprenticeship lasting from four to seven years (five was the median in 1909), with training supplied by journeymen engineers and, less often, foremen.[53]

As in Detroit, British engineers could and did learn their trade by "migration" (semiskilled workers moving from shop to shop and machine to machine until they could perform at the skilled rate) or by "following up" (helpers learning the full range of skills from the craftsman they assisted). But the majority of Britain's fitters, turners, and patternmakers in the early twentieth century were "time-served" apprentices. Engineering unions favored this route to skill over the various methods of "stealing" a trade, and many locals tried to police apprenticeship by limiting the ratio of apprentices to journeymen. Some met with limited success, but in general engineers were hard-pressed just to defend their shop rules in the late nineteenth and early twentieth centuries, much less impose training regulations on management. Apprenticeship programs, in short, were not a craft-union contrivance to artificially restrict the labor supply. Employers began training workers long before the engineering unions achieved significant power, and they continued apprenticeship training into the twentieth century because they found it a relatively cheap way to replenish their work force: in contrast to American firms, where skilled labor was in short supply and training therefore required special teachers and costly training facilities (notably, the Ford Trade School), British firms had an ample supply of craftsmen to tutor the apprentice in the shop. "Given the initial existence of skill," More concludes, "it cost little or nothing to train skilled workers."[54]

The cost was reduced still further by a prevailing craft culture that prepared boys for skilled labor before they reached the firm. Public education played only a limited role in England, though Bill Stevenson recalled taking algebra in Glasgow's schools by age fourteen and learning manual skills "necessary to get a job as a tradesman." More important were the family ties that reproduced skilled labor. One-third to one-half of British engineers in the late nineteenth and early twentieth centuries followed their fathers into the trade, and "hereditary succession" also prevailed among boilermakers, printers, and some building trades—in the latter case, the work rules explicitly provided free apprenticeship for at least one son. For employers, this lowered the cost of recruitment and, when the son entered the same firm, further reduced the already minor cost of supervision. For the crafts-man's son, the high wages and social status of skilled work encouraged emulation even if the boy chose a different craft. Ernie Woodcock's father and uncle were molders, but Ernie apprenticed as an engineer. John McGivern, on the other hand, followed his father into engineering. After emigrating from Belfast to Detroit in 1915, his father and mother followed—along with brothers Eugene, also a toolmaker, James, an electrician, and Francis, also an electrician. These Anglo-Gaelic immi-grants brought with them a craft culture rooted in family ties and passed from one generation to the next. Craft and family also over-lapped for American-born metalworkers, but the craft universe was far smaller (particularly outside New England and the mid-Atlantic states) and considerably more beleaguered.[55]

The craft culture of British engineering was not static. It could not be, since product technologies and production methods were constantly changing after 1890. Turret lathes, milling machines, surface grinders, and other "American" machine tools suited to repetition work began to enter the shops. These did not automatically undermine the crafts-man's position, since new methods and new products often demanded greater precision and complex fitting. But the new machines did gradu-ally transform the old dichotomy between skilled and unskilled labor, adding new strata of semiskilled specialists and less-skilled "handy-men." Wartime "dilution" of engineering promised additional changes in industry practices but had a surprisingly limited impact on postwar trends. During the war, the mass production of shells, cartridges, small arms, and other military hardware made feasible specialized machinery and female machine operators. But this practical demon-stration of mass production's apparent efficiency was not entirely persuasive, for the goal of such industrial innovation was military rather than commercial efficiency. Indeed, dilution was pressed even when it proved quite inefficient and costly—the primary aim being maximum production of war material, at *any* cost, with a minimum of draft-age males. The return to "varied and variable" output after the war encouraged a return to craft-intensive practices—and the Restora-tion of Pre-War Practices Act made it mandatory. Thereafter, a steady erosion of the craftsman's realm was evident (particularly in the Mid-lands), but not the rapid dismantling which many had predicted.[56]

A product of this craft environment, the Anglo-Gaelic immigrant brought to Detroit a corresponding sense of self-worth, even ar-rogance, matched only by German tradesmen, Yankee mechanics, and, perhaps, Ford's Trade School graduates. Admittedly, "self-worth" is hard to measure, and the Anglo-Gaelic immigrant may well have lost some of his pluck in the long months of unemployment following World War I. Nevertheless, he came from an industrial environment where craft had not been routed from direct production. In contrast, American-born toolmakers trained in Detroit must always have felt the supreme precariousness of their position—in recent memory, mechanization had wiped out dozens of production crafts, some overnight. As a group, this could only make them more defensive and less assertive than their British counterparts.

British toolmakers soon learned that Detroit was a very different place from Glasgow and Tyneside. Alan Strachan found his first job at Freuhauf Trailer, where he discovered his shop classification not only was limited to the turret lathe he operated but was further restricted by the machine's brand name and size—Warner and Swasey 2-A. "Remembering the advice of my uncle to take the first job that came along and then look around, I decided to ignore, temporarily, this slight to my more elevated credentials in the world of machine-shop practice." Bill McKie was also unprepared for life in a Detroit factory. Lunchtime on his first day at Ford brought a rude awakening. "It was the time when you relaxed," McKie's biographer, Philip Bonosky, wrote of Bill's expectations. "Talked with your buddies, maybe even snatched forty winks before going back to the job. In England, you sent the boy out for hot tea." Instead, McKie's co-workers had only fifteen minutes to eat, "swallowing rapidly, their eyes fixed in a stare, among the dirt and dust and open barrels of cyanide." Plunged suddenly into this alien world, the Anglo-Gaelic craftsman could measure these conditions against his British experience and readily find fault with Fordist management. American-born tradesmen, particularly those trained in Detroit, had no comparable benchmark for critically evaluating management practice.[57]

Automaking in Detroit left little room for craft culture, yet many Anglo-Gaelic workers continued to assert themselves as craftsmen. In 1935, when Mat Smith and John Anderson debated the future course of MESA, Smith could hurl no greater insult at his opponent than the charge he had "disowned his trade" by claiming he was a tool and die maker when he was really an electrician—and a "half-arssed" one at that. The previous year, when Smith took his membership out on strike, the union organized a ritual of solidarity that no other group of workers in the "craftless" auto industry could or would have considered.[58] Joe Brown described this singular episode in Detroit's labor history:

Introducing a new technique into strike strategy, the workers went to the struck shops . . . got their tool boxes and marched out with them, going to their local union offices. There, receipts were issued and the boxes were all stored in a bonded warehouse until the strike is over. That means the men cannot work, that every striker knows that every other striker will stay out until all go back together.[59]

There is no available evidence indicating the particular authors of this unique strategy, but there is every likelihood they were the same Anglo-Gaelic immigrants who dominated the leadership and much of the membership of MESA. For the 3,000 workers who so pledged their solidarity in this strike, their tools, as Hobsbawm said of British tradesmen, "symbolized . . . the relative independence of the artisan from management." No other group of autoworkers possessed such a powerful and tangible symbol of their independence on the job. MESA, by invoking collective control of these tools, welded its members into a union capable of challenging the world's most powerful industrial corporations.[60]

Class Consciousness

Craft consciousness strengthened the cohesion of Anglo-Gaelic tradesmen, but in the U.S. context it also restricted their organizational base. American conditions called for more inclusive membership, and the new-model industrial unionism, combining the IWW's charismatic-industrial practice with the organizational stamina of the Anglo-Gaelic tradesman, required a broader vision. The languages of class provided such a perspective, and Anglo-Gaelic workers spoke this idiom with a particular fluency.

"Pride is one of the essential ingredients of class consciousness." Historian Marc Bloch made this statement in reference to feudal nobility, but it could apply just as readily to British workers in the opening decades of the twentieth century. "We're fit and ready to govern," one South Wales miner boasted during the postwar strike wave. "We 'ave classes in Marx and all the others right 'ere and now we're ready to take over the job of runnin' the country."[61]

If the majority of workers were less familiar with Marx and far less certain they were "ready to govern," most shared the miner's implied disdain for the rich and powerful. In the day-to-day routine of working-class life, this was more often expressed in ironic terms. "There's many a swell in Park Lane tonight," sang the tramp in one

1902 music-hall tune, "Who'd be glad if only he had my appetite." As a penniless beggar who sleeps in Trafalgar Square, the singer drew attention to the social gulf separating "them and us." But as Standish Meacham points out, this awareness of difference didn't always imply antagonism. "He is not singing in order to raise a mob: let the swells stay where they are. He likes it where he is." If Trafalgar Square is "good enough for Nelson, it's good enough for me."[62]

Workers in continental Europe and North America also expressed themselves in class terms, whether in anger or in resignation, as in the two cases above. But their vocabulary was not so exclusively dominated by the "languages of class," as Gareth Stedman Jones puts it:

Unlike Germany, languages of class in England never faced serious rivalry from a pre-existing language of estates; unlike France and America, republican vocabulary and notions of citizenship never became more than a minor current, whether as everyday speech or as analytic categories; unlike the countries of southern Europe, vocabularies of class did not accompany, but long preceded, the arrival of social democratic parties and were never exclusively identified with them.[63]

In the United States, critics debated *whether* and to what degree the concept of social class was relevant in a society of "interest groups" and ethno-religious subcultures; in nineteenth- and early twentieth-century Britain, the posing of such a question would have seemed absurd. No other criterion could match the explanatory power of class: there were no sizable racial minorities or foreign-language ethnics to fragment society along these lines (particularly outside London), and religious distinctions lost their legal definition with Catholic Emancipation in 1829. Factory owners and landed nobles openly claimed the privileges of class rule and disagreed only over how the subordinate classes should be managed. Conservatives defended legal barriers against plebeian interlopers, while Liberals advocated a cross-class alliance with "respectable" workers. The working class, for its part, was not a homogeneous mass, but cultural distinctions between Anglo and Gaelic, Protestant and Catholic, Lowlander and Highlander were less determining than comparable racial, ethnic, and religious cleavages in American society. Only the "Irish question" fundamentally disrupted Britain's class-bound discourse, and even here, centuries of common language, migration, and intermarriage had eroded the salience of this conflict in England and Scotland, though not in Ireland. In all other respects, Britain, the pioneer of capitalist industry, was the exemplar of class society and the model for Marx's theory. The existence of social class was a given; debate focused on whether class rule should be protected, "humanized," or abolished.

That debate grew more heated as class relations were redefined in the late nineteenth and early twentieth centuries. This "remaking" of the British working class coincided with the Second Industrial Revolution, referred to in Chapter 3. City populations in the industrial areas of northern and central England doubled between 1870 and 1900, and working-class neighborhoods bore the brunt of this increase. Continuing growth after the turn of the century saw many workers moving to new residential suburbs linked by tram and train to factory districts; a few bought modest homes in terraced developments, but the majority, particularly those in older inner-city slums, lived in crowded tenements, often three to a room, with one communal water tap for an entire block, and outdoor privies shared by several households.[64]

These expanding and overcrowded neighborhoods were the context for a distinctive kind of sociability, not unrelated, says Meacham, to the older forms of mutual responsibility found in rural villages. "Unlike those earlier communities, however, there was to be no resident governing class, imposing its own will—philanthropic, condescending, authoritarian—upon the rest." At the turn of the century, middle-class reformers discovered that British workers were establishing a distinctively proletarian culture, both "rough" and "respectable." The former found expression in music halls, pubs, horse-betting, the sporting papers, football, and other forms of male sociability; the latter in workingmen's clubs, friendly societies, unions, co-ops, choirs, the Labour party, and, when the husband's wage permitted, "the mum at home." None of this sprang up all at once (the Labour party was a late arrival), and regional variations stand out. The Scots were more devoted to football, drank less in pubs, and preferred whiskey to beer; unions, co-ops, and friendly societies were more salient in the working-class culture of the North than in London, where workers "trapped in the twilight world of small workshop production," as Jones puts it, more often favored the music hall and the racetrack.[65]

While capable of sustaining working-class organization in the shop and the neighborhood, this was usually a conservative culture. Socialists like Bill McKie won the respect and sometimes the leadership of British workers, and episodes of peak mobilization between 1910 and 1926 could inspire the revolutionary rhetoric of the Welsh miner quoted above. But the prevailing consciousness, summarized by Jones, was one of "the separateness of a caste rather than the hegemonic potentialities of a particular position in production." Inward-looking and defensive, this consciousness was also stubbornly resistant to the crusading zeal of middle-class reformers. Settlement houses, sanitary legislation, housing inspection, penny savings banks, pub regulations, evangelical campaigns, and temperance crusades produced only modest returns on the enormous energy expended to "reform" the working class. Even labor aristocrats who advocated thrift, self-improvement, and political moderation did not thereby succumb to simple embourgeoisment. Rooted in such collective institutions as the trade union, the co-op, and the friendly society, these skilled tradesmen articulated a "negotiated version" of the ruling ideology, a hybrid of mutualistic norms for securing individual improvement. This "process of negotiation," as Robert Gray points out in his study of Edinburgh's Victorian labor aristocracy, "presupposes strong and autonomous protective class institutions."[66]

There were far fewer such institutions in Detroit. Like Flint, Pontiac, and other Michigan cities that grew with the automobile, Detroit acquired most of its population after 1900, much of it drawn from rural areas of Europe and North America with little history of sustained working-class organization. As late as 1930, 59 percent of the Detroit-area population was either foreign-born or the children of foreign-born parents, led by the Poles. This immigrant community was negotiating its own amendments to the dominant culture, but the resulting compromise was significantly different from Britain's working-class culture. The Polish variant incorporated the church, ethnic lodges and sports clubs, and a newly articulated national identity built upon the immigrant's initial (and far narrower) loyalty to village and region. This ethnic identity did not preclude class consciousness and union organization, but such hybrid formations as the "Polish Laborers' Alliance" were more episodic and, by definition, more exclusive to a particular portion of the working class.[67]

Detroit's dominant ideology was also quite different from what Anglo-Gaelic immigrants had known in the United Kingdom. Rather than the "languages of class" spoken by all sectors of British society, native Americans favored the language of democratic opportunity. Even factory owners favored this idiom. "The Ford Motor Company was started by a working-man [*sic*] for working-men," one half-page ad declared in the *Detroit News*. "Its chosen field . . . has been the average American family, for which it has consistently provided car facilities which formerly only the wealthy could buy." Walter Chrysler also proclaimed his humble origins "as a former shop worker" in a 1933 statement boosting the company union. This was not a language that Anglo-Gaelic immigrant workers could easily adopt, for Britain's factory workers did not often rise to the leadership of industrial corporations. Nor, for that matter, did American workers, though the hothouse growth of Detroit and its auto industry had, in living memory, afforded greater opportunities for such upward mobility than the stagnant economies of North England and Scotland. Henry Ford, Walter Chrysler, Henry Leland, and the other former mechanics who had risen through the auto industry's managerial ranks gave a certain credibility to the rags-to-riches folklore of popular culture, even if the opportunities for such advancement were widely exaggerated. The "true" American knew (or was supposed to know) that individualistic striving and acquisitive behavior prepared one for success, and once achieved (even when inherited), success warranted any means to protect and expand it. "America is far too big a proposition to take in all at once," James Connolly concluded during his eight-year stay in this country. Accustomed to the "civic interest" that animated even the ruling classes in Europe, Connolly confessed his surprise at the aggressiveness of American employers and their resolute opposition to working-class organization. "In no country is individualism so systematically pursued, both as a theory and as a policy."[68]

Individualism was by no means foreign to Anglo-Gaelic culture, though it took muted forms in a society where pedigree made the stronger claim to status. The Anglo-Gaelic immigrants who rose to leadership in Detroit's auto unions were ambitious men, marked by their decision to acquire craft skills, emigrate to America, and risk union activism in Detroit. But through the 1930s, their ambition did not, in most cases, seek goals outside the universe of blue-collar labor and its allied organizations (union, Odd Fellows, labor politics, and so on). There were some American autoworkers, often skilled tradesmen, who also rose to leadership from a working-class milieu. But there were many other American-born leaders who came to the auto industry from a world that straddled the white-collar professions.

Unlike their Anglo-Gaelic counterparts, these "aspiring professionals" had attended college, worked in white-collar jobs, or taken positions in sales or management before they became active in union organization. Some came from working-class backgrounds, others from families that had already acquired middle-class status, either as professionals or as petty entrepreneurs. In either case, if the economy had remained buoyant into the 1930s, these aspiring professionals would have entered the pulpit, the classroom, the bar, or management. But the depression short-circuited their careers and threw them into the ranks of blue-collar labor.

Chicago-born John Zaremba, a graduate of Browns Business College and a Cass Tech night student in metallurgy, worked in the 1920s as a time-study man for General Motors, a clerical worker at Dodge, a foreman at Dominion Forge of Canada, and a construction inspector for the City of Detroit; when the depression narrowed his white-collar options, he took a production job at Dodge in 1931 and later became recording secretary of UAW Local 3. Richard Frankensteen, president of the Dodge local and later vice president of the UAW, was another aspiring professional who straddled the worlds of blue- and white-collar work. Son of a singer-composer who led the Dodge Corporation's band, Frankensteen attended the University of Dayton and graduated in 1932 to pursue a career as a schoolteacher and coach; unable to find a job in his chosen profession, he hired into Dodge and attended law school at the University of Detroit before turning to union leadership as a new career. Leon Pody was a "ruined businessman" before taking a job at Briggs and becoming a strike leader in 1933; George Miller and Joe Rubin, members of the Dodge Local 3 Executive Board, were both aspiring lawyers. Wisconsin-born John W. Anderson ("little" John Anderson, not to be confused with Glasgow-born "big" John Anderson), the future strike leader at GM Fleetwood, graduated from the University of Wisconsin in 1931 and applied for work as a corporate personnel manager; after a futile job search and a stint selling vacuum cleaners door-to-door, he returned to work as a metal finisher in Detroit. Nestor Dessy, the future recording secretary of UAW Local 235 at Chevrolet Gear and Axle, had graduated from the Pittsburgh (Kansas) Business College and worked for GM as a clerical worker before the depression forced him to take a production job. Homer Martin, the future president of the UAW, had also entered the blue-collar work force during the depression. A graduate of William Jewell College and the Baptist Theological Seminary, Martin left the pulpit in 1932 after antagonizing some of his Leeds, Missouri, congregation with his prolabor sentiments; hiring into a GM plant, he quickly rose to president of the local, was fired, and moved to Detroit in 1934.[69]

Martin and other aspiring professionals who became autoworkers had to abandon their careers and renounce or modify the language of democratic opportunity. Nestor Dessy was better prepared than most for the transition to factory life and class conflict: the son of a UMW member, he spent a stretch of time during his childhood living on garden tomatoes and canned beans while his father was on strike. "Little" John Anderson's depression-era troubles ("during the summer and fall of 1934 I almost starved") also galvanized a reappraisal of his working-class roots, leading him to join the IWW in 1933. But for many other aspiring professionals, the language of class was a foreign idiom, learned with difficulty and merged in practice with the language of democratic opportunity. The result was an equivocal, sometimes con-tradictory dialect. Richard Frankensteen began his union career as leader of Dodge's company union. "In the beginning, Dick Franken-steen thought that all unions were infested with racketeers," recalled John Zaremba. Harry Ross, also an early union leader at Dodge, re-called Frankensteen's initial conviction that "we did not need any outside unions. 'If we treat the company right, they will treat us right.'" When Frankensteen finally concluded that only an indepen-dent union could force change on Chrysler, he turned to Father Coughlin for support, not to the existing "class" organizations already in the field. Homer Martin's gyrations are well known and landed him in the same company of Father Coughlin (long after Frankensteen, to his credit, had abandoned the demagogue). A lesser-known figure like Mike Manning is perhaps more representative. Manning, who worked through the 1920s as an inspector at Continental Motors, never entirely abandoned his aspirations to join the lower ranks of management, even after he became president of the AFL Federal Labor Union at Kel-sey Hayes Wheel. Since 1930, he had worked at Kelsey as a night-shift inspector, "so actually I was considered to be a supervisor." In 1935, faced with the opportunity for promotion to foreman, Manning offered his resignation as president, "since some of you," as he put it in an open letter, "have doubts as to the propriety of my continuing as an officer." He later reemerged as vice president of Local 174 only because the local's Communist and Socialist factions wanted a "neutral" for the post, and Manning, the former supervisor, was drafted to fill the void.[70]

Manning, by his own account, never tried to master the languages of class and opposed every leftist in his local, including the two he re-called from his home plant—"one of them an Englishman by the name of Jimmy Hindle." Anglo-Gaelic workers were by no means the only socialists in the labor movement, but they were, as Chapter 5 will indi-cate in more detail, unusually prominent in left circles—so much so that autoworker Frank Marquart recalled how the Marxian Club he be-longed to in the 1920s was dubbed "the tea drinkers" because its numerous British members favored the beverage. Even those Anglo-Gaelic workers who shunned socialism still favored the "class" dis-course of trade unionism. Before 1929, their "languages of class" marked these militants as foreign, no less so than their heavy accents and their penchant for tea. But after 1929, it was a different matter, par-ticularly inside the factory. Here, ethnic, racial, and occupational distinctions could still divide workers, but the extreme insecurity of employment was such a universal experience that these distinctions lost some of their urgency. Job-shop owners and accommodating foremen could sometimes personalize work relationships, but the "boss" still hired and fired, and individual rights had no bearing. Class lines could be traced all the more readily in bigger factories, where a relative handful of managers wielded unilateral power over hundreds or thousands of workers. When the economy had been growing, opportunities for promotion or job hopping had sustained the individualistic strategies of skilled tradesmen and production workers. Now, mass unemployment foreclosed these strategies. In this environment, the languages of class seemed most appropriate—and Anglo-Gaelic union leaders were their most fluent interpreters.[71]

Organizational Know-How

"The skilled workman was superior material for the spread of unionism," industry observer William Chalmers noted of Detroit's toolmakers in the 1930s. "A majority of them have come from Germany, Scotland, and England. Their training included membership in the unions there."[72]

There were, of course, American workers who had experience in unions, but far fewer. As indicated in Table 4.1, Britain's union movement dwarfed its American counterpart in both absolute numbers and

TABLE 4.1
NUMBER OF UNION MEMBERS AND PERCENTAGE OF THE LABOR FORCE,
BRITAIN AND AMERICA, 1900–1930

	United Kingdom		United States[a]	
Year	No. members (000s)	Percentage of labor force	No. members (000s)	Percentage of labor force
1900	2,022	12.7%	869	5.5%
1910	2,565	14.6	2,102	10.1
1920	8,348	45.2	4,775	16.7
1930	4,842	25.4	3,162	8.9

SOURCE: George Sayers Bain and Robert Price, *Profiles of Union Growth: Comparative Statistical Portrait of Eight Countries* (Oxford, 1980), 37, 88.

NOTE: Percentages for both the United Kingdom and the United States apply to a labor force of all wage earners, employed and unemployed, excluding armed forces.

[a]U.S. figures are based on surveys of the National Bureau of Economic Research, which Bain and Price (79–81) deem more accurate than the Bureau of Labor Statistics data for the period covered. U.S. figures for 1900 and 1910 include Canadian membership, which slightly inflates totals.

proportion of the labor force organized. In 1920, when both movements peaked, Britain's unions had 75 percent more members than the American labor movement, even though its labor force was one-third smaller. Industry-by-industry data are not strictly comparable, but a rough measure of union density in metalworking is revealing: in 1929, after unions on both sides of the Atlantic had suffered a serious decline in membership, Britain's "metals and engineering" unions still represented 30.2 percent of the industry labor force, compared with just 8.8 percent for American unions in "metals and machinery." The contrast was all the greater for Anglo-Gaelic immigrants coming from North England and Scotland, where union density was higher than the national average, and arriving in Detroit, where civic and corporate leaders claimed pride of place as America's open-shop capital.[73]

For Anglo-Gaelic workers emigrating from the British environment to Detroit, the absence of unions in their new home was not only lamentable but unnatural. Harry Southwell's incredulity was characteristic:

I immediately made inquiries as to the existence of a union, which an expert grinder ought to have been able to find without difficulty, based upon my experience in England. I was rather amazed to find that while there was such an organization nationally, it had very few members and was very inactive. . . . This caused me quite a bit of concern because I had been led to believe through my upbringing that every group of workers aspired to some form of security through a union.[74]

Bill Stevenson, initially employed at the Chrysler Jefferson plant, found the absence of a union "odd," since in Glasgow's shipyards you could not get a job *unless* you were a union member. "As far as I was concerned," Stevenson later recalled of his union upbringing, "I literally sucked this in with my mother's milk because my father before me was interested in the labor movement." Harry Southwell learned about unions in the same context of family instruction. Raised by his grandfather, Harry would accompany him "to various union meetings, and he would always instill in me the necessity of becoming an active union member in any trade that I might become involved in." Doug Fraser Sr., the Scottish electrician and socialist who emigrated to Detroit in 1923, also took his son, Doug Jr., to union and political meetings; in such families, it was an automatic part of the child's education. Even an aspiring professional like Stan Coulthard, who came to the United States to acquire training as a dentist, felt a natural affinity for union organization when a change in plans took him into Detroit's auto plants. "After all, I'd been brought up on trade unionism, fed on it with a knife, fork and spoon. It was a part of me," recalled Coulthard, whose father was a branch officer in the Amalgamated Society of Railway Servants and an ILP city councilor in Birkenhead.[75]

As a result, while many Americans accustomed to AFL inertia believed industries like auto and steel were "unorganizable," many Anglo-Gaelic workers not only believed it could be done but found it uncanny that it had not already happened. When Coulthard's workmates at Fisher Body complained of the lack of ventilation, it was Coulthard who suggested "having a go" at management; when the skilled workers in his department selected a spokesman to articulate their grievances, they picked Coulthard—even though he was "little more than a laborer minding a machine." The potential for a mass-based mobilization of workers was, for him, a practical experience, not a theoretical proposition: as a teenager and young man, his family had gone through the violent—and victorious—strikes of 1911 and 1919 that established industrial unionism on Britain's railroads.[76]

This "sense of the possible" that animated Coulthard and his Anglo-Gaelic workmates amplified the initial militancy of autoworker protest; thereafter, the organizational know-how these immigrants brought to Detroit provided much of the mortar that held the early unions together. The Anglo-Gaelic contribution to Detroit's early auto unions was evident in two critical areas of organization: the microorganization of routine business and the macroorganization of union structure.

Routine Business

It is all too easy to overlook the details of union organization while focusing on the big picture of sit-down strikes and political action. But no organization can sustain itself without establishing rules for the conduct of routine business. This is especially true for newly formed unions, since the conduct of "routine" business is jeopardized by external threats to the organization's very existence and by internal dissension over goals and strategy. Meetings cannot be conducted when opposing factions are either ignorant of parliamentary procedure or ignore its prescriptions for keeping contentious debate under control. Likewise, the formulation of policy and the routine accounting of income and expenditures require the ability to conduct a certain minimum of record keeping—minutes of previous meetings, account books, and so on.

Four overlapping groups had members who possessed these vital organizational skills: socialists, skilled workers, Anglo-Gaelic immigrants, and aspiring professionals. In both of the first two groups, there were American-born workers and immigrants from continental Europe, but the majority of native-born and immigrant workers had little experience with union organization. "We were all uninformed," recalled Dan Gallagher, an American-born production worker at Timken Axle and a future organizer for Local 174. He and most of his co-workers in 1936 were "naive, ignorant shop people who knew nothing about unions, organization, or anything else except that we knew our problem, each of us." Blaine Marrin, the American-born toolmaker at Fisher Body and future president of Local 157, recalled that in 1933, when he first joined MESA, "I didn't know unionism from rheumatism." John Zaremba was equally in the dark. "I had not the experience in organizing the workers," he later recalled; initially, his only guide was written instructions from Eugene Debs, with whom he had corresponded in the 1920s. Michael Manning, representing Detroit autoworkers at the 1934 National Conference of AFL Federal Labor Unions, was completely bewildered by the proceedings. "These people are all hollering about industrial union charters and I didn't even know what they were talking about. That's how green on that matter I was!"[77]

Many Anglo-Gaelic union activists found this lack of organizational know-how exasperating. Stan Coulthard concluded that his Polish co-workers at Dodge "must have been peasants" since "they didn't even understand the *idea* of trade unionism." Bill McKie initially concluded that the production workers at Ford, most of them immigrant and second-generation ethnics, had a consciousness that harkened back to "the political outlook . . . [of] Britain in the early eighteenth century. . . . So long as they are working they appear to be quite content." These harsh assessments of immigrant production workers were probably influenced by ethnic bias and the language barriers that prevented communication. But Walter Dorosh, a diemaker at Ford, a future president of Local 600, and a self-described "Polak," offered a similar assessment of his co-workers. "We were," he put it bluntly, "greenhorns."[78]

So, apparently, was Mike Lukatch, first recording secretary for the AFL's Federal Labor Union at Dodge Main. His minutes for the meeting of 1 December 1933 record a motion to pay what he called a "capital tax"—apparently, his version of the "per capita" levy required of any AFL affiliate. Lukatch's inexperience, compounded by his poor grammar and, perhaps, his difficulty mastering English as a second language, is evident throughout the minutes he kept for the union's first five months. An entry for the 16 December meeting of that year is characteristically garbled: in an uncertain and wobbly script, Lukatch recorded that the "minutes were Read and they were exception Just as they were Read By a Motion and Seconded. And it was so ordered." This phrase can be deciphered, but a subsequent entry for the same meeting gives only the murkiest indication of what happened: "A Motion was Maid to hold the dishion of the next hall of Meetings for Gittingg in New Members." One can sympathize with Lukatch's short-comings as a scribe and admire his perseverance in what must have been a very uncomfortable task. But his minutes, which were sparse as well as garbled, would be of little use to the union's officers when they needed to consult this record.[79]

This lack of organizational experience could also make the conduct of meetings virtually impossible. UAW organizer Stanley Nowak recalled the union's 1937 convention:

There was a great deal of enthusiasm, but at the same time, lack of discipline, a great deal of anarchy . . . [and] noisy meetings. If the workers did not like you, they were quite intolerant. They would just shout you down. If they liked you on the other hand, they would applaud for five, ten minutes and they would carry you on their arms out of the hall or to the platform. It was very, very shocking.[80]

Early MESA meetings could also be chaotic, despite the presence of experienced Anglo-Gaelic union activists. At one point when proceedings during the union's 1935 convention became especially muddled, a delegate with a gift for metaphor admonished his brothers for their lack of procedural discipline, observing that "we are building dies without blueprints." The contrast with the proceedings described by Nowak is one of degree: in early MESA conventions, confusion often reigned; in early UAW conventions, bedlam.[81]

There were, of course, American-born autoworkers with organizational skills and/or union experience. Harry Ross, Mike Lukatch's replacement at the Dodge local, was one; Stanley Nowak, the second-generation Polish-American, was another. Nestor Dessy's upbringing in a UMW family and his education at business school both drew the attention of fellow union activists at Chevrolet Gear and Axle. When they noticed him taking shorthand at an early meeting, they drafted him to fill the vacancy left by one Joe Katchenowski—the previous recording secretary at UAW Local 235, who "lost interest" (and perhaps confidence) in handling the job.[82]

American-born leaders with union experience were in short supply. At the Chrysler Jefferson plant, the AFL's Federal Labor Union turned to British-born Alan Strachan to help fill the void. In 1934 he became recording secretary, joining two other skilled tradesmen who filled out the local's top positions: John Panzner, an American-born sheet metal worker and former Wobbly who had served time for refusing to fight in World War I, and Jack Kennedy, an American-born carpenter and former craft-union member. As president of the local, Kennedy understood "the importance of orderly procedure," recalled Strachan. Reviewing the local's minutes years later, Strachan was struck "by the procedural pattern which ran consistently through them. 'Motion by Panzner seconded by Strachan. Motion by Strachan seconded by Panzner.' And so it went on week after week. . . . Other than Jack Kennedy, we were the only ones who knew how to make the simplest motion or amendment."[83]

A similar constellation of leadership conducted organizational affairs in other factories and locals. At the Ford Dearborn plant, Bill McKie became first president of the AFL Federal Labor Union, with fellow Scotsman Dave Miller as vice president. At Kelsey Hayes Wheel, Michael Manning recalled the initial leaders of the Federal Labor Union in 1933 as "either skilled people or inspectors." When organizers from Ford and Kelsey Hayes amalgamated with other shops in 1936 to form UAW West Side Local 174, the same groups dominated the early years of organization. Toolmaker and Socialist party member Walter Reuther was president, presiding over a leadership coalition that encompassed Anglo-Gaelic immigrants (McKie, Miller, Harry Southwell), aspiring professionals (Manning), skilled workers (Reuther, McKie, electrician Frank Manfred), and socialists (Communist party member McKie, allied with Miller, Stanley Nowak, and Irene Young; Socialist party members Reuther, brother Victor, George Edwards, and Robert Kantor; former Wobbly "little" John Anderson). In this and other locals, there were production workers in some leadership positions (Gallagher in Local 174, Harry Ross and many others at Dodge), but the majority came from the four groups identified above. As Chapters 5 and 6 will indicate in more detail, the mix varied from case to case, and over time. At Dodge, there were fewer craftsmen and more semiskilled production workers in leadership, and the initial predominance of aspiring professionals, led by Frankensteen, gave way to Anglo-Gaelic immigrants, led by Pat Quinn. In MESA and UAW Locals 155 and 157, the key leaders were predominantly Anglo-Gaelic.[84]

Public speaking was a vital skill for any organizer, and Anglo-Gaelic leaders were well versed in the oratorical arts. Bill McKie had learned to overcome his youthful reticence by speaking at meetings of the Edinburgh Sheet Metal workers and SDF. Mat Smith's wit and pointed sarcasm became legendary in union circles and gave pause to any opponent who contemplated a public challenge to the MESA leader. John Anderson's speaking skills also won him a wide following in Detroit union halls, where his thick brogue was certainly no liability. "He realized it was an asset," recalled Henry Kraus, editor of *The United Automobile Worker.* "So he just put it on stronger and stronger." The result was apparently quite engaging. "Brother John Anderson of Local 155 gave us a masterful speech Tuesday," *Dodge Main News* reported during Local 3's 1937 sit-down strike. Many in the audience spoke highly of his "gift of gab. Perhaps we can get him back."[85]

That would not be easy in the winter and spring of 1937, when more than 120 sit-down strikes swept Detroit industry. The need for skilled and experienced organizers put a premium on the limited number of socialists, skilled tradesmen, and Anglo-Gaelic workers with union experience. As one strike followed the next, individuals from these overlapping groups found themselves leading widely disparate groups of strikers: organizers from the East Side Tool and Die Local 155, for example, leading 500 women workers occupying the Parke Davis Pharmaceutical plant, or Patternmakers helping organize the more than 1,000 men and women who barricaded themselves inside Detroit's industrial laundries. Only in 1938 would Local 155 begin to pick through the jurisdictional chaos produced by this whirlwind of organization, turning over 1,425 members to CIO affiliates representing everything from electrical, creamery, and chemical workers, to riggers, truck drivers, and hardware workers.[86]

The acute shortage of organizers would only be alleviated over time as American "greenhorns" and immigrant production workers learned the rudiments of leadership through experience and emulation. the UAW launched crash education programs to teach parliamentary procedure, public speaking, and other organizational skills, drawing on current and former staff of the Bryn Mawr School for Women Workers and the Brookwood Labor College. But in the meantime, it was often Anglo-Gaelic workers who tutored their less-experienced brethren. Nearly twenty years before, Frank Marquart had learned "the ABC's of unionism" at Continental Motors from "Limey," the English immigrant who led an early organizing drive in the plant. In the mid-1930s, it was much the same for Blaine Marrin. As he later recalled, "I learned how to organize and hold meetings from the communists and socialists from England." American-born leaders in UAW Local 2 at Murray Body learned the ropes in much the same way. In Plant 5, covering nearly 500 workers in the tool and die departments, the UAW organizing committee was led by Tommy Hampsen, a Scottish toolmaker and socialist who also played a leading role on Local 2's Shop Committee. "He was way out front," recalled Russell Leach, an American-born co-worker of Hampsen. "Very intelligent, experienced in Scotland. He was over fifty at the time of the 1937 sitdowns, so he had . . . wisdom and he had a temper. Those days I guess it was a good mixture." Two other Anglo-Gaelic immigrants, Elmer Thomas and "Red" McKinna, were on the Plant 5 committee, along with Charlie Lesser, an American-born toolmaker of British parents, Walter Finch, a German-American, and Russ Leach, then a hi-lo driver. In 1938, Elmer Thomas, the British-born socialist and former IWW member who emigrated to America as a boy, organized classes under WPA auspices to teach parliamentary procedure, public speaking, and collective bargaining to prospective young leaders in the local. The teachers, recalled Leach, "were all men and they were mostly Scotch. They never would admit it but you could tell by their teaching that they were educated in the socialist circles. . . . They would tell you about their struggles in Scotland."[87]

Union Structure

Those struggles, in Scotland and elsewhere within the United Kingdom, had produced an enormously varied array of union organizations. In the United States, the organizational debates of the 1930s were often posed in the simplistic terms of craft versus industrial unionism, but in Britain the argument over union structure could not be so readily dichotomized. In engineering alone, G.D.H. Cole identified forty-two different unions representing skilled workers in the prewar years—everything from the dominant Amalgamated Society of Engineers (ASE), with 205,000 members in 1915, to the "Mathematical, Optical, and Philosophical Instrument Makers," with a minuscule membership of just 360. The situation was complicated even further by the nearly one dozen additional unions that organized less-skilled workers in engineering and other industries.[88]

Within this organizational maze, four basic forms of union structure coexisted: craft societies, amalgamated craft unions, general unions, and industrial unions. Craft societies represented either one "section" of highly skilled labor, such as the Patternmakers, or one narrowly defined specialization, such as Scientific Instrument Makers. Amalgamated craft unions, in contrast, combined varied sections of skilled labor from a wide range of metalworking industries: the ASE, the leading example, represented patternmakers, toolmakers, fitters, turners, machinists, electricians, scientific instrument makers, millwrights, machine tool operators, hammer forgers, and "all other workers engaged in the metal industry and trades constituting societies who may hereafter agree to amalgamation." General unions organized everyone else, particularly laborers and less-skilled workers whom craft unions ignored, but also semiskilled machine operators and even some craftsmen. Industrial unions took all of the above within a particular branch of industry.[89]

A rough chronology defined this elaboration of union organization. Craft societies traced their roots to the beginning of the industrial revolution, initially representing "fully skilled" tradesmen, and then fragmenting into more narrowly defined sections as skill specialization became more pronounced. Efforts to amalgamate these sections began almost immediately and continued throughout the period, culminating in the 1920 merger of the Engineers, Toolmakers, Smiths, Steam Engine Makers, Machine Workers, and Instrument Makers into the Amalgamated Engineering Union (AEU). General unions grew to significance in the 1890s and the second decade of the twentieth century; in 1922 they achieved a special prominence with the merger of twenty-three unions into the Transport and General Workers Union. Industrial unions, on the other hand, failed to establish a significant prewar presence in the British labor movement. Blocked by the preceding growth of craft and general unions, industrial unionists surpassed these barriers to wider organization only in mining and railroads.[90]

The predominance of amalgamated unions and general unions was formally ratified in 1927, when the TUC majority, noting the diffuse boundaries between many industries and the alleged jurisdictional confusion this would cause, rejected left-wing calls for industrial organization. The TUC thereby put its stamp of approval on a status quo that had already produced enormous organizational confusion. In some respects, the result bore a superficial resemblance to the AFL's model for dividing autoworkers into Federal Labor Unions and skilled-trades organizations, but with these crucial differences: first, FLU's were a temporary arrangement, designed to net a mass base in the industry before distributing skilled workers to their appropriate craft union; second, instead of combining skilled trades into an amalgamated structure, as in Britain, AFL policy contemplated an array of sectional craft societies—one for patternmakers, one for electricians, one for machinists, one for metal polishers, another for sheet metal workers, and so on.[91]

The unanticipated emergence of MESA changed all this. Known initially as a "tool and die" organization, MESA soon became an amalgamated craft union, combining patternmakers, electricians, pipe fitters, industrial carpenters, sheet metal workers, and metal polishers with the core membership of tool and die makers. This was a craft union, but its concept of craft was augmented by a class-conscious inclusiveness that incorporated the full range of metalworking and maintenance trades. As such, MESA represented a distinct alternative to the AFL's moribund "sectional" crafts, which pigeonholed tradesmen by job classifications in separate organizations. As a permanent amalgamation of skilled workers, it also represented an alternative to the CIO model of industrial unionism, particularly as MESA tried to establish coordinated strategies with such "general unions" as the Automotive Industrial Workers Association.[92]

For Detroit autoworkers, then, the debate over structure was at least three-cornered rather than two-sided. In addition to the AFL and CIO models, there was a "TUC" proxy in the form of MESA. Ultimately, the CIO model of industrial unionism prevailed, but the terms of debate were significantly altered by the presence of this "British model": both because the final form of autoworker unionism in Detroit synthesized several of its key features, and because British union leaders *opposed* to the TUC model gave a substantial boost to the cause of industrial unionism.

Isolating this Anglo-Gaelic influence is no easy matter, but at least five features of the British model are evident in the early structures of autoworker unionism in Detroit.

Local Autonomy.   If the British and American labor movements had metamorphosed into human form in 1920, the former would have possessed a muscular body with an undersized head, the latter an elephantine skull on a midget's frame. Whereas the AFL's national leaders imposed sole jurisdiction and rough lines of demarcation upon a far smaller membership, the TUC's Parliamentary Committee lacked any comparable authority over its larger membership. The TUC, in fact, had only just established its *first* full-time officer. Centralizers who wanted a genuine executive body to replace the part-time lobbying of the Parliamentary Committee contrasted the TUC's undernourished central organization with the AFL's substantial headquarters in Washington. In 1920, they finally persuaded the annual TUC meeting to establish the General Council. But until 1924 the council had no authority to coordinate union strategy in industrial disputes, and its authority to adjudicate jurisdictional conflicts remained uncertain.[93]

Most British unions wanted it this way, guarding their autonomy even more tenaciously than AFL organizations. The same applied to the districts and branches within many TUC affiliates. Local autonomy was a hallowed and, for national leaders, a troublesome tradition. Before 1910, centralized collective bargaining was nearly as rare in Britain as in the United States, even though Britain's far smaller size and more established labor movement made coordinated bargaining more feasible. Until the 1890s, the National Executive of most craft unions, including the ASE, busied itself primarily with financial matters related to benefits and contributions. Actual bargaining (or "trade policy," as it was called) "remained a local matter," according to historian H. A. Clegg, "firmly in the hands of the men whom it would directly effect." Even after the national settlement of the Engineers' 1897 lockout, the union's District Committees still negotiated their own local wage rates: forty-one shillings a week in prewar Belfast, forty in London, thirty-nine in Manchester, thirty-eight in Glasgow, and so on, with variations for different areas of large cities and for different sectors of engineering. Pressure for centralized negotiations grew as larger employers expanded the scale of their operations, but a countervailing movement to expand the power of district organization took control of the Engineers in 1912–1913 and expelled the "centralizers" on the National Executive. This bitter confrontation didn't permanently settle the conflicting claims of national policy and local autonomy. Even as districts reasserted their claim to the whole spectrum of collective bargaining issues, leaving only procedural matters and broad principles to national negotiators, war and government regulation gave added impetus to centralized negotiations. In 1919, these two trends clashed in the Glasgow Forty-Hours strike, when the District Committee of the Engineers defied the ASE Executive by joining the Strike Committee and working with such "unofficial" bodies as the Clydeside stewards. It was precisely this sort of situation that prompted Winston Churchill to exclaim in February of that year that "the curse of trade unionism was that *there was not enough of it*, and it was not highly developed enough to make its branch secretaries fall into line with the head office."[94]

This decentralized structure gave British union organization a distinctively "chaotic" appearance, at least to American eyes. Since there was no equivalent to the AFL's principle of sole jurisdiction, British union organization grew in weedlike proliferation, with dozens of purely local societies competing for membership with larger national bodies. Adding to the confusion of these overlapping jurisdictions was the practice of multiple memberships—the latter exemplified by the skilled engineer Charles Duncan, who was simultaneously a member of his craft union, the ASE, and a founding officer of a general organization, the Workers' Union.[95]

The competing claims of these varied organizations could produce gridlock when it came to developing coordinated strategies, but local autonomy also gave British unions a distinctive resiliency. In 1897, the Engineers lost a nationwide struggle to protect their traditional control of the machine; yet over the next fifteen years, despite explicit language in the national Terms of Settlement, the dogged resistance of local ASE branches and districts robbed employers of their victory, forcing upon them rules that banned less-skilled workers from machines the Engineers claimed for themselves. "That this was so," said G.D.H. Cole, "is clearly revealed by the fact that these rules and regulations, although most of them did not exist in writing, required for their enforced suspension during the war period, not only an Act of Parliament, but also a very great deal of national, local, and workshop negotiation."[96]

Detroit's Anglo-Gaelic union leaders drew on this tradition of decentralized authority when they wrote the MESA constitution. The "District Committee" mandated by the founding convention bore the same title as the citywide bodies that defended local autonomy in Britain's ASE, and Article V of the MESA Constitution gave this district body—not the national executive—the authority to approve local-union bylaws.

As Chapter 6 will indicate, the same claim to local autonomy would serve the UAW in 1938–1939, when the union's tool and die locals, led by Anglo-Gaelic militants, confronted the world's largest industrial corporations as well as their own president, Homer Martin.[97]

Shop Stewards.　　At the local level, where the union branch represented members drawn from many shops within a specific area, there was no formal shop-floor organization in Britain until late in the nineteenth century. Stewards first appeared in ASE shops in the 1890s, when branch officials in Belfast and Scotland began appointing particular workshop members to collect dues and ensure that new hires joined the society. This became a form of direct shop-floor representation as the ASE officially propagated the steward system after 1896, and as stewards gradually took on the unofficial function of a plant bargaining committee. The branch's remoteness from rapidly changing shop-floor conditions was remedied by this organizational innovation, though branch secretaries and the ASE Executive didn't always appreciate the corresponding erosion of their authority. This tension became acute during World War I, as wholesale changes in work practices demanded immediate attention, and as stewards began to convene on a multiunion basis to meet the challenge. The wartime shop-steward

movement took two forms as it spread among other unions and industries: the "official" movement worked within the structure of districts
and branches, winning uneasy approval from District Committees and
grudging recognition from employers and the government; the "unofficial" movement adopted left-wing political demands and led
unsanctioned strikes against the government's wartime policies. After
the war, the official stewards movement won recognition in the founding constitution of the AEU, while the unofficial movement provided
key leaders of the British Communist party at its founding in 1920–
1921. The militancy of both movements "strengthened the rank and
file . . . at the expense of officialdom," historian Walter Kendall concludes, though, in his estimate, "it did not decisively shift authority."[98]

The same could be said of MESA, though with greater emphasis on
the shop-floor authority of MESA stewards. Mat Smith was a charisma-
tic and dominating presence in the union throughout its history, but he
could not, as indicated in the following section, ignore stewards and
other shop-based leaders when they pursued goals he opposed. The
MESA constitution not only mandated a stewards committee in every
workplace but also gave stewards equal representation with other
local-union delegates on MESA's citywide District Committee. While
Detroit unionists in medium-sized shops and Big Three plants could
look to other precedents for a steward system, none was so immediate
or so compelling as the one MESA had already put into practice. MESA
was the first union in medium shops like Midland Steel, as Chapter 5
will indicate, and it was from this organizational beachhead that the
UAW expanded its base in 1936. In the smaller job shops represented by
UAW Locals 155 and 157, the steward system came in toto from the
MESA structures established after 1933.

Subsequent contracts protected this system in language mandating
wider representation than most other UAW agreements. The 1937 and
1938 supplements to the UAW-GM contract, for example, authorized
only one district committeeman (the equivalent of a chief steward) for
every 400 workers, with up to three committeemen for plants of 500 or
fewer workers and a maximum of seven for plant populations as large
as 2,800. The role of line stewards was specifically ruled out in language that gave them "no function under the grievance procedure." In
contrast, the master contract that Locals 155 and 157 jointly negotiated
in 1938 for Detroit's tool and die jobbing shops mandated Shop Committees "elected in any manner determined by employees," with a
minimum of three and a maximum of seven committeemen for plants
which rarely exceeded 250 workers and often had fifty or fewer. The
contract ratified a system that in Local 155 already boasted 279 shop

stewards, committeemen, and unit leaders for the 6,571 members under contract in 1937. For the thirty-six shops represented by Local 155, the average ratio of shop representatives to members was one in twenty-four.[99]

Rank-and-File Control.   Distrust of top union officials has never been unique to one labor movement. Full-time officers removed from the shop floor necessarily develop a different perspective—for good or ill—from members who tend to judge union performance by the standards of their immediate shop experience. In Britain, with a larger and more established labor movement than any other industrial nation, this rank-and-file distrust of leadership was correspondingly more developed. Within many TUC unions, it found institutional expression in a unique structure of "lay leadership." Before 1890, many craft societies had limited their central leadership to a general secretary, responsible for routine correspondence and the conduct of financial affairs, and monitored by an executive committee of "lay" members still working in the trade. For reasons of economy, this lay committee was drawn from the immediate district where the national headquarters was located— in the ASE's case, London. In 1892, the ASE expanded the Executive Committee to include national representation, followed by the Boilermakers and other metalworking crafts. In some unions, the lay executive was easily manipulated by the general secretary, but "the executive of the Engineers," says Clegg, "could sometimes prove a thorn in the flesh of the secretary." The AEU's 1920 constitution retained the same principal of lay leadership in its National Committee of rank-and-file members, meeting once a year to review leadership decisions and guide future actions.[100]

MESA incorporated the same kind of body in its formal structure. The union's 1935 convention established the National Administrative Committee, composed of one rank-and-file delegate from each local. These NAC members monitored the actions of full-time officers and served as jury members in final appeals of internal disputes. Salaried officials could make recommendations to the NAC, but they had no vote and were subject to dismissal if the NAC so ordered and a membership referendum concurred.[101]

"The MESA has a very definite policy of complete internal control," the NAC boasted during 1938, "in accordance with which men actually working in the shops make up the governing body of the society." This principle operated at all levels of the union, in marked contrast to the top-down procedures in the AFL autoworker unions, the UMW, or the CIO steel-organizing committee. Each of MESA's higher bodies—its District, State, and National Administrative Committees—drew their delegates directly from local-union elections, and these locals retained recall rights for all their delegates. MESA's membership could even cut the general secretary down to size, as in 1934 when Smith persuaded the Detroit District Committee to expel his chief rival, Communist leader John Anderson, but then had to countermand this order when Anderson's Local 7 voted narrowly (sixty-nine to sixty-four) to reinstate him. Delegates to the union's 1935 convention were equally assertive, refusing to accept a proposed per-capita levy to fund the National Office until Smith, in an eleventh-hour gesture during the convention's closing session, threatened to resign if the levy was not passed. The following year, the NAC exercised its right to veto the actions of MESA's full-time officers by rejecting a proposed merger with the Associated Auto Workers of America; surrendering MESA's name, the NAC ruled, was not worth "a few hundred Association members who would join the merger." At the local level, MESA's constitution also ensured that the decision to strike or settle could only be made by a membership vote, not, as in AFL auto unions, by full-time national officers.[102]

Distrust of AFL officialdom was reportedly endemic among tool and die makers, many of whom expressed their opposition in phrases borrowed from Communist party polemics. The success of party propaganda can be legitimately inferred from this, but it can also be overstated. Among MESA's numerous Anglo-Gaelic members, many with experience in British metalworking unions, distrust of union officialdom expressed a cultural predisposition, a mark of their previous experience. It made them receptive to proposals that protected "lay control" of the organization at the local level and, through the NAC, at the national level. It also made them uniquely receptive to Communist party attacks on the top-down interventions of AFL national leaders, though at the same time, as journalist Joe Brown observed, "a great majority of these same [skilled trades]men were definitely anti-Communist in their position." As described in Chapter 6, this commitment to the rhetoric, and sometimes the practice, of rank-and-file control would strengthen the UAW-CIO's tool and die locals in their resistance to Homer Martin.[103]

General Secretary. This artifact of the TUC "model" deserves attention solely as a measure of the Anglo-Gaelic presence in Detroit's early auto unions, particularly in MESA. Whereas the American labor movement, drawing upon republican precedent, usually named its authoritative executive a president, the British labor movement, drawing upon parliamentary and friendly-society models, gave comparable status to the general secretary. Arrangements varied union by union, but in most the secretary was empowered to "correspond" with outlying districts and administer programs mandated by the national delegate body; more often, the president served a largely ceremonial function by presiding at meetings.

The same applied in MESA, with Mat Smith, the union's general secretary, completely overshadowing the little-known president, Jesse Chapman of Toledo. "It was his [Smith's] British influence that resulted in the Secretary's job being the most important job inside the MESA," Elizabeth McCracken recalled. "He did not have the tradition behind him that the President was tops." Neither did the many MESA members and convention delegates whose previous union experience was the ASE or some other British organization. At MESA's second convention in 1934, they readily accepted a series of amendments that eliminated the president's control over other national officers, and transferred the vital task of signing checks to the general secretary. In elections the same year, three candidates for general secretary represented the spectrum of Anglo-Gaelic immigrants: the Belfast Irishman John McGivern, the Scotsman John Anderson, and the Englishman Mat Smith.[104]

Amalgamated Crafts.   This feature of British unionism, described earlier, prevailed in MESA despite the efforts of craft and industrial unionists to amend it. When the former concluded they could not steer MESA onto the straight and narrow path of "sectional" unionism, they departed in 1935 and, led by J. J. Griffen, the American-born MESA co-founder, formed a "sweetheart" outfit, the Society of Tool and Die Craftsmen. The following year, industrial unionists also bolted when MESA refused to merge with the UAW.

The union they left behind was founded, according to Mat Smith, "on the British plan of labor organization, which in turn derived much from the German labor unions." This "German" influence was more evident in the rhetoric than the substance of Smith's claim that MESA was neither a craft nor an industrial organization, but a "fabricated metal workers union." The CIO's brand of industrial unions, "that is, a separate union for each allied division of the metal products industry," would result, Smith predicted, only in bitter jurisdictional disputes between "pseudo" industrial groups. His arguments echoed the TUC's 1927 judgment on the "incoherence" of industrial-union jurisdiction. "Whether this is any advance on the battles of the past between various craft unions," Smith added, "we leave you to be the judge." But judging by the examples Smith cited, only *skilled* metalworkers were sufficiently mobile to achieve cross-industry amalgamation. When striking toolmakers from the United Electrical workers' RCA local in Camden, New Jersey, came to Detroit and sought MESA's help in finding auto-industry jobs, Smith claimed this incident proved his contention "that for labor purposes there is only one metal industry." He ignored the obvious fact that these union men were uniquely mobile precisely because they were "skilled" rather than "industrial" workers. "The MESA is the only real industrial union in the metal industry," another broadside claimed in 1936, predicting that separate unions for workers in auto, aircraft, machine tools, and electrical appliances were "doomed to failure"— and citing as the only "example" for this the fact that "all men capable of making tools and dies *must* be in one union." Smith was particularly blunt on this score in a statement made to the *Free Press* in January 1936, when he justified his call for a "fabricated metals industrial union" by noting that in auto, aircraft, and shipbuilding, "skilled men can jump from one to another of these industries and their interests are identical."[105]

The rhetoric of all-grades cross-industrial unionism, and the continuing practice of craft amalgamation, were both prominent in the British model that Smith so frequently invoked. Britain's Engineers, like their counterparts in the AFL Machinists, had to confront the troubling alternatives for dealing with semiskilled workers: incorporate them into the union and risk diluting craft prerogatives, or exclude them entirely and risk making them allies of management. In 1901, the ASE Delegate Meeting voted by a small majority to endorse the first alternative by establishing a special Machinist Section for semiskilled workers. Members qualified for this "Section E" if they earned at least 75 percent of the district rate; they paid lower dues than full members and also got lower benefits. In 1912, the ASE went a step farther and established a Section F for unskilled workers. Neither innovation worked. Shop stewards still hued to the model of an amalgamated craft union, and their passive refusal to sign up less skilled workers meant Section E boasted fewer than 11,000 members in 1914 and Section F a paltry 1,254. In 1917, the ASE dropped the obvious pretense of its claim to unskilled workers and abolished Section F. It was not until 1926 that the AEU reopened its ranks to unskilled workers with the establishment of Sections V and Va, and not until the 1930s that these sections began to accrue substantial membership. Even then, many of these "industrial" workers were actually skilled men who wished to evade the higher dues of the craft sections.[106]

Smith drew heavily on this British experience when he analyzed the labor movement in the United States. In a 1936 article in MESA's Toledo paper, he argued for wider organization through amalgamation and reminded his readers that "in England, when the Amalgamated Society of Engineers decided to merge with the Toolmakers' Society and the Steam Enginemakers' Union, it was found necessary to pension off displaced officials in order that they would not prevent amalgamation taking place." Since, Smith argued, it was the craft-oriented leaders of the AFL who blocked industrial organization in the United States, "it would be cheap at almost any price to pension off the Greens, Whartons, Hutchinsons, and Wolls."[107]

But in fact, opposition to industrial organization also existed among MESA members, some of whom—Smith included—exhibited the same resistance to wider recruitment that the ASE confronted in previous years. Formally, MESA moved quickly to adopt an industrial structure, first in 1934 when its convention established a separate Section II for production workers, and again in 1935 when the convention abolished that section and merged production and skilled workers into "industrial" locals. However, as with the ASE, the reality belied this formal commitment. With the notable exception of John Anderson and a few others, MESA organizers generally failed, neglected, or refused to recruit less-skilled workers. Whatever formal endorsements the national convention made, "on the ground" many MESA organizers still projected a skilled-trades agenda. A leaflet distributed by the Detroit District Committee in December 1934 is revealing. Calling upon workers to boycott the Automobile Labor Board's representation elections, MESA cautioned its readers that "skilled men are always in a minority in any auto plant, and any basis of proportional representation would place them in a hopeless position as far as numbers are concerned on any so-called Collective Bargaining committee." MESA had other good reasons for opposing the ALB elections (which sanctioned company unions), but this particular argument hardly conveyed a welcoming attitude toward production workers. The less skilled, after all, would be the majority in any industrial union's plant local and could dominate the collective bargaining committee accordingly. The only alternative was a committee that gave *disproportionate* representation to skilled workers—which may have been the only form of unity MESA craft stalwarts would have accepted.[108]

MESA never transcended this craft agenda. After MESA Locals 7, 8, and 9 bolted to the UAW in 1936, only a handful of MESA shops, including Kelvinator, Detroit Gasket, and GM Diesel, had a sizable production-worker membership. First and foremost an amalgamated craft union, Detroit MESA made little effort to accommodate production-worker members. Among the featured events at the union's 1940 picnic at Cedar Point was "Selection of the Skilled Mechanics Contest Winner." There was also a "Ladies Clothes Pin Race," a "Husband Calling Contest," and a "Fat Mens Race," but nothing for production workers of any size.[109]

Such a union, based primarily on skilled mechanics, had sufficient leverage in the 1930s to initiate genuine collective bargaining in Detroit and win a precarious recognition from employers. But craft amalgamation proved to be a durable structure only in the job shops, where craftsmen outnumbered less-skilled workers. It was otherwise in the big captive shops, where the skilled trades represented a small fraction of the surrounding plant populations. Here, MESA was a near total failure. One of the few exceptions was Fisher Body, which concentrated thousands of tool and die makers in its Detroit toolrooms, far removed from the main concentration of GM production workers in Pontiac and Flint. Skilled workers were the overwhelming majority of Fisher's Detroit work force, many of them (particularly in Plant 23) building complex body-panel dies that Fisher could not easily outsource. Otherwise, captive-shop tool and die makers could not afford to go it alone. Ford provided a telling example: when 500 MESA supporters donned union buttons in April 1934, Ford transferred the men to another department, then announced the "closing" of this new department and fired the entire group. Ford had a range of options that job shops lacked: well-organized coercion, transfer of work to other Ford toolrooms, outsourcing, mechanization of simple tasks, and upgrading of production workers into certain repetitive jobs. When Ford, responding to the public pressure MESA applied through the National Labor Board, rehired half of the former MESA men, many of these thoroughly cowed craftsmen must have realized that only an industrial union able to shut down the entire company could bring Ford to heel. MESA, in any case, never recovered its beachhead at the Rouge. Bill McKie, as founding president of the Federal Labor Union at Ford, pursued an industrial-union strategy from the start: to thwart the AFL policy that would eventually divide skilled workers into separate craft societies, he signed up every member as a "production worker" and sent phony names to the AFL's chief auto organizer, Francis Dillon. It is not known what Dillon thought of a local headed by a skilled tradesman but made up entirely of "production workers."[110]

It is known what Mat Smith and his followers thought of industrial-union advocates favoring merger with the UAW. Smith dismissed these opponents as "cloud kissers" and "politicians"; Ralph Covert, another craft stalwart, denounced them as "Reds" and told the *Detroit News* in 1936 that his MESA Local 6 would "clean house" of the pro-UAW faction.

The split found Anglo-Gaelic leaders on both sides, reflecting similar divisions in the British labor movement. Smith, the Englishman, faced an opposition led by three Scotsmen: John Anderson, Bill Stevenson, and James Murdoch. Murdoch, a past national president of MESA and, in 1936, secretary of Stevenson's Local 91 (combining Locals 8 and 9), chided Covert in the press for "raising the old cry of 'Red' just to block the merger." These verbal exchanges escalated to fisticuffs in early May during a District Committee meeting, when John Anderson answered Smith's taunts with a punch in the face. Anderson got the better of Smith in this encounter and certainly won the greater prize when he took the bulk of MESA's Detroit membership into the UAW's tool and die locals. Thereafter, Mat Smith and his MESA stalwarts directed an unyielding invective against the UAW, characterized by a sneering contempt for the "kindergarten diplomats" and "nondescript self-starters masquerading as leaders in the UAW-CIO." No amount of name calling could help MESA recover the initiative after 1936, however, and with the union's decline, the "British model" of craft amalgamation/general unions fell by the wayside. Even so, many of its elements survived in the UAW. Particularly in those plants or industry sectors where MESA had established the first organizational beachhead, UAW locals inherited MESA's emphasis on local autonomy, shop-steward representation, rank-and-file governance, and craft amalgamation. In this respect, the British model had a significant impact on the structure and durability of Detroit's auto labor movement.[111]

A few examples will suggest how that influence worked in many small ways. Al Hughes, a skilled tradesman at Ford Rouge, is referring to his Scots-born father, who emigrated to Detroit in the 1920s and hired into the Ford toolrooms:

I remember a story my father told me, he used to work in the B Building, he was a die maker by trade, and Walter Reuther was a tool maker. He used to go in the lunchroom and debate unionism. My dad would take the English version of unionism and Reuther would take the German method of unionism and they used to have people standing in the doorways of the lunchroom because if any of the plant guards caught them debating unionism . . . they would have been fired.[112]

Without confirming evidence, it remains a matter of speculation what the frequency and content were of these debates over "English" methods (probably craft-amalgamation/general unions) and "German" (probably metalworkers federation). Other fragments of evidence suggest that "British methods" carried considerable weight with American-born workers searching for precedents. Russell Leach, who learned the toolmaking trade at Murray Body and later won the presidency of Local 155, remembered that when he was a boy, British labor was the chief focus of the books given him by his aunt and uncle. Both were American-born socialists, he a skilled woodworker at Fisher Body, she a secretary for the Wayne County Federation of Labor. The first book they gave the teenaged Russell was British writer Robert Tressell's *The Ragged Trousered Philanthropist*, a moral tale of a young housepainter's conversion to socialism. Two other books followed on British labor history, and a third on the German metalworkers union. These readings were chosen with care, Leach recalls of his aunt and uncle, "because both . . . talked about how the labor movement would be successful in the U.S. by 1940. They both had that kind of date." There was no doubt in either's mind where Americans could learn about this future. "I could remember my aunt saying the history of the British labor movement was . . . what would happen in America."[113]

Personal Commitment

A final attribute of the Anglo-Gaelic union leaders' sensibility was his intense personal commitment to the union. "Commitment," a coveted but ill-defined virtue among trade unionists, can be understood as a personal identification with the labor movement that goes beyond a narrow calculation of material benefits. Since many workers have equated union organization with such nonmaterial benefits as "fair play" and "dignity," commitment is necessarily a relative measure, varying by intensity and focus. Among union leaders in auto, the most intensely committed were disproportionately drawn from a left-wing milieu and/or a skilled-trades subculture; Anglo-Gaelic immigrant workers straddled both categories. Many of them saw unions as the foundation for a broader movement that would transform society along socialist lines. Others focused more narrowly but no less intensively on the union as a vehicle for, and a measure of, their personal dignity as craftsmen.

Bill McKie exemplified the first dimension of commitment. In 1932, he worked long hours after his shift to meet with Ford workers and, with his wife's help, publish the *Ford Worker*—all of this at a time when every other AWU shop paper in Detroit had collapsed and many sympathetic observers regarded the organization of Ford to be impossible. McKie recognized the obstacles that demoralized many others but focused his energies on a political goal that went well beyond collective bargaining. "We didn't go in to organize Ford's pure and simple to organize a trade union," he recalled some twenty years later. "We realized that if we could not build the [Communist] Party there that the trade union movement would go the way of all trade unions and be pure and simple a bureaucracy." McKie's presumption that the 2,000 to 3,000 party members he hoped to recruit at the Rouge would necessarily prevent such an outcome seems like polemical cant today. But in McKie's experience, formed primarily by the exuberant growth of socialist organization in late nineteenth- and early twentieth-century Britain, the party could more credibly be identified with social emancipation and proletarian democracy.[114]

Ernie Woodcock exemplified the second dimension of commitment, a perspective that equated the worker's personal dignity with his membership in the union. Leonard Woodcock recalls how his father stuck with the 1935 MESA strike at Motor Products until the bitter end:

I'll never forget after the strike had been going on and was completely dead by this time . . . . There were only four of them left out in the die room and my mother, who was a solid union supporter, said to him, 'look, that strike is over, it's broken. Don't you think it's time you and the other three go back to work?' And I never saw my father in such a fury. He said, 'woman, my union called me *out*, and my union will put be *back*.' "[115]

His union could not put him back, and Woodcock was fired. He must have known then, as did his wife, that there was no prospect of victory. What he struggled to protect, therefore, were the personal values of solidarity and "manly" honor that he equated with union discipline. He could not return to work as a supplicant for mercy and expect to keep these.

There were American workers who exhibited the same personal devotion to the union. As indicated earlier, many of these were skilled tradesmen, socialists, or both. Former members of the UMW also staked their honor on the high ground of union discipline. But when they looked for help raising this standard, there was usually a "Scotty" or a "Limey" from the toolroom already on the scene.

5

CONFRONTING THE LIBERAL STATE

"When Pat Quinn came to this country from Old Ireland he brought with him more than just that keen Irish wit," said the program notes to a 1941 testimonial dinner honoring Dodge Local 3's president. "He brought with him some of that 'sterner stuff' . . . the fervor and zeal of an oppressed people fighting in the Cause of Freedom."[1]

Testimonial dinners rarely produce sober assessments of the guest of honor. But for all its apparent hyperbole, this characterization captures a unique quality in the Anglo-Gaelic union leader, something his American workmates recognized and valued. In 1930s Detroit, UAW organizers had to confront the determined and sometimes violent opposition of city police, Ford Servicemen, and Perrone-gang thugs. Understandably, many a "greenhorn," as Walter Dorosh termed his fellow American-born unionists, would hesitate before confronting these formidable foes. Pat Quinn had already been tested as an IRA captain and revolutionary leader, ultimately landing in a prison of the Irish Free State.

Quinn, unlike most Anglo-Gaelic union leaders, had carried his confrontation with the State to the point of armed struggle. Many of his fellow UAW leaders from the United Kingdom, though they had not crossed this line, had still traveled farther on the road to rebellion than their American-born counterparts. The Dublin Lockout of 1913, the wartime strikes on the Clyde, the Forty-Hours strike of 1919, the General Strike of 1926—these had challenged State authority as much as (in 1926, more than) a particular group of employers. The veterans of these confrontations knew firsthand what it meant to defy the State's coercive potential. Bill McKie had organized pay protests in the British

155

Army and participated in a near mutiny when his regiment refused duty in Ireland; in 1926, he led Edinburgh's labor movement in the General Strike. Fellow Scotsman Dave Miller served a prison term at hard labor for refusing army service during World War I. Mat Smith organized fellow apprentices into the Engineers, led several wartime strikes, became a union officer, and paid for these actions in several jail terms for his refusal to serve in the British Army. When told by his jailers to put on an army uniform, Smith put it on inside out. "Sterner stuff," indeed.[2]

These personal and collective confrontations with the State were not revolutionary actions, except in Ireland, but they were politicized in a way that prepared the Anglo-Gaelic unionist all the more for leadership in Detroit. American workers had also confronted government authorities during strikes, but these confrontations were different in at least two respects from the U.K. experience. First, in the American setting, public authority before 1932 was more often wielded by a municipal or state government, usually on behalf of a court injunction; second, American public officials, particularly judges and state leaders, more often identified with overtly antiunion ideologies that equated labor militancy with criminal conspiracy. In the United Kingdom, on the other hand, industrial conflict more frequently drew the attention of the national State between 1910 and 1926, and the public officials who wielded that State power were (by American standards) predominantly Liberal-Centrist.

Put another way, the Anglo-Gaelic union leader not only had considerable experience confronting the coercive power of the State but also knew the co-optive potential of the liberal welfare state. American-born and Eastern European unionists, in contrast, had considerably less experience with this more subtle adversary. At points, many would succumb to a naive faith in the New Deal and President Roosevelt. Here again, Anglo-Gaelic union leaders had the benefit of experience. Having known Lloyd George and Ramsey McDonald, they had a better idea of what to expect, for good or ill, of FDR. They had a firmer grasp on the role of militancy in galvanizing support and strengthening the labor movement's bargaining position, and a corresponding impatience with American-born union leaders who approached the New Deal with cautious solicitation. While prominent American-born union leaders boasted of their opposition to strikes and their unwavering loyalty to the Democratic party, Anglo-Gaelic union leaders, by advocating strikes and independent political action, gave a vital boost to young militants—native- and foreign-born—willing to pursue confrontational strategies.

The Liberal Welfare State

It would be hard to define exactly when Britain's welfare state emerged from the piecemeal reforms that preceded it, but the year 1906 marked a prominent turning point in that process. In the half-decade following the Liberal party's landslide victory of that year, a reform-minded Parliament passed legislation that substantially transformed the State's role: an Old Age Pension Act provided State-funded retirement income for persons seventy years and older; a Trades Board Act established minimum wages and collective bargaining in various "sweated trades"; a Labour Exchanges Act provided a voluntary clearinghouse for job seekers and employers; and finally, a National Insurance Act, funded by mandatory contributions from employers, workers, and the government, provided medical, sickness, and disability benefits for all workers, and unemployment benefits for a select group of industries (principally, construction, engineering, and shipbuilding). Advocates of these measures argued that the continued growth of urban poverty and cyclical unemployment would overwhelm the limited resources of Poor Law taxpayers and friendly-society members, and that only State assistance could protect the nation's human assets in a time of worldwide economic and military competition. Expediency, urged on by the model of Bismarkian welfare and by a fear that inaction might produce an unruly discontent among the lower orders, overcame laissez-faire principles. "The Liberals," as George Dangerfield described the Asquith government, "still . . . believed that state intervention was unforgivable, and watched with a growing apprehension the abyss which was growing between their theory and their practice. . . . [A]s a kind of capitalist left wing, they advanced upon social reform with noisy mouths and mouselike feet."[3]

The result, as James Cronin puts it, was not yet a modern welfare state but "a sort of bastardized liberalism or, perhaps more accurately, a form of corporatism without Keynes, without the state, and without the cash." The rudiments of public regulation had been established, but with only a minimal administrative apparatus. Government labor exchanges and the Post Office were administrators of last resort for, respectively, unemployment and health/sickness insurance, but the rest of the administrative burden was to be carried by trade unions, friendly societies, and commercial insurance companies. Benefits were also pegged at miserly levels to punish the shirker and goad the able-bodied to self-sufficiency. At a time when the average worker earned twenty-four shillings a week, unemployment benefits equaled less than three shillings a week, and only covered 2.5 million workers.[4]

If Liberals expected "the humble people" to show their gratitude for these paltry benefits, this initiative in public welfare was a failure. Instead of gratitude, a multifaceted unrest confronted successive Liberal, Coalition, Labour, and Conservative governments in the years 1910–1926. Profuse and varied grievances sparked this upheaval: low wages, denial of union recognition, victimization of leaders, dilution of skilled work, hiring of nonunionists, layoffs, conscription, emergency wartime measures, and rising rents and food prices. Until 1920, generally high employment levels and government policies favoring union organization also helped fuel the militancy. But behind these immediate grievances and opportunities, contemporary observers also detected an underlying resentment, a "psychological revolution," as George Dangerfield termed it, against Victorian respectability and deference.[5]

This included a change in how many Anglo-Gaelic workers viewed the State. For it was in the years after 1910 that the consolidation of proletarian life-styles and class consciousness described in Chapter 4 fused with a distinctive extraparliamentary strategy of confrontational bargaining and "sympathetic" action against the government. This growing attachment to Direct Action had several causes. The State's increasingly active role after 1900 and particularly after 1914—intervening in the economy, regulating social welfare, and mediating industrial conflicts—gave political action of some form a high priority for the labor movement. The Labour party was the first and most enduring response to this challenge, and by 1910, with the recent affiliation of the Miners, it had gained the formal allegiance of Britain's major unions and socialist organizations. But parliamentary action was no longer the sole option that workers might reasonably consider. After 1910, the militant suffragettes of the Women's Social and Political Union forced the government to act on their demands by breaking windows and burning buildings; at the same time, militant Ulsterites forced Parliament to exempt them from Irish Home Rule by threatening armed rebellion and fomenting army mutinies. Extraparliamentary strategies won the approval—and sanction—of these two elite groups, and in both cases, Direct Action proved enormously successful.[6]

In this context, the frustration of working-class parliamentary politics was all the more glaring. Having already failed to substantially improve the minimalist welfare programs of the Asquith government, the Labour party suffered the additional burdens imposed by the 1909 Osborne judgment, which prohibited union expenditures on political campaigns. Until 1913, when the Liberal government finally overturned Osborne, financial support for parliamentary representation was legally foreclosed to Britain's unions—a telling argument in favor of the Direct Action practiced by striking coal miners, dockers, railway workers, and thousands of others in these years. When the 1913 Trade Union Act restored the labor movement's right to collect a political levy, the mood of many union activists had changed. ASE delegates favored political action but rejected a levy for the Labour party and denounced its leaders as "political sham fighters" and "nothing but Liberals." The Labour party's subsequent participation in the wartime coalition further tarnished its standing among many workers; "they voted Labour," as Standish Meacham said of prewar supporters, "and agreed that Labour accomplished almost nothing."[7]

Even when the party broke from the coalition in 1918 and adopted a socialist platform, its impressive showing in the popular vote failed to deliver a corresponding representation in parliament: Labour tripled its support from 7 percent to 22 percent of the vote total but added only twenty-one seats to the forty-two it had won in 1910. These results, as the government's Home Office acknowledged in 1919, "brought into being an underground movement for Direct Action on the plea that the House of Commons had ceased to represent the country as a whole." Even when the Labour party won 191 seats in 1923 and formed a minority government the following year, the failure to produce any significant legislation, besides a public housing program, served only to convert more workers to the banner of Direct Action. Despite its socialist pretensions, the Labour party had no alternative program when it took its first tenuous hold on power, and this dismal record was repeated during the second Labour government of 1929–1931. "It would be difficult to state clearly what socialism meant to any of them," historian David Howell has said of the Labour party's interwar leaders, including Ramsey McDonald, ILP secretary and prime minister. "At best, it was a broad human fellowship; at worst, an easy rhetorical device for silencing critics." McDonald's socialism did not include nationalization of industry or government support for striking workers. With no alternative conception to guide government policy, his two minority governments invoked the familiar Liberal party nostrums: balanced budget, protection of the colonies, defense of the gold standard, and continued free trade. When McDonald's second Labour cabinet, confronting worldwide depression, voted by a slim majority to appease bankers and cut unemployment benefits in 1931, the Labour party repudiated these measures and the "national" government that McDonald subsequently formed. Only in the depression decade that followed did the Labour party repudiate laissez-faire economics and adopt a Social Democratic model of Keynesian growth and "public-utility" socialism. In the meantime, its previous failures had enhanced the alternative strategy of Direct Action. Goals which many felt they could not win in Parliament—shorter hours, minimum wages, shop-floor rights, government subsidies, nationalization—workers sought to win in the mass picket lines and sympathetic strikes of 1919–1926.[8]

Amid some spectacular failures, particularly after 1921, the strikes and political mobilizations of 1910–1926 also consolidated some hard-won, if lesser (and sometimes unanticipated) gains. The Labour party grew from fringe group to government-in-waiting, supplanting the Liberals; welfare regulation expanded with enactment of rent controls, creation of public housing, and the fivefold extension of unemployment insurance to twelve million workers in 1920; permanent unionization took root in a wide range of industries—including railways and the docks—where previous organization had been fitful or nonexistent; national agreements became more common; wages fell slower than prices after 1920; and during the war and its immediate aftermath, shop-floor representation flourished in multiple form, from the left-wing Shop Committees referred to in Chapter 4, to the "Joint Works Councils" recommended by the government's Whitley Report. The unrest provoked official repression against Irish rebels and left-wing shop stewards but also forced the liberal State to grope toward some kind of bargained adaptation, an accommodation that incorporated new forms of protest within reformulated norms. The Ministry of Munitions frankly acknowledged this latter goal in its official history of the war years: the Shop Stewards' Agreement it forced upon engineering employers and unions in 1917 gave recognition to a restricted form of shop-floor representation in the hope that "officially approved works committees . . . would help check the more revolutionary tendencies of the shop stewards' movement by bringing it into an ordered scheme." Similar considerations motivated the government's promotion of joint labor-management Whitley councils. "There was a substantial fear in some quarters," historian Rodger Charles says of Britain's wartime government, "that the end of the war would lead to a real challenge to the existing order. Some acceptable alternative must be found. The Whitley Councils provided it."[9]

In the rest of industrialized Europe, shop-floor factory organization proved to be equally contentious, and malleable. To German and Italian revolutionaries, the left-wing factory councils that grew during the war and its aftermath represented embryonic Soviets, lacking only a political program to guide them from syndicalist futility to revolutionary potency. But during the war, European governments also sanctioned official forms of shop-floor representation, both to preempt more militant movements and to facilitate the ongoing renegotiation of work rules and manufacturing technology for military production. After the war, government leaders in Germany and Italy worked to incorporate these new forms of shop-floor representation in the restricted norms of the Weimar government's 1920 Factory Councils Act and the Giolitti government's stillborn parity commission of the same year. Factory councils, Charles Maier observes, "could thus hold either old union beer or new revolutionary liquor. Bourgeois leaders were prepared to drain a glass if the workers agreed to the weaker potion."[10]

The Anglo-Gaelic workers who left this European context for Detroit carried with them the contradictory potentials of their recent past. As participants and, in some cases, leaders in the strikes and mass mobilizations of 1910–1926, many Anglo-Gaelic immigrants had gained the experience of confronting the government and forcing change. Some, including Bill McKie and Pat Quinn, had pursued a revolutionary agenda in their confrontations with the State; the majority had more modest goals. Historians and participants have since debated whether Britain's revolutionary minority could or should have led the majority into explicitly insurrectionary acts. Against the backdrop of insurrection in Ireland and general strikes in Europe, it was easy to equate the Red Clyde in 1919 with Red Petrograd, but the alluring congruence of form—factory committees and mass struggle—obscured a divergence of goals and resources. Russian, Eastern European, and, to a lesser degree, German and Italian metalworkers were recent arrivals in the factory, and the previous prohibition or restriction of their political rights had prevented or slowed their identification with liberal reformism. In contrast, British metalworkers had won piecemeal improvements in their conditions through a long history of gradual reform, dating back to the 1850s. They were impatient and rebellious after 1910, and many would support extraparliamentary Direct Action, but their rebellion generally focused on the *policies* of management and the State, not the legitimacy of these well-established institutions.[11]

James Hinton describes the characteristic ambivalence that many an Anglo-Gaelic engineer must have carried from wartime Britain to Detroit. In war industries where skill was in short supply but craft practices were under attack, "it was the combination of a very powerful bargaining position with a very strong sense of insecurity that made engineers . . . such an explosive force." Their protest merged two agendas, that of the "revolutionary engineer" and of the "militant craftsman." The first backed left-wing stewards and favored the demand for "workers' control" because this slogan transposed the craftsman's prideful assertion of workplace hegemony into class terms that included the ascendant semiskilled. The second, the militant craftsman, also backed left-wing stewards and demands, but only if they defended craft prerogatives against encroachment by both management *and* the semiskilled. These two agendas, as Hinton observes, "certainly describe categorically different stages of consciousness; but both states may well have coexisted, and interacted, in the same head." If so, the consequent ambivalence usually resolved itself in favor of demands that protected "past practices" and craft privilege—the wage differential, control of the machine, restoration of prewar shop rules, and defense of the craftsman's exemption from military service. The craft tradition, Hinton concludes, failed "to yield up its revolutionary ore without the clinging dross of exclusiveness."[12]

"Revolutionary methods appear," said George Dangerfield of the prewar unrest, "but not revolutionary intentions; distrust and respect for political democracy are hopelessly intermingled; the Government is simultaneously attacked and defended, and by the same people." If, as Steve Jefferys says of American auto-labor history, worker resistance and subordination share the same moment, Anglo-Gaelic union leaders in Detroit oscillated between these two potentials at a point closer to resistance than their native-born and Eastern European counterparts in the 1930s. The mainstream of British (if not Irish Nationalist) labor may have been marked, as Rodger Charles argues, by "a respect for conciliation, for negotiation, for proper procedures, for finding justice within the British system of law and politics," but, he adds, "it has been made to fight every bitter inch of the way."[13]

That fight was sufficiently bitter between 1910 and 1926 to mark a generation of Anglo-Gaelic immigrants with a unique capacity for confronting the liberal State.

Confronting the New Deal State

The identity and specific roles of secondary union leaders in the 1930s cannot easily be confirmed when documentary evidence is lacking. More often than not, the local union's written records are spotty or nonexistent for the initial period of union formation. Contemporary newspaper accounts can fill some of the gap in Detroit, where the frequency and magnitude of militant action sensitized some reporters to the shop-floor basis of autoworker organization. But more often, editors either ignored this story altogether or, when a strike demanded their attention, were satisfied with misinformed reporting on the spontaneity of crowds, the actions of top leaders, or the murky presence of radical subversion. Left-wing papers often reproduced the same themes with different conclusions, celebrating the spontaneity of the masses and congratulating their own leadership at the expense of all others. Individual participants also have their own ax to grind when describing past events, and even the most considerate usually convey only the immediate circumstances of his or her experience.

This lack of clear documentary evidence often prevents definitive conclusions about the influence of Anglo-Gaelic union leaders on events. How determining a role, for example, did Bill McKie play in organizing the Ford Hunger March of 1932? Fellow Scotsman and party member Billy Allan, reporting some twenty years later in the *Daily Worker*, wrote that McKie, "along with others," played a pivotal role. Other evidence strongly supports Allan's claim. McKie, like many Anglo-Gaelic radicals, had past experience leading unemployed demonstrations and "hunger marches" in Britain. Given this background, he would have been a natural candidate for implementing the same tactic in Detroit. McKie's leadership of awu and Communist party cadre at Ford Rouge—the target of the march—and his active participation in Detroit's unemployed councils also suggest the likelihood that he played an important role in planning the demonstration. But how determining was his British experience in shaping the Ford Hunger March? The Rouge may have been targeted, in part, because McKie's leadership had sustained the only functioning awu organization in Detroit's factories. But the prominence of Henry Ford also made the Rouge a natural target, and the widespread unemployment and near-starvation of 1932 made others besides McKie capable of formulating a hunger-march scenario. McKie, in fact, may have played only a modest role, "along with others," in developing a strategy endorsed by the Communist party and implemented by the entire Michigan leadership.[14]

Fortunately, there are cases where the evidence allows more definite conclusions. Three such moments are described below: the 1933 "riot" of mesa strikers; the 1936 sit-down strike at Midland Steel; and the 1937 sit-down at Dodge Main. In all three, the leadership role of Anglo-Gaelic militants in confronting the liberal State can be identified with reasonable certainty.

The 1933 mesa Riot

At 10:00 a.m. on Monday, 30 October 1933, in the sixth week of mesa's inaugural strike, an unusual motorcade made its way to the Koestlin Tool and Die Corporation on Detroit's West Side. The *Detroit*

Free Press later reported that the cars were "of the large, expensive type, and were two or three years old," reflecting, apparently, the last remnant of predepression status still owned by the tool and die makers who drove them. Packed into these automobiles were, according to subsequent police estimates, several hundred MESA strikers. Acting "with the precision and speed of a motorized military force," they disembarked at Koestlin and, joined by picketers already at the site, "surged about the building, crashing bricks and stones through the windows." To ensure that management could not continue production with strikebreakers, the attackers broke into the plant, carried the blueprints for work in progress out into the street, and burned them in a bonfire. As they left, they also overturned several cars owned by plant managers and set one on fire. "They want an Open Shop?," one striker asked as he pitched a milk bottle through a window, "We'll give them an 'Open' Shop."

The motorcade then split in two and departed for other targets. Until late in the afternoon, the strikers eluded the police while moving from one strike-bound plant to the next, storming the gates and burning blueprints at seven shops. Finally, the police intercepted MESA's "flying squadron" at the Murray Body plant and, after a brief clash, arrested eight men. With this confrontation, the "riot" ended.[15]

J. J. Griffen, the American-born diemaker and MESA leader, condemned the attacks and told the press that "none of the Society's members was in that group." No one believed this disclaimer, though subsequent events strongly indicate that Griffen was not an enthusiastic supporter of the "riotcade." Communist party opponents of MESA's leadership condemned the strategy of "Smith and Griffen" and warned that such violent actions would only "give the police the excuse they want to shoot down honest militant workers." But MESA members probably drew different conclusions about this strategy, for within days of the riot, the previously deadlocked negotiations between the union, the employers, and the federal government suddenly produced the compromise settlement that gave MESA de facto recognition. Mat Smith, unlike Griffen, did not deny the allegation of his Communist opponents that he had sanctioned the attacks; years later, he frankly admitted that MESA had "not opposed" the action and had only repudiated it for the public record.[16]

The "wild ride" of the Mechanics Educational Society was significant on several counts. First, it was a rare case of "collective bargaining by riot," a form of worker protest practiced in Britain during the first half of the nineteenth century but virtually extinct by the twentieth century. Second, this brazen defiance of public authority was undertaken by a union of foreign-born tradesmen, predominantly British, led by a Lancashire engineer who refused to become an American citizen. Finally, although the rioters targeted the property of specific employers who refused to bargain with MESA, it was the federal government's newly established regulatory machinery that, by failing to force collective bargaining on the employers, provoked the anger of MESA strikers.

The federal government's role was especially important in this strike, for like other major industries, auto was now embedded in a web of public regulation that was both complex and largely untested. Under guidelines established in June 1933 by the National Industrial Recovery Act, the federal government allowed the National Automobile Chamber of Commerce to draft a "code of Fair Competition" to govern the industry's recovery. Other industries used this code-drafting process to implement restrictive trade practices previously prohibited by antitrust laws, but the auto industry, having already achieved oligopolistic stability, limited its code to regulation of labor practices. In the final form which President Roosevelt signed in August, the Automobile Code in a mere four pages did little more than establish a minimum hourly wage of forty-three cents, an average workweek of thirty-five hours, and a maximum limit for any one week of forty-eight hours. The code also diluted the NIRA's Section 7a by adding a provision allowing the companies to treat employees "on the basis of individual merit, without regard to their membership . . . in any organization." Implementation of this code was the responsibility of the Detroit area NRA Compliance Board, but matters were complicated by the fact that the Automobile Code covered only the captive tool and die shops of the big companies, not the independent job shops still covered by the blanket code of the President's Reemployment Agreement. Moreover, at the request of the jobbers, this latter code's regulation of maximum hours was diluted in September, shortly before the MESA strike, to allow longer hours than the Automobile Code and to exempt altogether "individualist" employees working to complete dies "on schedule." These contradictions in regulatory procedure, with different sectors of the tool and die industry covered by different codes and different policies, would frustrate and prolong efforts to settle the 1933 strike.[17]

MESA's confrontation with this new regulatory apparatus developed through four stages. In the first, Mat Smith and other MESA leaders entertained the hope that the NRA Compliance Board might pressure the employers to negotiate a single agreement covering both captive- and job-shop workers in the three cities—Detroit, Pontiac, and Flint—where MESA was on strike. The union delegation to the Compliance

Board, consisting of Smith, Griffen, and Harry Spencer, the London-born machinist and chairman of the Pontiac strike committee, was soon disappointed. General Motors indicated that it would not merge negotiations covering its plants in Flint and Pontiac with those covering Detroit, and captive-shop employers in Detroit refused to include the jobbers in their negotiations. MESA opposed separate settlements, since the ability of manufacturers to shift their tool and die work between job shop and captive shop, or one city and the next, meant they would favor whichever sector settled first or lowest. Abner Larned, chairman of the Compliance Board and a retired clothing manufacturer, lacked the power and the will to bring the employers to the bargaining table.[18]

The union thought it might get a more sympathetic hearing from the second federal mediator who now arrived on the scene, John Carmody, an industrial engineer sent from Washington by the chairman of the National Labor Board, Senator Robert Wagner. Carmody's appearance at an early strike gathering in Detroit's Arena Gardens drew an ovation from 7,000 MESA members. Ten days later, however, Smith and MESA attorney Maurice Sugar issued a public statement condemning Carmody for failing to take an assertive role and acting, instead, "as a mere conveyor of messages from one party in the dispute to the other." In the meantime, said Smith and Sugar, the companies had violated Section 7a by refusing to bargain, had routinely circumvented code limitations on overtime, and were now hiring strikebreakers on "yellow dog" contracts and providing some with firearms. "It would indeed be regrettable," the statement warned, "if the National Administration would . . . take . . . action in this matter only if and when disturbances and violence make their appearance."[19]

In response to the union's public complaint, Carmody, who had two days previously told the *Detroit News* "the situation needs just a little more time to ferment," promptly reversed himself and called on the National Labor Board to hear the case in Washington. Having already jumped through two regulatory hoops, the union approached this third round of federal mediation with considerable skepticism. The five-man MESA delegation to Washington consisted of Griffen, Sugar, and three Anglo-Gaelic leaders: Smith, Spencer, and the Scottish engineer Frank McCracken. When they arrived in the hearing room on 18 October they discovered that GM and the National Automobile Chamber of Commerce had declined the NLB's "invitation." On top of this snub, NLB members, led by employer representative Gerard Swope of General Electric and labor representatives William Green and George Berry of the AFL (no friends of a "dual union"), told MESA the NLB could do nothing for the union because, instead of properly formulating its demands and delivering them to the employers before the strike, it had only finished this process of formal notification several days after the strike began. The union delegation was told to return to Detroit and send a second notice of its demands to each employer, with a formal request for individual, company-by-company negotiations.[20]

Four days later, Mat Smith and Maurice Sugar reported to a mass meeting of MESA strikers at Deutsches Haus, the East Side German hall where the union held frequent meetings and social gatherings. Both condemned the NLB in blunt terms for attempting to break the strike with delaying tactics and for favoring employers who ignored the law and refused to even attend NLB hearings. The strikers' mood certainly was not brightened by the additional news that the NLB had just established yet another regulatory body, the Detroit Regional Labor Board, with five employer members and five labor members—all of the latter representing AFL craft unions. MESA had been frozen out a fourth time.[21]

The strikers could vent their frustration with these events at the wrestling match and fund-raiser the union organized two evenings later at Deutsches Haus—the "Main Attraction" consisting of "A 'Rat'" who would "challenge from the ring to Wrestle any striker in the audience." Four nights later, Saturday, 28 October, the strikers at another Deutsches Haus meeting chose a far more tangible target for their anger. "Shortly before midnight," labor journalist Joe Brown wrote, after speakers had again denounced the NLB and the employers, "the suggestion was made by a member of the Auto Workers Union that following adjournment the strikers visit the Brigg's Vernor Highway plant and 'if a few windows are broken and some rats mussed up so much the better.'" The strikers, Brown reported, adopted this suggestion "with a whoop" and piled in their cars or made their way to the plant on foot. There, a large crowd—one estimate claimed 3,000—broke windows and set a strikebreaker's car on fire before being dispersed by police. Some 500 strikers then made their way to the Federal Engineering plant, also on the East Side, and smashed windows with rocks and milk bottles.[22]

This mini-riot gave organizers a rough blueprint for the highly organized "riotcade" of the following Monday, 30 October. Despite the Communist party's subsequent denunciation of the motorcade, the contributing role of AWU members at the Deutsches Haus meeting of 28 October indicates that "Direct Action" had won significant rank-and-file approval in both of MESA's main factions—Scotsman John Anderson's left-wing radicals (allied with the Community-led AWU) and

Englishman Mat Smith's more moderate radicals. When the motorized strike force embarked on its "wild ride" that Monday morning, it departed directly from the MESA union hall.[23]

Thereafter, the union was indelibly stamped with a reputation for militancy. "We don't meander with the NRA," Smith later declared, "but fight any encroachment of the bosses by direct action in the plants concerned. . . . We feel that labor can obtain its needs only by the power of organization." The strike also confirmed Smith's preeminent leadership position in MESA. At the start of the 1933 walkout, as chairman of the strike committee in Flint (where he was temporarily based as an organizer), he shared the limelight with fellow Englishman Harry Spencer, chairman of the Pontiac strike committee, and J. J. Griffen, the American-born strike leader in the union's Detroit stronghold. At the close of the strike's first week, however, Smith was elected sole chairman of a joint strike committee covering all three cities, and Griffen began the gradual decline in influence that ended with his separation from the union. Smith rose to solitary command of the union not only because he was willing to lead or, when events sometimes outran him, tolerate militant action, but also because he publicly ridiculed the cautious diplomacy of AFL leaders and adopted instead the blunt, threatening tone of an angry mechanic. "No strike is a lost strike," he would warn. "You weed out the chaff and find out who are your 'real' unionists." This kind of hard-edged rhetoric, hurled at owners and government officials alike, must have given embattled MESA members a vicarious outlet for their own frustrations. But whatever the rhetoric, the union did not adopt the hyperactive and uncritical militancy of the AWU, which followed the then current (until 1935) Communist party practice of attacking all New Deal liberals and agencies as betrayers of the working class. Even after the disappointments of federal intervention in the 1933 strike, MESA pursued a strategic halfway approach to the Regional Labor Board. At the close of the strike, when the Detroit Federation of Labor's Frank X. Martel, one of five union representatives on the board, generously offered his seat to MESA while he was out of town, the union accepted and put the Belfast engineer John McGivern in Martel's place. In January 1934, the NLB expanded the Regional Labor Board and, with Martel's endorsement, appointed Mat Smith to the new position. Smith did not remain for long, however. In May he resigned, explaining in a letter to Senator Wagner that "even one-horse employers treat Board recommendations with derision."[24]

The confrontational bargaining that characterized MESA strategy toward the New Deal contrasted sharply with the cautious diplomacy of most American-born auto-union leaders. In March 1934, when Presi-

dent Roosevelt established the Auto Labor Board (ALB) and sanctioned
company unions, Mat Smith publicly denounced the settlement as "a
shabby joke"; William Collins, AFL organizer in auto, called it "the biggest victory [autoworkers] have ever won." Collins, in contrast to
Smith, thought no strike could ever end in victory. "I never voted for a
strike in my life," he told auto manufacturers. "I have always opposed
them." So did his successor, the American-born patternmaker Francis
Dillon. "We do not seek strife or trouble," said Dillon, "but wish to carry on our work and negotiations with management in an orderly and
business-like way." Steeped in a tradition of defeat and marginaliza-
tion, American-born union leaders initially approached the New Deal
as grateful supplicants, and until 1935, local leaders in the AFL's Federal
Labor Unions were overwhelmingly in agreement with this strategy.
Roosevelt's 1934 ALB settlement disappointed many activists and members, but most American-born local leaders agreed with Collins that,
given the union's narrow membership base, they should avoid confrontation and rely on the president's promise to protect them. "He
asked us to trust him," Indiana-born Richard Byrd, secretary of the
Pontiac FLU, said of Roosevelt, "and we will." In June of that year, when
the AFL convened the National Conference of UAW Federal Labor
Unions, a sizable majority of the delegates favored continuation of direct AFL control and, with it, continued reliance on federal protection as
an alternative to strikes. Among the eleven men elected at this meeting
to the newly formed National Council, there was even greater support
for the AFL's cautious approach. "In fact," concluded one internal
memo of the Detroit AFL office, "there is almost no indication [among
them] of any inclination to object to Federation policies." Two groups
of dissidents did challenge AFL authority after the conference, but only
one of these, the Cleveland District Auto Council organized by Wyndham Mortimer, represented a demand for greater militancy. The
second, led by Auto Labor Board member Richard Byrd of Pontiac and
Arthur Greer of Hudson Motors, took the AFL to task for being *too* critical of management and the ALB. The Associated Automobile Workers
of America, formed by Byrd and Greer that summer, pledged itself to
even greater cooperation with employers and the federal government.[25]

It could be argued that the contrasting militancy of MESA's Anglo-
Gaelic union leaders may have reflected not their past experience in
Britain's combative labor movement, but their superior bargaining leverage and self-esteem as skilled tradesmen. There is certainly no doubt
that skilled tradesmen, both foreign- and native-born, possessed more
bargaining leverage in 1933–1939 than production workers. But the

presence *within* MESA of visible ethnic divisions between American-born and Anglo-Gaelic leaders also indicates the contributing role of culture. These divisions were prominent in the breakaway movement led by the American-born diemaker J. J. Griffen. By 1935, Griffen had apparently concluded that MESA was too militant to suit his moderate tastes and too devoted to Mat Smith to suit his leadership ambitions. When the MESA convention of that year voted to reduce the number of top officers from five to three, Griffen was one of the two officeholders cut from the roster. Two months later, he quit the union and dropped from sight. In 1937, he reappeared as the "general chairman" of a new union, the Society of Tool and Die Craftsmen (STDC). Opinion varied on the origins and intentions of this organization. Mat Smith claimed that job-shop employers funded Griffen's operation. "Whenever the MESA or the UAWA distributed leaflets in front of a tool and die shop," Smith told journalist Joe Brown, "within 24 hours J. J. would have an agreement for a closed shop for his outfit." Griffen, on the other hand, declared that the STDC was the only legitimate craft union in the tool and die industry. There is no evidence, however, that Griffen ever led the STDC on strike against an employer; most of his polemical energy was directed instead at "the communist element" in the labor movement. Griffen hoped that his proclaimed purpose of "creating harmony, cooperation, and contact between employer and employee" would win his union recognition without strikes. But if this made the STDC a company union, it was not an organization that most companies wanted: in its first year, the STDC signed only sixteen contracts with Detroit jobbing shops. The evidence suggests, therefore, that the STDC, whatever the merits of Smith's allegations, represented the same conservative, anticommunist, and craft-oriented union principles advocated by the AFL—which also disavowed strikes, proclaimed its common purpose with management, and signed sweetheart contracts at the expense of MESA and the UAW. There is little doubt, in any case, where the STDC stood in relationship to the Anglo-Gaelic immigrants who predominated in MESA and the tool and die locals of the UAW. "This Society has been built by and for the American craftsman," the STDC announced in an early leaflet. "In our . . . shops . . . we are governed by . . . American union principles."[26]

In practice, those principles subordinated auto-union strategy to the "procedural action" of State-regulated mediation. Griffen, Collins, Dillon, Byrd, and many other American-born leaders looked upon President Roosevelt as their protector and hoped the NIRA and the ALB would strengthen their fledgling organizations. They had no taste for confrontational bargaining and little confidence they could achieve their goals through strikes. When federal mediation proved to be ineffectual, these leaders either were unprepared for Direct Action or, like Griffen, recoiled from the violent potential of mass mobilization. Federal labor policy did move away from mediation toward arbitration after 1933, but this gradual policy shift had little to do with the cautious strategies of Griffen and Dillon. It had a lot to do, however, with the kind of militancy displayed in the MESA strike. Even before the riotcade of 30 October, NLB secretary William Leiserson cited the MESA walkout as a key example of the federal government's flawed strategy. "Mediators have failed," he wrote NLB chairman Robert Wagner,

because employers insisted they would not recognize unions of employees or strikers' committees. When the cases [MESA and two others] came before the Board, therefore, they should have been handled as matters for arbitration . . . [to determine if] Section 7(a) did or did not require recognition. . . . Instead, the Board attempted to mediate, with the result that the whole matter . . . was left as something to be fought out in industrial conflicts . . . as it was before Congress enacted Section 7(a).[27]

Leiserson's remarks must have acquired even greater urgency when the MESA strike escalated into violence on 30 October. With this spectacular evidence that mediation was a failure, advocates of arbitration and more direct federal intervention began to gain the upper hand among policymakers. Other events and social forces shaped the evolution of New Deal labor policy, but the Direct Action of MESA's Anglo-Gaelic leaders and members helped jump-start the process.

In the meantime, Griffen's conservative brand of "American" trade unionism was the dominant perspective among native-born union leaders in 1933–1934. By 1935, when Griffen left MESA, and certainly by 1937, when he formed the Society of Tool and Die Craftsmen, this cautious outlook was rapidly losing ground to a "nativist" articulation of militant industrial unionism. Many American-born "greenhorns," reacting to the AFL's failure, adopted the new idiom of confrontational bargaining from MESA's example. In the sit-down strikes and organizing drives of 1936–1937, these American-born leaders would play a far larger role in Detroit's autoworker militancy. But the Anglo-Gaelic influence would still be prominent and at key points decisive.

The 1936 Sit-down at Midland Steel

At 11:30 A.M. on Friday, 27 November 1936, first-shift workers at the Midland Steel Products Company, maker of body frames for Chrysler and Ford, stopped work and seized control of their plant. Demanding uniform wage increases for all departments, sit-down leaders announced that the strikers, reportedly numbering between 600 and 1,200, would remain inside the two-story plant until management renegotiated its earlier wage offer. The first sit-down strike in Detroit and Michigan, and only the second in the nation's auto industry, had begun. Victory here and in the Flint General Motors strikes that followed catalyzed a steadily growing wave of sit-downs in Detroit, where some 35,000 strikers (by newspaper estimates) in more than 120 workplaces "sat down" during the next four months. Detroit, the citadel of the open shop, suddenly became a union town.[28]

"Revolutionary methods appeared," to again paraphrase George Dangerfield, "but not revolutionary intentions." Autoworkers marched in the streets with American flags, and sit-downers occupying the Woolworth department store sang "America" when their boss refused to negotiate. Resistance and subordination occupied the same moment as sit-downers simultaneously defied the sanctions of private property but adopted patriotic symbols to sanction their lawlessness. They broke the law to uphold it: denied their workplace rights under the Wagner Act, the strikers seized the workplace and held it hostage until the owners agreed to obey the union's interpretation of the law. "We are determined to win and hold these rights," UAW Local 157 announced in response to conservative calls for legislation banning sit-downs, "knowing full well these rights must be established outside the courts before they will be recognized within the courts." The Anglo-Gaelic toolmakers who dominated the leadership of Local 157 noted the long history of British legislation restricting workers' rights, from England's fourteenth-century Statute of Artificers to its 1799 Combination Acts—the latter marking "the extreme in oppressive labor legislation." They rejected any claim that sit-downers were guilty of illegal trespass or that Congress should outlaw sit-downs. "It is the height of absurdity," Local 157 declared in its lengthy brief against such legislation, "to contend that a worker who . . . [has] contributed a substantial part of his strength and energy to his employer's enterprise has the same status as a mischievous stranger or interloper." Against the owner's property rights, Local 157 counterpoised "the property right of the worker in his job" and insisted that "the courts and armed forces of the state shall not be used to enforce the demands of the employer that the premises be vacated."[29]

This right to "withhold our labor power upon the premises of the employer," as Local 157 put it, won growing support from diverse groups of workers during the winter of 1937. But the previous fall, in November of 1936, only a handful of organizers and a minority of workers were prepared to initiate such bold action. At Midland Steel, it was the Scotsman John Anderson who led the way, backed by former MESA members in the toolroom. Union organization in the plant went back to 1933, when Midland's 120 tool and die makers joined MESA's citywide walkout. After the strikers attacked Midland during the "riot-cade" of that year, the company settled with MESA but refused to increase wages. Thereafter, Midland's tool and die makers formed a vital core of John Anderson's support in MESA Local 7. In 1934, when Mat Smith and the Detroit District Committee moved to suspend Anderson for his Communist activities, it was Midland's skilled tradesmen, along with workers from Ternstedt and Clayton Lambert, who testified against Smith in Local 7 hearings and voted for Anderson in the balloting that narrowly reinstated him.[30]

When Anderson took Local 7 out of MESA in May 1936, and merged it with the newly chartered UAW Local 155, Midland's workers already had a significant history of organization. They continued to meet at the ABC ("Arbeiter Bedung Club") Hall on Mack Avenue that previously served MESA Local 7, and their fourteen chief stewards became a UAW bargaining committee. They also continued to look to Anderson for leadership. He had not yet taken a formal position in the leadership of Local 155, but as a full-time organizer for the national UAW his duties made him the de facto leader of the East Side tool and die makers, the chief negotiator for the Midland workers, and the founding editor of their shop paper, *The Midland Flash*. As before, tool and die makers gave the union its initial base at Midland, led by the Yorkshire machinist Sam Brear, the Kentucky-born diemaker Tom Dyer, and the German-born toolmaker Anton Boll.[31]

"In the tool room a precedent has been set that all employees should be in the union," the first edition of *The Midland Flash* reported in November 1936, just before the sit-down.

When a non-union oiler was sent in, there naturally was objection from the other workers. The boss of the tool room stated that he had no objection to anyone joining the union but he didn't know what could be done about the matter. The Shop Steward replied: "There is a simple solution to the problem. Just send the man to me with $2. We will take him into the union and you will get your machines oiled by union labor."[32]

With this organizational base, UAW Local 155 was able to win bargaining rights at Midland without a strike. The company had a reputation for liberal policies on labor and other personnel matters, and on 14 November (two weeks before the sit-down) management agreed to open negotiations with the UAW. The two sides quickly reached agreement on key union demands: an eight-hour day (down from ten), time and a half for overtime, seniority rights, and union recognition. The only snag concerned the company's proposed five-cent wage increase for hourly workers and 10 percent increase for piece-rate workers. The union objected to the uneven impact of this two-tier wage proposal and called for across-the-board increases in all departments. Welders were especially unhappy with management's offer of a $.95 base rate, since it failed to meet their demand for $1 an hour and fell well below the $1.25 the union said Chrysler paid its welders.[33]

Even with these problems, Midland's mid-November offer would have produced a settlement with many UAW organizers. The union had not yet signed a single contract in Detroit, and here was a company willing to grant recognition, the eight-hour day, seniority, and wage increases—terms the UAW would accept in many other first contracts over the coming months. Yet Anderson proceeded with secret plans for a sit-down strike. His motives are hard to determine in the absence of known documentary evidence, but personal and political ambition may well have played a role. As a full-time organizer on the UAW's national staff, Anderson certainly was aware that a successful sit-down strike in the stronghold of the open shop would accrue considerable prestige for himself and the Communist party. But these circumstances could also indicate an opposing, or at least parallel, scenario: a successful Detroit sit-down would clearly advance the UAW's organizational goals, and Anderson was in a unique position to engineer such a victory. His long association with Midland's toolmakers and his successful efforts, even before MESA Local 7 jumped to the UAW, to organize production workers gave the union a stronger base at Midland than most other plants in Detroit. Midland's work force of 1,900 made it a significant target, without posing the formidable organizational and leadership problems found in the large assembly plants of Chrysler and Ford. And a sit-down strike at Midland would certainly draw attention, since the plant was a key supplier for chassis frames to Dodge, Plymouth, Chrysler, Lincoln, and Ford Truck. A successful sit-down here would quickly cripple production in Detroit's biggest assembly plants, providing immediate and compelling testimony for a tactic that workers, until then, had only read about in reports from France, Akron, and South Bend.[34]

These larger strategic concerns probably had a greater impact on the decision to call a sit-down than the immediate issues in the wage dispute. Anderson made that decision with the knowledge of the UAW's national director of organization, Richard Frankensteen, but with little support or input from the union's top leaders. National officers and staff in the UAW's Detroit offices were preparing for a showdown with General Motors and remained largely unaware of Anderson's plans. Then, "all of a sudden," recalled Henry Kraus, editor of the union's national paper, "we hear there's going to be a strike at Midland Steel." Kraus saw an "anti-red" attitude in the indifference most showed toward this news. "Weak as the union was," he recalled, "I was really shocked that they would have this attitude toward John. . . . I think [he] realized very much that he was being boycotted by the whole crowd in the International."[35]

When the sit-down began, many Midland workers were also surprised by its sudden arrival. "There is still some confusion in the minds of some of the fellows as to why we are striking," the *Midland Flash* acknowledged in its first Strike Edition. "Some of the men think everybody is happy except the welders." This frank admission by the union's strike publication indicates a considerable gap between the sit-down's stated aims, which some workers found unconvincing, and its larger strategic goals, which apparently went unstated. A. L. Faulkner, sent by the federal Conciliation Service to mediate the strike, was equally puzzled by the circumstances of the sit-down. "I found a peculiar situation," he reported in his 30 November letter to the Labor Department. "Anderson and Frankenstein [sic] who are 'under men' in the union organization, are 'over men' with the workers in Detroit." Faulkner had discovered that Homer Martin, the UAW president, and others in the national office had little knowledge and less control of the Midland strikers. It was the "under men," Anderson and Frankensteen, who were calling the shots, and Faulkner recognized that they apparently wanted to prolong the strike and cut off the supply of frames to Detroit's biggest assembly plants. "Looks as if Anderson and Frankenstein would hold back until they got all the others out and then step in and make a settlement." In fact, by the fifth day of the strike, Plymouth and Lincoln had announced sharply curtailed production, Chrysler assembly operations were virtually closed down, and more than 50,000 workers were temporarily idled—joined, according to Faulkner's estimate, by 10,000 more every day. Faulkner tried to circumvent the "under men" and restore stability by appealing to the UAW's top leaders. "I contacted Martin over the heads of Anderson and Frankenstein as I knew there was no use trying to settle with them. . . . Martin agreed it [the strike] was a mistake and would do everything possible to bring about a settlement."[36]

Anderson had other difficulties besides Martin's hasty impulse to settle. Sustaining the necessary unity to conduct a strike is never an easy matter, but Anderson faced a particularly daunting array of divisive issues. In addition to the confusion surrounding the strike's goals, there was the differential impact of the company's wage offer. Certain departmental and occupational groups fared better than others, and some, as noted above, thought everyone was happy except the welders. However, this potential for friction was neutralized by the experience and discipline of Midland's veteran activists. "Though several of the departments were satisfied by the original terms granted by the company," *The United Automobile Worker* reported, "they were willing to strike in full support of the demands of others whose grants [sic] were not sufficient. The tool and die makers and others were among the most self-sacrificing in this respect and are to be honored."[37]

The greater challenge to a unified strike came from the unique racial and gender divisions in Midland's work force. While all but a handful of Detroit auto manufacturers concentrated black workers in marginal or noxious occupations, Midland's liberal personnel policies gave African-Americans significantly wider representation in its production departments (though not in skilled trades). The 500 black workers at Midland represented roughly 30 percent of the work force, a far higher percentage than the national auto-industry norm of 4 percent. As in many auto plants, some were segregated in all-black jobs, but as historian Peter Friedlander found in "mapping" the ethno-occupational topography of Midland, many blacks worked as assemblers and welders on the integrated Plymouth-Dodge frame lines. This unusual incidence of job integration accounts in part for the unusually high participation of black workers in the Midland sit-down. Unlike the situation at other plants, where blacks were either absent in significant numbers or physically segregated from the initial centers of union growth, many black workers at Midland Steel labored in close proximity to the East Europeans, Italians, and migrant Protestants who predominated in semiskilled production jobs. At the same time, John Anderson's left-wing and industrial-union politics obligated him and his followers to a strategy that incorporated these black workers into the union. The tangible representation of this integration was Oscar Oden, the young black assembly worker who served on the strike committee.[38]

Union organizers paid far less attention, however, to the 150 women who worked as small-press operators in the Midland plant. "There were anti-feminine elements in the shop that kept the women [out]," recalled Henry Kraus, one of the few International staff who worked with Anderson on the strike. "Didn't even ask them. . . . 'Who cares whether we have them or not?'" Initial press reports indicated that local union leaders asked all 150 women to leave the plant at the start of the sit-down and set up a strike kitchen at the nearby Slovak Hall. Apparently, however, things were not so cut-and-dried, for a sizable number of women did not welcome this move or the sit-down strike. Dorothy Kraus found considerable confusion, and some resentment, among the night-shift women she encountered outside the plant on the sit-down's first day. "Dorothy approached them," her husband Henry recalled, "and they said . . . 'what do they [the sit-downers] think they're doing , without asking us, just striking, shutting the plant . . . , not letting us work,' . . . you know, words to that effect." Dorothy persuaded the women to come with her to Slovak Hall, where they found Anderson conducting a large strike meeting. "I see some ladies in the back here," he said after some time, as Dorothy recalled. "I wish you would come forward. Maybe you can help us." When the strike leaders asked the women to prepare food for the sit-downers, Dorothy led a group to the back of the hall, where they established a makeshift kitchen. Out of these ad hoc events, the UAW established its first Women's Auxiliary.[39]

There was a recent precedent for this innovation. During the 1933 tool and die strike, MESA had formed an auxiliary and addressed leaflets to the wives of the strikers. Noting that "recently in a court of England" a scab had been defined as a traitor to his trade, "an enemy to himself, to the present age and to all posterity," MESA had asked that wives support their husbands and back the strike. "Your husband will be needed on the picket line. . . . Expect him to be a man." Three years later, when the UAW reconstituted the Women's Auxiliary at Midland during the sit-down, it marked an equivocal step toward widening the UAW's base. The auxiliary brought the wives into the union and strengthened the strike's "home front"; but by also relegating women *workers* to the auxiliary's kitchen, the union's male leadership made it clear where they thought these women belonged.[40]

John Anderson was not immune to these beliefs. "My impression of John was that he was anti-feminine," recalled Dorothy Kraus. "I'm not talking about him as a union organizer . . . [but] as an individual. He gave that impression quite often . . . that somehow or other we weren't in the same society. . . . They [the men] were sort of the elite, you know." But in the sit-down strike, when normal rules of law and behavior were suspended and the union had to mobilize every available resource, attitudes changed. "In the strike, he was terrific, he was very grateful and mentioned the women ever so many times, practically every time he spoke to the members, he always . . . [said] what wonderful work we did." Many members also came to rely on the auxiliary. "They would come up," Dorothy remembers, "and ask me and the others if it's possible . . . to go and visit their wives." These house visits and the daily routine of food preparation engaged many of Midland's women workers throughout the strike, but the younger women soon began to abandon the kitchen for the picket line, leaving wives and older women to perform the traditional "women's jobs." Some wives also joined the picket line or visited their husbands at the plant as they delivered food, clothing, and razors.[41]

In the meantime, federal mediation of the strike proceeded, with a second commissioner of conciliation, James Dewey, joining A. L. Faulkner in talks held at the downtown Book-Cadillac Hotel. With each day, the sit-down was closing more plants and bringing considerable notoriety to the Midland strikers. "The greatest demonstration of solidarity came on Wednesday night," *The United Auto Worker* reported, "when two departments of the Dodge local, after their meeting, got into their cars and formed a caravan of some 300 autos, parading before the plant amid tremendous cheers." The next day, Midland's president, F. J. Kulas, arrived from the company's Cleveland headquarters to join the talks. A settlement quickly followed on roughly the same terms as the company's mid-November offer, with an improvement in the hourly wage increase (from five to ten cents), but with the same bad news for welders, who got only half the increase. In addition, Kulas publicly promised to eliminate all piecework wages and prepare a straight hourly pay schedule "as soon as practicable." The union made much of this concession, but it may only have been for public consumption: when Midland's workers agreed to a new contract one year later, the agreement still provided for piecework incentive wages.[42]

Even though the sit-down's contract gains were a disappointment compared with what the union had already won in previous negotiations, they still marked a decisive victory in the eyes of union militants. The important lesson was that union recognition and collective bargaining could be won in the heartland of the open shop, and John Anderson's sit-down strategy was the symbolic agent of this victory. Equally telling, the courts and "the forces of the state," as Local 157 put it, had not been used to evict the strikers, though later sit-downs would confront this challenge. Above all, the Midland sit-down gave the union valuable experience in the tactical dynamics of Direct Action and confrontational bargaining, including the vital role of community mobilization, publicity, and the organization of women. The sit-downs that immediately followed at Kelsey Hayes Wheel, led by tool and die maker Walter Reuther, and at General Motors, where the UAW won its single most important victory, built upon the Detroit precedent of John Anderson and the Midland toolmakers.

In the wave of sit-down strikes that followed these watershed victories, Locals 155 and 157 established their initial base in Detroit's tool and die job shops. Their success built upon the previous years of MESA organization and the momentum of "sit-down fever" generated by the strike at General Motors. Generally, little in-plant preparation was necessary. "I did not even know they were organizing our plant," recalled Orrin Peppler, a machinist at Buell Die and Machine, "until one morning when I went into work the place was closed and there was a sign out front, 'This Place is On Strike.'" After a two-week occupation, the union won recognition and a signed agreement for Buell's 250 workers.[43]

Local 157 quickly exploited the victory at Buell with sit-downs at other major job shops on the West Side, including Star Tool and Die and Koestlin, while Local 155 led sit-downs at Richard Brothers, Joseph Lamb, and a half-dozen other plants. As at Buell, strike tactics required little advance preparation. Direct Action was the order of the day, and union organizers dispensed with even the pretense of State-sanctioned mediation or certification. With the knowledge of only a few inside supporters, Local 157 would send a dozen outside organizers into the plant and call a sit-down. "We told them to sit down and then we would call the meeting," recalled Blaine Marrin. "We would have a hall close [by], for instance a beer garden near that place. We would bring these people in and get them signed and go into management." Organizers were prepared to use "brute force," Marrin remembered, but "there was very little resistance." MESA's previous organization had prepared the way, and many smaller shops signed agreements without a strike.[44]

Out of the initial chaos of organization, Locals 155 and 157 established a rough jurisdictional boundary along Woodward Avenue, Detroit's principal north-south roadway. Local 155 represented shops on the East Side and 157 covered the West Side, but this geographic division was apparently amended by a political demarcation. According to Russ Leach, "the Socialists would have the West Side and the Communists the East Side," and some plants that fell within the geographic realm of one local opted for membership in the other on these political grounds. Local 155 was thereafter known as the organizational center of Detroit's Communist party, led by Scotsman John Anderson and the American-born business agent Nat Ganley. Local 157, in contrast, was characterized by a diffuse "left-wing" politics that encompassed the Socialist party and support for the Spanish Republic. American-born organizers took leadership roles in both locals, but Anglo-Gaelic leaders were predominant, particularly in Local 157. Scotsman Bill Stevenson quickly rose from recording secretary to president, defeating incumbent Howard Barbour for that position in March 1937. The Belfast Irishman Robert Crothers replaced Stevenson as recording secretary, while Clydesider George Handyside served as vice president and chairman of the Executive Board, London-born William Hulle served as financial secretary, and fellow Londoner Alan Strachan (transferred from Chrysler Local 7) served as trustee.[45]

The 1937 Sit-down at Dodge Main

In the early afternoon of Monday, 8 March 1937, three weeks after the UAW's Flint victory at General Motors, John Zaremba's foreman called him to the phone in the Heat Treat Department of Dodge Main. "My hand is on the left lapel," said the voice of Frank Reid, Executive Board member of UAW Local 3. Acting on this coded message, Zaremba set in motion carefully laid plans for the biggest sit-down strike in American history. After telling his men to bank their furnaces, Zaremba, the local's recording secretary, sent word of the sit-down to the hundreds of union stewards in the plant. Within a half hour, some 25,000 workers had stepped back from their machines and work stations, bringing production to a standstill throughout the cavernous complex straddling the border of Detroit and Hamtramck. Many workers left the plant. Those who remained—the union claimed 10,000—began to barricade the gates. Simultaneously, UAW leaders called sit-downs at Chrysler's eight other Detroit plants and at Hudson Motors. According to newspaper accounts, some 17,000 Detroit workers had occupied ten of the city's biggest factories, with many more gathering in the streets.[46]

The Dodge sit-down marked the apex of Detroit's sit-down wave, and the culmination of three years patient organizing. Unlike Midland, tool and die makers did not lead the way. Dodge Local 3 traced its lineage not to MESA, but to a company-sponsored union based among production workers. Established in 1933, Chrysler's "Works Council" had successfully preempted the AFL's Federal Labor Union at Dodge. But by establishing a plant-wide structure of elected representatives, it also gave any Dodge worker—or group—the opportunity to seek a wider following. This proved to be a fatal weakness in the company's strategy. In 1935 the Works Council's hourly representatives, encouraged by the right-wing populist Father Coughlin, declared their independence and rechristened themselves the Automotive Industrial Workers Association (AIWA). Soon after breaking with Coughlin and merging with the UAW in 1936, the Dodge local demonstrated its appeal by winning forty-eight of fifty-three seats in Works Council elections, after which the UAW delegates resigned their positions and called on Chrysler to begin negotiations with Local 3. The company agreed to talk but reserved the right to also negotiate with other "minority" representatives, including the rump Works Council. Holding to the old Auto Labor Board's proportional-representation formula, which the NLRB had since repudiated, Chrysler refused to grant sole bargaining rights to a union that, despite its success in winning Works Council votes, still had only a minority of dues-paying members in the work force.[47]

Only a few of these were tool and die makers. Several of their number played an important role in building the union at Dodge, but as a group, toolmakers had no significant impact on events. Compared with General Motors and Ford, Chrysler "outsourced" more of its tool and die work, reducing the absolute size of its captive shops; and compared with Midland or Fisher, Dodge's work force in the toolroom was dwarfed by the thousands of production workers concentrated in the plant's foundry, forge, press rooms, paint departments, trim shops, and assembly operations. MESA was rarely able to establish a continuing presence in captive toolrooms, and this was especially true at Dodge, where the AIWA and the UAW also failed to garner significant support in the toolroom. At the time of the sit-down strike, Local 3's membership was concentrated in the same production departments where the local drew its leadership: five of the top eight officers came from the Body Trim Department, two more came from Pressed Steel Parts Assembly, and one from Heat Treat. Trim and Pressed Steel had also been the strongholds of the AIWA, which gave its first two "locals" the numbers 99 and 76, respectively, after their departmental designations. Tool and die members remained on the periphery of organization. Lacking the bargaining leverage that tool and die makers possessed at Fisher Body or Midland, and lacking the votes to capture leadership in the union, tool and die makers at Dodge may well have preferred the relative benevolence of Walter Chrysler and K. T. Keller (former machinists, after all) to the rough-and-tumble politics of a production-worker union they could not control. Three weeks before the sit-down, E. H. Wilsher, chairman of the Works Council, reported to management that tool and die workers were only just beginning to consider a change in allegiance. His source on this score was diemaker George Miller, who told Wilsher that only a few of his co-workers in Department 57 "have been interested in the union in the past, but

[they] are beginning to feel it may be advisable to join as they are under the impression that production workers who are organized have enjoyed more rate increases than they have."[48]

Among these beleaguered diemakers there must have been Anglo-Gaelic tradesmen whose ambivalence toward production workers—"fellow proletarians" or competing "upgraders"—resolved itself in favor of a defensive aloofness from production-worker organizing. But if the craft dimension of the Anglo-Gaelic sensibility here inhibited union activism, the class-cultural dimension of that sensibility still impelled individuals toward union leadership. Bert Manuel, a Scottish coal miner who emigrated to Detroit in 1923, earned a reputation as "Mr. Union" in the Dodge body shop, where he organized secret meetings in 1935, was a key leader in the 1937 sit-down, and subsequently rose to unit chairman, member of the Plant Committee, and member of Local 3's Executive Board. Tom Hanlon, the Tyneside engineer who emigrated in 1926, was chief steward and sit-down leader in the toolroom and served as plant committeeman and publicity director during the 1939 strike. David McIntyre, a skilled welder and twenty-seven-year-old Clydesider when he emigrated in 1919, rose to local leadership from his base in the Maintenance Department. Initially a chief steward with no position on the Executive Board, McIntyre was nevertheless one of a half-dozen men who dominated Local 3's business meetings in the months immediately before the sit-down. His prominent role apparently stemmed from leadership of the in-plant stewards' organization. Formally established in January of 1937, it provided for the election of 180 chief stewards, who in turn appointed some 800 line stewards. These stewards confirmed McIntyre's pivotal position in the embryonic shop structure shortly after the sit-down's conclusion, when they voted him their overwhelming support to become Local 3's first chairman of the Plant Committee. Pat Quinn, the former Irish revolutionary and president of the AIWA's Paint Department local, played an even more prominent role in union organization at Dodge, rising during the sit-down strike from chairman of the Food Committee to sole "inside" leader. Quinn thereafter won election to the union's top posts, becoming chairman of the Plant Committee in 1938 (succeeding McIntyre) and president of the local in 1939.[49]

It was the 1937 sit-down that catapulted McIntyre and especially Quinn into prominence. This large-scale undertaking in collective defiance of the law required careful planning and steady leadership for its success. But despite plans that specified, as Zaremba put it, the "what, when, and where" of each person's role, the sit-down produced considerable confusion as strikers took possession of several million square feet of factory space. The first order of business was to pare down the number of sit-downers to a manageable size. When the union made its first rough census of the occupying force on the sit-down's second day, it had dwindled to 4,000, and this, leaders announced, had to be cut nearly in half to reduce the cost of feeding the strikers. The union contracted with the plant's regular caterer, the Conant Factory Lunch Company, to feed the sit-downers for the first two days of the strike, after which the Local 3 Women's Auxiliary, aided by Dorothy Kraus, prepared meals in the plant cafeteria. The Food Committee that directed their efforts was led by Pat Quinn, who first appeared in the plant's daily strike paper, *Dodge Main News*, as one of the "Brain Trusters" who brought order to this vital task. "Brother Quinn of the Paint Division is to be congratulated on his handling of the food detail," the paper commented on the strike's third day. Another anonymous scribe referred in the same edition to "Our Hero . . . 'Con' Quinn . . . [who] is not a confidence man, but we have LOTS OF CON-FIDENCE IN PAT!" Two days later, Department 91 placed a notice in the paper thanking Quinn, "the old Hunger Striker," for "his valiant efforts in providing the most excellent mulligan."[50]

The daunting logistics of feeding more than 2,000 sit-downers was only one of several problems the union faced. Another was the very uneven support for the sit-down. Some departments had more participants than they could handle, particularly the perennial strongholds, Trim and Pressed Steel. The latter reported that one-third of its members sat in, and "when one-half of these were forced to go home there was a fight for the privilege of remaining." Other departments, however, had only a handful of sit-downers. Chief steward Tom Hanlon, the Tyneside engineer, reported that only thirteen men had joined him in the Department 31aa toolroom, and none from the toolroom in George Miller's Department 57. "Knowing that Department 57 was unable to organize quite as quickly, their moral support and a few of their men at the gates to assure us of the same, would be appreciated." A subsequent report indicated that a few of the Department 57 toolmakers did join the sit-down, but most held back. Even men who had supported the union in its previous organizational efforts stayed away, according to local officer John Zaremba, out of fear that participation in this illegal act would cost them their jobs.[51]

Zaremba later recalled a far more dangerous problem which he and other leaders soon became aware of: "Dave McIntyre registered a complaint at a regular meeting of the stewards' body on the inside of the plant, during the strike, that things were leaking out of this body to the corporation, and that a check had to be put on it as soon as possible."[52]

Company spies had been a problem for union activists since 1933, when half of the twenty-eight participants in the Federal Labor Union's first meeting were fired the next day. One company-paid spy, Jack Andrews, had even won union office and become a close personal friend of local leader Dick Frankensteen. Andrews was no longer in the union, but the company, it appeared, still had spies in the plant.[53]

Equally troubling was the uneven discipline among the sit-downers. Trim, one of the better-organized departments, reported that its members "were under sort of C.C.C. Camp Rules," but in some departments chaos reigned. The first two issues of *Dodge Main News* reported numerous cases of minor pilferage: candy machines pried open and plundered, storerooms broken into, small parts stolen. Some workers also found the sudden and total elimination of plant supervision an irresistible opportunity for such "undisciplined horseplay" as racing jitneys around the plant and driving new cars parked in the storage lot. These episodes, combined with several small fires and the ever-present possibility of police attack, prompted a countermovement for tightened discipline in the plant. On the fifth day of the sit-down, Fred Roe described in *Dodge Main News* how Pat Quinn's Paint Department had already established the means to produce such results. Exhorting others to instill discipline as "a practical daily affair," and not just a "theoretical viewpoint," he announced that "we men who constitute Departments 92–93 have set up a Kangaroo Court which has as its objective the teaching of discipline by practical application." Punishable crimes included failure to carry out assigned duties, to accept orders, or to keep the immediate area clean. "An Army without discipline is a *beaten* Army," Roe reminded his readers, "and we men and brothers of Dodge Local 3 are an Army . . . though we may not parade in uniforms and brass buttons, nevertheless we are engaged in a battle of far greater magnitude than the one in which many of us took part, over in France." The sit-downers were fighting, said Roe, not only to secure an "American standard of living" but also for posterity—"the breaking off of the shackles of Labor Slavery!!"[54]

Quinn became the man who would lead Local 3's "army" into this battle. "From the fourth day of the sit-down until evacuation," said a later program "Testimonial" for Local 3's president, "Pat Quinn was Chairman of all the activities in the Plant." Daily reports in the *Dodge Main News* began to refer to him as the "Police Chief," a title he initially shared with Carl Bennett, a leader in the Pressed Steel Department. Quinn used his position to strengthen discipline and, simultaneously, increase the staff for strike-kitchen duties. "To all district Kangaroo Courts," the strike paper announced: "Send all men guilty of minor infractions to the kitchen. We can use some Kitchen Police." By the end of the sit-down's first week, the strike paper was full of notices urging discipline and reporting the deliberations of various departmental kangaroo courts. These measures apparently worked, at least in the eyes of the strike paper's unnamed editor. "Well, under the leadership of C. Quinn, Bennett [*sic*] we are getting things started pretty good. Everything is running to perfection." Thereafter, notices continued to appear reminding sit-downers to stay in their departments after 9:00 P.M., primarily to reduce loitering and the attendant "grief and confusion" for men "placed under suspicion." Strikers were not to operate machinery unless "appointed by the Police Chief," C. Quinn or Carl Bennett.[55]

The strike paper also tried to clarify the aims and methods of the sit-down, particularly with respect to the law. On the third day of the sit-down, the correspondent from Department 76, Pressed Steel, expressed his opinion on this larger matter: "The men in the factory seem to be real Americans, good citizens, some property owners. They want to have real collective bargaining which rightfully belongs to them and guaranteed [*sic*] by the United States Government. They want to have fair play with management; they have Democracy within their union."[56] Chrysler, of course, did not regard the sit-down as "fair play." On the strike's third day, the company petitioned the Wayne County Circuit Court for an injunction against the occupation, announcing simultaneously that the sit-downers had "terminated their employment" and were "no longer employees of the plaintiff." The company made it clear that it regarded the sit-down as a revolutionary challenge to property and due process. "This is a damnable lie!" *Dodge Main News* thundered at the close of the sit-down's first week. "We are Union men on strike for RECOGNITION. Strikes are legal. Chrysler is trying to crush all strikes by labeling them REVOLUTION! This is an old trick used by the big-shots, dragging in the RED SCARE. STICK TO THE SHIP BOYS!!!" Having rejected revolutionary intentions, the paper nevertheless invoked revolutionary slogans. "You know what Patrick Henry said. 'I do not know what course others may take, but as for me, Give me recognition or give me ????' "[57]

The sit-downers' resolve would soon to be tested. On the occupation's eighth day, circuit judge Allen Campbell issued an injunction against the occupation and ordered the men to leave the plants. "There can be no compromise between the rule of law and the rule of violent self-help," he announced in his public statement accompanying the injunction. "Even if the Wagner Act is valid, it can hardly be contended that failure to abide by its terms give the defendants the right to seize and appropriate $50,000,000 of property." The judge gave the strikers until 9:00 A.M. on 17 March to comply with his order. George Wilson, president of Local 3 and one of the few union leaders in the courtroom, said the Dodge sit-downers would vote immediately on whether they would obey or resist.[58]

Their decision was made clear that day in the strike paper's instructions for defense of the plant. As each department took its assigned responsibility for defending a particular entrance, the sit-downers began to wedge skid boxes full of steel against the gates. "We had bins of steel of the throwable size right across the front end of the Campau [Street] side, on the sixth floor," recalled Walter Duda, a sit-downer from the Trim Department. If it came to a police attack, "we were gonna drop it on 'em." The strike paper speculated that Governor Murphy would not call out the National Guard to enforce the injunction, "but if he does, remember that the Flint strikers won out even though the Guard was there." The paper further warned against those who spread the "propaganda" that the sit-downers should leave the plant and rely on an outside picket line, as specified in the court injunction. "Boys, this is TREASON. Let's get these rumors stopped, also the stoolies that are spreading it." The paper also left no doubt whom the strikers were to look to for leadership in their coming confrontation with the State. "Our Chief of Police, Patrick Quinn, a former member of the Irish Republican Army, knows just how to deal with traitors. Get on your toes and let Pat do his stuff." The sit-downers' police chief had now become their general.[59]

When Judge Campbell's deadline expired at 9:00 A.M. on 17 March, the county sheriff found an estimated 10,000 picketers massed at the Dodge plant, with at least 2,000 sit-downers barricaded inside. Thousands of picketers also concentrated at the seven other Chrysler plants still held by sit-downers and named in the court order. At Dodge, the UAW flag was raised to a position beneath the American flag on the plant's roof, while picketers stretched their line around the entire two-mile circumference of the complex. An effigy hanging from the fence, labeled "Rat No. 1, fence-jumper," reviled those sit-downers who had quit the plant. New signs also appeared on the gates: "Give us liberty or give us death" and "Welcome Sheriff, we are here to stay!" *Dodge Main News* articulated the ethical grounds for this open defiance of the courts. "We believe that the agencies of government . . . should concern themselves with 'HUMAN RIGHTS' as well as the 'RIGHTS OF PROPERTY.'"[60]

With the sheriff powerless to enforce the injunction, the sit-downers remained in open defiance of the State. Frank Murphy, Michigan's recently inaugurated governor, took note of this on 17 March when the court deadline expired. "It must not be overlooked," Murphy announced, "that more important even than the interests of the parties directly involved . . . is the maintenance of public order and respect for public authority, as represented by the police and the tribunals." Finding fault on both sides, Murphy specifically singled out "backward employers who refuse to recognize properly the right of collective bargaining." But this staunch New Dealer, while he pledged himself to the defense of human rights, also made it clear that he equated these with "the authority and integrity of our courts" and the protection of private property. There were limits, the governor emphasized, to his forbearance in using force to reassert authority. Murphy soon met with top leaders from both sides, urging the UAW's Homer Martin to evacuate the plants in return for the governor's guarantee they would remain closed during negotiations. Few believed that Governor Murphy would risk potential bloodshed by forcing the sit-downers out of the Chrysler plants, but the political pressure for some kind of settlement was mounting rapidly. In Michigan's state capital, the Democratic floor leader in the Senate, William Palmer of Flint, introduced legislation that would make it a felony to participate in a sit-down strike. Palmer denied this was an Administration bill, but his high rank in the state Democratic party created speculation about Murphy's relationship to the initiative. In the meantime, across the border from Hamtramck, Detroit police began evicting sit-downers from several smaller plants, one of them, Bernard Schwartz Cigar, in the immediate neighborhood of Dodge Main. Tensions inside the Dodge plant rose sharply in the early morning of 19 March, when the sit-downers discovered a sizable fire in a tunnel beneath the main factory building. The *Detroit News* reported that the sit-downers allowed the Hamtramck Fire Department to enter the plant but barred the city police. It took the firemen four hours to extinguish the blaze, which sit-downers accused company guards of setting.[61]

As pressure for a settlement grew, *Dodge Main News* reminded the sit-downers of previous cases where the UAW had been lured into premature evacuation, principally at Cadillac in Detroit and GM's Guide Lamp in Anderson, Indiana. On 23 March, after two weeks inside the plant, the Dodge sit-downers voted "unanimously," according to the paper, to stay behind their barricades until the company granted sole recognition. The following day, however, it became clear that the in-plant leadership was not unanimously behind the sit-down. On 24 March, *Dodge Main News* announced under the headline "Smoke Out the Rats!" that "Carl Bennett, Chief Shop Steward in Department 76 has been expelled from the Union for being a company stool pigeon." The paper further cautioned that those advocating evacuation before a contract was signed "are possibly Stool Pigeons!!"[62]

An accompanying poem in the same edition of the paper, entitled "A Respectful Soul," described in verse how the sit-downers had dealt with a lesser rat, one Joseph Rubin:

> 'Stand Prisoner,' they said to him
>   'And listen to Chief Quinn
> You learn that with a life of crime
>   A post you will never win.'
>
> Patrick Quinn rose up with rath [*sic*]
>   Already written on his face
> 'Are you another man like Bennett
>   Do you seek his place??
>
> To the kitchen, off with him
>   For hours he shall slave
> With honest toil and sweat-dewed brow,
>   His soul may help his self.'[63]

Proposals to evacuate the plants apparently sparked an increasingly bitter debate among the sit-downers and their supporters. Judging by the content of the strike paper, much of this dissension focused on the participation of Communists in the strike. *Dodge Main News* was emphatic on the topic. "If you find a man that is always damming the communists," the paper warned on 25 March, "that is a red-baiter. He is one of two things; he is either a STOOL PIGEON OR A DAMN FOOL!!" When some objected that the *Daily World* was finding its way into the plant, McIntyre countered that if the government allowed it in the mails, the union should allow it in the plant. But the issue suddenly became moot when the UAW's top leadership announced a tentative settlement. During the morning hours, union leaders visited the plants to explain that state troopers would padlock the gates after the sit-downers evacuated, ensuring that the company could not recommence production during negotiations. The *Detroit News* reported bitter antagonism toward the settlement at two plants, Chrysler Jefferson and Dodge Main. At the latter, where 2,000 sit-downers were still barricaded behind the gates, "union leaders met considerable opposition when they first broached the evacuation plan. They debated with the men for several hours, and gradually the opposition subsided." When a vote was finally taken, UAW leader Dick Frankensteen claimed there were only twenty "no" votes.[64]

Two weeks later, John L. Lewis and Walter Chrysler signed an agreement which both sides called a victory. The UAW foreswore future sit-downs, while the company agreed to recognize the union and not to "aid, promote, or finance any labor group . . . for the purpose of undermining the UAW." This did not meet the sit-downers' original demand for sole recognition, but supporters of the agreement claimed that the company had, in effect, abandoned its company union and recognized the predominant power of the UAW. The sit-down had forced the company to accept this face-saving compromise, which marked the end of the Auto Labor Board's "proportional representation" plan in the Big Three auto industry. This was not clear at the time, however, and many sit-downers felt they had been betrayed. Pat Quinn soon emerged as leader of this militant opposition within the local. At the first business meeting following the sit-down, local officer Dick Frankensteen, the "administration" candidate for president in upcoming local elections, attacked an unnamed "clique" that was trying to take over the local. Pat Quinn immediately rose in response. While opposing cliques of any kind, Quinn also announced that the members "want officers who are and will be progressive." Quinn lost to Frankensteen by a 2-to-1 margin in the elections that followed, but his continued prominent role in the stewards' body and on the local's first bargaining committee gave him the opportunity to steadily build his base. By 1939, when the UAW confronted Chrysler in its final battle for recognition, it was Quinn who led the union at Dodge Main, the principal arena for this showdown.[65]

In that year, Local 3 had the full spectrum of Anglo-Gaelic leadership: the Irishman Pat Quinn was president, while the Scotsman David McIntyre and the Englishman Tom Hanlon held two of five positions on the Plant Committee and generally dominated its proceedings. As Chapter 6 will indicate in some detail, these three men played the decisive roles in the union's 1939 victory. Over the previous three years, UAW activists at Dodge had not been able to rely on the New Deal state—the Wagner Act was not ratified by the Supreme Court until after the sit-downs, and the NLRB's regulatory powers had not yet been confirmed. Dodge workers had turned, therefore, to confrontational bargaining with employers and the State, and as they did so, they came to rely on the proven ability of Anglo-Gaelic leaders to speak the language and implement the practice of Direct Action.

Building a Labor Party

For a movement that had to break the law or change it, the obvious complement to Direct Action was Political Action. During the Chrysler sit-down, union leaders were emphatic on this score. "Get ready to line up union members for elections to come," Homer Martin announced at a massive downtown rally on 23 March. "I want you not only to work together, but to fight together, march together, strike together and vote together." From the same speaker's platform, Frank Martel, president of the Detroit AFL, called particular attention to Detroit police commissioner Heinrich Pickert, who had directed police assaults on several occupied plants. "After the next election," Martel promised, "we will have a police commissioner who will put human rights above property rights." Leo Krzycki, CIO representative and vice president of the Amalgamated Clothing Workers, told the crowd how this could be done. "Organize politically into a labor party and your rights will be protected."[66]

Before 1929, only a minority of American-born workers would have drawn this link between workplace rights and the need for a labor party. But for roughly half of Britain's industrial workers, such a link had become axiomatic by 1929, when the Labour party won 37 percent of the vote and a plurality in Parliament with 288 seats. In contrast to the AFL, which divided its efforts between nonpartisan lobbying and fitful endorsement of Democratic and Progressive candidates, British labor had achieved a level of sustained, independent political organization surpassed only by the German labor movement. The accompanying transformation of British politics was still a recent memory for Anglo-Gaelic immigrants: the 1918 municipal elections, which first established the Labour party's urban base, had occurred just fifteen years before the advent of the New Deal and the promise of a similar transformation in Detroit.

As with workplace organization and Direct Action, the presence in Detroit of experienced political activists from Great Britain and Ireland would help advance the political mobilization of American workers in the 1930s. Relatively speaking, however, their impact was less determining in the political realm than in the workplace. There were at least two reasons for this. First, although American-born workers were comparatively unfamiliar with the idiom and practice of shop-floor organization, the majority had some experience with electoral politics and a minority knew the rudiments of political discourse and mobilization. The nature and scope of their experience was certainly different from that of their British counterparts. In Detroit, saloon keepers, temperance advocates, ethnic leaders, Americanizers, Progressives, socialists, "Good Government" reformers, municipal contractors, realtors, trade unionists, businessmen, and grafters all vied for power and influence in a political spoils system. In Britain, on the other hand, the paternalistic and ethno-religious politics of the nineteenth century had given way to a new class-bound discourse as the Labour party won British workers and Irish Catholics away from the Liberals. Consequently, British workers spoke a different political dialect. But "politics" was not a foreign language in Detroit, and American-born union activists were correspondingly less dependent on their immigrant tutors from Britain.

Second, although the Anglo-Gaelic union leader had greater experience with the *independent* organization of labor politics within the welfare state, the unique structure of American politics made it difficult to replicate that independence in Detroit. In terms of program, Anglo-Gaelic immigrants were well suited to speak the language of New Deal reformism, but organizationally, they confronted a two-party system that had long frustrated the efforts of native born social democrats and labor radicals. Britain's Labour party had forced its way into a two-party system, but the structure of parliamentary politics placed fewer obstacles in the path of such a challenge. British voters did not directly choose the holders of executive office, but voted for parliamentary candidates whose party affiliations determined which party—or parties—would subsequently form a government and select a prime minister. Starting from its regional strongholds in Scotland and the North, the Labour party's initially small delegation could still wield some influence on events by "brokering" its support to the Liberals; since the latter were hard-pressed to maintain a majority in the face of Conservative and Unionist opposition, the Labour party's handful of representatives wielded a disproportionately greater influence on events. A vote for Labour was not, in this sense, a wasted vote, particularly since the party had a secret pact with the Liberals to avoid head-to-head confrontations between 1903 and 1918.[67]

The contrast with American politics is striking. Here, direct election of executive leaders on a winner-take-all basis put a premium on building the broadest possible coalition: even a 49 percent showing in a two-party presidential election left the losing party with nothing to show for its efforts. Third parties could mount local campaigns that won municipal office, but the multiple tiers of state and federal government diminished the power of these lower officials, and local elites often rallied behind antisocialist "fusion" tickets to defeat third-party challenges. Only a national party with a credible chance of winning the White House and the governor's mansion could sustain long-term political loyalty, and the necessary resources for such a coast-to-coast campaign dwarfed the financial and organizational assets of America's undernourished labor movement. In 1912, the American Socialist party won 6 percent of the vote, leaving them a distant fourth in the presidential balloting and with no congressional seats; two years previous, the British Labour party with just 6.4 percent of the vote sent forty-two representatives to Parliament and secured a minor role as the Liberal government's junior partner.[68]

In the American setting, unionization of factory workers was a difficult yet achievable goal that Anglo-Gaelic union leaders could help advance; but the mobilization of Detroit's workers into an independent labor party was a far more difficult task. In 1930s Detroit, Anglo-Gaelic union leaders were no more capable of overcoming the two-party system than their American counterparts. Failing to establish an independent political base for labor action, they eventually joined the Democratic party as left-wing advocates of the New Deal welfare state. In this context, their impact on the political agenda of Detroit's labor movement was evident in just two dimensions. First, to the degree that Anglo-Gaelic leaders more often identified themselves publicly as communists or socialists, they heightened the visibility of a left-wing agenda within the New Deal coalition; second, to the degree they were disproportionately represented among early organizers of independent political action, they strengthened the organizational leverage of the left-wing agenda within the Democratic party.

"Most of us had socialist leanings," Elizabeth McCracken recalled of the MESA leadership, "very definite socialist leanings." This was also true of many American and foreign-born union activists, but the socialism of Anglo-Gaelic immigrants was more widely held and more assertive. Socialism, usually the eclectic and rather fuzzy variety associated with the ILP, was the secular faith of many union activists at all levels of the British labor movement, an emblem of their rationality, class pride, and "independent" thinking. Bill Stevenson's induction into this cognitive orientation occurred in the same workplace and organizational context that Bill McKie had known twenty years before.

The boys serving an apprenticeship in most of the shops on the Clydeside probably came under the supervision of a shop steward who at lunch time had classes on the industrial history of England, and on Political Science. This is where we gradually began to pick up the drift of the whole system of capitalism and its economic impact on society. So this was our training.[69]

The diffusion of socialist ideology among British workers was uneven. Some turn-of-the-century unions, including the Cotton Spinners and some London Trades, backed the Conservative party because they opposed the free-trade and temperance planks of Liberal reform. The miners union, on the other hand, supported the Liberal party until 1908, and 43 percent of its membership voted against paying the union's political levy to the Labour party in 1913. Socialism found a readier acceptance among metalworkers. As early as 1912, more than half the representatives to the ASE's Delegate Meeting endorsed socialist measures and "class-war" tactics to counter the power of big business; over the next decade, British engineers played a disproportionately large role in the leadership and membership of the prewar Marxist sects, the wartime shop-stewards' movement, and the postwar Communist party. This, in turn, gave the socialists among Anglo-Gaelic metalworkers a distinctive assertiveness, since their constituents were well acquainted with, and generally supportive of, a political agenda freighted with socialist rhetoric.[70]

In this respect, it is no coincidence that the brief list of "public" and self-avowed Communists in Detroit's labor movement was dominated by Bill McKie, John Anderson, and Billy Allan, all of them from a Scottish milieu defined by metalworker militancy and left-wing politics. McKie found the "closet" communism of American party members wrongheaded and bewildering:

The mistake we made in the beginning, most of the leaders denied being members of the Communist Party. . . . I don't know what the psychology is of the American people generally, but such a thing would be just impossible in the old countries. They knew I was a communist in the trade union movement way back and there was no reason to say something else. After all, you're fighting for something; you have to be in some party, in some organization, so you'll be able to let them know exactly of your thinking of these things.[71]

McKie was consistent and vocal in his public identification with the Communist party, eventually choosing to leave union office rather than renounce his membership under Taft-Hartley requirements. John Anderson was equally blunt. As a candidate for governor on the 1934 Communist party ticket and a frequent party representative at public events, Anderson was perhaps Detroit's best-known Communist in the UAW, rivaled only by the full-time business agent in his local, New Yorker Nat Ganley. "I make no apologies for my honest beliefs," Anderson told UAW delegates at the 1941 convention, where he opposed (unsuccessfully) proposals to bar Communists and Nazis from union office. "And if those Red baiters want to see this Scotchman crawl," he added, no doubt in his deepest brogue, "their whiskers will trip them before that day comes." Anderson openly conducted Communist party meetings at Local 155's Schiller Hall and fully sanctioned

Ganley's considerable commitment of time and resources to party activities. In the eyes of some members, these practices made Schiller Hall the UAW's "Moscow Square," an epithet Anderson, in contrast to most UAW communists, probably accepted with pride. His membership, with a sizable plurality of British engineers, either seconded or selectively tolerated Anderson's communist views and consistently returned him to office between 1937 and 1947.[72]

The same assertiveness was evident among Anglo-Gaelic socialists outside the Communist party. Mat Smith, a former ILP member, identified himself as a socialist and publicly declared that MESA must become a "revolutionary industrial organization or it will decay like conservative unions." If this militant rhetoric was divorced from actions or programs that advanced explicitly revolutionary goals, then Smith was simply true to his ILP heritage. British-born Alan Strachan, like many of his American-born comrades in the Socialist party, chose Democratic governor Frank Murphy over the Socialist party ticket in 1938. But among the stalwarts who still raised the banner of the Socialist party in the 1940s was Michael Magee, an officer in Ford Local 600 who hailed from Belfast. A factional opponent of Bill McKie, Magee shared with his Communist rival a dogged devotion to socialist organization. His 1947 campaign as Socialist party candidate for Detroit City Council emphasized that he had been active in the British Labour party, had been an organizer for the Transport Workers Union, and had taken "a leading part in the general strike of 1926."[73]

Independent labor action found many of its most vocal adherents among Anglo-Gaelic union leaders. When a left-union coalition, the United Labor Conference for Political Action, ran a "Labor Slate" in the nonpartisan City Council elections of 1935, the three candidates on this labor ticket represented the same ethno-occupational-political alliance found among early union organizers: the Scots-born Bill McKie and Pennsylvania-born Fay O'Camb were both skilled tradesmen (sheet metal and metal polisher) and left-wingers (O'Camb in the Socialist party), and Michigan-born labor lawyer Maurice Sugar had a long history in the Detroit Socialist party and left-wing politics. Mat Smith and MESA provided the most consistent union backing for the Labor Slate, including the use of three MESA halls (Schiller, ABC, and Scotia) as distribution points for campaign literature and volunteers. In 1936, when this coalition formed the Michigan Farmer Labor party (FLP) and ran Sugar for Congress, Smith was pictured in the opening issue of *Farmer-Labor Challenge* as one of the party's "leading participants," along with Sugar and Judge Edward Jefferies. Toolmaker James Murdoch, the Clyde valley engineer and MESA vice president, was FLP treasurer and with O'Camb (secretary) and Walter Reuther (vice chair) represented one of three skilled metalworkers among the FLP's top seven officers. The party did not survive the November elections, but the United Front coalition carried over into the 1937 municipal campaign when a UAW-dominated Labor Slate of five City Council candidates generated considerable enthusiasm and 145,000 votes for its top candidate, Sugar. The Labor Slate candidates took between 30 and 35 percent of the vote, and Sugar came in tenth among eighteen candidates, narrowly missing the cut for the nine-member council. The Labor Slate candidates were all American-born trade unionists or socialists, including future UAW presidents Walter Reuther and R. J. Thomas, with Englishman Alan Strachan acting as campaign manager.[74]

McKie, Smith, and other Anglo-Gaelic socialists saw reason to believe these initiatives were, as Smith termed the 1937 campaign, "a prelude to starting a Labor Party that will eventually control the city." Sugar's campaigns in particular drew the widest possible range of support between 1935 and 1937—from the AFL Building Trades, the UAW-CIO, and, most consistently, MESA. Every Anglo-Gaelic militant knew that the British Labour party had sprung from just such local campaigns as these, though the Detroit version took on two features peculiar to the American setting. Farmers were not a significant constituency in British labor politics, but they played a sizable role in America's populist tradition—and a troublesome one in Michigan's FLP when they temporarily bolted to the right-wing ticket of National Union candidate William Lemke. Ethnic and foreign-born workers also played a key role in the Labor-Slate/Farmer-Labor campaigns. "We met Germans, and Finns, and Rumanians, Ukrainians, Italians, Jewish Americans, all types," McKie recalled of the ethnic halls he and Sugar visited during the 1935 campaign. John Anderson, as secretary of Detroit's left-wing mutual-insurance society, the International Workers Order, helped open the doors to dozens of IWO halls in the city's ethnic neighborhoods. With this combined union-ethnic block, the 1935 Labor Slate predicted that Detroit's workers would soon produce a movement "which shall become on the political field, what the Trade Unions are on the economic field, and shall join hands with the many similar movements for a Labor Party now in the process of development the country over."[75]

This movement for a Labor party was, of course, stillborn. Labor support in Detroit was evident across a wide spectrum between 1935 and 1937, but it was successive rather than simultaneous. The Detroit Federation of Labor endorsed Sugar's campaign for Recorders' Court in the spring of 1935, but not the City Council slate in the fall; in 1937, the

DFL also backed out of the City Council campaign when the national rivalry between the AFL and CIO spiked all efforts at local unity. The Farmer Labor party won continued MESA support in 1936, but it alienated CIO leaders and most workers with broadstroke attacks on Frank Murphy, "a Democratic candidate and a part of the EMPLOYERS' political machine." In this respect, the Farmer Labor party faced the same dilemma as the Socialist party and later the Michigan Commonwealth Federation (MCF): each tapped the active support of left-wing workers frustrated with the conservative drift of the New Deal, but could not convince a sizable number of voters that third-party politics wouldn't undermine the New Deal majority and return the Republicans to power. Much as the British Labour party initially represented a "laborist" extension of the Liberal party's left wing, so did the FLP articulate a "radical" New Deal program of low-cost housing construction, expanded unemployment and welfare relief, taxes on profits and the rich, and federal action against right-wing groups and corporate spying on unions. FDR's Second New Deal took some of these issues from the FLP, while conservative attacks on Roosevelt and Governor Murphy portrayed the incumbent Democrats as being every bit as radical as their left-wing critics. In the United States, a cultural stigma was easily attached to overtly "class" politics, and the prevailing anticommunism of the employer-controlled media ensured that Detroit's Labor Slates and FLP paid dearly for their proletarian independence. All these factors, combined with the previously mentioned structural obstacles to third-party challengers, undermined Detroit's embryonic Labor party.[76]

Under these circumstances, while many Anglo-Gaelic immigrants joined the independent political initiatives of the FLP and later the MCF, many others went with the Democratic party. Harold Snudden and his son Geoffrey both considered themselves socialists, yet both concluded, as Geoffrey put it, that socialists "would never make it, so you were just throwing your vote away." Ernie Woodcock, a former member of the British ILP, came to the same conclusion. "I understand what you're doing,' he told his son Leonard, who served on the Executive Board of the Socialist party in the late 1930s, "but in this country you're wasting your time." The Socialist party lost a considerable number of members in 1938, when many left-wing workers backed Governor Frank Murphy's reelection campaign and ignored the futile independence of the Socialist party ticket. The Communist party backed independent initiatives in Detroit's nonpartisan elections but supported liberal Democrats in partisan contests and backed FDR between 1935 and 1939.[77]

The ultimate failure of labor's third-party initiatives in Detroit and elsewhere had a decisive impact on the future course of New Deal politics, particularly when compared with the British case. If nothing else, the Labour party's working-class base, rooted as it was in a densely unionized work force, gave Britain's liberal-labor welfare state a more durable structure than the American version. But this does not mean that the Detroit campaigns of 1935–1937 had no impact. Even though these initiatives did not produce a Labor party, they still helped galvanize a new structure of labor political action that made unions an active rather than passive participant *within* the Democratic party's New Deal coalition. For the 1937 municipal Labor Slate, Alan Strachan, chairman of the UAW Detroit District Council's newly formed Political Action Committee, established an enormously ambitious campaign organization. Funded by a per capita levy on UAW locals, Strachan hired more than forty female clerical workers—all of them UAW strikers from Yale and Towne who were paid fifty cents an hour ("more than they got at Yale and Towne," Strachan told reporters)—and set them to work creating a file-card system for the estimated 200,000 UAW members in the city. Strachan then directed UAW shop stewards to establish precinct and ward committees and contact every member in their designated area to ensure that they were registered to vote and went to the polls on election day. Special committees for Polish, Jewish, Negro, and other ethno-religious-racial groups supplemented the citywide organization. With only a few months to establish this elaborate structure, Strachan's Political Action Committee registered 12,000 new voters, distributed four editions and 1.7 million copies of a *Vote Labor* paper, conducted hundreds of meetings, and organized poll-watching committees in 800 of the city's 912 precincts. Labor had never before mobilized for political action on such a scale, and though the Labor Slate's top candidate narrowly missed election, "it must nevertheless be understood," Strachan observed, "that the tremendous vote gained by labor was something of which to be very proud." This grass roots mobilization was also, he added, "the secret of any successful political machine. The basis for organization has been laid."[78]

Indeed it had, and the Wayne County CIO subsequently perfected this machine into one of the nation's most oft-cited models for political action. Its power within the Michigan Democratic party grew accordingly. In 1940, the first sizable group of labor delegates appeared at the party's state convention. Four years later, ten of thirty-eight Michigan delegates to the national Democratic party convention were CIO members and leaders, with UAW vice president Richard Frankensteen chairing the delegation and seconding FDR's nomination to a fourth term. Finally, in 1948–1950 the CIO-PAC joined with reform liberals and took over the Michigan Democratic party, electing nearly 500 CIO delegates to the state convention and ousting the "old guard" cadre of ethnic politicians and Teamster officers. Blue-collar workers and union leaders made up 47 percent of the State Central Committee between 1949 and 1959, and 80 percent or more of Detroit's Eastern European and African-American voters favored Democratic candidates. Even so, this was not a Labor party: liberal businessmen dominated top leadership positions and wealthy shaving-cream heir G. Mennen "Soapy" Williams led the state ticket to victory in six general elections between 1948 and 1960. Yet it was certainly different from the conservative patronage party it replaced. Together with similar transformations between 1944 and 1949 in Minnesota and Wisconsin, where left-labor third parties (Farmer-Labor, Progressive, and Socialist) merged into the Democratic party, the events in Michigan marked a transition toward more issue-oriented and programmatic two-party politics in the upper Midwest.[79]

Anglo-Gaelic union leaders helped initiate this transformation by their early prominence in the political-action campaigns of 1935–1937. But as suggested above, their political skills were more nearly matched by their American-born counterparts, and the Anglo-Gaelic contributions was correspondingly less determining in the narrowly construed realm of "politics" than it was in the "workplace." But these two realms were not so easily separated, particularly after 1933 as liberal Democrats established a new structure of public welfare and government regulation of collective bargaining. For the first time in a peace economy, workplace organization confronted not only employer opposition but also a liberal State that both sanctioned and confined union activity. Anglo-Gaelic union leaders had considerably more experience with such a welfare state than other immigrant or native-born leaders. Whereas many of the latter initially invested their faith in Franklin Roosevelt and the Democratic party, Anglo-Gaelic leaders showed a marked disposition toward the same confrontational bargaining and independent political action that had won Britain's labor movement a measured role in that nation's polity. In Detroit, labor's Direct Action helped push the New Deal from its passive toleration of merit clauses and company unions in the early 1930s toward an interventionist policy in the late 1930s that adjudicated disputes, enforced majority rule, and sanctioned industrial organization through sole recognition.

There were other factors that contributed to this shift in policy, but in

Detroit, Anglo-Gaelic leaders played a prominent and, at key moments, a leading role in the confrontational bargaining that strengthened the hand of pro-CIO New Dealers. To the degree they helped build Detroit's auto unions, their *indirect* impact on labor's ability to mobilize political action was correspondingly huge. For without a UAW-CIO there would not have been a CIO-PAC in Michigan, at least not of the same scope and nature. And without the British craftsmen in GM's Detroit toolmaking plants and the Anglo-Gaelic union leaders in Detroit's jobbing shops and Dodge Main, the UAW-CIO might not have survived 1939.

6

CRISIS, RECOVERY, ECLIPSE

Francis Dillon, general organizer for the AFL and past president of the UAW, had much to look forward to in June of 1938, or so he thought. "The CIO is in its death throes," he predicted shortly after UAW president Homer Martin suspended five opponents from the union's Executive Board. Dillon believed he saw in this not just a factional split in the CIO's leading affiliate, but "the sign of disintegration of the entire CIO movement." Editorial writers across the country drew much the same conclusion.[1]

The survival of the UAW was not a moot point in 1938–1939, for the union faced the external threats of recession and employer counterattack, and the internal threat of Homer Martin. In this context, the New Deal's swing toward interventionist labor policies played a far more positive and determining role than in 1936–1937. Direct Action would still have a decisive impact in 1938–1939, but the available range of confrontational strategies narrowed as factionalism and recession thinned UAW ranks, as the Supreme Court outlawed sit-downs, and as the NLRB asserted a more prominent role in adjudicating disputes. Government intervention would grow more confining over time, but in 1939 the NLRB gave significant assistance to a labor movement still weakened by recent factionalism and heavy layoffs.

Even with this support, however, Homer Martin loomed as a formidable foe, enjoying the tacit backing of General Motors and Chrysler, and the covert support of Ford's security chief, Harry Bennett. Against weaker opponents, Martin might have made the UAW more akin to the company-dominated unions later established in 1950s Japan. When he failed in this and took his few loyalists back into the AFL, he might still have diluted autoworker militancy by making the

UAW-AFL a more potent rival of the UAW-CIO. Fortunately, Martin and the auto companies met their match in the UAW's "Unity" caucus. Foreign-born tool and die makers were especially prominent in this resistance to Homer Martin, but with some variation across nationality groups. Many German-born craftsmen stayed on the margins of union activism, and those who articulated a political consciousness more often split between left and right. Anglo-Gaelic immigrants, in contrast, were far more prominent in their support of the Unity caucus. In the decisive 1939 strikes at General Motors and Dodge, their leadership and disciplined militancy carried the day. Afterward, as the union incorporated large numbers of previously unorganized workers, individual Anglo-Gaelic leaders continued to play a prominent role in Detroit's largest locals. But collectively, the Anglo-Gaelic presence was eclipsed by the rise of native-born leaders and the growing majority of production-worker members.

Crisis

The factional struggle that racked the UAW in 1937–1939 split the union along distinct occupational and cultural fault lines. Politically, Homer Martin's "Progressive" caucus followed the lead of Jay Lovestone, former Communist party head now turned Red baiter, whereas the opposing "Unity" caucus drew most of its initial support from the many Socialist party and Communist party activists in the union. Programmatically, Martin favored centralization of union authority and moderation of its bargaining strategy; the Unity caucus also publicly opposed wildcats and the indiscriminate use of Direct Action, but defended local-union democracy and, unlike Martin, opposed wage cuts and company firings of wildcat leaders. Martin found his strongest support among native-born Protestants, particularly in assembly-line departments and in regions (Indiana, southern Ohio, or Flint) where southern workers concentrated; Irish and German Catholics also favored Martin in some cases, particularly those in such ancillary occupations as transportation and inspection. The Unity caucus, in contrast, had its strongest following among those who gave the UAW its initial base: the Eastern European immigrants and their American-born offspring concentrated in Detroit and Cleveland; the semiskilled trimmers, cushion builders, and metal finishers in the body plants; and, above all, the Anglo-Gaelic immigrants who predominated in the tool and die job shops of Detroit.

Carl Haessler, editor of the UAW's *Tool and Die Engineering News*, linked the anti-Martin sentiments of these Anglo-Gaelic craftsmen with their unique cultural disposition. Job-shop tool and die makers, he observed, "had the greatest contempt for Homer Martin as a preacher trying to make like a union man." Such posturing could only alienate Anglo-Gaelic tradesmen trained in the secular culture of British artisanship: "Being from Glasgow and other such places," as Haessler put it, "they had a rather godless attitude."[2]

Another contemporary journalist, W. L. White, also detected a British dimension to Martin's opposition. Writing in *The New Republic*, White singled out John Anderson's Local 155 as a leading center of Unity caucus support in Detroit, noting that Martin had "ousted from feeble unions Unity officials of an almost indistinguishable shade of pinkness, but he has not touched the avowed 20-minute-egg Reds of tool and die." White speculated on why Martin did not try to purge Detroit's toolmakers of their left-wing leadership: "Maybe because these labor aristocrats—about 75 percent British-born and with deep trade union traditions—are too tough to crack. . . . If he removed their elected officers, any steering committee he put in charge would, according to one Unity spokesman, 'be blown out of there. And I mean *blown.'*"[3]

However "hard-boiled" these British militants in Local 155, support for the Unity caucus was not unanimous among tool and die makers. Within the craft, ethno-cultural distinctions also contributed to political differences and factional identities. Some American-born toolmakers, as indicated in the preceding chapter, shunned the militancy and Direct Action of MESA and the UAW. Many German-born toolmakers also favored greater moderation than their Anglo-Gaelic coworkers, particularly in those plants where the owner or manager was a right-wing German. In a few such shops, management apparently demanded more than mere "moderation." MESA staffer Elizabeth McCracken recalled at least two tool and die job shops that gave hiring preference to workers who showed management a swastika. "The same thing applied in the Murray Body Corporation at their Ecorse plant," McCracken remembered. "If you had one of those [swastikas] . . . you would be hired, but not," she added, "if you had a British accent or Scotch. The English and the Scotch . . . could not get by the personnel manager."[4]

Most German-born metalworkers were not Nazis, but compared with Anglo-Gaelic immigrant workers, many followed a more cautious union agenda. Russ Leach recalled how relatively few German-born tool and die workers took leadership roles in the union, as compared with the Scots. "The Scotch were way out in front. . . . 'I'm a volunteer, I'll help sign people up, man the picket lines, take on the cops. . . .' But not the Germans, they were more docile. . . . Many of them wanted the union, but not . . . to the extent [of] joining flying squadrons and manning picket lines." There were several reasons for this diminished role. Most obvious, recent German immigrants who might otherwise have become union activists often did not speak fluent English and found it difficult to communicate with their fellow workers. Henry Geile, a German-Catholic toolmaker from Westphalia who emigrated in 1928, was just such a case. As a young mechanic drafted by the wartime government and assigned to the engine room of a German battleship, Geile participated in the 1918 mutiny that eventually spread from the northern ports across the country, hastening Germany's surrender. Freed from prison by the success of the November revolution, Geile served in an irregular military unit, apparently loyal to the Social Democrats, guarding public buildings in Bremen. He never rose to leadership in the Social Democratic movement or in the union that organized a closed shop at Kupperbusch Stove, where he worked before and after the war. But his participation as a low-level activist in the organizational routine of the German metalworkers' union, together with his experience in the wartime strikes to end the war, qualified Geile as a candidate for steward or local-union office in Detroit. He was certainly prounion—"I grown [sic] up with that"—but he nevertheless avoided union office, primarily because he never mastered the language of his new home. "That was in me personally," Geile explained years later in slow and heavily accented words, "don't take any [union] job while you don't speak a clear, good English."[5]

Language set many other German-born workers apart, and their isolation was prolonged if they worked in one of the many German-owned job shops where even the blueprints were in the mother tongue. Equally significant, the anti-German hysteria of World War I was a recent and sobering memory for German-Americans on Detroit's East Side. "Germans didn't want to become prominent at all," recalled Kurt Keytal, editor in the 1930s of Detroit's daily German-language newspaper, the *Abend Post*. "They simply ducked under. . . . For one thing, they got out of politics. They were politically very active in the time of World War I, and then they gradually dropped out." This caution must have been communicated to newly arrived German metalworkers as they settled into Detroit's East Side Deutscheum. Some immigrants learned the need for caution the hard way. George Barth, a German-born toolmaker who emigrated to the United States in

1923, was arrested in Detroit eight years later for allegedly violating wartime measures—still on the books—that prohibited aliens from distributing Communist literature. The hapless Mr. Barth, who carried an unsigned membership card in the Unemployed Councils, was doubly stigmatized as a "subversive alien" and a German. His difficulties were no doubt compounded when he tried to explain to the arresting officers that he was not a Communist and the literature was intended for Canadians in neighboring Windsor. "He is not well versed in the English language," admitted Barth's lawyer, Patrick O'Brien (the future Labor Slate mayoral candidate of 1937), "being unable to read, write, or fully understand it, and speaks . . . it only imperfectly." Barth's incoherent pleading must have confirmed his "Un-American" identity in the eyes of his captors.[6]

In the eyes of other Detroiters, there was additional reason to keep Germans at arms length in the 1930s. Added to the legacy of wartime hysteria against the German Hun and the Alien Red was a growing anti-Nazi sentiment, especially among Eastern European workers who viewed the "new" Germany's militarism with understandable alarm. For any German-born toolmaker who contemplated a high-profile role in union organizing, the anti-German sentiments of these and many other workers must have dampened his enthusiasm for union activity. Many tuned inward, devoting themselves to their craft. While Scots-born tool and die makers, according to Leach, "were more interested in going to the bar and talking about rebuilding the world," their German co-workers wanted instead "to be the top mechanic." Many, in short, retreated to a craft realm where manual skills and precision work carried more weight than language skills and ethnic pedigree. If the prototypical Scotsman rose to union office, his German counterpart rose within the toolroom, becoming die leader, supervisor, or job-shop owner.[7]

There were German-born toolmakers who overcame the barriers of language and anti-German feeling to become prominent union organizers. Chief among them was Paul Diechgraeber, a thirty-two-year-old toolmaker from Berlin when he emigrated in 1928. After landing in New York City, he immediately applied for U.S. citizenship and soon moved to Detroit, where he Americanized his name to Dykes. Six years later, speaking "broken English," as one fellow unionist recalled, Paul Dykes was signing up members for MESA Local 9. By 1937, he was a general organizer for the UAW and an International representative in several sit-down strikes organized by Local 155, most prominent among these a wild and sometimes violent series of plant occupations by several hundred men and women at Ferro Stamping.[8]

Other lesser-known activists with German names appeared in the minutes and reports of the UAW's two tool and die job-shop locals, particularly Local 157. Along with the Anglo-Gaelic immigrants who predominated in local leadership, most of these German-born union activists probably sided with the Unity caucus. But in some supplier plants and captive-shop toolrooms, German-born workers sided with Homer Martin. This was certainly the case at Midland Steel, where the newly chartered Local 410, led by German-born diemaker Anton Boll, followed Martin into the AFL. As the leader of a predominantly German- and Irish-Catholic faction centered on the maintenance trades and transportation, Boll kept Local 410 in the UAW-AFL until December of 1939. In that month, Boll's faction lost to a CIO coalition of semiskilled production workers, leftists, immigrant Eastern Europeans, and second-generation blacks and Poles—led by, among others, Sam Brear, the British shaper hand, and Tom Dyer, the Kentucky-born diemaker.[9]

At Ford, German toolmakers were sharply divided in their organizational loyalties. Walter Dorosh recalled several pro-CIO Germans in the toolroom where he worked, including Frank Gau, a German trade unionist who actively organized for the UAW, and "Doc" Doczkal, a left-winger who first emigrated to Czechoslovakia and worked briefly in the Skoda works before coming to Detroit. "I was just like you," Doczkal told the youthful Dorosh. "I figured that we were going to have socialism in Germany. Instead we got fascism." To Doczkal's chagrin, fascism had also come to the Rouge, where a sizable number of German-born toolmakers openly sided with the Nazi government. Ford Rouge was something of an incubator for the American Nazi movement, providing jobs for many right-wing Germans fleeing Weimar in the 1920s, and sanction for Nazi propaganda in the public statements of Henry Ford. Funded initially by the earnings of expatriate Germans at Ford and other auto plants, the American Nazi movement took its first organizational form with the 1924 founding of the National Socialist Teutonia Association, headquartered in Detroit. Teutonia's leaders saw the United States as a temporary refuge from Weimar and looked forward to returning to Germany, as many members did after 1938. By then, Nazi supporters had shifted their national headquarters from Detroit to New York City and changed their name to the American-German Bund. Founder Heinz Spanknobel and subsequent Bund leader Fritz Kuhn were both German immigrants who had worked at Ford Rouge—Kuhn, a Freikorps veteran, as a chemical engineer. Although they could count only a few adherents among German-Americans, immigrant Germans gave them a modest following in Detroit and other urban centers of the Northeast.[10]

In the Ford Rouge toolrooms, their presence provoked some bitter feelings among other ethnic groups and anti-Nazis. "They used to like to razz me," recalled Walter Dorosh, a Unity caucus supporter and American-born son of Russian-Polish parents. " 'You know what Hitler just done?' . . . [they'd] say. 'He bought some police dogs . . . [to] piss on the Poles.' " British toolmakers also found themselves on the receiving end of German taunts. The Germans, Dorosh remembered, "were kind of haughty, you know, 'Germany is not going to be a second rate power no more,' and there was an animosity between the English and the Germans. I used to hear them shoot wisecracks at each other. 'When Hitler's ready, we're going to go over in a rowboat and take England.' " Similar tensions prevailed at Fisher Body's Plant 21, where toolmakers from Germany were the predominant immigrant group and many, by 1937, had joined the Bund. Led by John Schreiber, a German-born toolmaker, they established an organizational presence in the plant that directly opposed the UAW. According to union organizer Blaine Marrin, the Bund's presence was the chief reason that UAW organization at Plant 21 lagged behind that at neighboring plant 23. Bund opposition was overcome only when some 700 diemakers from the predominantly Anglo-Gaelic work force in Plant 23, upon hearing a Bund meeting was in progress in Plant 21, marched across the street and shut the plant down. Following this intimidation, Bund activity apparently abated. But two years later, the Bund presence still drew the ire of UAW members during the tool and die strike at General Motors. In a front-page cartoon featuring a fish with a swastika on its tail, the Plant 21 strike bulletin highlighted the "Nazi Fisherman," John Schreiber, and asked rhetorically if his absence from the picket line meant he had gone fishing. "Sure you're not putting swastikas on their tails? Well, John, this is America and if you don't make the picket line, watch *your* tail."[11]

Nazi workers were not necessarily pro-Martin; more often, they rejected the union altogether. "We had some of these German Bund people," recalled Russ Leach of the Murray Body toolroom in Detroit, "[but] they just didn't want to attend meetings. They didn't care about the union." Bundists followed a political agenda that made them opposed or indifferent to the UAW's aims, but these Nazis were a small, if troublesome, proportion of the immigrant German work force. "We had a lot of Germans in our plant who were pro-union," Leach recalled, "and they [the Bundists] just weren't able to convince the vast majority . . . to be against the union." Leach and the Anglo-Gaelic leaders who predominated on his Shop Committee did their best to ensure this outcome. "We always tried to . . . pick out the most aggressive of the German group to be sure they had at least one member in that [shop] committee."[12]

Among the larger population of German toolmakers, the prevailing sentiment was characterized not by antiunionism, but by ambivalence toward union militancy and industrial organization. This ambivalence more often resolved itself in favor of positive—if passive—support for the militancy advocated by left-wing Anglo-Gaelic leaders during the union's heady success of 1936–1937. With the recession and union collapse of 1937–1938, however, this ambivalence moved many to support Homer Martin's conservative agenda, especially in captive shops and supplier plants where toolmakers felt threatened by semi-skilled "upgraders." It was this changing environment that activated potential behavior ranging from industrial militancy to craft caution, but with a central tendency located to the right of the Anglo-Gaelic sensibility.

The same dynamic shaped the consciousness of other skilled tradesmen—including the Anglo-Gaelic—within parameters unique to each nationality group. Craft concerns, in particular, became more compelling in the altered conditions of 1937–1938 as skilled tradesmen from every ethnic group contemplated the frustrated hopes of the preceding strike wave. On the plus side, tool and die workers did win sizable increases in hourly wages after the sit-downs, from an average $1.03 in tool and die job shops surveyed by the employer association in May of 1936, to $1.21 by June of 1937. But the higher minimums and the twenty-cent blanket increase negotiated by the UAW's job-shop locals could not compensate for larger problems. Many skilled workers could not find a job in the fall of 1937, when the recession hit the auto industry especially hard. Combined with the seasonal downswing that still plagued tool and die workers, this slump emptied many of Detroit's shops. In November of 1938, Bill Stevenson reported that the entire work force of Fisher Plant 23 had been laid off, leaving just 20 of 1,600 men on the job. General Motors and other carmakers sharply curtailed their annual model changes, leaving job shops to scramble for die-repair work and nonautomotive contracts. UAW organizers believed Detroit's carmakers further cut their tooling budgets by using identical dies in several models and by redesigning cars and stampings to produce larger parts and a smaller total number of dies. They also charged that automakers were sending work out of town or to low-wage alley-shops. The simultaneous impact of these seasonal, cyclical, and long-term changes was severe unemployment and a sharply curtailed production season, amounting to only three to four months for many toolmakers. The UAW, by signing a citywide job-shop contract in 1938 that renewed the previous year's rates, at least prevented the massive wage cutting that characterized the early depression. But the sharp reductions in employment caused a corresponding fall in dues-paying members for the job-shop locals, precipitating a financial crisis and forcing cuts in clerical staff, organizer salaries, and office expense accounts.[13]

These setbacks provoked a general complaint that the union had not yet reversed the long-term erosion of the toolmaker's power and status. In captive shops and larger supplier plants, this apprehension became more acute as thousands of production workers joined the UAW in 1937, shifting the union's internal politics away from the skilled trades. Captive-shop toolmakers were "mixed up with a lot of production workers and unskilled workers," as Orrin Peppler, a chief steward in Local 157, put it. "The production workers elected the leaders. Therefore, the skilled workers in the captive shops fell way behind the jobbing shop men." They also fell behind in maintaining the wage differential that separated them from production workers. A. R. Duckworth, a committeeman and toolmaker in the Engineering Laboratory at General Motors, complained in an October 1937 bargaining session that production workers at GM had received higher percentage increases than the skilled trades. Citing cases where semiskilled workers earned as much as $1.08–$1.15 an hour, only pennies below the $1.19 he earned, Duckworth asked a question many other captive-shop toolmakers must have pondered. "Of what use is our skill," he inquired of these unequal wage increases, "if we cannot obtain a higher percentage?" Equally alarming, the continuing subdivision of toolroom tasks was creating ever more specialized work on lathes, milling machines, and grinders, and much of this work required only semiskilled machine operators. Since many of the workers who took these jobs saw them as a first step to "stealing" a trade, fully trained craftsmen saw them as a threat. In the Midland Steel toolroom, conflict between these two groups took on an ethnic dimension, with Germans concentrated in the fully skilled positions and second-generation Poles predominant in the entry-level jobs. The dispute had factional implications as well, since the Germans tended to support Homer Martin, whereas the Poles usually sided with the Unity/CIO caucus.[14]

In a context of intense factionalism and economic stagnation, the craft concerns articulated by skilled workers at Midland and elsewhere posed a serious threat to industrial unionism. Some UAW tradesmen openly rejected their alliance with production workers, insisting that craft amalgamation suited their interests better. At General Motors, a group of tool and die makers, sheet metal workers, patternmakers, and maintenance men in the company's experimental engineering plants petitioned the UAW in 1938 for an independent local, separate from the production workers with whom they were currently merged. "We are unable to get the Engineering workers to come to the Production workers' meetings," the petitioners complained. "The meetings are not interesting." Only a separate, company-wide local for experimental engineering workers could address their needs. "By associating at social affairs," the petition argued, engineering tradesmen "would fraternize with people of their own trade or occupation. They would develop economic power of their own free will instead of being forced into the union by a picket line." Only a company-wide craft local, the petitioners concluded, "could solve many of the small problems that the production workers do not understand."[15]

The craft sentiments articulated in this document expressed the underlying anxiety that many other tool and die makers felt toward industrial unionism. In the Ford Dearborn toolrooms, this anxiety turned some fully trained craftsmen into supporters of Homer Martin. "A lot of the tool and die makers thought that the CIO was a production union," Walter Dorosh recalled, "'and God damn it' [they said] 'we don't need a production line.'" Factional debate was particularly heated around the issue of toolroom classifications. These had proliferated over the years for at least three reasons: first, plant managers created phoney "go-for" jobs to accommodate family members and friends; second, the company pursued continual subdivision and specialization of toolroom labor; and third, managers defined these subdivisions in the narrowest possible terms, designating each tool-machine operator not only by type of machine (shaper, lathe, etc.) but by the machine's trade name (Cincinnati shaper, Milwaukee shaper, etc.). Wage rates proliferated accordingly, from one "micro" classification to the next, and from one worker to the next within the same classification. Dorosh and others in the Unity/CIO caucus wanted to eliminate trade-name distinctions and consolidate tool-machine classifications into general categories—shaper operator, lathe operator, and so on. The "true tradesmen," as Dorosh derisively recalled pro-AFL workers in the toolroom, opposed such changes and charged CIO organizers with "trying to dilute the craft." In all likelihood, pro-AFL craftsmen were not defending the craft so much as their individual position within it. They conceded the inevitability of subdivision in tool-machine jobs and circled their wagons around the diemaker, the benchworker, and those specialized jobs that required a high degree of skill. For their narrowly defensive purposes, the byzantine trade-name classifications acted as a bulwark against the ocean of production workers at the Rouge: each narrowly defined classification made the tool-machine operator more dependent on machine-specific skills, more vulnerable to layoff, and less able to "steal" truly skilled work.[16]

In this, the Rouge's pro-AFL tradesmen no doubt had much in common with the Midland Steel toolroom's pro-Martin Germans. But according to Dorosh, the factions in Ford's toolrooms cut across ethno-cultural lines. Among his opponents he recalls both conservative Germans—many of them die leaders—and some Scots-born workers, including George Campbell, a Mason, and John Fitzpatrick, a Catholic. In the Unity/CIO corner were left-wing Germans and Scottish tradesmen of varied hue, including former coal miner Joe McCusker, an Irish-Catholic toolroom apprentice, and Bill McKie, the Communist party activist and UAW organizer for the Rouge's tool and die makers.

Factionalism and the Craft Agenda

Through at least the spring of 1938, Martin could win significant support, sometimes a majority, in some of the UAW's biggest production-worker locals in Flint, Pontiac, and Detroit. But he could not attract such a following in the amalgamated Locals 174, 155, and 157, the Detroit strongholds of the Unity caucus.

Yet the militant trade unionism of Locals 157 and 155 had its Achilles' heel, and Martin made a bold move to exploit this weakness in the summer and fall of 1938. Appealing directly to the craft concerns of tool and die makers, he established new organizations at all levels of the union—national, regional, and local—that focused exclusively on skilled-trades issues. Unable to challenge the Unity caucus within Locals 155 and 157, Martin hoped to dilute caucus influence with a plethora of overlapping and competing craft organizations.

He launched his campaign in June by establishing a National Tool and Die Organizing Committee. This initial step was well chosen, since the Anglo-Gaelic leaders of Detroit's toolmakers had been calling for greater efforts in this direction for some time and were therefore in no position to oppose Martin's initiative on factional grounds. Not surprisingly, Martin passed over John Anderson, Bill Stevenson, and other prominent leaders—all pro-Unity—who might have led such a national effort, and selected instead George Mitchell, a former ally of Anderson's in MESA and the heretofore obscure financial secretary of Local 155. Of the six men chosen to serve under Mitchell on the Organizing Committee, only two, Frank Trusell and Jack Greany, had achieved some prominence among Detroit's toolmakers. Both had served on the five-man Joint Negotiating Committee of Locals 155 and 157 that bargained the citywide job-shop contract in May 1938. Greany was also on the Local 157 Executive Board, where he soon identified himself as a pro-Martin presence. When the board voted on 18 August to send Unity caucus newspapers to the membership, Greany lodged the solitary vote in opposition.[17]

Martin opened a second front in his campaign in the late summer. Focusing on the local level, he chartered a new organization, Local 588, open to job-shop tradesmen but closed to the production-worker units Locals 157 and 155 had included in their amalgamated structure. This splinter movement began in August when Frank Trusell, shop chairman of the Local 157 unit at Buell Die and Machine, began circulating a petition to other job shops calling for the new craft local. The executive officers of Local 157 immediately responded on 3 September by suspending Trusell and convening, in a membership meeting two days later, a Trial Committee to review his case. But the pro-Martin breakaway won additional momentum when one of the eleven Trial Committee members, Jack Greany, shop chairman at Swartz Tool Products, subsequently took his twenty-member unit into Local 588. Several other shops also bolted, including Local 155 units at H. R. Kreuger, Motor City Tool, and Barker Tool and Die. The German names of three of the five shops (Buell, Swartz, and Kreuger) associated with Local 588 suggests that German tradesmen may have provided the splinter group with a disproportionate number of its members; in addition, Blaine Marrin remembered Greany as being German, though Marrin failed to recall whether this meant German-born or German parentage. Certainly German names predominated in the leadership of the Swartz unit, with H. Reich serving as recording secretary and A. Bechtel filling in for Greany as alternative delegate to the citywide tool and die committee. Trusell, who later joined Martin's staff, was apparently American-born.[18]

Following the formation of Local 588, the Anglo-Gaelic leaders of Locals 155 and 157 acted quickly to remove Trusell and Greany from their citywide Joint Tool and Die Committee. When John Anderson convened an emergency meeting of this body on 11 September, Trusell had already been replaced as recording secretary by the Belfast Irishman Robert Crothers. Discussion focused "on the question of the chartering of a local confined to job shop men only," and concluded two hours later with a resolution "that this body go on record against any split in 155 and 157 and that we also go on record against the chartering of a tool and die job-shop local."[19]

Martin's followers proceeded nevertheless with their breakaway strategy, establishing Local 588 headquarters in an empty garage on Cass Avenue, not far from Local 157's Sproat Street hall. They escalated their challenge to the Unity caucus in mid-October when Martin launched a third organizational initiative designed to attract craft-conscious toolmakers. Convening an open meeting at the Cass Technical High School auditorium, he announced the formation of regional "Tool and Die Councils" to implement programs of the National Organizing Committee and coordinate these, in Detroit, with Local 588. The councils would serve several purposes, according to Martin. "Amalgamated locals were set up as organizational methods during the infancy of the union," he explained to an audience of 700 members, with obvious reference to Locals 155 and 157. "But the problems of the tool and die workers are different from those of the production workers." Detroit's Tool and Die Council would help Local 588 address these problems on a regional basis and would also unite job-shop workers with tradesmen from the captive shops. The council would therefore give the captive-shop tradesmen a greater voice in the union, and Local 588 would remove job-shop craftsmen from "Communist controlled" groups led by John Anderson and Nat Ganley. Under this plan, Martin concluded, the uaw could organize every tool and die maker in the automobile industry.[20]

While Martin spoke, ten pro-Martin men from Packard Local 190 patrolled the aisles and kept the crowd in reasonable order. But when Martin left the hall, Frank Trusell, chairman of the meeting, faced an increasingly unruly opposition. As men in the back of the hall rose in their seats and shouted for a "discussion," a particularly outraged individual leapt to the stage and tried to replace Trusell at the podium. "The newcomer," according to the *Detroit News*, "was hurled back into the audience." But Trusell now confronted a far more formidable opponent. "[John] Anderson, a six-footer, stormed down the aisle and climbed onto the stage, shoving Trusell aside." The chairman was joined by a member of the Packard local's security force, and both "attempted to shove Anderson back, but were rebuffed."[21]

Anderson had taken control, and the acknowledged leader of Detroit's uaw tradesmen proceeded to repudiate President Martin's craft agenda. Declaring that "neither the uaw International executive board nor the cio executives were consulted about the meeting," Anderson said Locals 155 and 157 would cooperate with the National Tool and Die Committee in organizing the unorganized, "but not in setting up craft unions or disrupting existing organizations that have contractual relations with employers." As his departing opponents cut the auditorium lights and the sound system, Anderson, as the *News* put it, "continued the meeting in the dark," heaping particular scorn on the president's Red-baiting. "The false charge of Communist control," he concluded, "is . . . perpetuated by those who wish a continuance of factionalism and splitting tactics."[22]

In the weeks that followed this meeting, Anderson and his allies aggressively countered Martin's "splitting tactics." Yet even as they did so, they had to simultaneously represent a united UAW to employers. Just two weeks after Anderson confronted Martin and Trusell in the riotous meeting at Cass Tech, fellow Unity caucus leader Bill Stevenson joined George Mitchell, national director of Martin's Tool and Die Organizing Committee, and Elmer Dowell, Martin's director of the UAW's General Motors department, in a Detroit conference to formulate contract demands for GM tradesmen. Stevenson and at least four other delegates from Local 157 joined thirty-two representatives from GM toolrooms concentrated in the Detroit area and Flint. Whatever their factional loyalties, the delegates set these aside and, with Chairman Mitchell ruling on the appropriate parliamentary procedure, focused their attention on captive-shop issues. Since none of these skilled-trades concerns were addressed in the 1937 contract or the supplemental agreement of 1938, the delegates had considerable ground to cover. One particularly troublesome issue concerned classifications. After rejecting an initial draft of proposed language, the conference adopted a proposal that divided toolroom occupations into twenty-three classifications, ranging from die barbers and grinders at the low-end rate of $1.05 an hour to die leaders and patternmakers at the top rate of $1.35. The delegates called on General Motors to "plan and cooperate with employee representatives" to achieve full employment and "avoid as far as possible seasonal peaks and slack-period layoffs." No layoffs should occur in any case until the workweek had been reduced to thirty-two hours, and then only by seniority within corporate divisions. But the delegates ruled that seniority was not to extend under any circumstances across the divide between skilled labor and production workers. They also rejected a proposed 1:20 ratio of apprentices to journeymen, agreeing on the more restrictive ratio of 1:30. All agreed that overtime premiums had to be paid for Saturday and Sunday work, that the company should use only tools and dies bearing a union label, and that negotiations with General Motors should begin immediately. Before any contract was signed, it would have to be ratified by the conference delegates—a blunt expression of the distrust many tradesmen felt toward Martin's International. To oversee the negotiations, the conference chose a committee of ten, including Stevenson and four other Detroit delegates. Talks with the company began that November.[23]

By December, however, factional conflict had intensified dramatically, and in January of the new year the UAW split in two. Martin finally overplayed his hand when, at the invitation of Detroit's right-wing "Radio Priest," Father Coughlin, he opened secret negotiations with Harry Bennett to establish a sweetheart union at Ford. When the International Executive Board demanded an accounting of these unauthorized meetings, Martin precipitously suspended fifteen of the twenty-four board members. The Unity caucus majority ignored Martin's action and removed the president from office. Shortly after, Martin took his remaining supporters into the rival AFL, calling a convention of the rump organization in early March.

As this factional turmoil began to boil in December, General Motors broke off negotiations for the supplementary tool and die agreement. It was no longer possible, the company insisted, to identify the legitimate representatives of the union. Other employers followed suit, and for all practical purposes, effective union representation lapsed in most General Motors plants and many other major factories. Intense and sometimes violent factional warfare dominated the agenda in most Detroit locals, including 155 and 157. After Martin supporters demolished the headquarters and seized the records of Plymouth Local 51 in January 1939, Local 157 organized a twenty-four-hour guard at its Sproat Street hall, with each of the union's shop units rotating daily responsibility for this task. The local also called for a LaFollete Committee investigation "of the Ford Motor boys' tie-up with Martin" and established a three-man committee, composed of Melvin Bishop and the Scotsmen Stevenson and Handyside, to edit all shop papers. When the International Executive Board removed Martin from office, the local heartily endorsed the action and subsequently ruled "that any member of Local 157 attending the Martin [AFL] convention as a representative of this Local be expelled."[24]

With Martin's departure, the Anglo-Gaelic leaders of Locals 155 and 157 regained the initiative among Detroit's tool and die makers. The Detroit and Wayne County Tool and Die Council remained in operation and still promised to represent the "particular" interests of job-shop and captive-shop craftsmen. However, the Unity caucus had banished Frank Trusell from the council and replaced him with a new president, Bill Stevenson. Craft concerns still animated Detroit's skilled tradesmen and gave continued life to MESA, the Society of Tool and Die Craftsmen, and, for a time, Local 588. But Stevenson and others moved to reharness the craft impulse to the UAW-CIO, reaffirming in May 1939 that the Tool and Die Council "is not based on job-shop men nor on major-shop men, but on the basis of tool and die makers in general and their problems." As the UAW-CIO recovered momentum, Martin's Local 588 began to collapse. At the February 1939 union meeting of Swartz Tool Products, members moved and seconded "that this unit resign from Local 588 and return to Local 157." A secret ballot of the eleven men in attendance (the total unit had eighteen members) produced a vote of six in favor, two opposed, two abstentions, and one vote unaccounted for.[25]

The following month, chief steward Jack Greany reported to his constituents that Local 157 had welcomed the Swartz unit back, "it being understood that we were never officially suspended from the local." In the months that followed, other wayward units also returned to the fold.[26]

Recovery

A revitalized UAW-CIO officially reconstituted itself in March and April of 1939 at the union's Special Convention in Cleveland, Ohio. The union that emerged from these proceedings was substantially different from the fledgling organization of 1937. By abolishing three vice-presidential posts, the convention pared the national Executive Board of both its left and right wings, eliminating Wyndham Mortimer, the highest-ranking representative of Communist party influence in the union, and Walter Wells, a skilled tradesman and leader of an informal Masonic "caucus" within the union. The Communists, hoping to preserve the CIO's left-center alliance, acquiesced in Mortimer's removal. Wells, however, refused to accept his demotion and threatened to lead his men into either the Martin camp or an AFL craft union. "But he had no men, so nothing happened," recalled labor journalist Carl Haessler. "The Masonic power was more among foremen in the plants and executives than among the ordinary rank and file."[27]

The delegates to this convention also represented a significant change in the union's internal life. At the previous convention in 1937, the delegates, according to Dan Gallagher of Local 174, "were all naive, uninformed people from the shops who had no idea in the world what the union was. . . . [That] convention, I think, was more directed and led by the officers." In the intervening two years, however, the "greenhorns" of 1937 had matured. "Now the opposite . . . could be found in the Cleveland Convention. . . . [The delegates were] determined, conscientious, reasonably well-informed workers who were determined on writing a constitution that would give the union to the workers and completely take away from its leaders any dictatorial powers." The constitution that issued from their deliberations scaled back the authority of the president, restricted the International's power to impose receivership, increased the powers of the Executive Board and the rights of local unions, brought back the yearly convention, and strengthened the members' role in collective bargaining through a structure of intracorporation delegate councils drawn from the plants. The Unity caucus had many reasons for favoring these changes, the most obvious being Homer Martin's abuse of power under the previous constitution. But however much Martin's negative example shaped the reform agenda at the 1939 convention, the *positive* articulation of rank-and-file control drew some of its inspiration from Anglo-Gaelic sources. The prominent role in the Unity caucus of Anglo-Gaelic leaders must have given their prescriptions for a revived UAW special weight. But the more persuasive influence would have been Maurice Sugar, the UAW attorney who oversaw the writing of the constitution. While Sugar drew upon an extensive experience in Detroit's labor movement, dating back to World War I, his most intensive exposure to rank-and-file unionism had been as Mat Smith's ally during MESA's founding and growth. Sugar could not have found a more compelling, battle-tested model of democratic unionism from which to borrow.[28]

As the union's chief counsel, Sugar would also play a prominent role in the UAW-CIO's subsequent campaign to recover its base in auto. Unlike the union's organizing methods in 1936–1937, the strategy in 1939 would rely to a sizable degree on procedural action under the law. R. J. Thomas, the union's new president, previewed the new strategy in his address to the convention. Based on the UAW-CIO's growing support in Detroit's Chrysler locals, Thomas expressed confidence that "through NLRB elections a death blow could be struck against dual and company unionism." The anticipated increase in NLRB elections at Chrysler and elsewhere prompted Sugar's proposal, three weeks after the close of the Cleveland convention, that the UAW-CIO establish a legal department to handle the expanding litigation that would accompany this strategy. In his previous work for MESA and the UAW, Sugar had always stressed that legal remedies were dependent upon and subordinate to militant Direct Action, but in 1939 he and other radical lawyers placed a new emphasis on exploiting the law. "It is my opinion," he wrote on 24 April in his report to the UAW president, "that the National Labor Relations Act offers the opportunity for the prosecution of a large number of cases against antiunion employers with real prospects of success. . . . The organization of workers into our Union, and their retention, once organized, often depends upon action or lack of action under the Act."[29]

There were many compelling reasons for this new reliance on the NLRB. These included the nature of the board itself, for with the backing of the Supreme Court, the NLRB had finally established its authority to intervene in labor disputes. The board's executive secretary, radical lawyer Nathan Witt, still had the backing of board members Edwin Smith and William Madden, and Witt would remain in charge of NLRB operations until 1940, when FDR appointed Harry Millis to replace the retiring Madden. In the meantime, the NLRB was aggressively pro-union and generally favored the CIO over the AFL.[30]

At the same time, the political and economic climate for union growth had chilled since the spring of 1937. This shift, already apparent in the defeat of Detroit's Labor Slate that fall, accelerated in 1938 as the slumping economy deflated the New Deal's promise of full recovery. The newly organized House Committee on Un-American Activities held Michigan hearings on Governor Murphy's so-called treasonable action in refusing to suppress the Flint sit-down, providing enemies of the governor and the UAW with a public forum for opposing Murphy's upcoming reelection. A string of anti-Murphy witnesses charged that the governor had the backing of "Soviet agents" and would "Turn Michigan over to [the] Reds" if voters returned him to office. This clumsy Red-baiting failed in Detroit, where Murphy won 59 percent of the vote, but carried enough weight in rural and small-town districts to defeat the governor by a margin of 53 to 47 percent. Murphy's defeat reflected the larger crisis of New Deal liberalism in 1938. Nationally, the Republicans won twelve governorships, eight Senate races, and doubled their House representation from 88 to 170 seats. The Democrats still controlled Congress, but liberal representation in the House was halved. Following these losses came the Supreme Court decision in February 1939 that definitively placed the sit-down strike outside the law, eliminating any legal defense for a tactic that the altered political climate already made problematic.[31]

Under these conditions, NLRB elections offered a means of demonstrating the UAW-CIO's majority without risking the potential backlash that Direct Action might provoke. There was a catch, however. At Chrysler, where effective union organization had come earlier than elsewhere, and where the Detroit base of the Unity caucus strengthened the UAW-CIO, the union was reasonably confident it could win such an election. But General Motors was the single most important target in the union's campaign to reestablish its presence in the industry, and at that company there was considerable doubt whether the

UAW-CIO could win majority support. The union presence was more recent at GM and always more uneven than in Detroit, and the social composition of Flint's work force had given Homer Martin a sizable following in GM's home city. The 1937–1938 recession and the intense factionalism of these years had weakened the union, and CIO activists were demoralized by the failure to consolidate the gains of 1937. Socialist party organizer Ben Fischer may have exaggerated when he told party officials in a June 1938 report that the Unity caucus in Flint "is virtually dead"; he had reason to exaggerate, since the party's top leaders were temporarily swayed toward Martin by his endorsement of their antiwar program. But there was no denying that supporters of the Unity caucus had lost the initiative in Flint. Elsewhere at General Motors, disappointment and cynicism had also dampened enthusiasm for a revival of the UAW-CIO. The situation was complicated all the more by the presence of competing shop committees in eleven of the company's biggest plants—one committee representing the UAW-CIO, the other representing Homer Martin's UAW-AFL. In twelve smaller plants, Martin's rump group had the field to itself; in only three plants did the UAW-CIO have uncontested representation.[32]

"Confidence in our International union was destroyed," R. J. Thomas later remarked. By his estimate, in June 1939 only 8 percent of the 200,000 workers at General Motors were UAW-CIO members, with another 4 percent signed up under Martin's UAW-AFL. Because it was weak, the UAW-CIO could not inspire the ranks; and because it could not inspire the ranks, the union remained weak. General Motors was well aware of this dynamic and did all it could to exploit the situation. When the NLRB announced a new policy in June of 1939 that permitted employers to petition the board when competing unions contended for bargaining rights, the company made a decisive turnaround in its previous policy opposing NLRB intervention. Announcing that it faced precisely the situation specified by the NLRB, the company became the first employer to ask the board for an election under the new policy.[33]

The UAW-CIO, despite its general position favoring NLRB elections, wanted no such balloting at General Motors. The union had already decided upon an alternative: a "strategy strike" limited solely to GM's tool and die makers. The strategy relied on the UAW-CIO's one undeniable base of support within GM—tool and die makers and other skilled tradesmen, particularly those concentrated in Detroit's Fisher Body plants. Direct Action by these Local 157 members could paralyze the company's preparations for the 1940 model year without risking the difficult task of mobilizing the more numerous production workers. There simply were not enough tool and die makers during the rush season to replace the entire work force at GM, and any effort by the company to shift its die program to Detroit's job shops would confront the formidable opposition of Locals 155 and 157.[34]

Sole credit for this strategy is usually given to Walter Reuther. The thirty-two-year-old diemaker and president of Local 174 did play a crucial and highly visible role in developing the union's strategy, particularly in his new capacity as director of the union's General Motors department. Even so, although Reuther's personal experience as a skilled tradesman and his past experience in Detroit's labor movement gave him ample reason for favoring a tool and die strike, it is highly unlikely that he devised this strategy in isolation. Reuther had left Detroit in 1933 before the MESA tool and die strike, but the leaders of that practical demonstration in skilled-trades bargaining leverage were still on the scene, many of them in Locals 155 and 157. One such man was Bill Stevenson, former MESA strike leader at Fisher 23 and recently elected strike chairman of the UAW-CIO's National GM Bargaining Committee. Stevenson later recalled the strategy-strike idea as originating in collective discussions at the local level, and then proceeding upward through the UAW and CIO hierarchy: "We happened to have an idea of striking the [General Motors] plants using the skilled workers. We had long talks with Walter about it and finally went down to see Phil Murray in his office in Pittsburgh. From there we saw Sidney Hillman in his office in Washington and got the okay."[35] Blaine Marrin also recalled a collective planning process, with Stevenson, Reuther, and others participating in a key meeting during a recess of the state CIO convention in Bay City, Michigan.[36]

In early June, Reuther called on GM to recommence negotiations for a supplemental tool and die agreement. Reuther stressed that internal factionalism was a thing of the past in the UAW-CIO, and since the union was not demanding sole recognition for all GM workers, the NLRB had no role to play. There was, he pointed out, no jurisdictional dispute to muddy the water, since "[Homer] Martin's so-called charter from the AFL deprives him of any jurisdiction over tool and die makers." For the public record, Reuther insisted that the union was simply bargaining for skilled tradesmen, though he and executives at General Motors were well aware that success in this strategic realm would win the UAW-CIO de facto recognition for production workers as well as skilled. "If William Knudsen insists that only the courts can decide who shall speak for GM workers," Reuther warned, "we will be compelled to tell him to see if the courts can make his tools and dies." When Knudsen subsequently questioned the urgency of resolving this strike threat, Reuther drew attention to the fleeting nature of the skilled workers' bargaining leverage. "Within a few weeks, General Motors will have completed its tool and die program and will then, as in other years, throw its most skilled employees on the streets for nine and ten months of unemployment." The union's national bargaining council for GM workers, chaired by the Scotsman Bill Stevenson, had already identified the issues it expected the company to address, drawing on the bargaining resolutions of its 1938 conference.[37]

Union balloting between 27 June and 2 July produced prostrike majorities of 87–96 percent among tool and die workers at eight General Motors plants in Detroit and Pontiac. When efforts by U.S. Department of Labor mediator James Dewey—by now, an experienced hand in Detroit strikes—failed to produce any movement in preliminary negotiations, the union called out its first contingent of strikers on 5 July. "The watchwords," said the UAW *Strike Bulletin*, "are solidarity and discipline. . . . Power under control!"[38]

Fisher Body Plant 21 led the way. Many dies for General Motors were nearly finished or were being completed in outside job shops, but the company's only maker of checking fixtures for stamping and body-welding operations was Plant 21. "They couldn't do a damn thing unless they could use the checking fixtures after the die," recalled Marrin. "We were the key plant." On a hot July morning the day after Independence Day, Marrin and his committee went to the top floor of the six-story factory, located a half mile east of General's Motor's headquarters in mid-Detroit. "We blew a whistle and walked out—one floor at a time." The following day, members of Local 157 shut down neighboring Fisher 23, and UAW strikers closed GM toolrooms at the Detroit Gear and Axle Plant and Pontiac Fisher. To sustain a sense of momentum and widening support, the union held back the next round of plant walkouts until 7 July, when strikers closed the Fisher 37 Stamping Plant and the captive toolrooms at Cadillac, Fleetwood, and Ternstedt. Except for the 400 diemakers in Pontiac, the union's first contingent of nearly 6,000 strikers was concentrated in Detroit, where Unity caucus and CIO backing were strongest. These Detroit plants were joined on 10 July by toolroom strikers in Cleveland and Saginaw, Michigan, but it was not until 24 July—three weeks into the walkout—that diemakers in Flint's Fisher Plant 1 joined the strike.[39]

In Detroit, the walkout had overwhelming but not quite unanimous support. At the Fleetwood plant, the company claimed that only 50 of 250 tool and die makers walked out, but the union said the entire toolroom was emptied and the only men in the plant were nonstriking production workers. Elsewhere, the company retained the loyalty of only a handful of tradesmen, a few of whom crossed the picket line, while others stayed home and refused their picket duty. Shop bulletins for each striking unit damned these shirkers, while praising the stalwarts who did their turn on the picket line. "William Curran is a happy man these days," the *Fisher 21 Key Hole* said of one especially punctual Anglo-Gaelic striker. Under the title "Hoot Mon," the bulletin explained that "Scotty" Curran's new electric razor not only made shaving a pleasure but enabled him to get to the picket line at the start of his shift—reason enough, the *Key Hole* concluded, for some of his tardier mates to get electric razors. Those who never made it to the lines were subjected to a withering attack. The *Key Hole* featured a few in front-page profiles with appropriate nicknames: Jim McQueen, the "Wall Street Lizard," or John Schreiber, the previously mentioned "Nazi's Fisherman." The editors heaped particular scorn on the "Reverend" Christian Fink, "who apparently served his time in the pulpit." Articulating the anticlerical bias of many tradesmen, the *Key Hole* reminded "good deacon" Fink of the slang meaning in his name, and warned him to either "change his tune" about the union or take his tent and go "bull s--- innocent victims out of their nickel." Other strike units also pt pressure on nonstriking co-workers. The *Ternstedt Picket* published an "S" list of their names beneath a picture of a rat, with one Clyde O'Brien, among others, warned to "recall what happens to spies. Some Irishmen have a short memory," the *Picket* continued. "Remember when 'pal' Broden fired you, Clyde, m' boy?" The *Cadillac Steward* went beyond such printed invective and announced a "Visiting Committee" to picket the homes of nonstriking workers. "You can never tell whose home they will picket next," the *Steward* warned. "Better be on the safe side." Most were. "The number of scabs has decreased from eight to four out here," the GM *Picket* reported from Fleetwood on 23 July. "And the four aren't very comfortable."[40]

While the strikers effectively immobilized preparations for the 1940 models, production of GM's 1939 models continued, though with mounting difficulties. Initially relegated to the sidelines by the union's strike strategy, production workers became more central to the conflict as the UAW grew confident it could mobilize them for the union and as the company tried to mobilize them for strikebreaking. General Motors, hoping to galvanize a backlash against the skilled tradesmen, publicly linked every strike-related disruption with the production-worker layoffs that followed. On the strike's second day, the company announced that cutter grinders at the Gear and Axle Plant had joined the walkout, causing a shortage of sharpened tools and requiring the imminent layoff of 5,500 production workers. None of these workers, said the company, would be eligible for the new program of interest-free loans that it had recently made available to laid-off production workers. The union detected a "divide and conquer" strategy in these actions and probably got the better of the company in the public-relations campaign that followed. "Like Shylock who demanded his pound of flesh," the UAW declared in one leaflet aimed at production workers, "Knudsen withdraws his loan arrangement in hopes that it will stir up hatred of Production workers against skilled workers." Emphasizing that only a victorious skilled-trades strike would "make GM talk turkey for production workers," the union asked these nonstrikers to support the tradesmen by refusing to set new dies or perform maintenance work, and by immediately registering for unemployment benefits and notifying the union if they were laid off. The UAW also asked production workers to cooperate with pickets by showing their badges when they went to work, allowing the union to screen out skilled-trades strikebreakers. In Detroit, these measures won the backing of most production workers, including some 2,500 at the Gear and Axle Plant who joined the picket lines on 6 July before going into work. But in Pontiac, a violent confrontation erupted on the strike's fourth day when the company ordered both night- and day-shift production workers to report for work at 7:00 A.M. Alarmed by this unusual move, 1,000 UAW picketers physically blocked the gates to prevent their entry. After repelling the Pontiac police and county sheriffs, the stone-throwing picketers did not surrender control of the streets until two days later when the Michigan State Police arrived in force. The company was able to bring production workers into the plant, but the union said only 150 responded to the call and the company claimed no more than 450.[41]

With its own toolrooms embargoed by the strike, General Motors turned to its one remaining option, the job-shop toolrooms of Michigan and neighboring states. Securing their services would be no easy matter. On 10 July, Local 14 in Toledo had already ordered its men at the Toledo Machine and Tool Company to "lay aside" die work from General Motors and that night a citywide meeting of Detroit's job-shop stewards voted to do the same. Local 155 and 157 members picketed "within their own jobbing shops," as reporter Carl Haessler later put it, quarantining GM tools and dies. When some shops began laying off workers who refused work from General Motors, Locals 155 and 157 threatened a citywide job-shop strike; when the automaker tried to retrieve its dies from the Frederick Coleman & Sons plant on the West Side, Local 157's 300 shop members barricaded the factory and repelled several police efforts to break their embargo. Only after George Addes arrived on the scene and explained the company's legal right to retrieve its unfinished dies did the pickets relent and let the trucks through.[42]

Efforts to mobilize AFL members as strikebreakers also failed. Among the few AFL craftsmen inside General Motors, most had joined the walkout, including 135 patternmakers at Fisher Body and sixty electricians at Ternstedt. AFL construction tradesmen also refused to cross CIO picket lines and work on plant renovations for Fisher. Top AFL leaders ordered these men back to their jobs, provoking picket-line scuffles at several plants, but some AFL members and local leaders still refused to scab. "Our members are not going through the picket lines," said Patternmaker leader Frank Tise. "We don't have to take orders from the AFL." After federation leaders rebuked Tise for this open defiance, he dutifully attacked the CIO for its "extralegal" tactics but said his men still refused to cross UAW picket lines for fear of physical violence.[43]

The failure to find workers who could or would complete GM's die program ultimately forced the company to settle with the UAW-CIO. But before this failure was fully evident, other events had already forced the company to resume negotiations with the union. Chief among these was the NLRB's refusal to expedite consideration of GM's case. When the board announced on 10 July that its investigation would take two or three months, the company was left with no legal strategy for refusing to bargain. On 12 July, federal mediator Dewey convened a meeting between Knudsen and CIO vice president Murray, and after a "rough" session, as Dewey termed it, the two agreed that negotiations would resume that afternoon. The GM *Picket* welcomed Murray's presence in negotiations, noting that the CIO leader was a former coal miner, "but he feels at home among tool and die makers. He's Scotch—with a burr from here to Glasgow."[44]

While the company still pursued its search for alternative ways to weaken the strike, negotiations snagged on GM's refusal to negotiate company-wide wage rates or compromise on overtime premiums and the union label. But the company's public support was steadily eroding. Even its success turned against it: GM's announcement in late July of a $134 million profit for the first six months of 1939, triple the $44 million figure for the same period in 1938, gave credence to UAW charges of corporate greed. The company's bargaining strength slipped further on 4 August, when the Michigan Compensation Commission ruled against it and declared laid-off production workers eligible for benefits. Preparations for the 1940 model year had meanwhile come to a halt, while Ford and Chrysler forged ahead. When strikers at Pontiac retrieved an early-model GM car from the dump and paraded it as a "1940 Pontiac produced from scab tool and dies," their mocking gesture aptly conveyed GM's predicament.[45]

On 3 August, the company and the union reached a tentative agreement, and strikers ratified the settlement the next day by a 5,500 to 50 margin. In the single most important concession won by the four-week strike, General Motors agreed to recognize the UAW-CIO as the exclusive bargaining agent in those plants (now numbering forty-one of fifty-nine) where there was no competing AFL committee. In this regard, the company promised that any substitution of committeemen "would only be made by the Local union and must be certified by the Chairman of the plant committee and the officers of such Local Union," thereby foreclosing a return of Martin's rump group. Bargaining rights in the eleven plants where dual committees still existed would be determined later. In return for this de facto recognition, the UAW-CIO promised it would "not cause or permit its members to cause" any strikes during the contract "until all negotiations through the regular established procedure have failed." The union thereby pledged itself to the delicate task of opposing wildcat strikes.[46]

The rest of the agreement included some partial concessions from the company but fell short of the UAW's initial demands. General Motors agreed to substantial increases in overtime pay, including double-time for Sunday work, but refused to accept the demand for a union label on all of its dies. The agreement postponed discussion of seniority and apprenticeship standards, and proposed a compromise on the union's demand for company-wide classifications and wage rates. Although General Motors refused to negotiate such a company-wide system, it agreed to accept the classifications and wage rates already negotiated in Fisher Plant 23 as "a pattern" for plant-by-plant negotiations elsewhere. Hourly minimums for the twenty-six classifications covered by the Plant 23 agreement were five to twenty cents lower than the minimums called for in the union's October 1938 meeting and included such "brand name" classifications as "Lucas and Ingersoll" (boring mills), "Giddings and Lewis" (planer-type mills), and "Ingersoll planer and mill." But the company did agree to bring Ternstedt, Fleetwood, Fisher Pontiac, Flint Fisher 1, and other Detroit Fisher plants up to these rates; other tool and maintenance workers would be raised to minimums no more than five cents below the Fisher 23 benchmark. The union did not win an across-the-board wage raise of ten cents, but wage increases to meet the Plant 23 standard would average out to five cents an hour.[47]

These pennies hardly mattered when measured against the strike's incalculable gains for the UAW-CIO. With this first tangible victory since 1937, the union galvanized an immediate revival of the momentum it had lost in the intervening two years. By the time it reconvened for its 1940 convention, the UAW-CIO had won NLRB elections in 110 plants covering 227,000 workers. More than half of these victories came on a single day in April 1940, when the NLRB finally held balloting in fifty-eight GM factories across the country. With the momentum won in the tool and die strike, the union now welcomed the NLRB ballot and had good reason to celebrate the results: the UAW-CIO won in forty-eight plants, the UAW-AFL in only five, and MESA in one. The voting highlighted previous patterns of regional and occupational support for the contending factions. Of the approximately 23,100 voters in GM's fourteen Detroit plants, only 1,456 (6.3 percent) chose the UAW-AFL, while Martin's 9,940 votes in Flint represented nearly 30 percent of the total vote in that city—well above the 21 percent he won nationwide. The UAW-AFL's handful of victories were all outside Michigan (Ohio, Missouri, and Connecticut); the sole nonunion plant was in Buffalo, New York, and the no-union vote was high enough to force runoffs in Indiana and Maryland.[48]

Ironically, while the skilled workers at General Motors gave the UAW-CIO its biggest relative margins in favor of industrial unionism, they also voted for craft unions in several departmental elections. The UAW-CIO swamped the UAW-AFL by votes of 837 to 10 at Fisher Plant 23 and 263 to 6 at Fisher Plant 21, both strongholds of Local 157. But the AFL Patternmakers League won four of nine craft-unit elections in Michigan and Ohio for patternmakers, and MESA won a plant-wide majority of the predominantly skilled work force at GM's Detroit Diesel Plant. Skilled workers would not vote for Homer Martin, but a minority still believed that craft rather than industrial unionism was the better vehicle for representing their interests. "We are," said Patternmakers League president George Lynch, "skilled craftsmen, not auto workers."[49]

Showdown at Dodge

With its strike victory at General Motors, the union turned to Chrysler, the second-largest employer under UAW contract. Here, as at General Motors, management had also exploited UAW factionalism and Martin's "dual union" as the pretext for suspending collective bargaining. But in this case, the UAW-CIO could not count on the bargaining leverage of skilled workers to recover the initiative—Chrysler's skilled work force was too small and too cautious to spark such a revival. At

Dodge, the company's flagship plant, the outcome hinged on the more than 20,000 production workers who labored in the massive complex. But even here, individual craftsmen would play a vital leadership role, and Anglo-Gaelic leaders a prominent one.

"The factional strife is over," Scotsman David McIntyre announced at an All Stewards meeting in early February, shortly after Martin's final split with the International Executive Board. McIntyre's sanguine assessment of the situation in the Dodge local was premature but indicative of a growing certainty that upcoming elections would finally decide the issue. Martin's supporters had already lost control of the local's incumbent Executive Board: a 19 January roll-call vote to rescind President Frank Reid's unauthorized scheduling of a pro-Martin mass meeting passed by a 10 to 9 margin favoring the Unity caucus; two weeks later, after Martin's supporters in Local 51 had demolished the Plymouth local's nearby hall, a resolution committing Local 3 to the CIO and R. J. Thomas passed by a substantially wider vote of 13 to 7. Thereafter, as Martin's support weakened on the local Executive Board, his Progressive caucus split between diehards favoring the former president's AFL "dual" union and moderates favoring a Progressive slate within the UAW-CIO. The former came to the attention of the Local 3 Executive Board on 26 February when they tried to pack a critical meeting with black members and some whites holding falsified dues receipts; after questioning by alert officers who detected an "unusual" number of black participants (testimony to the union's failure to recruit African-American workers), the gate crashers confessed they had been sent by officers Ed McCann and O. D. Hamel with instructions to break up the meeting. In the meantime, Henry Bartell, a member of the Plant Committee and another diehard Martinite, leafleted the plant with flyers naming John Zaremba and other Unity caucus leaders as Communists. Not surprisingly, the pro-CIO board immediately convened a hearing and collected ample evidence to condemn these men for their splitting tactics. Equally telling, the moderate Progressives took McCann off their slate for the upcoming elections in Local 3 and replaced him with Joe Mehlic as candidate for vice president.[50]

Their efforts to distance themselves from McCann and other "dual" unionists proved unconvincing to the majority of Dodge workers. In the local balloting that followed, Pat Quinn's CIO slate routed the Progressive caucus, winning every executive office and electing pro-CIO candidates to all six positions on the Plant Committee. Anglo-Saxon and Gaelic names still predominated in the leadership ranks, but two Polish Americans won reelection to top office: John Zaremba, recording secretary, and E. J. Danielowski, financial secretary. As in previous years, the only candidate that every faction could support was David McIntyre, who ran for convention delegate on both the Unity and the Progressive slates. He was joined on the new Plant Committee by another Anglo-Gaelic tradesman, the English toolmaker and sit-down leader Tom Hanlon.[51]

Confronted by this irrefutable endorsement of the CIO, many Progressives retired from leadership or redefined their role and cooperated with Quinn's new administration. This second alternative did not necessarily indicate rank opportunism, since Frank Reid, Barney Hopkins, and others who had supported the International union's elected president found Martin's subsequent endorsement of the AFL ample reason to repudiate their former leader. The diehards, however, still had to be dealt with. O. D. Hamel and fourteen others who openly sided with Martin's UAW-AFL were charged with "dual unionism" in April and placed in the hands of David McIntyre and six other members of a special Trial Board. Other Progressives who remained in the UAW-CIO but continued in small ways to favor Martin by word or deed posed a more difficult problem. In late April, the Executive Board suspended one chief steward merely for indicating he was "neutral" concerning the UAW-AFL, an action deemed in violation of the Executive Board's strong endorsement of the CIO. But three board members abstained from this decision and seven others, prominent Unity leaders among them, voted against suspending the man, apparently feeling it was too harsh a punishment for such a passive expression of opposition. Pat Quinn led the thirteen-vote majority favoring suspension, and he relied on this backing for a second motion empowering the Executive Board to appoint future replacements for any steward suspended on charges of dual unionism. Quinn, the "police chief" of 1937, would tolerate no quislings.[52]

Other suspensions followed, but Quinn and his supporters were well aware that only a resounding victory in the upcoming NLRB elections would settle the issue once and for all. The local began to prepare for the September balloting by establishing a Propaganda Committee. Quinn led the three-man operation, joined by two former Progressives: Barney Hopkins, a production worker from the pressroom, and George Miller, the diemaker, aspiring lawyer, and former Works Council supporter of 1937, now active on the local's Executive Board. In early August, the "Labor Vote Committee," as it was rechristened, expanded to five members and acquired extraordinary powers to commandeer the resources of the local. The new members were both drawn from the Plant Committee: Englishman Tom Hanlon, the toolmaker, joined by Harold Curry. On 1 August, the Executive Board not only ceded to this reconstituted committee control of the local's sound truck, newspaper, and all printed matter produced for the upcoming election, but also gave it the right to call meetings and to control the local's paramilitary "Flying Squadron." To cover any further contingencies, a final motion stipulated that "all the facilities of the office of Dodge Local 3 be placed at the disposal of the Labor Vote Committee." Dodge Local 3, in effect, had created a five-man executive committee to steer the union through its most decisive campaign for State-certified recognition. The leadership cadre the local drew upon had the same characteristics identified in previous episodes of union organization: in a local of Eastern European production workers, the Labor Vote Committee was led by two Anglo-Gaelic workers and two tool and die makers, with the balance drawn from native-born production workers.[53]

Their efforts helped produce the categorical destruction of the UAW-AFL in Chrysler. In the September balloting conducted by the NLRB, Martin's union could only win narrow majorities in two small Indiana plants with a total of 1,220 voters. In the company's eight Detroit-area plants, the UAW-AFL had only 9.4 percent of the 45,000 ballots cast, and two-thirds of these were concentrated in the Plymouth plant. Martin won only 4.7 percent of the 8,300 ballots at the Chrysler-Kercheval plant, and only 4.0 percent of the 20,585 votes at Dodge. The UAW-CIO's nearly 37,000 votes were 82 percent of the total in Detroit, with only 8.8 percent voting no-union.[54]

The NLRB election ended all debate over the UAW-CIO's majority status at Dodge; immediately following the vote, the Executive Board opened negotiations with the remnants of the UAW-AFL for reinstatement of approximately 300 members who wished to return to the CIO. But the election left unresolved the boundaries of the collective-bargaining relationship it mandated. In the fall of 1939, Pat Quinn, president of Local 3, with David McIntyre and Tom Hanlon, leaders of the Plant Committee, launched a campaign to extend these boundaries toward joint deliberation of production standards.[55]

At stake was more than just job descriptions and work loads in a single plant. Beyond these, as the conflict at Dodge spread throughout the corporation, the company and the union contended for alternative conceptions of "who controlled the plants." The company's position on this matter was the clearer for being unqualified. Chrysler would more readily, though still grudgingly, compromise on wage issues than accept any dilution of its previous unilateral right to manage production. "Production schedules are the management's function," said Herman Weckler, Chrysler vice president in charge of operations. "You

may as well know now that we do not intend to give your union control
of production." Dodge Local 3 made no such unilateral claim for control of production but demanded instead "joint fixing of production
standards by the corporation and the union."[56]

Since "joint" procedures could not be unilaterally imposed, the
union's position had to remain ambiguous so long as the company refused to negotiate the matter. But Local 3 gave some indication of its
intentions that fall when the union issued proposals for new local by-
laws. The key changes concerned the respective roles of the six-
member Plant Committee, the roughly 180 chief stewards (also called
district committeemen) scattered among the Dodge plant's many departments and sections, and the approximately 700 "blue button" and
"white button" deputy stewards who worked on the line, collected
dues, and reported to their departmental chief steward. During the factionalism of previous years, the local's divided Executive Board had
favored centralized bargaining, stipulating that chief stewards could
take no action in their district without the permission of the Plant Committee. Proposed rules governing the actions of chief stewards had
been opposed by some Unity caucus leaders, but the board majority
determined that any steward who led an unauthorized work stoppage
would be reprimanded by the local. The local Executive Board had also
relegated deputy stewards to a minor role, recommending they be barred from plant-wide meetings of chief stewards. Committeemen and
stewards had not always abided by these rules. At one "All Stewards"
meeting in May 1938, presided over by Quinn, then chairman of the
Plant Committee, the body had rejected the local Executive Board's recommendation that only Plant Committee members and chief stewards
be admitted to the room; contrary to the wishes of the Executive Board,
the deputy stewards were invited to remain. But the tension between
departmental and centralized bargaining continued, with an emphasis
on the powers of the Plant Committee.[57]

The following year, after Quinn and his Unity caucus followers took
control of the Executive Board, the local shifted the emphasis toward
decentralized representation and increased powers for chief stewards.
The new bylaws issued in the fall stipulated that the Plant Committee
could not "invade" the jurisdiction of a chief steward without permission, and chief stewards could not settle a grievance without "the
approval of the majority of the union men affected." The chief steward
had the right to "appoint or elect, if the group wishes, as many deputy
stewards as may be necessary to aid in his or her duties," at a ratio of "at
least one deputy steward for a group of twenty or less." The bylaws
also defined the plant-wide Steward's Council in the broadest possible

terms to include the union's Executive Board, Plant Committee, chief stewards, assistant stewards, and deputy stewards. In effect, the new bylaws called for "sectional bargaining," as historian Steve Jefferys has called it, with the initial negotiation of work standards and other matters delegated to the chief stewards rather than the Plant Committee.[58]

Chrysler would have none of this. The densely organized steward system at Dodge posed an alarming challenge to managers schooled in the unilateral ways of scientific management. In an October public statement, Herman Weckler, vice president at Chrysler, focused his entire remarks on the "army" of union stewards in the plant. Their sheer numbers, he complained, surpassed the company's force of shop-floor superintendents and foremen. Deputy stewards worked "under shop committee men and district committee men who defy the factory management and tell foremen what the men will and will not do." Obviously outraged by this innovation in union organization, the company's vice president described how these leaders used the departmental washrooms as "a 'command post' from which to direct orders." Deputy stewards acted on these commands with "lightning speed" but were otherwise, in Weckler's eyes, a generally chaotic bunch, lacking firm "rank" or stability of tenure. "Men may wear the 'white button' today and not tomorrow," as Weckler put it. "This body of self-appointed operators of our business have tried to take over control of our production, getting steadily more and more arrogant and openly defying the management." Chrysler's president K. T. Keller, was no less emphatic in an open letter to the company's car dealers, writing of men who "tell their foreman what they will do and what they will not do." Keller vowed to prevent these stewards from taking "into their own hands the running of the plants."[59]

In August and September 1939, as Chrysler brought its 1940 models into production, these issues came to a head over production standards. Negotiations for a new agreement had gone nowhere since the old contract expired in March, and the union said the company, in the interim extensions of the contract, had increased work loads and eliminated jobs. New-model introductions always generated some conflict over the alteration of job descriptions and work standards, but the number of such disputes proliferated at Dodge, as elsewhere in Chrysler. In some departments, according to the union, output simply increased over the previous standard, with no matching increase in labor force or fixed capital; in others, output remained the same but the number of workers fell. In still others, the speed and work force remained the same, but the work intensity increased nevertheless: in Heat Treat, because there were too few relief men; in the Crankshaft

Department because shafts were four pounds heavier, requiring handlers to lift two additional tons in a single shift. The union estimated the overall "speedup" at 20 percent. The company said there was no speedup, and that stewards were organizing resistance to reasonable work orders. The dispute contributed to a growing number of grievance hearings, and these rarely produced a timely resolution of the issue. In a front-page article in *Dodge Main News*, Tom Hanlon, secretary of the Plant Committee, complained that management, rather than negotiate grievances, referred the Plant Committee to a newly designated "labor relations supervisor." This individual was always available, "but he only has the power to investigate or replace a worn-out clock," said Hanlon. "It usually takes about two weeks for an answer, which is generally 'no.'" Hanlon dubbed this labor-relations system a "Comic Opera Maginot Line," staffed by "powerless Gilbert and Sullivan generals." Even by the company's reckoning, only one-third of all grievances were settled in the workers' favor, and without mandatory arbitration, the union had just two alternatives when the company refused to budge: accept management's unilateral rulings, or employ Direct Action to compel negotiation.[60]

There was little doubt that Local 3 would ultimately resort to the latter. The tone had already been set in May, following the Cleveland convention, when the newly elected Plant Committee confirmed Pat Patrick as chairman despite his recent firing for "insulting and intimidating remarks to [a] foreman." In practice, however, Patrick's removal from the plant made it difficult for him to lead the Plant Committee, and by October he was organizing Chrysler workers in Kokomo, Indiana. During his absence, Harold Curry became temporary chairman of the Plant Committee, but it was McIntyre who most often represented the committee at Executive Board and steward meetings. On 9 September, McIntyre reported to the board at length on the "serious situation" in the Pressed Steel Department and the foundry, where management claimed slowdowns were in progress. Claiming no knowledge of any slowdown, McIntyre stated "most emphatically that the Plant Committee does oppose all speed ups." His recommendation that the local's top officers needed to join the negotiations, and that the International be brought in if necessary, were both carried by the board. That same day, at an All Stewards meeting chaired by Pat Quinn, McIntyre told the assembled body "that the Plant Committee would not sanction any slowdowns, but would aggressively oppose any speed-ups." McIntyre, whose lengthy report dominated this strategy session, linked the many disputes over production standards with the pending negotiations on a new contract: "In some of the departments, the machine has made slaves of men, which should be the reverse. The contract was not written for such a purpose and the Plant Committee was elected to protect the members of this local." He then articulated the union's strategy in its confrontation with Chrysler management: "Keep [the] plant operating no matter what happens, because a walk out is just what the company desires. If the plant is to be shut down, allow the company of having that privilege."[61] Workers should produce only what had been expected of them under the old production standard; in this sense, they were not slowing down so much as they were refusing to speed up. By remaining on the job and withholding some of their labor, rather than initiating a walkout, they invited management to take the first overtly aggressive act.[62]

Management obliged them. On 6 October, one week after the last contract extension had expired, the company fired a group of men on the body welding line for refusing to meet the new production standard. As in the sit-down two years before, the body plant, paint department, and trim shop were the centers of union strength and the most disciplined practitioners of McIntyre's "work-to-past-practices." In the weeks preceding the firings, the slowdown (as the company called it) had spread from these union strongholds to other departments. "After the Labor Board elections on September 27," President Keller later complained, "the slowdowns got worse and more widespread." Chrysler's top executive couldn't help but be impressed, as well as outraged, by the union's disciplined strangulation of production. Four days before the firings, a union officer had warned one plant manager that the next morning the slowdown would spread to the motor lines and cut production 25 percent. "Promptly at the hour he named," said Keller, "output fell off by almost exactly as he had predicted. . . . Pistons, connecting rods, cam shafts, cylinder heads . . . all were short by an average of about 25 percent." "The 'slow down,'" Keller concluded in his public condemnation of these tactics, "is a blood relative of the 'sit down.'"[63]

With the first firings on Friday, 6 October, the Executive Board convened a special meeting the following Sunday morning to determine its response. After reports from the Plant Committee by McIntyre, Hanlon, and Curry, the board appointed a special five-man committee to make recommendations on how the union should address an emergency meeting of the membership. The presence of Anglo-Gaelic leaders and skilled workers on this "Committee of Five" was even more pronounced than the previous Labor Vote Committee: Quinn and the British tradesmen McIntyre and Hanlon made up three-fifths of the committee, joined by a third tradesman, George Miller, and by the chairman of the Plant Committee, Harold Curry. With the Executive Board temporarily adjourned, these five men determined the strategy and the organizational structure that would guide Local 3 through the crisis. When the Executive Board reconvened that afternoon, it accepted each of their recommendations: that the fired men should report for work on Monday; that the rank and file be given instructions which, though unspecified in the board minutes, apparently reconfirmed McIntyre's earlier injunctions to stay on the job and "work to past practices"; and that the Plant Committee and five Executive Board members constitute a ten-man Strategy Committee to conduct the strike.[64]

By 12 October, the company had fired 105 stewards and other union supporters, but these disciplinary actions only intensified the conflict. In some departments, the company claimed production fell to 50 percent of capacity after the firings, with workers on the paint line allowing every second car to go by untouched. The backup of unfinished work soon choked off production, forcing management to shut the plant.[65]

The union called it a lockout. Management called it a strike. It wasn't until 15 October, when UAW members voted official strike authorization, that the two sides could even agree on the nature of their dispute. The margin of victory in the strike vote, coming less than three weeks after the union's landslide NLRB victory, must have given the company pause. Turnout was high, and the 13,751 Dodge workers who favored strike action overwhelmed the 1,324 who opposed it. If the company thought the UAW's base had irrecoverably eroded during two years of faction fighting, it had miscalculated. It now had a major battle on its hands as other Chrysler locals joined the walkout, and the UAW reiterated its corporate-wide demands: negotiation of production standards; arbitration of unresolved grievances; union shop; general wage increase of 10 percent; special rate adjustments for skilled workers; paid vacations; and reinstatement of fired workers.[66]

For six weeks, Chrysler tried to fend off defeat. It had few allies in this endeavor. Father Coughlin called the strike un-Christian and Moscow-inspired; Homer Martin rallied black supporters for a back-to-work movement; and the *Detroit Free Press* termed the walkout "a conscious effort . . . to impose communistic control in those plants." These fulminations mattered little when the UAW could count among its supporters Archbishop Mooney and key Protestant ministers from African-American congregations. The NLRB also backed the UAW by designating Chrysler's eleven plants as a single unit, overriding the company's insistence on separate contracts for each plant. As the NLRB foreclosed on the company's divide-and-rule strategy, and as General Motors and other competitors accelerated production of their 1940 models, Chrysler resorted to increasingly desperate actions. On 27 and 28 November, these culminated in a clumsy effort to bring black strike-breakers into the Dodge foundry. This provocative act backfired when the predominantly white UAW picketers ignored the company's invitation to a race riot and allowed the handful of strikebreakers to enter the plant. Thoroughly discredited, the company capitulated the next day.[67]

Chrysler could take little solace in the agreement that ended the strike. The company successfully resisted demands for the union shop and paid vacations, and bargained the general wage increase down from ten cents to three. But the union won many of its key demands, including a new four-member Joint Appeal Board to rule on unresolved grievances, and reinstatement of all those fired in the "slowdown." Equally important, the settlement established new procedures for shop-floor representation and adjustment of production standards. The contract expanded recognition for chief stewards and assistant chief stewards, granting them super seniority and the right to leave their jobs for union business at no loss in pay. Workers could protest new production standards through the grievance procedure, and chief stewards could now negotiate revised standards with the general foreman or departmental superintendent. If these negotiations failed, the dispute went to the Plant Committee and higher-level management.[68]

By ratifying the "sectional" bargaining called for in Local 3's September bylaws, the contract gave the Dodge steward system a unique potency. At General Motors, where a sustained union presence among production workers came years after the organization of Dodge, the steward system had shallower roots and a smaller impact on in-plant negotiations. The GM contract of 1937 and the supplement negotiated in March of the following year mandated only one member of the Shop Committee for every 400 workers and specifically ruled that line stewards had no role in the grievance procedure. Only in 1940, following the victories in the tool and die strike at General Motors and the slowdown at Dodge, did the new GM agreement incorporate a similar expansion of union representation. There would now be one committeeman and alternate for every 250 workers, with the understanding that these committeemen could appoint "as many assistant dues collectors as are necessary." Significantly, however, these front-line union representatives were mandated by their title only to perform the specific function of collecting dues. At Dodge, the contractual structure was similar, but the actual representation was far denser. The contract recognized roughly the same ratio of formal representatives as at General Motors (plant committeemen and chief stewards at Chrysler) and made no mention of line stewards. But there was also no effort to denature the line steward with specific language or titles restricting his or her role. Consequently, in addition to collecting dues, the "deputy" stewards designated by the local's bylaws carried the union's mandate to "aid [the chief steward] in his or her duties." In this respect, the structure expressed a vitality more akin to the shop-floor representation in tool and die job shops. There were many influences that contributed to this decentralized form of shop-floor bargaining at Dodge: the early company sanctioning of departmental representation in the Works Council; the AIWA's early arrival and its initial organization into departmental "locals" with their own unit officers; the wider participation of union supporters in the 1937 sit-down (compared with those at General Motors); the sheer concentrated mass of the plant work force—second only to Ford Rouge—which required some form of organizational extension beyond the committee structure; the elaboration of that extension in a steward system that predated the procedural norms of arbitration/umpire systems; and Chrysler management's failure to promote alternative structures of centralized bargaining.[69]

In addition, there is ample reason to hypothesize a vital role for the individuals who founded and led this steward system. Two men stand out in this regard: Dave McIntyre, the local's first chairman of the Plant Committee and a key leader of the 1939 slowdown, and Pat Quinn, the second chairman of the Plant Committee and the predominant local leader during both the sit-down and the slowdown. Unlike Richard Frankensteen and other "outside" leaders who initially held the limelight as executive officers, McIntyre and Quinn built their base inside the plant, as organizers and leaders of the stewards. Their formative role establishing this in-plant organization gave both men an unusually wide base, making Quinn the top vote getter in local elections and McIntyre a consensus candidate for every faction. In 1939, they purged the steward system of Martinites and "neutrals," and schooled their followers in the disciplines of shop-floor leadership. It was McIntyre, joined by Curry, who recommended to the Executive Board in June of 1939 that classes be established to train stewards, with a stenographic record of these classes to be used as a stewards's handbook. There is no record of who taught these classes, but McIntyre was the obvious candidate: not only was he the sole member of the Plant Committee to have served continuously since 1937, but as a twenty-seven-year-old skilled welder when he emigrated from the Clydeside in 1919, he undoubtedly brought with him some experience with Scottish shop organization. Quinn had no such experience with British unions, but he definitely brought with him the combativeness of an IRA veteran. Tom Hanlon, the Tyneside engineer who emigrated in 1926, brought a facility for the "language of class" that made him the local's propaganda chief in 1939, articulating the union's position in front-page articles for *Dodge Main News*.[70]

Like the Anglo-Gaelic leaders of Detroit's toolmakers, these men were uniquely qualified to speak the language and teach the practice of "power under control."

Eclipse

"I may be so bold to say," Bill Stevenson observed in later years, "had it not been for the determination of the skilled workers in 1939, we might not be where we are today."[71]

Given his prominent role in the events of 1939, Stevenson had personal reasons for highlighting the contribution of his constituents in the skilled trades. Even so, there are no creditable grounds for disputing his claim that without the successful tool and die strike of that year, the UAW would have been a fundamentally different union. General Motors would not have been reclaimed to the CIO, and failure here would certainly have diminished the UAW's recovery elsewhere. Defeat in 1939 would have made the preceding victories of 1937 less of a watershed and more akin to the spasmodic union advances of 1885 and 1919. NLRB action or government intervention during World War II would have given the UAW-CIO a second chance to organize General Motors, but victory through procedural action would have reinforced the already visible drift toward bureaucratic norms in union organization. Instead, the victory of the tool and die strike enabled the union to win—on its own terms—a secure position in the auto industry's leading firm. While the union's shop-floor representation at GM was comparatively weak, it owed whatever vitality it possessed to a presence won through Direct Action rather than federal intervention.

The tool and die strike posed in the most dramatic manner the role of strategic groups in leading a mass movement. There were, by the union's estimate, roughly 200,000 workers at GM in 1939; the approximately 6,000 skilled tradesmen who carried the union to victory represented just 3 percent of the total work force. Distinguished from the production-worker majority by their craft knowledge, these skilled workers also represented a distinct ethno-cultural minority. As indicated in previous chapters, Detroit's skilled workers were predominantly foreign-born, with the most prominent of their leaders coming from Britain and northern Ireland. Their preeminent role in the 1939 tool and die strike was perhaps the clearest indication of how Anglo-Gaelic leaders and activists played a disproportionate part in founding Detroit's auto unions. In other key events and organizational initiatives, their determining role is substantial but sometimes less obvious. At Dodge, where skilled workers collectively played a small role, the strategic occupational groups were semiskilled body welders, finishers, painters, and trimmers. But individual tradesmen and Anglo-Gaelic leaders played a significant role in defining the union's in-plant organization and strategy.

"Power under control," the slogan of the 1939 tool and die strike, can be taken as the motto of these Anglo-Gaelic militants. Even when union strategy called for violence, as in MESA's 1933 strike, the targets were carefully chosen, the attacks carefully coordinated. Like their American-born counterparts, Anglo-Gaelic leaders discouraged random violence and impulsive militancy. American-born leaders, however, generally put more trust in procedural action as an alternative to such improvised acts, whereas Anglo-Gaelic leaders favored disciplined Direct Action. This did not mean that Anglo-Gaelic leaders counterpoised Direct Action *against* procedural action. "Power under control" implied something more subtle: a recognition that Direct Action could strengthen the union's position in procedural action, while procedural action could protect and ratify the gains of Direct Action. Imbalance in either direction could weaken the union. Excessive reliance on procedural action could attenuate the capacity and will for Direct Action, and make the union overly dependent on a legalistic process where lawyers and government regulators defined the issues. On the other hand, excessive use of Direct Action could exhaust membership and public support, and provoke extreme countermeasures from employers and the State. This delicate interdependence of union strategy was not lost on a growing number of American-born militants. But many arrived at this understanding in the 1930s only after painful trial and error. Their Anglo-Gaelic counterparts, in contrast, had already learned some of these lessons in the years 1910–1926, when British and Irish workers challenged both employers and the State on a scale that dwarfed comparable union efforts in Detroit and the rest of the United States.

Individual Anglo-Gaelic leaders would continue to play a prominent role in Detroit's auto unions after 1939. At Ford Rouge, where Bill McKie led the first union organization in 1934, Anglo-Gaelic leaders and skilled tradesmen had a virtual lock on the Local 600 presidency in the 1940s. Most were drawn from the Tool and Die unit's Building Committee. In 1941, at least four of nine committeemen were Anglo-Gaelic: W. G. Grant, an English-born toolmaker; Joe McCusker, the former Lanarkshire miner and apprentice in the Ford toolroom; George Campbell, the Clydeside engineer and former AFL supporter; and John Fitzpatrick, another Scots engineer who had previously supported the craft-oriented AFL. Among the American-born tradesmen on the Building Committee was Paul Ste. Marie, a die patternmaker active in the Association of Catholic Trade Unionists. The committee was already split between left and right, with Grant joining the German-born toolmaker Frank Gau and the American-born Walter Dorosh on the left, and Campbell and Fitzpatrick joining the former CIO organizer Joe McCusker on the right. What these men shared, however, was a capacity for leadership that elevated three of them to the presidency of Local 600: first Ste. Marie, followed by Grant in 1944, and McCusker in 1945 for the first of two terms. In 1947, McCusker was succeeded by another Anglo-Gaelic leader, production worker Tommy Thompson, the former coal miner from England. Even Thompson's opponent, the Irishman Michael Magee, came from the United Kingdom.[72]

A similar pattern prevailed in many of Detroit's biggest UAW locals. Norman Mathews, an electrician from Cornwall, won office in Packard Local 190 in 1943; Dave Miller, the Scottish tram driver from Dundee, became the first president of Cadillac Local 22 when it separated from West Side Local 174; and Harry Southwell, the Lancashire grinder hand, won the Local 174 presidency in 1947 and held it for the next sixteen years. Some rose higher still. McCusker, Mathews, and Bill Stevenson all became regional directors and members of the International Executive Board in the 1940s. Three other Anglo-Gaelic leaders also served on the IEB in that decade: Jack Thompson, a veteran of the Irish labor movement who worked at Ford before moving to Toledo and becoming a founding leader of UAW Local 12; William McAuley, a Scottish miner and former UMW member who worked as a body trimmer at General Motors and became a union organizer in Flint and Pontiac; and Alex McGowan, a Clyde shipyard worker who emigrated to New York and became first president of GM Local 664 in Tarrytown. Bill Stevenson also later served as assistant director of the UAW Skilled Trades Department, a post previously held by fellow Scotsman George Campbell.

There was a difference, however, between the leadership role these

Anglo-Gaelic immigrants filled in the 1940s and 1950s, and the role they and others played in the 1930s. Until 1939, the UAW was fighting for its existence, aided only sporadically by the federal government and consistently opposed by employers. This began to change between 1939 and 1941 as the NLRB certified the gains of Direct Action, and as union strike victories forced General Motors, Chrysler, and Ford to begin genuine collective bargaining. Procedural action quickly took precedence over Direct Action. This was inevitable in some respects, since employer acceptance of the union (however grudging) reduced the number of occasions where Direct Action seemed necessary. Employers wanted stable, predictable labor relations, and so did union leaders if such stability allowed for adequate adjustment of grievances. Spurred by the strike militancy of 1939, management agreed to cooperate in the establishment of quasi-judicial mechanisms for dispute resolution: an arbitration board at Chrysler in 1939, and a permanent umpire system at General Motors in 1940. These achievements of "industrial democracy" legitimated the union's presence but gradually restricted its role to the narrow realm of contract administration. After Pearl Harbor, the federal government also sharply restricted the scope of Direct Action. Arbitration became mandatory, with the War Labor Board the ultimate tribunal for resolving disputes. Union-sanctioned strikes resumed after the war, but these mobilizations were ritualistic affairs compared with the picket-line battles of the 1941 strike at Ford—the last occasion where a Big Three employer in Detroit used strikebreakers to counter a UAW walkout. Contracts grew longer and no-strike clauses more common. The Taft-Hartley Act proscribed mass picketing and secondary boycotts in 1947, and over time, the federal courts virtually prohibited Direct Action during the life of the contract. Under Taft-Hartley, the federal government even defined the acceptable range of political beliefs for union officers. And all the while, the accumulating "common law" precedent of arbitration and umpire decisions grew ever more determining in dispute resolution. The steward system grew correspondingly weaker as procedural action moved grievance handling off the shop floor, and as the dues check-off system eliminated the steward's "bread and butter" role.[73]

Some Anglo-Gaelic leaders accommodated to these trends. For them, the new stability represented an acceptable approximation of what they had hoped to achieve or thought was possible. After all, the UAW was not a revolutionary movement, even if many of its founders were members of ostensibly revolutionary parties. Moderate Anglo-Gaelic leaders could accept the grievance-arbitration systems and collective-bargaining arrangements established after 1939 as an acceptable version of the Whitley councils they had known in postwar

Britain. Left-wing Anglo-Gaelic leaders had envisioned a more radical transformation of work and society, but the wartime emergency, the Red Scare that followed, and the conservative political victories of the 1940s persuaded most to lower their sights and accept a Laborite model of piecemeal reform. It was, if nothing else, a model with which they were intimately familiar. The Democratic party was not a labor party, and the UAW was not an "equal partner" with management, but under the circumstances they came close enough to warrant continued faith in the deliberative model of industrial democracy.

Some Anglo-Gaelic leaders resisted the accumulating restrictions on Direct Action. Mat Smith was the most prominent of these. Bitterly opposed to the "world savers" who led the UAW, Smith condemned the CIO's voluntary no-strike pledge during World War II and committed MESA's remaining members to militant Direct Action. Earning a wartime reputation for strike activity second only to that of John L. Lewis and the UMW, Smith and MESA challenged the federal government's growing regulation of the labor movement. "We do not intend to refrain from striking," Smith told congressional investigators during the war, "as we have not as yet met any employers that are worthy of being given that pledge."[74]

Bill McKie was another of the irreconcilables. When the Taft-Hartley Act required union officers to sign a "non-Communist" affidavit, on pain of losing NLRA protection, McKie flatly refused. When the UAW directed its local leaders to comply and Local 600 seconded this order, McKie resigned. "It is certainly well known by most members of this local that I cannot abide by any such order," McKie wrote in his 1948 letter of resignation, "since I am, and intend to remain, a member of the Communist Party." McKie saw in the local's action an abdication of union autonomy. "By surrendering to . . . Taft-Hartley, [Local 600] proposes to cancel the election mandate which an exceptionally large majority gave me after full knowledge of the facts."[75]

Fellow Scotsman Bill Stevenson, regional director from Detroit's West Side when the UAW's Executive Board debated the Taft-Hartley affidavit, also opposed compliance. Later, however, Stevenson reversed his position as the political tides turned against resistance. His subsequent accommodation to the moderating trend in union policy followed a path traveled by other Anglo-Gaelic union leaders. In a 1942 conference where UAW officials defended both the no-strike pledge and their agreement allowing toolroom "upgraders" to operate specialized machines, W. G. Grant spoke in opposition from the floor, calling the "Equality of Sacrifice" program a surrender. By 1944, however, Grant had accepted at least part of the government's wartime program, agreeing to serve as chairman of the UAW's Committee to

Uphold the No-Strike Pledge. Grant had just won election as president of Local 600 with the backing of the Communist Party, which put him in the same camp as John Anderson and other supporters of the party's production-for-victory agenda.[76]

When the bitter factionalism generated by the no-strike pledge later polarized into caucuses of the "left" and "right" in the postwar years, Anglo-Gaelic leaders also divided into warring camps. McKie, Anderson, Miller, Stevenson, Grant, Quinn, Patrick Rice, Tommy Thompson, and others supported Secretary-Treasurer George Addes on the left; Mathews, Southwell, McCusker, Magee, Pat Hamilton, and Tom Doherty, among others, supported Walter Reuther on the right. The left naturally drew those who had joined or identified with the Communist party, and more of these seemed to be Scotsmen. The right won the support of more Irish-Catholics, particularly those allied with ACTU, though two IRA veterans, Quinn and Rice, identified with the left. These alliances were quite fluid, however, since "pork barrel" conflicts over staff appointments and leadership positions also determined factional loyalties. "You get in a factional fight," recalled Doug Fraser, a former member of the Addes caucus, "and sometimes you wonder what the hell the differences are. It becomes personality and loyalty. . . . That happened to me. With Dick Leonard, I left the Reuther caucus because we thought we were getting the short end. . . . It wasn't philosophical or ideological or anything like that." Reuther's victory in 1946–1948 also had a substantial impact, as former Addes supporters abandoned the left wing and joined the pro-Reuther majority.[77]

While factional splits fragmented the Anglo-Gaelic presence in the union, the simultaneous rise of American-born leaders in the skilled trades diluted that presence all the more. Local 157 retained at least one Anglo-Gaelic leader, the Scotsman John Fairbairn, as financial secretary through the 1950s. But the top leadership was American-born after 1942, when Stevenson rose to regional director and American-born Mat Hammond (1942–1947), Dale Harris (1948), and Blaine Marrin (1949–1969) occupied the president's office. After Stevenson lost his regional post in the Reuther victory of 1947, he returned to the shops and challenged Marrin for local president, losing by a 3 to 1 margin. The election generated some bitterness between Stevenson and his self-acknowledged protégé, with Stevenson later threatening court action for Marrin's "slanderous" accusation that the former Local 157 leader was a Communist. The transition to new leadership was also bitterly disputed in Local 155. In 1947, Russell Leach, the American-born diemaker from Murray Body, now working in the East Side job shops, challenged John Anderson for the presidency and lost by only fifty-nine votes of the nearly 3,900 cast. The following year, Scotsman Robert Allison, the popular secretary-treasurer of the local, switched to Leach's pro-Reuther slate. Anderson was further weakened, according to Leach, by his obligation to follow a Communist party platform that opposed negotiation of pension and hospitalization plans. "John started to waffle a bit," Leach said of Anderson's commitment to this portion of the party line, since neither he nor the members believed a left-wing government would soon come to power and introduce these benefits on a universal basis. To win him back to party doctrine, "Nat [Ganley] would really have to lock John into a office and give him hell." Anderson's personal prestige could not overcome the burden of such doctrinaire policies, and in the 1948 election he narrowly lost to Leach. With his future in the UAW foreclosed, Anderson became a negotiator for management in Detroit's tool and die job shops.[78]

Anderson's departure marked the end of an era. Although immigrant craftsmen would continue to play a role in the industry, they no longer predominated in the membership or the leadership. Skilled workers were increasingly American-born and American-trained—but they inherited the same problems their predecessors had faced. Many, in particular, felt beleaguered by the union's growing production-worker majority. The identical issues that Homer Martin exploited in 1938 continued to fester in the 1940s and 1950s: the diminished wage differential between skilled and less-skilled workers; the threat of production-worker "upgraders" diluting the craft and swamping the labor market; the refusal by management to establish acceptable apprenticeship standards; the failure of local-union leaders to support captive-shop tradesmen; and the apparent indifference of top UAW leaders to these and other skilled-trades concerns. The issues were similar to 1938–1939, but the outcome was not. In the earlier period, the UAW-CIO had channeled these craft grievances into Direct Action that finally won industrial unionism a firm place at General Motors. In the 1950s, however, the accumulated resentments of UAW tradesmen exploded in open defiance of the union's industrial structure. Between 1955 and 1958, protesting skilled tradesmen rejected contracts, demanded separate ratification of agreements, and finally petitioned the NLRB for craft-union status under the breakaway banner of the Society of Skilled Trades. The revolt was only defused in 1958 when the board ruled against unit-by-unit elections, requiring the SST to mount company-wide campaigns that overtaxed its modest resources. To deny future craft-minded unionists a base of support, the UAW International abolished the Skilled Trades Councils established by Homer Martin twenty years before. Thereafter, skilled tradesmen were further isolated in the union as civil rights activists contrasted the all-white work force in the toolrooms and maintenance trades with the growing minority work force in the auto industry's production departments.[79]

Long-term changes in the economy and in the demographics of the workplace have also diminished the prominent role of tool and die makers in manufacturing, and in the labor movement. The development of computer technologies and the simultaneous shift to technical and service-sector jobs have called forth new forms of "tooling," both mechanical and conceptual, that redefine the demand for skill. Accordingly, teachers, nurses, electricians, and computer programers have grown in numbers, and some of them in levels of unionization (notably teachers and, perhaps in the near future, nurses). Women comprise a growing percentage or a clear majority of the work force in many sectors of the economy, particularly in the rapidly expanding clerical and health-care occupations. Meanwhile, in the manufacturing sector, plant closings have sharply reduced overall employment, while computer technology has transformed the demand for skilled labor. The new realities of a "downsized" auto industry were evident in the seniority recall dates published in April 1988 by Pontiac Local 653. Even after a rash of plant closings in this multiunit GM local, electricians with less than four years seniority were still on the job. Computer-driven machines with electronic components and programmable controls demanded a sizable number of these skilled workers. For others, however, the new technology was more problematic. The seniority date for machine repairmen was 1981, for millwrights and machine welders, 1977, for tinsmiths, 1974. And for those without a trade, the combined impact of new technology and plant closings was disastrous. At Pontiac, production workers with up to twenty years seniority were still on layoff in the "boom"year of 1988; so were material handlers with nearly twenty-two years on the job.[80]

Like Anglo-Gaelic immigrants in the 1920s, many of these displaced autoworkers have migrated to the growth areas of a dynamic world economy. Very often, they have ended up in communities that are bitterly antiunion, much like Detroit in the early twentieth century. Particularly in the growing manufacturing centers of the South, the migrant autoworker produces a fermentation similar in some ways to the Anglo-Gaelic influence of the 1930s.

The yeastlike presence of these Michigan workers was described by

Robert Teeter, a political pollster working for Texas Republicans in the mid-1980s. Puzzled by his clients' repeated speculation and concern for the "black-tag" vote, Teeter asked who the black-taggers were. "Oh them," one Texan answered. "They're your people from Detroit—you know, they come down here with those black Michigan license plates on their cars, and their pro-labor ways."[81]

APPENDIX A

BIOGRAPHICAL DATA ON
ANGLO-GAELIC LEADERS IN MESA/UAW

Anglo-Gaelic immigrants rose to prominence within Detroit's labor movement, but most did not achieve the kind of sustained public visibility that encourages biographical investigation. Even for Matthew Smith and those few others who did achieve considerable public notice, much of the journalism that followed was superficial or careless. The *Detroit News* might report in 1933 that Matthew Smith came from Manchester, but in the same newspaper a year later, Smith's hometown had shifted to nearby Oldham.

At least in Smith's case we know it was Lancashire. For comparable information about lesser-known Anglo-Gaelic union leaders, we have to glean the "paper trail" of their migration: "Certificate of Arrival," "Declaration of Intention," "Petition for Citizenship," and other official records. Even these minimal data are hard to come by when the immigrant (as in Smith's case) never petitioned for citizenship; or when he crossed the border and petitioned for citizenship somewhere other than Detroit; or when he had a common name that buried his documents in a haystack of "Thompsons" or "Andersons." Census data are no help either, since most of these men immigrated in the 1920s, and the most recent Census available is for 1910.

Available sources therefore include immigration records, newspaper accounts, the oral histories and clipping files at the Reuther Library, published histories, union records, and interviews with relatives and co-workers. A complete listing of documentary sources accompanies the biographical profiles in the dissertation "Pointing the Way: Skilled Workers and Anglo-Gaelic Immigrants in the Rise of the UAW," Appendix A (Steve Babson, Wayne State University, 1989, 696–734).

Table A.1 summarizes the data for thirty selected leaders.

TABLE A.1
BIOGRAPHICAL DATA ON ANGLO-GAELIC LEADERS IN MESA/UAW

Name	Hometown or region	U.K. trade[a]	Year of last emigration	Age[b]	Marital status[b]	Port of entry	Highest leadership position[c]
			Scottish-born				
Allison, Robert	Clyde	tool	1923[d]	33	married	Canada	UAW 155, FS
Anderson, John	Clyde	elec.[d]	—	—	—	—	MESA 7, P UAW 155, P
Campbell, George	Clyde	tool	—	—	—	Conn.	UAW 600, unit VP UAW Intl., asst. dir.
Fairbairn, John	Edinburgh	tool	1926	26	single	Canada	UAW 157, FS
Handyside, George	Clyde	mach.	1927	26	single	Canada	UAW 157, VP
Manuel, Bert	Clyde[d]	coal	1923[d]	20	single	Canada	UAW 3, PC/EB
McCusker, Henry	Lanark	coal	1923	23	single	Pa.	UAW 600, unit P
McCusker, Joseph	Lanark	coal	1927	23	—	—	UAW 600, P UAW, IEB
McIntyre, David	Clyde	maint.	1919	27	single	Canada	UAW 3, PCH
McKie, William	Edinburgh	sh. metal	1927	51	married	—	AFL 19374, P UAW 98, P UAW 174, EB UAW 600, EB

Miller, David	Dundee	tram	1920	29	married	—	FLU 19374, VP UAW 174, EB UAW 22, P
Murdoch, James	Clyde	tool	1922	27	single	Canada	MESA, Natl. P
Stevenson, William	Clyde	tool	1923	22	single	Canada	MESA 91, P UAW 157, P UAW, IEB

English-born

Grant, Wilfred	—	tool	1929[d]	32	single	Canada	UAW 600, P
Hamilton, Patrick	North	paint	1925[d]	18	single	Canada	ACTU, EB
Hanlon, Thomas	North	tool	1926	28	single	Canada	UAW 3, PC
Hulle, William	London	tool	1910	29	married[d]	NYC	UAW 157, FS
Matthews, Norman	South	elec.	1920	24	single	NYC	UAW 190, P UAW, IEB
Parry, Thomas	—	mach.[d]	—	—	—	—	UAW 155, P
Shaw, Walter	North	tool	1919	42	married	NYC	UAW 600, EB
Smith, Mat	North	tool	1926	33	married	Canada	MESA, gen. sec.
Southwell, Harry	North	wood	1923	22[d]	married	—	UAW 174, P

(continued)

TABLE A.1 (Continued)

Name	Hometown or region	U.K. trade[a]	Year of last emmigration	Age[b]	Marital status[b]	Port of entry	Highest leadership position[c]
Spencer, Harry	London	mach.	1919	20	single	NYC	MESA, chrm. strike comm.
Strachan, Alan	London	tool	1926	24	single	Canada	AFL 18313, RS / UAW 7, EB / UAW 157, EB
Thompson, Thomas	—	coal	—	—	—	—	UAW 600, P
Woodcock, Ernest	North	tool	1924	40	married	Canada	AWU, chrm. strike comm.
Irish-born							
Crothers, Robert	Belfast	tool	1923	23	single	NYC	UAW 157, RS
Magee, Michael	Belfast	mech.	1930	34	married	Canada	UAW 600, EB
Quinn, Patrick	Donegal	labor	1924	23	single	Canada	UAW 3, PCH/P
Rice, Patrick	Belfast	labor	1922	21	single	NYC	UAW 600, VP

[a]tool = engineer/toolmaker, elec. = electrician, mach. = machinist, maint. = maintenance worker, sh.metal = sheet metal worker, mech. = mechanic.

[b]In year of emigration.

[c]P = president, VP = vice president, EB = member of Executive Board, FS = financial secretary, RS = recording secretary, PC = member of Plant Committee, PCH = chairman of Plant Committee, IEB = member of International Executive Board.

[d]Best estimate.

APPENDIX B

SETTLING IN

Map B.1 identifies the Detroit neighborhood where Anglo-Gaelic immigrants and leaders concentrated. As indicated, two-thirds of the twenty-seven immigrant union leaders for whom an address could be located in the years 1928–1932 lived within the specified boundary. Also outlined are the areas of residential concentration for the officers of Scottish Rite Masonry, the St. Andrews Society, and the Scotia and American Eagle Lodges of the Odd Fellows; for each organization, the boundaries encompass two-thirds of the individuals for whom occupational and residential information is available for the mid-1920s. Locations of major factories where the immigrants worked and halls where they congregated are indicated on the map as well.

For detailed maps, a description of sources, and a complete list of individuals by name, address, and occupation, see Steve Babson, "Pointing the Way: Skilled Workers and Anglo-Gaelic Immigrants in the Rise of the UAW" (Ph.D. diss., Wayne State University, 1989), 783–792.

MAP B.1. GROUP CONCENTRATIONS, FRATERNAL HALLS,
AND FACTORIES, DETROIT, 1920S

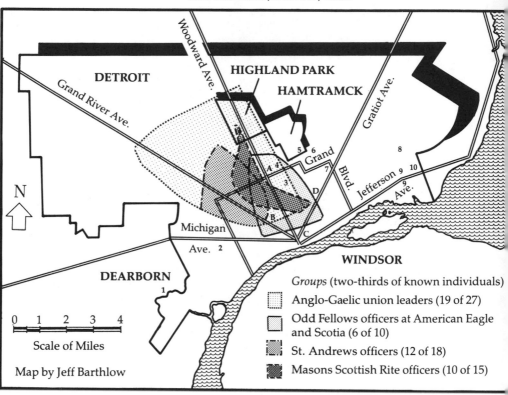

Groups (two-thirds of known individuals)

Anglo-Gaelic union leaders (19 of 27)

Odd Fellows officers at American Eagle
and Scotia (6 of 10)

St. Andrews officers (12 of 18)

Masons Scottish Rite officers (10 of 15)

Halls		*Factories*			
A.	American Eagle	1.	Ford Dearborn	7.	Packard
B.	Scotia	2.	Cadillac	8.	Briggs Vernor Ave
C.	St. Andrews	3.	Fisher Tool/Die	9.	Chrysler
D.	Schiller	4.	Murray Body	10.	Hudson
		5.	Dodge Main		
		6.	Midland Steel		

NOTES

![black bar]

"Reuther Library" indicates the Archives of Labor History and Urban Affairs, Reuther Library, Wayne State University, Detroit. Unless otherwise indicated, all collections cited are located in the Reuther Library. "Henry Ford Museum" indicates the Archives and Research Library, Henry Ford Museum at Greenfield Village, Dearborn, Michigan. "Burton Historical Collection" indicates the collections of the Detroit Public Library.

Introduction

1. The *United Auto Worker* passage was quoted in Mary Heaton Vorse, *Labor's New Millions* (New York, 1938), 92. Worker spontaneity is invoked by Jeremy Brecher, *Strike!* (San Francisco, 1972), 233–236 and passim, and by Art Preis, *Labor's Giant Step* (New York, 1972), 53–54 and 64–65, as a club to punish, in Preis's words, those "abject servants of the capitalist class," union officials; by Richard Boyer and Herbert Morais, *Labor's Untold Story* (New York, 1955), 290–291, to exalt the heroism of the sit-downers; and in passing by, among others, James Green, *The World of the Worker: Labor in Twentieth Century America* (New York, 1980), 155, and David Brody, *Workers in Industrial America: Essays on the Twentieth Century Struggle* (New York, 1980), 103, in lieu of a concept of leadership that encompasses more than just the union's national executive board.
2. See, among others, Sidney Fine, *Sitdown: The General Motors Strike of 1936–1937* (Ann Arbor, 1969); Peter Friedlander, *The Emergence of a UAW Local, 1936–1939: A Study in Class and Culture* (Pittsburgh, 1975); Nelson Lichtenstein, "Auto Worker Militancy and the Structure of Factory Life, 1937–1955," *The Journal of American History* 67, no. 2 (September, 1980): 335–353; and Ray Boryczka, "Militancy and Factionalism in the United Auto Workers Union, 1937–1941," *Maryland Historian* 8 (Fall 1977): 13–25.
3. On the role of Anglo-Gaelic immigrants in the nineteenth century, see Rowland Berthoff, *British Immigrants in Industrial America, 1790–1950* (Cambridge, Mass., 1953) and Clifton Yearly, *Britons in American Labor: A History of the Influence of the United Kingdom Immigrants on American Labor, 1820–1914* (Baltimore, 1957).
4. See Appendix A for a listing of union leadership positions held by Anglo-Gaelic immigrants. The ranking of uaw locals in Detroit is based on convention votes. See *Proceedings of the Seventh Convention of the UAW-CIO, 3 August 1942–9 August 1942 . . . Chicago, Illinois*, n.d., "Roll Call," 534–579.

5. Clifford Geertz, *The Interpretation of Cultures* (New York, 1973), Chapter 1, "Thick Description: Toward an Interpretive Theory of Culture," 28. Peter Friedlander's *The Emergence of a UAW Local* is among the earliest and best-known labor histories that explicitly draws on Geertz.

6. Charles Sabel, *Work and Politics: The Division of Labor in Industry* (Cambridge, 1982), 138, 138–139, 144, 188. Sabel's account relies on just two case histories: one, a study of union organization in Norwood, Ohio, has little relevance to Detroit; the second, Friedlander's study of an unnamed supplier plant in Hamtramck, is misidentified as a "Ford" factory and misconstrued as a pioneer local. For an excellent historical overview of mass production in the auto industry, see Steven Tolliday and Jonathan Zeitlin, eds., *The Automobile Industry and Its Workers: Between Fordism and Flexibility* (New York, 1987). Particular studies of skilled workers in Detroit include Harry Dalheimer, *A History of the Mechanics Educational Society of America in Detroit from Its Inception in 1933 through 1937* (Detroit, 1951); Sidney Fine, "The Tool and Die Makers Strike of 1933," *Michigan History* 42 (September 1958): 297–323; John Barnard, "Rebirth of the United Automobile Workers: The General Motors Tool and Die Strike of 1939," *Labor History* 27, no. 2 (Spring 1986): 165–187; and Kevin Boyle, "Rite of Passage: The 1939 General Motors Tool and Die Strike," *Labor History* 27, no. 2 (Spring 1986): 188–203.

7. Coulthard quoted in Tony Lane, "A Merseysider in Detroit," *History Workshop*, no. 11 (Spring 1981): 149.

8. Philip Bonosky, *Brother Bill McKie: Building the Union at Ford* (New York, 1953), 23, 41, 111, 117. Verbatim transcripts of interviews with McKie can be found in the Nat Ganley Collection, Box 33, Series 6, Folders 15–20, 22, 25, and 26.

9. "A Survey of Communist Activities in the City of Detroit and Vicinity," typescripts, 1 July 1936, 3, AFL-CIO Metropolitan Detroit Collection, Box 1, Folder "Communist Party, 1926–1930s."

10. *New York Times*, 10 March 1937. Jeremy Brecher cites this *Times* story and two subsequent reports on 17 and 27 March in *Strike!* (San Francisco, 1972), 206, as evidence of leadership temerity and worker spontaneity. The actual planning and organization of the sit-down are described in Chapter 5.

11. Richard Edwards, *Contested Terrain: The Transformation of the Workplace in the Twentieth Century* (New York, 1979), 52–54, describes union formation as a reaction to "oppressive conditions in day-to-day work" which "emboldened workers to engage in strikes and other concerted action for higher wages and shorter hours." If oppression always "emboldened" workers to resist, historians would have to explain why oppressors have nevertheless favored such counterproductive strategies. Charles Tilly, *From Mobilization to Revolution* (New York, 1978), articulates an alternative conception of "resources and opportunity" as key determinants of collective action.

12. G.D.H. Cole, *Trade Unionism and Munitions* (Oxford, 1923), 27–29; Allan quoted in Harry Sheer, "The Saga of a Labor Journalist," *Daily World*, 20 August 1981.

13. Ronald Schatz, *The Electrical Workers: A History of Labor at General Electric and Westinghouse, 1923–1960* (Urbana, 1983), 84–86; Joshua Freeman, "Catholics, Communists, and Republicans: Irish Workers and the Organization of the Transport Workers Union," in Michael Frisch and Daniel Walkowitz, eds., *Working Class America: Essays on Labor, Community, and American Society* (Urbana, 1983), 256–283.

14. The roles of McIntyre and Anderson are examined in detail in Chapters 5 and 6.

15. According to Mark Naison, *Communists in Harlem During the Depression* (New York,

1983), 5, four of the five initial leaders of the Communist party in Harlem were West Indians.

16. More detailed individual biographies and complete documentation for these Anglo-Gaelic immigrants can be found in Steve Babson, "Pointing the Way: Skilled Workers and Anglo-Gaelic Immigrants in the Rise of the UAW" (Ph.D. diss., Wayne State University, 1989), 694–734.

Chapter 1. Skilled Workers and the Rise of Auto

1. "Why Strikers Stand Pat," *Fisher Strike News*, 21 July 1939, 1, Walter Reuther Collection, Box 26, Folder 26-20.
2. Royal Russell, "Split the Line," *Chrysler Motors Magazine*, September 1935, 5, Joe Brown Collection, Box 34, Folder "Chrysler Motors Magazine."
3. Mortimer La Fever, "Workers, Machinery, and Production in the Automobile Industry," *Monthly Labor Review* 19, no. 4 (October 1924): 740; David Hounshell, *From the American System to Mass Production, 1800–1932* (Baltimore, 1984), 214; George May, *A Most Unique Machine: The Michigan Origins of the American Automobile Industry* (Grand Rapids, 1975), 92–93, 111–114; Jean-Pierre Bardou et al., *The Automobile Revolution: The Impact of an Industry*, trans. James Laux (Chapel Hill, 1982), 6.
4. George Walsh, "Automobile Machine Tools," *Iron Age* 81 (12 March 1903): 10.
5. On the Craftsman's Realm in nineteenth-century metalworking, see Steve Babson, "Pointing the Way: Skilled Workers and Anglo-Gaelic Immigrants in the Rise of the UAW" (Ph.D. diss., Wayne State University, 1989), Chapter 1. See also Hounshell, *From the American System to Mass Production*; Dan Clawson, *Bureaucracy and the Labor Process* (New York, 1980); and Daniel Nelson, *Managers and Workers: Origins of the New Factory System in the United States, 1880–1920* (Madison, 1975).
6. Walsh, "Automobile Machine Tools," 10. For biographical backgrounds of auto company founders, see May, *A Most Unique Machine*.
7. Bredo Berghoff, "Reminiscences," Accession 65-219, Henry Ford Museum, 3, 16.
8. Joseph Galamb, "Reminiscences," Accession 65, Henry Ford Museum, 4; William Ellison Chalmers, "Labor in the Automobile Industry: A Study of Personnel Policies, Workers' Attitudes, and Attempts at Unionism" (Ph.D. diss., University of Wisconsin, 1932), 89–90; Hounshell, *From the American System to Mass Production*, 235–237; Henry Ford quoted in David Gartman, *Auto Slavery: The Labor Process in the American Automobile Industry, 1897–1950* (New Brunswick, 1986), 23.
9. May, *A Most Unique Machine*, 117–120, 277, 293, 299; "Automobile Industry and Trade in Detroit," *The Automobile* 9 (12 October 1903): 617–618; Galamb, "Reminiscences," 7–8, 10, 23, 29, 143, 146; Hounshell, *From the American System to Mass Production*, 220. On the "unitary" nature of craft production, see Gartman, *Auto Slavery*, 24. On workers per factory, see Chalmers, "Labor in the Automobile Industry," 6.
10. May, *A Most Unique Machine*, 341.
11. Ibid., 81–82, 338–339.
12. Bardou et al., *The Automobile Revolution*, 39–40; May, *A Most Unique Machine*, 124, 135, 142, 254–255; *Historical Statistics of the United States*, Part 2 (Washington, D.C., 1975), 718.
13. La Fever, "Workers, Machinery, and Production in the Automobile Industry," 740, 749; "Influence of the Automobile on Machine-Tool Design," *American Machinist*, 24

February 1916, 341; "The Metallurgists' Contribution to Automotive Development," *Automotive Industries*, 15 July 1933, 64–68.

14. E. F. Lake, "The Foundry in Its Relation to the Automobile Factory," *The Horseless Age* 18, no. 11 (22 September 1906): 327–328.
15. La Fever, "Workers, Machinery, and Production in the Automobile Industry," 736, 749.
16. Tom Klug, "The Employers Association of Detroit, the Open Shop, and the Making of Managerial Authority, 1900–1916" typescript, 1981, History Department, Wayne State University, 5–7; Richard Oestreicher, *Solidarity and Fragmentation: Working People and Class Consciousness in Detroit, 1875–1900* (Urbana, 1986), 242–243.
17. Klug, "The Employers Association of Detroit," 10, 11–18.
18. Alan Nevins and Frank Hill, *Ford: The Times, the Man, the Company* (New York, 1957), 1: 377, 380–383. On the Machinists' strike and Olds, see May, *A Most Unique Machine*, 123.
19. On the EAD's open-shop campaign, see Klug, "The Employers Association of Detroit"; Tom Klug, "The Ideology and Practices of Labor Market Control and the Origins of Personnel Management in Detroit, 1900–1920," typescript, 1981, History Department, Wayne State University; Dennis Aron, "The Role of the Employers Association of Detroit in the City's Battles over the Open Shop during the 1900s," typescript, 1972, University of Detroit.
20. Klug, "The Employers Association of Detroit," 20–22, and Appendix; *Evening News*, 12 March 1904, EAD Scrapbook no. 2, Burton Historical Collection; and "Six Saloons Riot Cause: Rouge Strikers May Go Back to Work on Thursday," *Detroit Journal*, 26 June 1907, EAD Scrapbook no. 20, Burton Historical Collection. See also *Detroit Journal*, 20 June 1907, and *Detroit News*, 25 June 1907, EAD Scrapbook no. 20.
21. Klug, "The Employers Association of Detroit," 16–18, 21.
22. La Fever, "Workers, Machinery, and Production in the Automobile Industry," 741, 750; "The Metallurgists' Contribution to Automotive Development," 64–68; "Influence of the Auto on Machine-Tool Design," *The Automobile* 16, no. 25 (20 June 1907): 1012; "Influence of the Automobile on Machine-Tool Design," *American Machinist*, 24 February 1916, 341.
23. "Influence of the Auto on Machine-Tool Design," *The Automobile*, 1012; "Influence of the Automobile on Machine-Tool Design," *American Machinist*, 341.
24. Nevins and Hill, *Ford*, 1:367–368.
25. Eugene Farkas, "Reminiscences," Henry Ford Museum, 8–11, 15–16.
26. Nevins and Hill, *Ford*, 1:456; Board of Tax Appeals, "Petitioners Statement of Facts," typescript, 18 April 1927, Dodge Estate, Legal, Accession 96, Box 7, Henry Ford Museum, 73.
27. Hounshell, *From the American System to Mass Production*, 6; "Influence of the Automobile on Machine-Tool Design," *American Machinist*, 341.
28. Lake, "The Foundry in Its Relation to the Automobile Factory," 327; Charles Hyde, *Detroit: An Industrial History Guide* (Detroit, 1980), gives the following dates for construction of Detroit's major integrated plants: Packard, 1903–1911; Chrysler-Chalmers, 1907–1916; Ford Highland Park, 1909–1914; Dodge Main, 1910–1920; Cadillac Clark Street, 1921.
29. "The Metallurgists' Contribution to Automotive Development," 64–68; La Fever, "Workers, Machinery, and Production in the Automobile Industry," 748.
30. Blanche Bernstein, "Labor Market in the Auto Industry, 1937," typescript, W. Ellison Chalmers Collection, Box 2, 61.
31. W. W. Galbreath and John Winter, "Development of Modern Stamping Practice,"

American Machinist, 13 December 1923, 885, 883–887; "Pressed Steel Automobile Parts," *The Horseless Age* 24, no. 10 (8 September 1909): 263–264; La Fever, "Workers, Machinery, and Production in the Auto Industry," 749–750; Hounshell, *From the American System to Mass Production*, 59–60, 149, 190, 208–213, 274; Gartman, *Auto Slavery*, 31.

32. P. M. Heldt, "Many Automotive Production Problems Solved by Welding Processes," *Automotive Industries*, 24 September 1925, 506–511; W. Spraragen, "Welding Effects Economies in Construction of Jigs," *Automotive Industries*, 17 October 1931, 591; *Ford News*, 15 September 1927; La Fever, "Workers, Machinery, and Production in the Auto Industry," 742; Hounshell, *From the American System to Mass Production*, 149, 208.

33. Board of Tax Appeals, "Petitioners Statement of Facts," 76–77.

34. Horace Arnold and Fay Leone Faurote, *Ford Methods and Ford Shops* (New York, 1915), 41–42.

35. G. T. Bloomfield, "Shaping the Character of a City: The Automobile Industry and Detroit, 1900–1920," *Michigan Quarterly Review* 25, no. 2 (Spring 1986): 171, 174; Stephen Meyer, *The Five Dollar Day: Labor Management and Social Control in the Ford Motor Company, 1908–1921* (Albany, 1981), 75; Jack Russell, "The Coming of the Line: Rationalization and Labor at the Ford Highland Park Plant, 1910 to 1920," typescript, n.d., in author's possession, 9.

36. *Detroit Free Press*, 22 June 1913; U.S. Department of Commerce, *Fifteenth Census of the United States: 1930*, Part 1, Volume 3, *Population* (Washington, D.C., 1932), Table 69, p. 74, and *Abstract of the Fourteenth Census of the U.S., 1920* (Washington, D.C., 1923), Table 39, p. 126; *Polk's City Directory, 1929*, 1–15.

37. See Meyer, *The Five Dollar Day*, Chapters 5 and 6 passim; Russell, "The Coming of the Line," 64–81; and Jonathan Schwartz, "Henry Ford's Melting Pot," in David Hartman, ed., *Immigrants and Migrants: The Detroit Ethnic Experience* (Detroit, 1974), 252–260.

38. Chalmers, "Labor in the Automobile Industry," 6; Robert Dunn, *Labor and Automobiles* (New York, 1929), 49, 176–178; Jacob Solin, "The Detroit Federation of Labor, 1900–1920," (M.A. thesis, Wayne State University, 1939), 27–28.

39. John Laslett, *Labor and the Left: A Study of Socialist and Radical Influences in the American Labor Movement, 1881–1924* (New York, 1970), 157–159, 164–179; Mark Perlman, *The Machinists: A New Study in American Trade Unionism* (Cambridge, Mass., 1961), 34, 40–41, 64–65, 206; David Montgomery, *Workers' Control in America: Studies in the History of Work, Technology, and Labor Struggles* (Cambridge, 1979), 54–67, 82–83.

40. Walter Chrysler, *Life of An American Workman* (New York, 1937), 134. The *Carriage, Wagon and Automobile Workers Journal* (April 1912), describes the subdivision of painting, woodworking, and trim circa 1912. Copies of the *Journal* and the predecessor publication of the CWAW are available at the Johns Hopkins University Library. Except for 1899 and 1919, as noted, all citations of the *Journal*, *The Auto Worker News*, and the constitutions and convention proceedings of the Carriage and Wagon Workers and its successor unions are taken from Edward Levinson's typescript notes of these sources, contained in the Edward Levinson Collection, Box 1, in several files labeled "Auto Industry History."

41. "The Automobile," *Carriage and Wagon Workers Journal* 1, no. 2 (1 July 1899): 1, and William Logan, "Who and What We Are," *The Auto Worker* 1, no. 3 (July 1919): 1, in Levinson Collection, Box 2, Folder "Early Labor Papers"; *Carriage and Wagon Workers Journal*, 1 September 1899, 1 September 1900, 1 January 1901; *Carriage and Wagon Workers Constitution*, 1913.

42. Logan, "Who and What We Are," 1; *Carriage, Wagon, and Automobile Workers Journal,* January 1914.
43. Dunn, *Labor and Automobiles,* 188–190; Nevins and Hill, *Ford,* 2:149.
44. Roger Keeran, *The Communist Party and the Auto Workers Unions* (Bloomington, 1980), 32–35; *Auto Worker News,* issues of 15 May through 25 December 1919, and 29 January 1920, 9 December 1920, and 22 January 1921 through 14 April 1921.
45. On the membership decline in the UAAVWA, see "Early Unions," typescript, 1, Joe Brown Collection, Box 3, Folder 2.
46. Nevins and Hill, *Ford,* 2:149, 201, 209–210; Alfred Chandler, *Strategy and Structure* (Cambridge, Mass., 1962), 124; Bernstein, "Labor Market in the Auto Industry, 1937," 24–25.
47. George Mercer, "Standard Bodies Are Now Produced at One-Third Pre-War Cost," *Automotive Industries,* 24 September 1925, 492; Dunn, *Labor and Automobiles,* 16.
48. Mercer, "Standard Bodies," 493; *Fisher Body Service Manual* (Detroit, 1935), 1; Hounshell, *From the American System to Mass Production,* 274.
49. La Fever, "Workers, Machinery, and Production in the Automobile Industry," 750.
50. Joseph Geschelin, "160 Spot-Welds in 45 Seconds!" *Automotive Industries,* 28 July 1934, 105.
51. Bernstein, "Labor Market in the Auto Industry, 1937," 24.
52. "Developments in Production and Design Mark the New Briggs All-Steel Bodies," *Automotive Industries,* 25 April 1931, 656–658; John W. Anderson, "How I Joined the Labor Movement," in Alice and Staughton Lynd, eds., *Rank and File: Personal Histories of Working Class Organizers* (Boston, 1973), 43, 46.
53. Joseph Geschelin, "Trim Shop Is Automatically Scheduled to Fit Progress of Assembly Line," *Automotive Industries,* 29 November 1930, 788.
54. Bernstein, "Labor Market in the Auto Industry, 1937," 26–27.
55. Mercer, "Standard Bodies," 493.
56. "Auto Body Building in Detroit," *American Machinist,* 29 November 1923, 824h; La Fever, "Workers, Machinery, and Production in the Automobile Industry," 759.
57. Dunn, *Labor and Automobiles,* 101. On the declining proportion of skilled production workers in the auto industry's work force, see Babson, "Pointing the Way," Tables 3–4, 165–167.
58. Charles Reitell, "Machinery and Its Effect upon the Workers in the Automotive Industry," *The Annals. The American Academy of Political and Social Science* 116 (November 1924): 40.
59. Ibid., 38.

Chapter 2. The Citadel of Craft

1. Franklin Jones, ed., *Jig and Fixture Design* (New York, 1942), 3.
2. Frank Stanley, *Punches and Dies: Layout, Construction, and Use* (New York, 1950), 458; Charles Corey, *Die Design Manual,* Part 1 (Detroit, 1937), 1, 10, 13–14.
3. The following summary description of die characteristics and toolroom practices is drawn from a more detailed explanation in Steve Babson, "Pointing the Way: Skilled Workers and Anglo-Gaelic Immigrants in the Rise of the UAW" (Ph.D. diss., Wayne State University, 1989), 180–199.
4. Charles Cole, *Tool Making* (Chicago, 1943), 354; see also Logan Miller, "Reminiscences," Accession 65–152, Henry Ford Museum, 8. See Howard Raymond,

Modern Shop Practice (Chicago, 1945), 4:265–268, for the tool-design procedure in large plants.

5. Miller, "Reminiscences," 27–28.

6. Ibid., 27; "Skilled Workers Lose in Technological Advance," *Tool and Die Engineering News*, 14 February 1940; Howard Raymond, ed., *Modern Shop Practice* (Chicago, 1945), 2:196–197; Stanley, *Punches and Dies*, 453–454.

7. Irv Iverson, interview by author, tape recording, Royal Oak, Michigan, 30 October 1985.

8. Henry Burghardt, *Machine Tool Operation*, Volume 1, *Lathe, Bench, Forge* (New York, 1936), 292–298; Stanley, *Punches and Dies*, 503–536.

9. For a summary of these characteristic differences between skilled and less-skilled labor, see Charles Sabel, *Work and Politics: The Division of Labor in Industry* (Cambridge, 1982), Chapter 3, "Careers at Work."

10. *Automotive Industries* 41 (25 September 1919): 608–610; Burghardt, *Machine Tool Operation*, 1:153, 311.

11. Burghardt, *Machine Tool Operation*, 1:279.

12. Blaine Marrin, interview by author, tape recording, Madison Heights, Michigan, 5 November 1985; Russell Leach, interview by author, tape recording, Detroit, 22 October 1985 and 19 November 1985; Leonard Woodcock, interview by author, tape recording, Ann Arbor, Michigan, 3 December 1985; Alan Nevins and Frank Hill, *Ford: The Times, the Man, the Company* (New York, 1957), 2:451; E. A. Walters, "Reminiscences," Accession 65-200, Henry Ford Museum, 84–85.

13. Bureau of the Census, *Census of Manufacturers: 1929*, Volume 2, *Report by Industries* (Washington, D.C., 1933), 1154; Marrin, interview by author; Woodcock, interview by author; Leach, interview by author; Joe Oberg, interview by author, tape recording, Detroit, 26 November 1985; Cole, *Tool Making*, 170.

14. Iverson, interview by author.

15. Frederick Blackall, Jr., "The Special Tool, Die and Machine Shop Institute," *American Machinist*, 2 December 1936, 1003.

16. Miller, "Reminiscences," iii, 8; William Pioch, "Reminiscences," Accession 65-146, Henry Ford Museum, iii; Walters, "Reminiscences," iii; Alex Lumsden, "Reminiscences," Accession 65-169, Henry Ford Museum, iii, 8, 12–16.

17. Miller, "Reminiscences," 2–3; Lumsden, "Reminiscences," 4; Walters, "Reminiscences," 54–55; Charles Sorensen, *My Forty Years with Ford* (New York, 1956), 66–73.

18. Walters, "Reminiscences," 54.

19. Horace Arnold and Fay Leone Faurote, *Ford Methods and Ford Shops* (New York, 1915), 41.

20. C. B. Gordy, "Craftsmen Needed," *American Machinist*, 6 November 1935, 823; *Detroit Free Press*, 19 January 1913; *Detroit Labor News*, 5 March 1915.

21. *Detroit Labor News*, 16 June 1915; transcript of interviews at EAD, April 1928, in Robert Dunn Collection, Box 1, Folder "Employers Organizations"; William Ellison Chalmers, "Labor in the Automobile Industry: A Study of Personnel Policies, Workers Attitudes, and Attempts at Unionism (Ph.D. diss., University of Wisconsin, 1932)," 192.

22. Hyacinth Dubreuil, *Robots or Men? A French Workman's Experience in American Industry* (New York, 1977), 20; Frank Muellner, interview by author, tape recording, Detroit, 25 March 1986; Henry Geile, interview by author, tape recording, Detroit, 25 February 1986.

23. Transcript of interviews at EAD, April 1928, Robert Dunn Collection; Nevins and

Hill, *Ford*, 2:527–520; Edwin Norwood, *Ford, Men and Methods* (Garden City, 1931), 200.

24. *Detroit News*, 29 August 1926, Section 5; Leland Olds, "Machine Shops Average $31.31 a Week," Federated Press, 23 March 1928, Sheet 2; Alfred Sloan, *My Years with General Motors* (New York, 1965), 163–168; Chalmers, "Labor in the Automobile Industry," 43, 55; "Auto Industry Succeeding in Stabilizing Employment," *Detroit News*, 15 February 1936; Bureau of the Census, *Census of Manufacturers: 1929*, 2:1156.

25. Leach, interview by author; Muellner, interview by author; Albert Kanarz, interview by author, tape recording, Warren, Michigan, 27 August 1986; Geoffrey Snudden, interview by author, tape recording, Detroit, 14 February 1987.

26. Joe Brown, "Standard of Living among Tool and Die Makers (Analysis of MESA Data)," typescript, Joe Brown Collection, Box 15, Folder "MESA," 1. Of the seventy-three MESA members surveyed, 18 (25 percent) earned over $3,000. For income of production workers, see Robert Dunn, *Labor and Automobiles* (New York, 1929), 119–123.

27. Norman Shidle, "Automotive Factory Labor Costs Cut 10–50 Percent in Last Two Years," *Automotive Industries*, 10 September 1925, 401–403; William Patterson, "Wanted: Broader Training," *American Machinist*, 9 October 1935, 749.

28. Gartman, *Auto Slavery: The Labor Process in the American Automobile Industry, 1897–1950* (New Brunswick, 1986), 242–244.

29. Norwood, *Ford, Men and Methods*, Chapter 14; Kanarz, interview by author; Blanche Bernstein, "Hiring Policies in the Automobile Industry," Works Progress Administration National Research Project, Special Research Section, typescript, 1937, in Edward Levinson Collection, Box 2, Folder "Hiring Policies," 10–12, 37–38.

30. Chalmers, "Labor in the Automobile Industry," 67–71; General Motors Institute of Technology, *Bulletin, Evening and Afternoon Spare Time Courses, 1928–1929*, Henry Kraus Collection, Box 16, Folder "GM Institute of Technology Bulletin, 1928," "General Announcement," "Contents," and 46–53.

31. Bureau of the Census, *Fifteenth Census of the United States. Population—Michigan* (Washington, D.C., 1933), 1164; Bureau of the Census, *Fifteenth Census of the United Stated*, Volume 4, *Population: Occupations by States* (Washington, D.C., 1933), 783.

32. Lloyd Cofer, "We Face Reality in Detroit," *National Educational Outlook among Negroes* (November 1937): 36; Joyce Shaw Peterson, "Black Automobile Workers in Detroit, 1910–1930," *Journal of Negro History* 64, no. 3 (Summer 1979): 181, 179–181.

33. August Meier and Elliot Rudwick, *Black Detroit and the Rise of the UAW* (New York, 1979), 5–6, 12–13; Willis Ward, "Reminiscences," Accession 65-175, Henry Ford Museum, 9–10; Walter Dorosh, interview by author, tape recording, Dearborn, Michigan, 1 July 1986; Susan Watson, "From Rouge to Soviet Union and Back," *Detroit Free Press*, 26 June 1987; Bureau of the Census, *Population: Occupations by States*, (1933), 800, 803. McKie did not specify which trade the victimized black worker was a leader in. See Nat Ganley Collection, Box 33, Series 6, Folder 33–15, "Misc. Notes," interview transcript, 14–15.

34. Shidle, "Automotive Factory Costs Cut 10–50 Percent" (10 September 1925), 401–403; Bureau of the Census, *Fourteenth Census of the United States*, Volume 4, *Population, 1920, Occupations* (Washington, D.C., 1923), 14.

35. Walters, "Reminiscences," 4–5; Pioch, "Reminiscences," 1; Sorensen, *My Forty Years with Ford*, 67; *Detroit News*, 29 August 1926; *Detroit News*, 29 May 1927.

36. Oberg, interview by author; Iverson, interview by author.

37. Frank Marquart, *An Auto Workers' Journal: The UAW from Crusade to One-Party Union* (University Park, 1975), 13–14.

38. Bredo Berghoff, "Reminiscences," Accession 65-219, Henry Ford Museum, 32.
39. Sorensen, *My Forty Years with Ford*, 64–67; Lumsden, "Reminiscences," 12–16; Walters, "Reminiscences," 50.
40. Eugene Farkas, "Reminiscences," Accession 65, Henry Ford Museum, 9–13; Joseph Galamb, "Reminiscences," Accession 65, Henry Ford Museum, 5–6; Nevins and Hill, *Ford*, 2:440–441; *Automotive Industries*, 25 September 1919, 608–610.
41. Dorosh, interview by author; Muellner, interview by author; Geile, interview by author; "Tool and Die Aliens," typed document, John Blaich Collection, Box 1, Folder 1-4. It appears this list was compiled shortly before the 1941 Ford strike, by which time many immigrants had become citizens and many German-born tradesmen had returned to Germany.
42. On the Vernor Avenue Briggs plant, see "Table 1: Data Regarding Representative Groups of Tool and Die Makers," typed document, Joe Brown Collection, Box 15, Folder "MESA." Marrin, interview by author; Woodcock, interview by author; Leach, interview by author.
43. Leach, interview by author.
44. Iverson, interview by author; Oberg, interview by author; Marrin, interview by author.
45. R. S. Walshaw, *Migration to and from the British Isles* (London, 1941), 13–14. The proportion of skilled workers among Anglo-Gaelic immigrants is examined in the next chapter.

Chapter 3. Labor Routes

1. Information on Harold Snudden was provided by Geoffrey Snudden, interview by author, tape recording, Detroit, 14 February 1987; U.S. Immigration and Naturalization Service, "Declaration of Intention," no. 157757, document signed by Harold Snudden, 27 June 1924, and "Petition for Citizenship," no. 59547, document signed by Harold Snudden, 31 March 1931, National Archives, Great Lakes Region, Chicago, Illinois.
2. Compiled from U.S. Department of Commerce, Bureau of Census, *Historical Statistics of the United States, Colonial Times to 1970*, Part 1 (Washington, D.C., 1975), 105–106, Series C 89–119. For a detailed discussion of the Bureau of Immigration's alternative measures of immigration, see Steve Babson, "Pointing the Way: Skilled Workers and Anglo-Gaelic Immigrants in the Rise of the UAW" (Ph.D. diss., Wayne State University, 1989), Chapter 4, endnote 3, 331.
3. Compiled from *Annual Report of the Commissioner General of Immigration, 1923*, Table 10, 81–85; *1924*, Table 10, 75–79; *1925*, Table 29, 86–89, Table 33, 97–103; *1926*, Table 29, 79–83, Table 33, 91–97. For a detailed breakdown, see Babson, "Pointing the Way," Chapter 4, particularly Tables 15 and 16.
4. Compiled from *Annual Report of the Commissioner General of Immigration, 1924*, Table 11, 92–97.
5. Vice consul, Manchester, England, to secretary of state, Washington, D.C., "Emigration from the Manchester Consular District during the Period 1 July 1922 to 30 June 1923," letter, 12 July 1923, Box 190, File 53531/53, "Emigration England: Canada: 1924," Records of the Immigration and Naturalization Service, Record Group 85, National Archives, Washington, D.C. (hereafter NA/RG 85.)
6. Eric Hobsbawm, *Industry and Empire: From 1750 to the Present* (New York, 1986), 174; Standish Meacham, " 'The Sense of an Impending Clash,': English Working Class

Unrest before the First World War," *American Historical Review* 77, no. 5 (December 1972): 1350; James Cronin, "Insurgency and Reaction in Britain, 1919–1926: A Structural Analysis," typescript, 1980, 18; Noreen Branson, *Britain in the Nineteen Twenties* (Minneapolis, 1976), 69–72, 90; James Jeffreys, *The Story of the Engineers, 1800–1945* (London, 1970), 198, 209–210; Christopher Harvie, *No Gods and Precious Few Heroes: Scotland, 1914–1980* (Toronto, 1981), 24.

7. Branson, *Britain in the Nineteen Twenties*, 95–96; Hobsbawm, *Industry and Empire*, 213–223; Leslie Hannah, "Visible and Invisible Hands in Great Britain," in Alfred Chandler, Jr., and Herman Daems, eds., *Managerial Hierarchies: Comparative Perspectives on the Rise of Modern Industrial Enterprise* (Cambridge, Mass., 1980), 40–76.

8. Tony Dickson, ed., *Scottish Capitalism: Class, State, and Nation from before the Union to the Present* (London, 1980), 190–192; Hobsbawm, *Industry and Empire*, 179; Jeffreys, *The Story of the Engineers*, 118; Harvie, *No Gods and Precious Few Heroes*, 2–4.

9. David Landes, *The Unbound Prometheus: Technological Change and Industrial Development in Western Europe from 1750 to the Present* (Cambridge, 1969), Chapter 5; Frank Tipton and Robert Aldrich, *An Economic and Social History of Europe, 1890–1939* (Baltimore, 1987), 10–26; Hobsbawm, *Industry and Empire*, 127, 180–181; Harvie, *No Gods and Precious Few Heroes*, 1, 4; Jeffreys, *The Story of the Engineers*, 118, 198.

10. Hannah, "Visible and Invisible Hands in Great Britain," 61–69; Hobsbawm, *Industry and Empire*, 135–152, 187–192; Dickson, *Scottish Capitalism*, 248–255; Harvie, *No Gods and Precious Few Heroes*, 4. On the comparative cost of craft labor in the U.S. and U.K. auto industries in 1910, see Jean-Pierre Bardou et al., *The Automobile Revolution: The Impact of an Industry*, trans. James Laux (Chapel Hill, 1982), 66.

11. R. H. Campbell, *Scotland since 1707* (New York, 1965), 256–258, 262–263; Harvie, *No Gods and Precious Few Heroes*, 39–40.

12. Robert Keith Middlemas, *The Clydesiders: A Left Wing Struggle for Parliamentary Power* (New York, 1968), 97; Harvie, *No Gods and Precious Few Heroes*, 47–48; Bill Stevenson, "Oral History Interview," 6 July 1961, transcript, Reuther Library, 1–2.

13. Henry McCusker, interview by author, tape recording, Dearborn, Michigan, 12 November 1980.

14. Harry Southwell, "Oral History Interview," 16 April 1963, transcript, Reuther Library, 1–2.

15. Leonard Woodcock, interview by author, tape recording, Ann Arbor, Michigan, 3 December 1985.

16. George Sayers Bain and Robert Price, *Profiles of Union Growth: A Comparative Statistical Portrait of Eight Countries* (Oxford, 1980), 37; James Cronin, "Labor Insurgency and Class Formation," in James Cronin and Carmen Sirianni, eds., *Work, Community, and Power: The Experience of Labor in Europe and America, 1900–1925* (Philadelphia, 1983), 23. On the shop stewards' movement, see James Hinton, *The First Shop Stewards' Movement* (London, 1973). On the 1919 Forty-Hours Strike, see Middlemas, *The Clydesiders*, 90–96; Iain McLean, *The Legend of Red Clydeside* (Edinburgh, 1983), 118–122, 136–138; and Jeffreys, *The Story of the Engineers*, 187–188.

17. Elizabeth McCracken, "Oral History Interview," 23 December 1959, transcript, Reuther Library, 3.

18. Joshua Freeman, "Catholics, Communists, and Republicans: Irish Workers and the Organization of the Transport Workers Union," in Michael Frisch and Daniel Walkowitz, eds., *Working Class America* (Urbana, 1983) 256–283; *CIO Reporter*, clipping, January 1940, Vertical File "Hugh Thompson," Reuther Library; Connie Quinn, Jr., phone interview by author, 9 April 1988; Jim Quinn, phone interview by author, 27 June 1988.

19. Convention flyer, n.d., Vertical File "Jack Thompson," Reuther Library; campaign brochure, 1947, Vertical File "Michael Magee," Reuther Library.

20. U.S. Department of Commerce, *Historical Statistics of the United States*, 105–106.

21. Except where otherwise noted, discussion of U.S. immigration law in this period is drawn from Marion Bennett, *American Immigration Policies: A History* (Washington, D.C., 1963), Chapters 3–6, and Maldwyn Allen Jones, *American Immigration* (Chicago, 1960), Chapter 9. General Wood quoted in Robert Murray, *Red Scare: A Study in National Hysteria* (New York, 1964), 265. For a more detailed description of immigration law as it defined Anglo-Gaelic emigration to Canada and the United States via Windsor, see Babson, "Pointing the Way," Chapter 4.

22. *Annual Report of the Commissioner General of Immigration, 1928*, 190; *1924*, 3.

23. Kenneth Lines, *British and Canadian Immigration to the United States since 1920* (San Francisco, 1978), 6–12; Stanley Johnson, *A History of Immigration: From the United Kingdom to North America, 1763–1912* (London, 1913/1966), 62–66; Rowland Berthoff, *British Immigrants in Industrial America, 1790–1950* (Cambridge, Mass., 1953), 21; Walshaw, *Migration to and from the British Isles*, (London, 1941) 30–41.

24. Consul General, Liverpool, England, to U.S. secretary of state, letter, 1 May 1924, and attached "Editorial," *Liverpool Journal of Commerce*, 28 April 1924, Box 190, File 53531–53, "Emigration England: Canada: 1924," NA/RG 85.

25. American consul, Windsor, Ontario, to American consul, Manchester, England, letter, 11 May 1923, Records of Foreign Service Posts of the State Department, Volume 152, File 811.11, "Correspondence, American Consulate, Windsor, 1923," NA/RG 84: Bennett, *American Immigration Policies*, 61.

26. "Danger Seen in Migration across Line," *Hamilton Herald*, 28 January 1925, in clipping file, Box 348, File 55442/909, "Immigration Pessimism in Canada, 1925," NA/RG 85; *Annual Report of the Commissioner General of Immigration, 1923*, 27; *1924*, 4–13.

27. *Annual Report of the Commissioner General of Immigration, 1923*, 25; *1924*, 14–15; *1925*, 18; Lines, *British and Canadian Immigration to the United States*, 76–77.

28. American Consul, Windsor, to U.S. Representative John Jacob Rogers, letter, 29 November 1924, Quota Control, Volume 159, File 811.11, "Correspondence, American Consulate Windsor, 1924," Records of the Foreign Service, Record Group 84, National Archives, Washington, D.C. (NA/RG 84); American Consulate General, Ottawa, to American consul, Windsor, letter, 6 June 1925, Quota Control, File 811.11, "Correspondence, Windsor, 1925," NA/RG 84: American Consular Service, London, to American consul, Windsor, letter, 16 June 1925, Quota Control, File 811.11, "Correspondence, Windsor, 1925," NA/RG 84: American consul, Windsor, to American consul general, London England, letter, 7 May 1926, Quota Great Britain, File 811.11, Part V, "Correspondence, American Consulate, Windsor, 1926," NA/RG 84: American consul general, Dublin, to American consul, Windsor, letter, 6 January 1926, Quota Control, File 811.11, "Correspondence, Windsor, 1925," NA/RG 84.

29. Philip Bonosky, *Brother Bill McKie: Building the Union at Ford* (New York, 1953), 18; Dues Book, Bill McKie, Nat Ganley Collection, Box 33, Folder 33-1, "Contracts, 1928, 1941."

30. Tony Lane, "A Merseysider in Detroit," *History Workshop* 11 (Spring 1981): 148.

31. "Early Unions," typescript, Joe Brown Collection, Box 3, Folder 2; typescript summary of article in *The Auto Worker*, 16 September 1920, Robert Dunn Collection, Box 1, Folder "Organizing"; Chris Johnson, *Maurice Sugar: Law, Labor, and the Left in Detroit, 1912–1950* (Detroit, 1988), 91–92.

32. "Organ. tactics" [*sic*], typescript notes, Robert Dunn Collection, Box 1, Folder "Organizing"; "Record of Struggles," typescript notes, Henry Kraus Collection, Box 1, Folder "Auto Workers Unions—Causes and Results of Work Stoppages, April 1926–May 1929." Henry Kraus recalls (interview by author, tape recording, Detroit, 16 June 1986) collecting this latter report from Phil Raymond after the AWU dissolved and turned its papers over to the UAW. See also Chalmers, "Labor in the Automobile Industry," 208–212.

33. Alan Strachan, "On the Road to Becoming an American," typescript, n.d., 1.

34. Ratcliffe quote in Lines, *British and Canadian Immigration to the United States since 1920*, 30.

35. Olivier Zunz, *The Changing Face of Inequality: Urbanization, Industrial Development, and Immigrants in Detroit, 1880–1920* (Chicago, 1982), 349; McCusker, interview by author; Jim Quinn, phone interview by author.

36. Lane, "A Merseysider in Detroit," 143; Mat Smith, longhand manuscript, December 1934, Joe Brown Collection, Box 15, Folder 33-34.

37. Bill McKie, testimony before the Henderson Committee, Detroit, 1934, quoted in *New Masses*, 8 January 1935, 16–17, Joe Brown Scrapbooks, Volume 3; Strachan, "On the Road to Becoming an American," 243; Joe Brown, "The MESA: Tool and Die Makers Organize and Strike," Chapter 15, typescript, Joe Brown Collection, Box 23, Folder "Strikes, Tool and Die, 1933," 1.

38. *The Detroiter*, 27 September 1926, 5; Bill McKie, interview transcript, Nat Ganley Collection, Box 33, Folder 33-15, "Misc. Notes," 17; Walter Dorosh, interview by author, tape recording, Dearborn, Michigan, 1 July 1986; Strachan, "On the Road to Becoming an American," 43.

39. Snudden, interview by author; Zunz, *The Changing Face of Inequality*, Maps 13.2 and 13.3, 344–347, and Table 13.11, 370–371.

40. Snudden, interview by author.

41. Ibid. The *Detroit Free Press* reported the membership of the Amity Lodge at 2,200 in 1919 (24 October 1919, 10).

42. P.H.J.H. Gosden, *Self-Help: Voluntary Associations in the Nineteenth Century* (London, 1973), 3–104, 260–282.

43. Mary Ann Clawson, *Constructing Brotherhood: Class, Gender, and Fraternalism* (Princeton, 1989), 96–97, 118–123; *General Laws, By-Laws and Rules of Order of Amity Lodge, No. 335, I.O.O.F.* (Detroit, 1918), Burton Historical Collection.

44. *American Eagle Bulletin* 6, no. 12 (April 1918): 1–8, Burton Historical Collection. The *Bulletin* also contains a complete list of officers. Unless otherwise indicated, the annual editions of *Polk's City Directory* are the source for addresses and occupational information on officers of the Odd Fellows, St. Andrews Society, and the Masons. Occupations listed in the 1918 *Polk's City Directory* for the eleven blue-collar officers of the Eagle Lodge include: machinist, toolmaker, electrician, carpenter, confectioner, inspector, conductor, welder, laborer, and two foreman; the latter were skilled workers, one a printer, the other a machinist (as indicated in directories for previous years).

45. *Polk's City Directory* lists the addresses of MESA halls only sporadically. The full list is indicated in MESA literature, including a leaflet entitled "The Union Must Be Preserved," in the Maurice Sugar Collection, Box 10, Folder 10:g.

46. St. Andrews Society, *Grand Scottish Concert and Ball*, Program, 1926, 8, Burton Historical Collection; *American Eagle Bulletin*. Organizations affiliated with St. Andrews and American Eagle are listed in *Polk's City Directory* under "Societies & Misc. Information."

47. On Diamond Lodge meeting, see *Detroit Free Press*, 28 April 1919, 10; *American Eagle Bulletin*.

48. Melvin Holli, *Reform in Detroit: Hazen Pingree and Urban Politics* (New York, 1969), 17–21, 123–154; Stephen Sarasohn and Vera Sarasohn, *Political Party Patterns in Michigan* (Detroit, 1957). The American Eagle Lodge's moderation toward the foreign-born was not seconded by some in the statewide IOOF: at the 1919 Michigan convention, the keynote speaker roundly condemned all aliens and called for strict regulation of citizenship. (*Detroit Free Press*, 22 October 1919.) For a detailed description of the MESA, AFL, and UAW locals that housed their headquarters and meetings in Odd Fellow halls, see Babson, "Pointing the Way," Chapter 4, endnote 84, 341–342.

49. Albert Kanarz, interview by author, tape recording, Warren, Michigan, 27 August 1986.

50. Joe Oberg, interview by author, tape recording, Detroit, 26 November 1985; Strachan, "On the Road to Becoming an American," 102. On the Anglim saloon and ASE, see *Polk's City Directory*, 1910. On Bob Bolton's bar, thanks to Sam Stark, recalling his Scots-born dad, who was a MESA member, a local-union vice president in the UAW, and a regular at the Bolton establishment. *Polk's City Directory* for 1928–1929 lists a Robert Bolton, machinist, and wife, Agnes, living nearby at 6 W. Arizona. "Bob Bolton's Bar and Grill" is still open today, though regular customers say Bolton sold the bar in 1972 after forty years in the business. Several of the more senior patrons recalled that Bolton "was a Limey."

51. On Mooney versus Coughlin, see Charles Tull, *Father Coughlin and the New Deal* (Syracuse, 1965), and the *Detroit News*, 26 October 1985.

52. Jim Quinn, phone interview by author; Johnson, *A History of Emigration*, 264–270; Branson, *Britain in the Nineteen Twenties*, 11; *Annual Report of the Commissioner General of Immigration, 1921*, 66–71; *1923*, 81–85; *1924*, 75–79.

Chapter 4. Pointing the Way

1. William McKie, interview, transcript, Nat Ganley Collection, Box 33, Folder 33-26. Many folders in Box 33 of this collection, particularly folders 15–26, contain lengthy verbatim transcripts of interviews with Bill McKie, apparently—since most do not identify the interviewer—conducted by *Daily World* correspondent and fellow Scotsman, Billy Allan, and/or Philip Bonosky, author of *Brother Bill McKie: Building the Union at Ford* (New York, 1953). Bonosky used virtually none of McKie's extended and detailed description of his life in Scotland. Except where otherwise noted, the biographical sketch that follows relies on these interviews.

2. Bonosky, *Brother Bill McKie*, 127.

3. Robert Middlemas, *The Clydesiders: A Left-Wing Struggle for Parliamentary Power* (London, 1965), 48 and passim; Walter Kendall, *The Revolutionary Movement in Britain, 1900–21: The Origins of British Communism* (London, 1969), 4–16.

4. On the Edinburgh SDF in these years, see C. Desmond Greaves, *The Life and Times of James Connolly* (London, 1976).

5. On Leslie's politics and their influence on Connolly, see ibid., 38–39, 43, 50–55.

6. On the SLP, see Chushichi Tsuzki, "The Impossibilist Revolt in Britain," *International Review of Social History* 1 (1956): 377–397; L. J. MacFarlane, *The British Communist Party: Its Origin and Development until 1929* (London, 1966), 24–30.

7. MacFarlane, *The British Communist Party*, 20; Kendall, *The Revolutionary Movement in Britain*, 40–45.
8. Middlemas, *The Clydesiders*, 78–80; Iain McLean, *The Legend of Red Clydeside* (Edinburgh, 1983), 144–151; Kendall, *The Revolutionary Movement in Britain*, Chapter 17.
9. Tony Lane, "A Merseysider in Detroit," *History Workshop* 11 (Spring 1981): 142–143.
10. *Historical Statistics of the United States*, Part 2 (Washington, D.C., 1975), 716 (car sales); Richard Ortquist, "Unemployment and Relief: Michigan's Response to the Depression during the Hoover Years," *Michigan History* (Fall 1973): 210; Detroit Board of Commerce, "Industrial Employment Index, Detroit Metropolitan Area," 8 August 1934, W. Ellison Chalmers Collection, Box 1, Folder "Auto Industry Statistics." Index = 100 for 1923–1925 monthly average.
11. On general depression conditions for autoworkers, see Sidney Fine, *The Automobile under the Blue Eagle: Labor, Management, and the Automobile Manufacturing Code* (Ann Arbor, 1963); Joyce Shaw Peterson, "Auto Workers and Their Work, 1900–1933," *Labor History*, 22 (Spring 1981): 213–236; and Kenneth West, " 'On the Line:' Rank and File Reminiscences of Working Conditions and the General Motors Sit-down Strike of 1936–1937," *Michigan Historical Review* 12 (Spring 1986): 57–82. On Ford layoffs, Albert Kanarz, interview by author, tape recording, Warren, Michigan, 27 August 1986, and Frank Muellner, interview by author, tape recording, Detroit, 25 March 1986. On the growing use of the same dies and stampings for several models, see Blanche Bernstein, "Labor Market in the Auto Industry, 1937," typescript, W. Ellison Chalmers Collection, Box 2, Reuther Library.
12. United States Civil Service Commission, Form 375, document signed by Joseph H. Picconke, 15 October 1941, Joseph Picconke Collection, Box 1, Folder "Personal and Biographical Information, 1942–1947," Item 5, Supplement, 1-3.
13. "A Statement of Mat Smith, General Secretary of the MESA, before the President's Commission of Inquiry into Conditions in the Automobile Industry, Detroit, Michigan, December 16, 1934," typescript, Joe Brown Collection, Box 17, Folder "NRA—Decisions and Orders," 2; "Standard of Living among Tool and Diemakers (analysis of MESA Data)," Joe Brown Collection, Box 15, Folder "MESA."
14. "A Statement of Mat Smith"; Blanche Bernstein, "Hiring Policies in the Automobile Industry," typescript, in "Reemployment Opportunities and Recent Changes in Industrial Technique," New York, 1937, 13; W. E. Chalmers, "First Strikes in the Automobile Industry, IV," typescript, in W. Ellison Chalmers Collection, Box 8, Folder 8-3, 1–2, 7; "Patternmaker Parley Called," *Detroit News*, 8 August 1934.
15. Joe Brown, "The MESA: Tool and Die Makers Organize and Strike," typescript, 3, Joe Brown Collection, Box 23, Folder "Strikes, Tool and Die, 1933."
16. Orrin Peppler, "Oral History Interview," 16 March 1961, transcript, Reuther Library, 2.
17. "A Statement of Mat Smith," 2; Bill Stevenson, "Oral History Interview," 6 July 1961, transcript, Reuther Library, 8; Harry Dahlheimer, *A History of the Mechanics Educational Society of America in Detroit from Its Inception in 1933 through 1937* (Detroit, 1951), 2; Brown, "The MESA: Tool and Die Makers Organize and Strike," 3.
18. Tool and die makers' median annual wages were $2,433 in 1929 and $636 in 1933; in the same years, autoworkers' mean annual wages were $1,475 and $850, respectively. See "Standard of Living among Tool and Diemakers"; The Labor Advisory Board to Sidney Hillman, National Industrial Recovery Board, memorandum, 23 October 1934, W. E. Chalmers Collection, Box 2, Folder "U.S. Auto Labor Board, Correspondence, 8/34–12/34," 2. Captive-shop wages cited in "A Statement of Mat

Smith," 2. Hourly wages are hard to estimate for autoworkers in the early 1930s, since nominal rates bore little relationship to actual income. Production workers were paid a group piecework bonus that varied week to week according to a formula that was highly complex (and arbitrary, according to many). Workers also lost pay for the many hours of "dead time" when the assembly line stopped or parts ran short—a frequent occurrence at the start of a production season. Bill Stevenson recalled that "dead time" also eroded the weekly pay of skilled workers. Stevenson, "Oral History Interview," 9.

19.   Smith, "A Statement of Mat Smith," 5.

20.   Keeran, *The Communist Party and the Auto Workers Unions* (Bloomington, 1980), 77–81.

21.   "Patternmakers! Toolmakers! Diemakers!" typescript for leaflet, Henry Kraus Collection, Box 1, Folder "AWU—Organization of Tool and Diemakers, 1933."

22.   Phil Raymond, "The Briggs Auto Strike Victory," *Labor Unity* (March 1933): 21–24, Robert Dunn Collection, Box 3, Folder 3-23.

23.   Ibid.; Walter Reuther, "Auto Workers Strike," *The Student Outlook* 1, no. 4 (March 1933): 15–16, Walter Reuther Collection, Box 565, Folder 565-1; "Minutes," Briggs Waterloo Strike Committee, Henry Kraus Collection, Box 1, Folder "AWU—Briggs Strike Minutes, Jan. 11–17, 1933"; "Table 1: Data Regarding Representative Groups of Tool and Die Makers," Joe Brown Collection, Box 15, Folder "MESA"; Keeran, *The Communist Party and the Auto Workers Unions*, 84–85.

24.   Raymond, "The Briggs Auto Strike Victory," 23; *Auto Worker News* 7, no. 1 (27 January 1933), Joe Brown Collection, Box 34, Folder "Auto Workers News 1927–1933"; Leonard Woodcock, interview by author, tape recording, Ann Arbor, Michigan, 3 December 1985, Reuther, "Auto Workers Strike," 15–16; Keeran, *The Communist Party and the Auto Workers Unions*, 86.

25.   Reuther, "Auto Workers Strike," 16; Michael Manning, "Oral History Interview," 6 July 1960, transcript, Reuther Library, 1–2. For coverage of strike events in 1933, see Federated Press, *Detroit News*, *Free Press*, and *Detroit Times* news articles for 13 January 1933 through 4 March 1933 in the Joe Brown Scrapbooks, Volume 1, Reuther Library, and Keeran, *The Communist Party and the Auto Worker Unions*, Chapter 4. On the prominent role of metal finishers, trimmers, and other body plant workers in the auto strikes of the 1930s, see Nelson Lichtenstein, "Auto Worker Militancy and the Structure of Factory Life, 1937–1955," *Journal of American History* 67 (September 1980), 337.

26.   On the history of MESA and early Detroit UAW, see Dahlheimer, *A History of the Mechanics Educational Society of America in Detroit*; Fine, *The Automobile under the Blue Eagle*; Keeran, *The Communist Party and the Auto Workers Unions*; Victor Reuther, *The Brothers Reuther, and the Story of the UAW. A Memoir* (Boston, 1976); Frank Marquart, *An Auto Worker's Journal: The UAW from Crusade to One-Party Union* (University Park, 1975); Brown, "The MESA: Tool and Die Makers Organize and Strike"; Chalmers, "First Strikes in the Automobile Industry"; Steve Babson, *Working Detroit: The Making of a Union Town* (Detroit, 1986).

27.   Elizabeth McCracken, "Oral History Interview," 23 December 1959, transcript, Reuther Library, 2, 8; Brown, "The MESA: Tool and Die Makers Organize and Strike," 4. Smith's handwritten story of his first encounter with MESA, dated December 1934, has a note from Joe Brown indicating it was subsequently published in the *MESA Voice* of the same month. Joe Brown Collection, Box 15, Folder "MESA, 1933–1934."

28.   Dahlheimer, *A History of the Mechanics Educational Society of America*, 6–15; Fine, *The*

Automobile under the Blue Eagle, 163–171; Brown, "The MESA: Tool and Die Makers Organize and Strike"; Chalmers, "First Strikes in the Automobile Industry"; Joe Brown Scrapbooks, Volume 1, 27 September 1933–6 November 1933.

29. MESA's Detroit membership is discussed in Joe Brown, Federated Press, 26 February 1934, Joe Brown Collection, Box 15, Folder "MESA." On the 1934 strike, see Dahlheimer, *A History of the Mechanics Educational Society of America*, 18–25, and Joe Brown Scrapbooks, Volume 2, 5 April 1934–5 May 1934.

30. Stevenson, "Oral History Interview," 14; McCracken, "Oral History Interview," 14; United States Civil Service Commission, Form 375, document signed by Joseph H. Picconke, 15 October 1941, 2–3.

31. Dahlheimer, *A History of the Mechanics Educational Society of America*, 36–37; Babson, *Working Detroit*, 61–102.

32. McCracken, "Oral History Interview," 24; Reuther, "Auto Workers Strike," 15.

33. Barton Bernstein, "The New Deal: The Conservative Achievements of Liberal Reform," in Barton Bernstein, ed., *Towards A New Past: Dissenting Essays in American History* (New York, 1968), 263–288; W. E. Chalmers, "The Passage of the Automobile Code," Chapter 3, typescript, W. Ellison Chalmers Collection, Box 8, Folder 8-2; Babson, *Working Detroit*, 52–72. On the timing of the Flint GM sit-down strike to coincide with Murphy's inauguration, see Sidney Fine, *Sit-Down: The General Motors Strike of 1936–1937* (Ann Arbor, 1969), 137.

34. *Historical Statistics of the United States*, Part 2, 716; Gerald Lazarowitz, "Comments on Professors Elkiss' and Linton's Paper," paper delivered at the North American Labor History Conference, Wayne State University, Detroit, 1982, 1–2.

35. William Cronin, National Automobile Chamber of Commerce, to the National Recovery Administration, Detroit, letter, 1 October 1934, W. Ellison Chalmers Collection, Box 2, Folder "U.S. Auto Labor Board; *Detroit News*, 30 October 1935, Joe Brown Collection, Box 1, Folder "Apprenticeship"; "Labor Shortage Found in the Metal Plants," *American Machinist*, 5 June 1935, 432c; "Labor and Incentives," *American Machinist*, 14 August 1935, 592b; Homer Coy, "Skill—What Is It Worth?" *American Machinist*, 3 June 1936, 509.

36. Frank Martel quoted in *Detroit Labor News*, 10 April 1936, Joe Brown Scrapbooks, Volume 4, Reuther Library; Frederick Blackall, Jr., "The Special Tool, Die and Machine Shop Institute," *American Machinist* 80 (2 December 1936): 1003; "Minutes of November 5, 1934 Meeting," typescript, attached to "Memorandum" (from Abner Larned, state NRA compliance director, to John Swope, chief, Field Branch, 9 November 1934), Joe Brown Collection, Box 17, Folder "NRA Codes, Tool and Die."

37. W. E. Chalmers to Deputy Administrator A. W. Caesar, "Report," letter, 7 November 1934, Joe Brown Collection, Box 17, Folder "NRA Codes, Tool and Die," 1–5.

38. Coy, "Skill—What Is It Worth?" 509.

39. "Auto Industry Succeeding in Stabilizing Employment," *Detroit News*, 15 February 1936; "GM Manufacturers Fatten on Orders; Tool Shops Face Long Cold Winter," *American Machinist*, 20 November 1935, 860e–860f; Russell Leach, interviews by author, tape recording, Detroit, 22 October 1985 and 19 November 1985.

40. Blaine Marrin, interview by author, tape recording, Madison Heights, Michigan, 5 November 1985; *Fisher Body Service Manual* (Detroit, 1935–1936), 1.

41. C. B. Gordy, "Craftsmen Needed," *American Machinist* 79 (6 November 1935): 823.

42. "Open Letter to the M.E.S.A. Men at Buell Die & Machine Co.," leaflet, 19 August 1935, Joe Brown Collection, Box 15, Folder "MESA—1935," Reuther Library; "Tool and Die Makers! Let's Get Together for a Noon Hour Chat," leaflet, 1936, Joe Brown Collection, Box 15, Folder "MESA," Reuther Library.

43. Charles Tilly, *From Mobilization to Revolution* (New York, 1978), 81, 119–166.
44. MESA halls are listed, among other places, on a leaflet distributed to Murray Body workers on 21 February 1935, in Joe Brown Collection, Box 15, Folder "MESA."
45. Henry Pelling, *America and the British Left* (London, 1956), 25, 29; James Young, *The Rousing of the Scottish Working Class* (London, 1979), 42–44, 63, 108, 119, 132.
46. Pelling, *America and the British Left*, 56, 62, 103–105; Greaves, *The Life and Times of James Connolly*, 45, 86, 264–265, 271–272; Young, *The Rousing of the Scottish Working Class*, 148–155, 160, 164, 180–184; James Young, "Changing Images of American Democracy," *International Review of Social History*, Part 1 (1973): 83–84; Patrick Renshaw, *The Wobblies: The Story of Syndicalism in the United States* (Garden City, 1968), 224–225.
47. Chushichi Tsuzuki, "The 'Impossibilist Revolt' in Britain: The Origins of the S.L.P. and the S.P.G.B.," *International Review of Social History* 1 (1956): 377–397, 381; James Hinton, *The First Shop Stewards' Movement* (London, 1973), 122; Kendall, *The Revolutionary Movement in Britain*, 66–76; MacFarlane, *The British Communist Party*, 24–30.
48. James Jefferys, *The Story of the Engineers, 1800–1945* (London, 1970), 206–207. Charles More amends this figure to 50 percent. Charles More, *Skill and the English Working Class, 1870–1914* (London, 1980), 185–186.
49. Peterson, "Auto Workers and Their Work," 220; Nick DiGaetano, "Oral History Interview," 29 April 1959, transcript, Reuther Library, 50.
50. Wayne Lewchuk, "Fordism and the Moving Assembly Line: The British and American Experience, 1895–1930," in Nelson Lichtenstein and Stephen Meyer, eds., *On the Line: Essays in the History of Auto Work* (Urbana, 1989), 24–30. On the Workers' Union at Daimler and the low level of union organization in auto, see Richard Hyman, *The Workers' Union* (Oxford, 1971), 61, and Chapter 3, "Achievement, 1910–1914." For an excellent critique of Lewchuk, see Steven Tolliday, "Management and Labor in Britain," in Steven Tolliday and Jonathan Zeitlin, eds., *The Automobile Industry and Its Workers* (Cambridge, 1985).
51. More, *Skill and the English Working Class*, 32–34.
52. Ibid., 171–177.
53. Ibid., Chapters 3 and 5, and 101, 137–143, 148; Bureau of the Census, *Fourteenth Census of the United States, 1920*, Volume 4, *Population, Occupations* (Washington, D.C., 1923), 947–948.
54. More, *Skill and the English Working Class*, 34, 64, 145–149, 174, and Chapter 6.
55. Stevenson, "Oral History Interview," 2; More, *Skill and the English Working Class*, 66–67, and Chapter 10; Eric Hobsbawm, *Workers: Worlds of Labor* (New York, 1984), 265; Woodcock, interview by author. The McGivern family and their occupations are listed in the *Polk's City Directory* for 1920–1921 and 1928–1929.
56. G. D. H. Cole, *Trade Unionism and Munitions* (Oxford, 1923), Chapter 3 and 12; More, *Skill and the English Working Class*, 28–31; Jefferys, *The Story of the Engineers*, 118–127. More rejects Hinton's assertion (*The First Shop Stewards' Movement*, 62) that the wartime employment of unskilled workers "revealed the degree to which the genuine skill content of the craftsmen's work had declined." Hinton fails to acknowledge how the mass production of war material differed from the "varied and variable" production of capital goods.
57. Alan Strachan, "On the Road to Becoming an American," typescript, n.d., 7; Bonosky, *Brother Bill McKie*, 15.
58. Strachan, in "On the Road to Becoming an American," 109, recalls Smith's attack on Anderson. Mat Hammond, president of Local 157 in the mid-1940s, also describes

Anderson as an electrician. Mat Hammond, "Oral History Interview," 6 April 1961, transcript, Reuther Library, 4.

59. Federated Press, 16 April 1934, Joe Brown Collection, Box 23, Folder "Strikes, Tool and Die, 1934," Sheet 1, 2-1.

60. Hobsbawm, *Workers*, 264.

61. Marc Block, *Feudal Society* (Chicago, 1974), 292; Welsh miner quoted in James Cronin, "Insurgency and Reaction in Britain, 1919–1926," typescript, North American Labor History Conference, Wayne State University, Detroit, 1980, 10–11.

62. Standish Meacham, *A Life Apart. The English Working Class, 1890–1914* (Cambridge, Mass., 1977), 14.

63. Gareth Stedman Jones, *Languages of Class: Studies in English Working Class History, 1832–1982* (Cambridge, 1983), 2.

64. Meacham, *A Life Apart*, Chapter 2.

65. Ibid., 59, and Chapters 2 and 5; Hobsbawm, *Workers*, Chapters 10 and 11; Jones, *Languages of Class*, 236, and Chapter 4; Christopher Harvie, *No Gods and Precious Few Heroes: Scotland, 1914–1980* (Toronto, 1981), 118–127.

66. Jones, *Languages of Class*, 196–205, 224–229; Robert Gray, *The Labour Aristocracy in Victorian Edinburgh* (Oxford, 1976), 190, and Chapters 1, 7, and 10; Meacham, *A Life Apart*, 121–123, 196–199; Hobsbawm, *Workers*, 242–243.

67. Ronald Edsforth, "Divergent Traditions: Union Organization in the Automobile Industries of Flint, Michigan and Coventry, England," *Detroit in Perspective* 5 (Spring 1981): 7, 9–16; Babson *Working Detroit*, 27; Steve Babson, "Living in Two Worlds: The Immigrant Experience in Detroit, *Michigan Quarterly Review* 25, no. 2 (Spring 1986). With the rise of the CIO and the New Deal, ethnic identity would later incorporate the union and the Democratic party. On the Polish Laborers' Alliance, see Melvin Holli, *Reform in Detroit: Hazen Pingree and Urban Politics* (New York, 1969), 67. On the positive correlation between class and ethnic consciousness, see John Leggett, *Class, Race, and Labor: Working Class Consciousness in Detroit* (New York, 1968), 8, 16, and 106–117.

68. "The Ford Way of Doing Business," *Detroit News*, 11 February 1940, Joe Brown Scrapbooks, Volume 18, Reuther Library; Chrysler's letter accompanied the company's document, "Employee Representation in the Plants of Chrysler Motors, October, 1933," Joe Brown Collection, Box 6, Folder "Company Unions"; Greaves, *The Life and Times of James Connolly*, 153.

69. John Zaremba, "Oral History Interview," 11 August 1961, transcript, Reuther Library, 1, 14; Gary Fink, ed., *Biographical Dictionary of American Labor* (Westport, Conn., 1984), 235, 392; John W. Anderson, "How I Became Part of the Labor Movement," in Alice Lynd and Staughton Lynd, eds., *Rank and File: Personal Histories of Working Class Organizers* (Boston, 1973), 49–51; Nestor Dessy, interview by author, tape recording, East Detroit, 14 September 1986; Harry Ross, "Oral History Interview," 10 July 1961, transcript, Reuther Library, 14.

70. Dessy, interview by author; Anderson, "How I Became Part of the Labor Movement," 50; Zaremba, "Oral History Interview," 12; Ross, "Oral History Interview," 14–15; Manning, "Oral History Interview," 1–2, 30–31; Michael Manning to the officers and members of United Automobile Workers Federal Labor Union no. 18677, letter, 6 January 1935, Michael Manning Collection, Box 1, Folder "1935."

71. Manning, "Oral History Interview," 15; Marquart, *An Auto Worker's Journal*, 32.

72. Chalmers, "First Strikes in the Automobile Industry," 1.

73. George Sayers Bain and Robert Price, *Profiles of Union Growth: A Comparative Statistical Portrait of Eight Countries* (Oxford, 1980). 50, 96–97.

74. Harry Southwell, "Oral History Interview," 17 April 1963, transcript, Reuther Library, 3–4.

75. "Bill Stevenson," typescript biography, 20 August 1942, Vertical File, Bill Stevenson, Reuther Library; Stevenson, "Oral History Interview," 4; Southwell, "Oral History Interview," 3–4; "Doug Fraser, Jr.," *Current Biography* (October 1977): 16; Lane, "A Merseysider in Detroit," 146, 142–143.

76. Lane, "A Merseysider in Detroit," 144–145.

77. Dan Gallagher, "Oral History Interview," 26 January 1960, transcript, Reuther Library, 25; Marrin, interview by author; Zaremba, "Oral History Interview," 2; Manning, "Oral History Interview," 13.

78. Lane, "A Merseysider in Detroit," 144; Bill McKie to A. J. Muste, letter, 3 December 1929, Brookwood Papers, Box 28, Folder 2; Walter Dorosh, interview by author, tape recording, Dearborn, Michigan, 1 July 1986.

79. "Minutes," longhand minutes by Mike Lukatch, 1 December 1933, Harry Ross Collection, Box 2, Folder "Local 3 Minutes, 9/33–4/3?" [*sic*].

80. Stanley Nowak, "Oral History Interview," 2 June 1960, transcript, Reuther Library, 14.

81. Federated Press News Release, typescript by Joe Brown, 26 February 1934, Joe Brown Collection, Box 15, Folder "MESA."

82. Dessy, interview by author.

83. Strachan, "On the Road to Becoming an American," 72–74.

84. Manning, "Oral History Interview," 9. For identification of officers and organizers in Local 174, see "Executive Board, West Side Local 174, U.A.W.A.," typed minutes, 8 April 1938, Walter Reuther Collection, Box 1, Folder 1-19; "Report on Condition of Plants," typed reports by organizers, 24 February 1938, Walter Reuther Collection, Box 1, Folder 1-6; "Forward with Experienced Militant Leadership," election card, 1938, Walter Reuther Collection, Box 1, Folder 1-17; Victor Reuther, *The Brothers Reuther*, Chapters 12 and 15; Anderson, "How I Became Part of the Labor Movement," 35.

85. Bill McKie, interview transcript, 13–14, Nat Ganley Collection, Box 33, Folder 33-19; *Dodge Main News*, 25 March 1937, Harry Ross Collection, Box 2, Folder "Dodge Main News, 3/37."

86. *Detroit Labor News*, 25 December 1936, 29 January 1937, 26 February 1937, 30 April 1937, 7 May 1937, 4 June 1937, 25 June 1937; Nat Ganley, Local 155 business agent, "Report for 1938," Nat Ganley Collection, Box 4, Folder 4-18, 1.

87. Melvin Bishop, "Oral History Interview, 29 March 1963, transcript, Reuther Library, 5–9; Marquart, *An Auto Worker's Journal*, 16, 23–25; *Solidarity* 28, no. 10 (October 1985): 18; Marrin, interview by author; Strachan, "On the Road to Becoming an American," 74; Leach, interview by author.

88. Cole, *Trade Unionism and Munitions*, 27–31, 207.

89. Ibid., 42.

90. On the amalgamation movement in the British labor movement after World War I, see ibid., 206–209.

91. On the 1927 TUC decision, see John Lovell and B. C. Roberts, *A Short History of the TUC* (London, 1968), 99–103.

92. McCracken, "Oral History Interview," 18–19.

93. Lovell and Roberts, *A Short History of the TUC*, 56–58, 66–71, 75–83.

94. H. A. Clegg, *A History of British Trade Unions since 1889* (Oxford, 1964), 1:38; Jefferys, *The Story of the Engineers*, 167–171; Hinton, *The First Shop Stewards' Movement*, 83–84; Cole, *Trade Unions and Munitions*, 47–50; Churchill quote in James Cronin, "Coping

with Labour, 1918–1926," in James Cronin and Jonathan Schneer, eds., *Social Conflict and the Political Order in Modern Britain* (New Brunswick, 1982), 115.

95. Hymen, *The Workers' Union*, 12–30 describes other examples of such multiple membership in the Workers Union.

96. Cole, *Trade Unions and Munitions*, 46.

97. The MESA constitution is quoted in Dahlheimer, *A History of the Mechanics Educational Society of America*, 53–55.

98. Jefferys, *The Story of the Engineers*, 137, 165, 180–187, 193–194; Hinton, *The First Shop Stewards' Movement*, 76–83, 162–169, 221–115, 294–295, and passim; Hymen, *The Workers' Union*, 117; Kendall, *The Revolutionary Movement in Britain*, 142–143, 167.

99. "GM Supplement," typed contract, 12 April 1937 and 7 March 1938, Nat Ganley Collection, Box 7, Folder 7-11; *Agreement*, UAW Tool and Die Jobbing Shops, May 1938, Walter Reuther Collection, Box 28, Folder 28-22, 3; Nat Ganley, "Report for 1937 by Nat Ganley, Business Agent, Local 155," Ganley Collection, Box 4, Folder 4-18, 1.

100. Clegg, *A History of British Trade Unions*, 1:37–39, 476–478; Jefferys, *The Story of the Engineers*, 193.

101. Dahlheimer, *A History of the Mechanics Educational Society of America*, 28, 53–55; McCracken, "Oral History Interview," 35–37.

102. *Detroit Free Press*, 17 July 1938, Joe Brown Scrapbooks, Volume 13, Reuther Library; *Daily World*, 17 May 1934, Joe Brown Scrapbooks, Volume 2, Reuther Library; Dahlheimer, *A History of the Mechanics Educational Society of America*, 17, 25–28, 35.

103. Keeran, *The Communist Party and the Auto Worker Unions*, 106–107, quotes Joe Brown on the popularity among MESA members of Communist party attacks on the AFL, even though most MESA members opposed the party per se.

104. McCracken, "Oral History Interview," 22–23; "Report of the Revision Committee to Convention, May 26, 1934," and "Constitution and By-Laws of the MESA," Joe Brown Collection, Box 15, Folder "MESA 1933–1934;" "Primary Election of National Officers . . . for the Year Ending December 31, 1934," printed ballot, Joe Brown Collection, Box 15, Folder "MESA 1933–1934."

105. *Newsweek*, 21 February 1944, 66–69; "The State of the Union," 16 October 1936, Joe Brown Collection, Box 15, Folder "MESA 1936–1944"; "What MESA Is Doing," 1936, Box 15, Folder "MESA 1936–1944"; *Detroit Free Press*, 23 January 1936, Joe Brown Scrapbooks, Volume 4, Reuther Library.

106. Jefferys, *The Story of the Engineers*, 166, 208, 214; Cole, *Trade Unions and Munitions*, 41–43; Steven Tolliday, "Management and Labour in Britain, 1896–1939," in Steven Tolliday and Jonathan Zeitlin, eds., *The Automobile Industry and Its Workers* (New York, 1987), 47–48.

107. Mat Smith, "Industrial Unionism," *Industrial Unionist* (Toledo), March 1936, Joe Brown Scrapbooks, Volume 4, Reuther Library.

108. Dahlheimer, *A History of the Mechanics Educational Society of America*, 16, 28; Mechanics Educational Society of America, "Don't Vote!" leaflet with notation of "JB," 18 December 1934, Joe Brown Collection, Box 15, Folder "MESA 1933–1934."

109. "UAW Scabs at National Stamping," leaflet, circa March 1937, Joe Brown Collection, Box 23, Folder "Strikes, Auto Companies, 1937"; "Program, National Play Day and Outing," 14 July 1940, Joe Brown Collection, Box 15, "MESA 1936–1944."

110. McCracken, "Oral History Interview," 11–12; *Detroit News*, 4 May 1934, 14 May 1934, and *Detroit Free Press*, 5 May 1934, Joe Brown Scrapbooks, Volume 2, Reuther Library; Bonosky, *Brother Bill McKie*, 120.

111. *Detroit News*, 7 May 1936 and 28 May 1936, Joe Brown Scrapbooks, Volume 4,

Reuther Library; Kraus, interview by author; "To All G.M. Diemakers," leaflet, no date, Joe Brown Collection, Box 31, Folder "UAW Jurisdictional Disputes— MESA."

112. William Corey, "Apprenticeship—Past and Present," typescript, 21 November 1985, Wayne State University, Labor Studies Center, 8.
113. Leach, interview by author.
114. Bill McKie, "Monday, May 3rd Session," interview transcripts, Nat Ganley Collection, Box 33, Folder 33-20.
115. Woodcock, interview by author.

Chapter 5. Confronting the Liberal State

1. "Testimonial Dinner Honoring Richard T. 'Dick' Frankensteen and Cornelius P. 'Pat' Quinn," printed program, 15 March 1941, Harry Ross Collection, Box 3, Folder "Local 3 Misc., 1940."
2. Steve Babson, "Pointing the Way: Skilled Workers and Anglo-Gaelic Immigrants in the Rise of the UAW" (Ph.D. diss., Wayne State University, 1989), Appendix A. On Smith's prison experience, see Elizabeth McCracken, "Oral History Interview," 23 December 1959, transcript, Reuther Library, 30–31.
3. H. A. Clegg, *A History of British Trade Unions since 1889* (Oxford, 1964), 1:400–405, 2:100–103; Peter Hennock, "The Origins of British National Insurance and the German Precedent, 1880–1914," and Roy Hay, "The British Business Community, Social Insurance and the German Example," in W. J. Mommsen, ed., *The Emergence of the Welfare State in Britain and Germany* (London, 1981); George Dangerfield, *The Strange Death of Liberal England* (London, 1966), 28.
4. James Cronin, "Coping with Labour, 1918–1926," in James Cronin and Jonathan Schneer, eds., *Social Conflict and the Political Order in Modern Britain* (New Brunswick, 1982), 126; Hennock, "The Origins of British National Insurance," 93; Clegg, *A History of British Trade Unions*, 1:400, 2:101.
5. For varied assessments of working-class consciousness in this period, see Meacham, "'The Sense of an Impending Clash': English Working Class Unrest Before the First World War," *American Historical Review* 77 (December 1972): 1343–1364; Dangerfield, *The Strange Death of Liberal England*, 212–213; Cronin, "Coping with Labour," passim; Joe White, "1910–1914 Reconsidered," in James Cronin and Jonathan Schneer, eds., *Social Conflict and the Political Order in Modern Britain* (New Brunswick, 1982), 73–95; R. J. Holton, "Daily Herald v. Daily Citizen, 1912–1915: The Struggle for a Labour Daily in Relation to 'The Labour Unrest,'" *International Review of Social History* 19 (1974): 347–376. For differing interpretations of the State's repressive role in wartime, see Alastair Reid, "Dilution, Trade Unionism and the State in Britain during the First World War," in Steven Tolliday and Jonathan Zeitlin, eds., *Shop Floor Bargaining and the State: Historical and Comparative Perspectives* (Cambridge, 1985), versus Jeffrey Haydu, "Factory Politics in Britain and the United States: Engineers and Machinists, 1914–1919," *Comparative Studies in Society and History* 27, no. 1 (January 1985): 57–85, and James Hinton, *The First Shop Stewards' Movement* (London, 1973).
6. See Dangerfield, *The Strange Death of Liberal England*, passim.
7. James Jefferys, *The Story of the Engineers, 1800–1945* (London, 1970), 162; Meacham, "The Sense of an Impending Clash," 1364.
8. Home Office quoted in Cronin, "Coping with Labour," 115–116; David Howell,

British Social Democracy. A Study in Development and Decay (New York, 1980), 18, and Chapter 1 and 2; John Lovell and B. C. Roberts, *A Short History of the TUC* (London, 1968), 122–134; Gareth Stedman Jones, *Languages of Class: Studies in English Working Class History, 1832–1982* (Cambridge, 1983), 236–238, 246–247; Robert Middlemas, *The Clydesiders: A Left-Wing Struggle for Parliamentary Power* (London, 1965), 132–158; Allen Hutt, *The Post-War History of the British Working Class* (London, 1937), 67–99, 197–203.

9. Ministry of Munitions quoted in Haydu, "Factory Politics in Britain and the United States," 73; Hinton, *The First Shop Stewards' Movement*, Chapter 8; Rodger Charles, *The Development of Industrial Relations in Britain, 1911–1939* (London, 1973), 85, 95–129, 140–151.

10. Charles Maier, *Recasting Bourgeois Europe: Stabilization in France, Germany, and Italy in the Decade after World War I* (Princeton, 1975), 148, 138–192.

11. Hutt, *The Post-War History of the British Working Class*, and Chanie Rosenberg, *1919: Britain on the Brink of Revolution* (London, 1987), support the claims of contemporary revolutionaries that British workers were prepared for insurrection; Iain McLean, *The Legend of Red Clydeside* (Edinburgh, 1983), provides a convincing counterargument.

12. Cole, *Trade Unionism and Munitions*, Chapter 3; Hinton, *The First Shop Stewards' Movement*, 65, 335, 337.

13. Dangerfield, *The Strange Death of Liberal England*, 212; Steve Jefferys, *Management and Managed: Fifty Years of Crisis at Chrysler* (Cambridge, 1986), 2–16; Charles, *The Development of Industrial Relations in Britain*, 22.

14. William Allan, "'Grand Old Man' of UAW Is Victim of Reuther Factionalism," newspaper clipping, circa 1950, Nat Ganley Collection, Box 33, Folder 33-30.

15. Joe Brown, "The MESA: Tool and Die Makers Organize and Strike," typescript, 17–19, Joe Brown Collection, Box 23, Folder "Strikes, Tool and Die, 1933"; Joe Brown, "The Mechanics Educational Society Strike and Background," typescript chronology, undated, Joe Brown Collection, Box 15, Folder "MESA, 1936–1944," 5; *Detroit Times*, 30 October 1933, and *Detroit Free Press*, 31 October 1933, Joe Brown Scrapbooks, Volume 1, Reuther Library; Harry Dahlheimer, *A History of the Mechanics Educational Society of America in Detroit from Its Inception in 1933 through 1937* (Detroit, 1951), 11–12.

16. *Detroit Free Press*, 31 October 1933, Joe Brown Scrapbook, Volume 1, Reuther Library; Brown, "The MESA: Tool and Die Makers Organize and Strike," 19; Sidney Fine, *The Automobile under the Blue Eagle: Labor, Management, and the Automobile Manufacturing Code* (Ann Arbor, 1963), 170.

17. National Recovery Administration, *Code of Fair Competition for the Automobile Manufacturing Industry* (Washington, D.C., 1933), 5–9; W. E. Chalmers, "The Passage of the Automobile Code," typescript, undated, W. Ellison Chalmers Collection, Box 8, Folder 8-2, 1–10; "Memorandum of the Mechanics Educational Society of America . . . to the National Recovery Administration, Washington, D.C.," typescript, 8 October 1933, Joe Brown Collection, Box 17, Folder "NRA—Codes, Tool and Die," 2; Fine, *The Automobile under the Blue Eagle*, Chapter 2.

18. Fine, *The Automobile under the Blue Eagle*, 166–167; Dahlheimer, *A History of the Mechanics Educational Society of America*, 7–8; Chris Johnson, *Maurice Sugar: Law, Labor, and the Left in Detroit, 1912–1950* (Detroit, 1988), 140–141; *Detroit Times*, 29 September 1933, Joe Brown Scrapbooks, Volume 1, Reuther Library.

19. *Detroit Times*, 29 September 1933, Joe Brown Scrapbooks, Volume 1, Reuther Library; "Memorandum of the Mechanics Educational Society of America . . . ," 8–13.

20. Johnson, *Maurice Sugar*, 142–144; Dahlheimer, *A History of the Mechanics Educational Society of America*, 10–11; Brown, "The MESA: Tool and Die Makers Organize and Strike," 15–16.

21. *Detroit News*, 22 October 1933, and *Detroit Times*, 23 October 1933, Joe Brown Scrapbooks, Volume 1, Reuther Library.

22. MESA, "Wrestling Match: Three Star Bouts," flyer, 1933, Joe Brown Collection, Box 15, Folder "MESA 1933–34"; Brown, "The MESA: Tool and Die Makers Organize and Strike," 17–18. Brown says the Deutsches Haus meeting on the twenty-eighth heard Smith and Sugar's report on the Washington NLB hearing. But newspaper accounts indicate this occurred on the twenty-second, a more likely date, since the union had no reason to delay their report until ten days after the event.

23. On departing directly from hall, see the *Detroit Times*, 30 October 1933, Joe Brown Scrapbooks, Volume 1.

24. Smith quoted in Fine, *The Automobile under the Blue Eagle*, 173–174, 183. On the rise of Smith, see the *Detroit News*, 1 October 1933, Joe Brown Scrapbooks, Volume 1, Reuther Library; and Dahlheimer, *A History of the Mechanics Educational Society of America*, 8. On McGivern and Smith on the Regional Labor Board, see the *Detroit Times*, 4 November 1933 and 5 November 1933, Joe Brown Scrapbooks, Volume 1, Reuther Library, and Fine, *The Automobile under the Blue Eagle*, 183–184.

25. Fine, *The Automobile under the Blue Eagle*, 147–148, 187–188, 218–226, Smith quoted in *Detroit News*, 14 April 1934, Joe Brown Scrapbooks, Volume 2, Reuther Library; William Chalmers, Chapter 9, "The First National Conference of Automobile Unions," typescript, W. Ellison Chalmers Collection, Box 8, Folder 8-6, 1–17; "Development [of] Local Leadership," anonymous typescript, Henry Kraus Collection, Box 2, Folder "AFL Detroit Office, Development of Local Leadership and Review of Council Members, 12/20/34"; Roger Keeran, *The Communist Party and the Auto Workers Unions* (Bloomington, 1980), 109–110, 121–127. Keeran overstates the opposition to the AFL's cautious policies at the June 1934 national conference by lumping together Wyndham Mortimer's left wing and Byrd-Greer's right wing.

26. *Daily Worker*, 4 January 1935, 5 January 1935, and *Detroit Free Press*, 9 March 1935, Joe Brown Scrapbooks, Volume 3, Reuther Library; Mat Smith, interview by Joe Brown, typescript notes, 9 May 1938, Joe Brown Collection, Box 18, Folder "Society of Tool and Die Craftsmen"; *Craftsman's Clarion*, 11 April 1938, 1, Joe Brown Collection, Box 34, Folder "Craftsman's Clarion, Oct., 1937"; "The Society of Tool and Die Craftsmen," leaflet, n.d., Blaine Marrin Collection, no. 204.

27. Leiserson quoted in Christopher Tomlins, *The State and the Unions: Labor Relations, Law, and the Organized Labor Movement in America, 1880–1960* (Cambridge, 1985), 111–112. The other two cases were the Philadelphia Bakers and the Jamestown Art Metal Company.

28. *Detroit News*, 28 November 1936 and 4 December 1936, Joe Brown Scrapbooks, Volume 4, Reuther Library; Steve Babson, *Working Detroit: The Making of a Union Town* (Detroit, 1986), 68–90.

29. Babson, *Working Detroit*, 82; UAW Local 157, "Resolution on Sit-Down Strike Legislation," typescript signed by William Hulle, undated, Local 157 Collection, Box 5, Part 1, Folder "Minutes, 12/6/36–2/17/38," 1–3.

30. *Detroit Times*, 4 November 1933, Joe Brown Scrapbooks, Volume 1, Reuther Library; *Daily Worker*, 17 May 1934, Joe Brown Scrapbooks, Volume 2, Reuther Library.

31. Anderson remained a full-time organizer for the International through 1937. See Nat Ganley, "Report for 1937 by Nat Ganley Business Agent, Local 155," Ganley Collection, Box 4, Folder 4-18, 1. *Midland Flash*, November 1936, Henry Kraus Collection, Box 7, Folder "Midland Steel Strike, 11/36," 1, lists its address care of

Anderson and advertises a meeting at ABC hall preceding the sit-down. *Midland Flash* 1, no. 2, 1, lists Anderson, International Vice President Wyndham Mortimer, and Shop Chairman Frank Carr as negotiators. On Brear, Dyer, and Boll, see Peter Friedlander, "The Social Bases of Politics in a UAW Local: Midland Steel, 1933–1941," typescript prepared for the Annual Meeting of the Organization of American Historians, April 1977, author's possession, 6–7; Peter Friedlander, interview by author, Ferndale, Michigan, 20 December 1988. Sam Brear, whom co-workers recalled as "Scottish," was born and raised in the west Yorkshire town of Bradford, England. "Declaration of Intention," no. 5245, document signed by Sam Brear, 24 February 1917, National Archives, Great Lakes Region, Chicago, Illinois.

32. *Midland Flash*, November 1936, 3.
33. *Midland Flash*, December 1936, 1–3; *Detroit Times* 30 November 1936, and *Detroit Labor News*, 4 December 1936, Joe Brown Scrapbooks, Volume 4, Reuther Library.
34. Peter Friedlander, "Before the Institution: Politics on the Shopfloor, 1933–1936," typescript prepared for the Annual Meeting of the Industrial Relations Research Association, Atlanta, Georgia, 28 December 1979, 6–7, also puts the Midland strike strategy in the larger context of the UAW's organizational goals.
35. Henry Kraus, interview by author, tape recording, Detroit, 16 June 1986.
36. A. L. Faulkner to Mr. Kerwin, typescript summary of letter, 30 November 1936, and "Preliminary Report of Commissioner of Conciliation, Re the Midland Steel Products Corporation," document signed by A. L. Faulkner, 5 December 1936, Federal Mediation and Conciliation Service Case Files, Box 415, no. 182-1976, Records of the Federal Mediation and Conciliation Service, Record Group 280, National Archives, Washington, D.C.; *Detroit Labor News*, 4 December 1936, Joe Brown Scrapbooks, Volume 4, Reuther Library. Thanks to Peter Friedlander for copies of the FMCS correspondence and reports.
37. "Midland Victory Extra!," undated clipping, Harry Ross Collection, Box 2, Folder "Local 3 Misc., 1937."
38. Peter Friedlander, "The Social Bases of Politics in a UAW Local," 6; August Meier and Elliot Rudwick, *Black Detroit and the Rise of the UAW* (New York, 1979), 6–8, 35.
39. Henry Kraus, interview by author; Dorothy Kraus, interview by author, tape recording, Detroit, 16 June 1986.
40. MESA, "To the Wives of the Strikers," leaflet, 1933, Joe Brown Collection, Box 15, Folder "MESA, 1933–1934"; Johnson, *Maurice Sugar*, 145; Dorothy Kraus, interview by author.
41. Dorothy Kraus, interview by author; *Detroit Times*, 30 November 1936, Joe Brown Scrapbooks, Volume 4, Reuther Library.
42. "Midland Victory Extra!," undated clipping, Harry Ross Collection, Box 2, Folder "Local 3 Misc., 1937"; A. L. Faulkner to Mr. Kerwin, 30 November 1936; Wyndham Mortimer, *Organize! My Life as a Union Man* (Boston, 1971), 121–122; E. J. Kulas to Honorable Madam Frances Perkins, secretary of labor, letter, 4 December 1936, Henry Kraus Collection, Box 7, Folder "Midland Steel Strike, 11/36"; "Agreement," UAW Local 410 and Midland Steel, August 1937, UAW Local 410 Collection, Box 8, Folder "1937 Agreement."
43. Orrin Peppler, "Oral History Interview," 16 March 1961, transcript, Reuther Library, 6–7.
44. Mat Hammond, "Oral History Interview," 6 March 1961, transcript, Reuther Library, 4–8; Ganley, "Report for 1937," 2–4; Blaine Marrin, interview by author, tape recording, Madison Heights, Michigan, 5 November 1985.
45. Russell Leach, interviews by author, tape recordings, Detroit, 22 October 1985 and 19 November 1985; "UAW Local 157 Minutes," UAW Local 157 Collection, Part I, Box

5, Folders "UAW Local 157 Minutes, 12/6/36–2/17/38" and "UAW Local 157 Minutes, 2/18/38–2/29/40."

46. John Zaremba, "Oral History Interview," 11 August 1961, transcript, Reuther Library, 25–28; *Detroit News*, 8 March 1937.
47. Jefferys, *Management and Managed*, 49–71; Fine, *The Automobile under the Blue Eagle*, 155–162, 337–344; Zaremba, "Oral History Interview," 13; *Detroit Times*, 3 March 1937.
48. Local 3's officers for 1936–1937 are listed in the minutes of the "Regular Business Meeting, Sunday, June 6, 1937," Local 3 Collection, Box 3, Folder "Reg. Bus. Mtg. 27 Dec., 1936–24 Apr. 1938," 1; their departmental backgrounds are indicated in Works Council election lists for February 1935 and January 1936, Harry Ross Collection, Box 2, Folder "Local 3 Elections, 1935–1937." AIWA "Locals" 99 and 76 are indicated in Dick Frankensteen, *First Year Book and History of the AIWA, Featuring "Gypsy Moon"*, printed program, 14 December 1935, Harry Ross Collection, Box 2, Folder "AIWA-Dodge Amalgamation, 1935–1936." E. H. Wilsher's summary of George Miller's comments are in typescript notes, 18 February 1937, Harry Ross Collection, Box 6, Folder "Stool Pigeon Reports, 1931–1937."
49. On McIntyre's participation in Local 3 meetings before the sit-down, see the minutes for the Local 3 regular business meetings on 27 December 1936, 30 January 1937, and 28 February 1937, Local 3 Collection, Box 3, Folder "Regular Business Meetings, 27 Dec. 1936–24 April 1938." In these last three meetings before the sit-down, McIntyre's active presence is indicated eight times (to report, to move, to second, etc.), surpassed only by Richard Frankensteen and four other top officers (indicated 9, 9, 13, 18, and 24 times). On his stature among fellow stewards, see "Stewards Meeting, First, Second, and Third Shifts," typed minutes, 1 May 1937, Local 3 Collection, Box 4, Folder "Stewards Meeting Minutes, 1937–1940," 2, where he leads twenty-five other candidates in primary voting for the Plant Committee. On the establishment of Local 3's steward system, see "Steward Meeting," typed minutes, 25 January 1937, 1, and "Chief Shop Steward Meeting," typed minutes, 5 April 1937, Local 3 Collection, Box 4, Folder "Stewards meeting Minutes, 1937–1940."
50. Zaremba, "Oral History Interview," 25–26; *Detroit News*, 9–11 March 1937; *Dodge Main News*, 10 March 1937, and 12 March 1937, Henry Kraus Collection, Box 11, Folder "Chrysler Strike—Dodge Main News, 3/9–22/37." Unless otherwise indicated, all citations from *Dodge Main News* are from the Henry Kraus Collection, as indicated above.
51. *Dodge Main News*, 10 March 1937, 12 March 1937, 14 March 1937. Zaremba, "Oral History Interview," 10–15.
52. Zaremba, "Oral History Interview," 16.
53. Leo Huberman, *The Labor Spy Racket* (New York, 1937), 3–4, 76–78; Dodge Local 3, *The Story of Dodge Local 3* (Detroit, 1941), 3–4, Harry Ross Collection, Box 2, Folder "Dodge Local 3 History."
54. *Dodge Main News*, 9 March 1937, 10 March 1937, 13 March 1937, 17 March 1937.
55. "Testimonial Dinner Honoring . . . 'Pat' Quinn"; *Dodge Main News*, 14 March 1937, 17 March 1937, 23 March 1937.
56. *Dodge Main News*, 10 March 1937.
57. *Detroit News*, 11 March 1937; *Dodge Main News*, 14 March 1937.
58. *Detroit News*, 15 March 1937.
59. *Dodge Main News*, 14 March 1937, and 17 March 1937; Walter Duda, interview by author, tape recording, Detroit, 13 September 1979.
60. *Detroit News*, 17 March 1937; *Dodge Main News*, 18 March 1937.

61. *Detroit News*, 12 March 1937, 17 March 1937, 18 March 1937, 19 March 1937.

62. *Dodge Main News*, 19 March 1937, 23 March 1937, 24 March 1937.

63. *Dodge Main News*, 24 March 1937.

64. *Dodge Main News*, 25 March 1937; *Detroit News*, 25 March 1937.

65. *Detroit News*, 7 April 1937; "Regular Business Meeting," typed minutes, 25 April 1937, p. 2, Local 3 Collection, Box 3, Folder "Regular Business Meetings, 27 Dec. 1936–24 Apr. 1938."

66. *Detroit News*, 24 March 1937.

67. Howell, *British Social Democracy*, 19–22.

68. For an excellent summary of these issues, see Richard Oestricher, "Urban Working-Class Political Behavior and Theories of American Electoral Politics, 1870–1940," *Journal of American History* 74, no. 4 (March 1988): 1270–1272 and passim.

69. Bill Stevenson, "Oral History Interview," 6 July 1961, transcript, Reuther Library, 4.

70. McCracken, "Oral History Interview," 30; Hobsbawm, *Workers*, 154, 211, 266–267; Lovell and Roberts, *A Short History of the TUC*, 32–33; Jones, *Languages of Class*, 213.

71. Bill McKie, "Misc. Notes," interview transcript, Nat Ganley Collection, Box 33, Folder 33–20.

72. Anderson quoted in Keeran, *The Communist Party and the Auto Workers Unions*, 224; Leach, interview by author.

73. Smith quoted in the *Cleveland Plain Dealer*, 3 January 1935, Joe Brown Scrapbooks, Volume 3, Reuther Library. On Magee, see campaign brochure, 1947, Vertical File, "Michael Magee," Reuther Library.

74. Johnson, *Maurice Sugar*, 152–176, 228–230. On MESA halls, see "Final Instructions for District Campaign Workers," typescript notes, Maurice Sugar Collection, Box 10, Folder 10:20; *Farmer-Labor Challenge*, April 1936, 4, Joe Brown Collection, Box 34, Folder "Farmer-Labor Challenge, April, 1936"; Farmer Labor Party, "A Real American," campaign leaflet listing officers, 1936, Maurice Sugar Collection, Series 1, Box 11, Folder 11:2; "Analysis of Vote, November 2, 1937 Elections, City of Detroit," typescript, in Henry Kraus Collection, Box 12, Folder "Labor Slate in Detroit Elections, 1937 Vote Analysis."

75. Mat Smith, typescript notes, Maurice Sugar Collection, Box 10, Folder 10:21. On farmers, see *Farmer-Labor Voice*, n.d., 2, Joe Brown Collection, Box 34, Folder "Farmer-Labor Challenge, April, 1936." On Anderson and the IWO, see Johnson, *Maurice Sugar*, 153–156; Bill McKie, interview transcript, in Nat Ganley Collection, Box 33, Folder 33-16; 1935 quote in "United Labor's Choice," leaflet, Maurice Sugar Collection, Box 10, Folder 10:20.

76. FLP 1936 program in *Farmer-Labor Voice*, n.d., 1, Joe Brown Collection, Box 34, Folder "Farmer-Labor Challenge, April, 1936"; Johnson, *Maurice Sugar*, 167–171. On the AFL versus CIO in the 1937 elections, see Alan Strachan, "A History of the Work of the Political Action Committee in the Detroit Municipal Elections, 1937," typescript, Henry Kraus Collection, Box 12, Folder "(title)," 2–3, 13.

77. Geoffrey Snudden, interview by author, tape recording, Detroit, 14 February 1987; Leonard Woodcock, interview by author, tape recording, Ann Arbor, Michigan, 3 December 1985.

78. Strachan, "A History of the Work of the Political Action Committee," 4, 5, 11, and passim.

79. On the UAW and CIO roles in the Democratic party, see Frank Semperger, "Direct Political Action by Labor in Wayne County, 1941–1946" (M.A. thesis, Wayne State University, 1948); Fay Calkins, *The CIO and the Democratic Party* (Chicago, 1952); Selig Harrison, "The Political Program of the United Automobile Workers" (B.A.

thesis, Harvard University, 1948); George Douglas Blackwood, "The United Automobile Workers of America, 1935–1951," (Ph.D. diss., University of Chicago, 1951); Stephen Sarasohn and Vera Sarasohn, *Political Party Patterns in Michigan* (Detroit, 1957); John Fenton, *Midwest Politics* (New York, 1966), 1–43.

Chapter 6. Crisis, Recovery, Eclipse

1. Dillon quoted in Victor Reuther, *The Brothers Reuther and the Story of the UAW* (Boston, 1976), 191.
2. Carl Haessler, "Oral History Interview," 27 November 1959, transcript, Reuther Library, 54.
3. W. L. White, "Trouble in the UAW," *The New Republic*, 10 August 1938, in Joe Brown Scrapbooks, Volume 13, Reuther Library.
4. Elizabeth McCracken, "Oral History Interview," 23 December 1959, transcript, Reuther Library, 29–30.
5. Russell Leach, interviews by author, tape recordings, Detroit, 22 October 1985 and 19 November 1985; Henry Geile, interview by author, tape recording, Detroit, 25 February 1986.
6. Kurt Keytal, interview by author, tape recording, Detroit, 10 December 1985; Patrick O'Brien, "Brief for Appellant, George John Barth v. John L. Zurbick, District Director of Immigration at Detroit," U.S. Circuit Court of Appeals, Sixth Circuit, no. 6193, 1931, Maurice Sugar Collection, Series 1, Box 24, 1–3.
7. Leach, interview by author.
8. U.S. Immigration and Naturalization Service, "Petition for Citizenship," no. 81092, document signed by Paul Charles Adolf Diechgraeber, 4 June 1934, National Archives, Great Lakes Region, Chicago, Illinois; Blaine Marrin, interview by author, tape recording, Madison Heights, Michigan, 5 November 1985; *Detroit News*, 28 February 1937; Nat Ganley, "Report for 1937 by Nat Ganley Business Agent, Local 155," 1–2.
9. For German-named activists in Local 157, see "Executive Board and Local Meeting," typed minutes, UAW Local 157 Collection, Part 1, Box 5, Folders "UAW Local 157 Minutes, 12/6/36–2/17/38" and "UAW Local 157 Minutes, 2/18/37–2/29/40." On ethno-cultural dimensions of the factionalism at Midland Steel, see Peter Friedlander, "The Social Bases of Politics in a UAW Local: Midland Steel, 1933–1941."
10. Walter Dorosh, interview by author, tape recording, Dearborn, Michigan, 1 July 1986; Sander Diamond, *The Nazi Movement in the United States, 1924–1941* (Ithaca, 1974), 91–249; Michael Sayers and Albert Kahn, *Sabotage! The Secret War against America* (New York, 1944), 85.
11. Dorosh, interview by author; Marrin, interview by author; *Fisher 21 Key Hole*, Strike Edition, undated, Joe Brown Collection, Box 21, Folder "Strikes, GM, 1939."
12. Leach, interview by author.
13. Average wage rates quoted in "Tool and Die Job Shop Rates—1936–1943," in *Special Supplement for Organizational and Financial Reports*, 1, Carl Haessler Collection, Box 19, Folder 26. On general conditions, see articles clipped from the UAW's Tool and Die Edition of the *Automobile Worker*, "Technological Improvements Cause Heavy Loss in Die Work," 14 June 1939, Joe Brown Collection, Box 9, Folder "Employment-Unemployment," and "Research Committee to Provide Vital Facts," 14 February 1940, Joe Brown Collection, Box 18, Folder "Skilled Trades"; *Detroit News*, 6 August

1939, Joe Brown Scrapbooks, Volume 16, Reuther Library; "Detroit Tool, Die Sales Up Sharply," unidentified news clipping in Blaine Marrin Collection, Folder 204. On GM shifting die work to Grand Rapids, see Leonard Woodcock, interview by author, tape recording, Ann Arbor, Michigan, 3 December 1985; on membership loss, financial crisis, and cost-cutting measures in Local 157, see "UAW Local 157 Minutes," particularly the meeting of the Executive Board on 30 December 1937 and that of the executive officers on 15 September 1938.

14. Orrin Peppler, "Oral History Interview," 16 March 1961, transcript, Reuther Library, 9–10; UAW Local 235, Shop Committee, Experimental Division, "Second Meeting," typed minutes, 18 October 1937, John Panzer Collection, Box 1, Folder "Minutes, UAW & Chevrolet Experimental, Local 235, 10/15/37–12/8/37," 1, 3; "CIO Industrial Unionism Protects Skilled Trades," *Tool, Die, and Engineering News*, clipping, 28 February 1940, Joe Brown Collection, Box 33, Folder "UAW Skilled Trades Dept."; Peter Friedlander, "Before the Institution: Politics on the Shopfloor, 1933–46," typescript, prepared for the Annual Meeting, Industrial Relations Research Association, 28 December 1979, 11.

15. "An Argument in Favor of a General Motors Local of Engineering and Experimental Workers within the UAWA," typescript, Walter Reuther Collection, Box 1, Folder 1-25.

16. Dorosh, interview by author. Dorosh recalls upward of 2,000 classifications among the Rouge's 12,000 toolroom workers during World War II.

17. Press release, UAW Publicity Bureau, 24 June 1938, Joe Brown Collection, Box 18, Folder "Skilled Trades"; Local 157, "Executive Board Meeting," typed minutes, 18 August 1938. On George Mitchell's previous ties to John Anderson, see "Election Statement by Progressives to the Members of the Mechanics Educational Society of America," leaflet, undated, Joe Brown Collection, Box 15, Folder "MESA, 1936–1944," which lists Mitchell with Anderson as Progressive candidates for MESA office.

18. UAW Local 157, "Executive Board and Local Meetings," typed minutes, entries for 1 September 1938, 3 September 1938, 5 September 1938; Peppler, "Oral History Interview," 9–11; Mat Hammond, "Oral History Interview," 6 March 1961, transcript, Reuther Library, 10–12; Marrin, interview by author. There are no INS files indexed in Detroit for Greany or Trusell, through they could have entered the United States and filed for citizenship in another city. UAW Local 157, Swartz Tool Unit, typed minutes, UAW Local 157 Collection, Part 2, Box 24, Folder "Swartz Tool Product Company, Minutes, Local 157, 1938–1943."

19. "City-Wide Tool and Die Job Shop [Meeting], Locals 155 and 157, 9/11/38," typed minutes, 11 September 1938, UAW Local 157 Collection, Part 2, Box 25, Folder "City-Wide Jobbing Shops, Membership and Stewards, Minutes L.157, 1938–1956, #20." Crothers first appears as "temporary recording secretary" at this meeting. Previous minutes are signed by Trusell.

20. Hammond, "Oral History Interview," 11–12; "UAW Rally Ends in Row," *Detroit News*, 17 October 1938, Joe Brown Scrapbooks, Volume 14, Reuther Library.

21. "UAW Rally Ends in Row."

22. Ibid.

23. National GM Tool and Die Conference, typed minutes, 29–30 October 1938, Walter Reuther Collection, Box 18, Folder 18-19, 1–6; "Delegates Represent Tool and Die Workers in All GM Plants," clipping from unidentified UAW publication, 6 November 1938, Joe Brown Collection, Box 33, Folder "UAW Skilled Trades Dept."

24. *GM Strike Bulletin*, 3 July 1939, Walter Reuther Collection, Box 26, Folder 26-20, 2;

Hammond, "Oral History Interview," 10–11; UAW Local 157, "Executive Board and Local meetings," typed minutes, entries for 26 January 1939, 2 February 1939, 5 February 1939, 16 February 1939, and 5 March 1939.

25. "Detroit and Wayne County Tool and Die Council," clipping from *Tool and Die Edition*, UAW-CIO, 27 May 1939, Joe Brown Collection, Box 18, Folder "Skilled Trades"; "Regular Meeting of Swartz Tool Products Co.," typed minutes, 24 February 1939, UAW Local 157 Collection.

26. "Regular Meeting of Swartz Tool Products Co.," typed minutes, 31 March 1939; *Automobilizer*, 24 July 1939, Walter Reuther Collection, Box 26, Folder 26-20, 1.

27. Haessler, "Oral History Interview," 42; Peter Friedlander, *The Emergence of a UAW Local, 1936–1939: A Study in Class and Culture* (Pittsburgh, 1975), 130.

28. Dan Gallagher, "Oral History Interview," 26 January 1960, transcript, Reuther Library, 35–36; Chris Johnson, *Maurice Sugar: Law, Labor, and the Left in Detroit, 1912–1950* (Detroit, 1988), 234.

29. R. J. Thomas, *President's Report to the Special Convention . . . 1939*, 21–22; Johnson, *Maurice Sugar*, 239–240.

30. Christopher Tomlins, *The State and the Unions: Labor Relations, Law, and the Organized Labor Movement in America, 1880–1960* (Cambridge, 1985), 200–224.

31. Fine, *Frank Murphy. The Detroit Years* (Ann Arbor, 1975), 344–346, 502–508; James MacGregor Burns, *Roosevelt: The Lion and the Fox* (New York, 1956), 360–366.

32. Ben Fischer, "Confidential Report of the Socialist Party on the Inner Situation in the Auto Union," typescript, June 1938, Maurice Sugar Collection, Box 41, Folder 41-27, 1–3; Keeran, *The Communist Party and the Auto Workers Unions* (Bloomington, 1980), 196; R. J. Thomas, *Automobile Unionism (1939–1940): A Report Submitted to the 1940 Convention of the UAW-CIO*, St. Louis, 29 July 1940, Reuther Library, 20.

33. R. J. Thomas, *Automobile Unionism (1939–1940)*, n.c., n.d., 19–20; *Detroit Free Press*, 30 June 1939, and *Detroit News*, 1 July 1939, Joe Brown Scrapbooks, Volume 16, Reuther Library; Kevin Boyle, "Rite of Passage: The 1939 General Motors Tool and Die Strike," *Labor History* (Spring 1986): 191–194.

34. Two recent articles provide excellent overviews of the 1939 strike: John Barnard, "Rebirth of the United Automobile Workers," *Labor History* (Spring 1986): 165–187, and Boyle, "Rite of Passage: The 1939 General Motors Tool and Die Strike," 188–203.

35. Bill Stevenson, "Oral History Interview," 6 July 1961, transcript, Reuther Library.

36. *UAW Skill*, Fall 1985, 5.

37. "Statement of Walter P. Reuther," press release, 10 June 1939, Joe Brown Collection, Box 21, Folder "Strikes, GM, 1939"; *Detroit Free Press*, 12 June 1939, Joe Brown Scrapbooks, Volume 16, Reuther Library; *GM Strike Bulletin*, 3 July 1939, Walter Reuther Collection, Box 26, Folder 26-20, 1–2; Barnard, "Rebirth of the United Automobile Workers," 172; *Detroit Free Press*, 12 June 1939 and 30 June 1939, Joe Brown Scrapbooks, Volume 16, Reuther Library; UAW-CIO, press release, 26 June 1939, Walter Reuther Collection, Box 26, Folder 26-19, 2.

38. *GM Strike Bulletin*, 3 July 1939, 1–2, 6 July 1939, 1, and 15 July 1939, 2; also see [untitled], typescript list of GM tool and die plants, type of work, number of workers, local union, strike vote date, and date plant went on strike, Walter Reuther Collection, Box 26, Folder 26-18.

39. Marrin, interview by author; *UAW Skill*, 4; *Detroit News*, 7 July 1939, 10 July 1939, and 24 July 1939, Joe Brown Scrapbooks, Volume 16, Reuther Library.

40. *Detroit News*, 7 July 1939, Joe Brown Scrapbooks, Volume 16, Reuther Library; *Fisher 21 Key Hole*, undated "Strike Editions," Joe Brown Collection, Box 21, Folder

"Strikes, GM, 1939"; *Ternstedt S List*, no. 6, n.d., Walter Reuther Collection, Box 26, Folder 26-20; *Cadillac Steward*, "Strike Flashes," Walter Reuther Collection, Box 26, Folder 26-20; *GM Picket*, 23 July 1939, 1, and 22 July 1939, 1, Walter Reuther Collection, Box 26, Folder 26-20.

41. *Detroit News*, 6 July 1939 and 10–13 July 1939, Joe Brown Scrapbooks, Volume 16, Reuther Library; "Production Workers: Tool and Die Strike Is Your Fight Too!" leaflet, Walter Reuther Collection, Box 26, Folder 26-15; Bernard, "Rebirth of the United Automobile Workers," 179.

42. *Detroit News*, 10–13 July 1939, Joe Brown Scrapbooks, Volume 16, Reuther Library; Haessler, "Oral History Interview," 55; *Ternstedt Picket*, 31 July 1939, 1, Walter Reuther Collection, Box 26, Folder 26-20; Marrin, interview by author; Boyle, "Rite of Passage," 199–200.

43. *Detroit News*, 5–7 July 1939, 14 July 1939, 31 July 1939, 1 August 1939, and *Detroit Free Press*, 1 August 1939, 3 August 1939, Joe Brown Scrapbooks, Volume 16, Reuther Library.

44. Boyle, "Rite of Passage," 191–194; *Detroit News*, 12 July 1939 and 14 July 1939, Joe Brown Scrapbooks, Volume 16, Reuther Library; *GM Picket*, 13 July 1939, 1, Joe Brown Collection, Box 21, Folder "Strikes, GM, 1939."

45. Bernard, "Rebirth of the United Automobile Workers," 181–183; *Fisher Strike News*, 1 August 1939, 1, Walter Reuther Collection, Box 25, Folder 26-20; *Detroit News*, 20 July 1939, Joe Brown Scrapbooks, Volume 16, Reuther Library; *GM Picket*, 18 July 1939, 1, Walter Reuther Collection, Box 26, Folder 26-20. Boyle, "Rite of Passage," 195–201, gives a detailed account of the progress of negotiations.

46. "Memorandum of Settlement . . . August 3, 1939," typed contract, 1, Walter Reuther Collection, Box 26, Folder 26-17; Bernard, "Rebirth of the United Automobile Workers," 184–185; Boyle, "Rite of Passage," 195–196.

47. "Memorandum of Settlement . . . August 3, 1939," 3–5.

48. Thomas, *Automobile Unionism*, 20–21; *Detroit News*, 19 April 1940, clippings, Joe Brown Collection, Box 16, Folder "NLRB Elections, GM," Reuther Library.

49. *Detroit News*, 19 April 1940, clippings, Joe Brown Collection, Box 16, Folder "NLRB Elections, GM"; Federated Press, "AFL Hopes for Craft Foothold in Auto Industry," 16 April 1940, Joe Brown Collection, Box 16, Folder "NLRB Elections, GM."

50. "All Stewards Meeting," typed minutes, 11 February 1939, UAW Local 3 Collection, Box 4, Folder "Steward Meeting Minutes, 1937–1941," 1; Dodge Local 3, "Executive Board Meetings," typed minutes, 19 January 1939, 4–5; 2 February 1939, 3–4; and 28 February 1939, 1–7—all in John Zaremba Collection, Box 2, Folder "Dodge Local 3 Exec. Bd. Minutes, Jan.–Feb. 1939"; Dodge Local 3, "Executive Board Meeting, typed minutes, 2 March 1939, 1–14, John Zaremba Collection, Box 2, Folder "Dodge Local 3 Exec. Bd. Minutes, March–April, 1939"; "The 12 Point Program of the Dodge Local 3 Progressive Candidates," printed flyer, Harry Ross Collection, Box 2, Folder "Local 3 Elections, 1939"; Jefferys, *Management and Managed*, 81–82. There are no INS records in Detroit for McCann or Hamel, suggesting they were American-born. "Frank Reid," a Canadian-born toolmaker, did petition for citizenship.

51. For slate cards, election leaflets, and results for local officers, Plant Committee, and convention delegates in 1939, see Harry Ross Collection, Box 2, Folder "Local 3 Elections, 1939,"

52. Dodge Local 3, "Executive Board Meetings," typed minutes, 14 April 1939, 1, 27 April 1939, 2–4, 25 May 1939, 1, John Zaremba Collection, Box 2, Folders "Dodge

Local 3 Executive Board Minutes, March–April 1939" and "Dodge Local 3 Executive Board Minutes, May–June 1939."

53. Dodge Local 3, "Executive Board Meetings," typed minutes, 18 May 1939, 4, 1 August 1939, 6–7, 10 August 1939, 3, John Zaremba Collection, Box 2, Folders "Dodge Local 3 Executive Board Minutes, May–June 1939," and "Dodge Local 3 Executive Board Minutes, July–August 1939." A measure of the key role played by Quinn and Hanlon on the Labor Vote Committee is provided by the Executive Board minutes in the week before the September 27 vote, when these two leaders made the final reports on the committee's preparations. See Dodge Local 3, "Executive Board Minutes," 21 September 1939, 5, and 25 September 1939, 1, John Zaremba Collection, Box 2, Folder "Dodge Local 3, UAW Executive Board Minutes, September 1939." Joe Kozma, a machine repairman and union activist, knew Hopkins as a production worker in the pressroom (Kozma, phone interview by author, 13 May 1989).

54. *United Automobile Worker*, 4 October 1939, 1.

55. Dodge Local 3, "Executive Board Meeting," typed minutes, 5 October 1939, 5, John Zaremba Collection, Box 2, Folders "Dodge Local 3 Executive Board Minutes, October 1939."

56. Quoted in Steve Jefferys, *Management and Managed: Fifty Years of Crisis at Chrysler* (Cambridge, 1986), 84.

57. Dodge Local 3, "Executive Board Meetings," typed minutes, 10 November 1938, 3; 5 December 1938, 1; 29 December 1938, 2–3; and one-page supplement "No Copies to Be Made of This Motion"—all in John Zaremba Collection, Box 1, Folder "Dodge Local 3 UAW Executive Board Minutes, October–December 1938"; "All Stewards Meeting," typed minutes, 1 May 1938, 1–3; Jefferys, *Management and Managed*, 80.

58. "Proposed By-Laws for Dodge Local 3," *Dodge Main News*, 4 October 1939; Jefferys, *Management and Managed*, 82.

59. Chrysler Corporation, *Slowdown: A Documentary Record of the Strike in Chrysler Corporation Plants from October 6 to November 29, 1939* (Detroit, 1939), 36, 63–67.

60. *United Automobile Worker*, 4 October 1939, 11 October, 1939, 18 October 1939; Jefferys, *Management and Managed*, 83; Tom Hanlon, "Comic Opera Generals Stall Grievance Procedure," *Dodge Main News*, 1 November 1939, 1, Chrysler Corporation, *Slowdown*, 71.

61. Local 3, "Stewards' Council Meeting," typed minutes, 9 September 1939, Local 3 Collection, Box 4, Folder "Steward Meeting Minutes, 1937–1940."

62. On McIntyre's report to the Executive Board, see typed minutes, 9 September 1939, 1–2. Patrick's firing is first indicated in the board minutes of 7 May 1939, 1. *Dodge Main News*, 4 October 1939, reported on Patrick's assignment to Indiana.

63. Chrysler Corporation, *Slowdown*, 33–35.

64. "Special Executive Board Meeting," typed minutes, 8 October 1939, 1–2, John Zaremba Collection, Box 2, Folder "Dodge Local 3, UAW Executive Board Minutes, October 1939."

65. Chrysler Corporation, *Slowdown*, 35; Jefferys, *Management and Managed*, 83.

66. *United Auto Worker*, 18 October 1939; *Detroit News*, 29 September 1939, 21 November 1939; *Detroit Times*, 8 November 1939; *New York Times*, 20 October 1939.

67. *Detroit News*, 30 October 1939, 13–14 November 1939, 16 November 1939, 27–28 November 1939; *Detroit Free Press*, 25 November 1939.

68. "Text of New Contract," *Dodge Main News*, 6 December 1939; Jefferys, *Management and Managed*, 85–86.

69. UAW-GM Contract, "Supplement," 12 March 1937, and "Supplement," 7 March

1938, Nat Ganley Collection, Box 7, Folder 7-11; International GM Negotiating Committee and UAW GM Department, "Concessions Won in New GM Agreement," typescript, [1940], Walter Reuther Collection, Box 26, Folder 26-17; "Proposed By-Laws for Local 3," *Dodge Main News*. Jefferys, *Management and Managed*, 71–77 and 85–87, provides an excellent review of the factors influencing the Dodge and GM representation systems, but by failing to note the 1940 amendments to the GM contract, he overstates the contrast with the formal representation structure at Dodge.

70. "Executive Board Meetings," typed minutes, 22 June 1939, 2, and 29 June 1939, 3–4.
71. Stevenson, "Oral History Interview," 21.
72. On the Tool and Die Building Committee at the Rouge, see the slate cards and flyers in the John Blaich Collection, Box 1, Folder 1-3.
73. The decline of the steward system was already evident in the late 1940s. See B. J. Widick and Irving Howe, *The UAW and Walter Reuther* (New York, 1949), 238–240. On the role of wartime controls in mandating procedural action over Direct Action, see Nelson Lichtenstein, *Labor's War at Home: The CIO in World War II* (Cambridge, 1982).
74. Smith quoted in Martin Glaberman, *Wartime Strikes: The Struggle against the No-Strike Pledge in the UAW During World War II* (Detroit, 1980), 86.
75. Bill McKie to the General Council and membership of Local 600, letter, 16 February 1948, Nat Ganley Collection, Box 33, Folder 33-4.
76. Haessler, "Oral History Interview," 102–107; Keeran, *The Communist Party and the Auto Workers Unions*, 244.
77. Doug Fraser, interview by author, tape recording, Detroit, 26 July 1982.
78. Hammond, "Oral History Interview," 18–19; attorney Irwin Kasoff to Blaine Marrin, letter, 12 October 1949, Marrin Collection, Folder 204; Leach, interview by author; "Official Local 155 Election Results," 1947, Nat Ganley Collection, Box 6, Folder 6-12; election slates with penciled vote totals, 1948, Nat Ganley Collection, Box 6, Folder 6-13.
79. Seth Wigderson, "Reuther's Last Fight: The Skilled Trades Revolt of the 1950s," typescript prepared for the Organization of American Historians, April 1984; Stephen Amberg, "Skilled Auto Workers and Union Politics in the 1950s," MIT Department of Political Science (October 1983).
80. UAW Local 653, *The Leader*, 21 April 1988, 6.
81. Quoted in David Halberstam, *The Reckoning* (New York, 1986), 50.

INDEX